PEOPLE AND ENVIRONMENT
IN AFRICA

PEOPLE AND ENVIRONMENT IN AFRICA

Edited by
Tony Binns
University of Sussex, UK

JOHN WILEY & SONS
Chichester · New York · Brisbane · Toronto · Singapore

Copyright © 1995 by John Wiley & Sons Ltd,
Baffins Lane, Chichester,
West Sussex PO19 1UD, England

Telephone National 01243 779777
International (+44) 1243 779777

Other Wiley Editorial Offices

John Wiley & Sons, Inc., 605 Third Avenue,
New York, NY 10158-0012, USA

Jacaranda Wiley Ltd, 33 Park Road, Milton,
Queensland 4064, Australia

John Wiley & Sons (Canada) Ltd, 22 Worcester Road,
Rexdale, Ontario M9W 1L1, Canada

John Wiley & Sons (SEA) Pte Ltd, 37 Jalan Pemimpin #05-04,
Block B, Union Industrial Building, Singapore 2057

Library of Congress Cataloging-in-Publication Data

People and environment in Africa / edited by Tony Binns.
    p. cm.
    Includes bibliographical references (p.   ) and index.
    ISBN 0-471-95530-2 (ppc)—ISBN 0-471-95100-5 (pbk)
    1. Human geography—Africa. 2. Man—Influence on nature—Africa.
3. Rural development—Africa. 4. Environmental degradation—Africa.
5. Africa—Environmental conditions. I. Binns, Tony.
GF701.P46 1995   94-38627
304.2′096—dc20   CIP

British Library Cataloguing in Publication Data

A catalogue record for this book is available from the British Library

ISBN 0-471-95530-2 (ppc)
ISBN 0-471-95100-5 (pbk)

Typeset in 10/12pt Times by Dobbie Typesetting Limited, Tavistock, Devon
Printed and bound in Great Britain by Bookcraft (Bath) Ltd

Contents

Contents

About the contributors

W. M. (Bill) Adams is a Lecturer in geography at the University of Cambridge. He has carried out research on environment, conservation and development in Nigeria, Kenya and Tanzania, and has made a particular study of human use of floodplain wetlands, the environmental and socio-economic impacts of dam construction and farmer-managed irrigation. His books include *Green Development: environment and sustainability in the Third World* (Routledge, 1990) and *Wasting the Rain: rivers, people and planning in Africa* (Earthscan, 1992).

Clive T. Agnew is Senior Lecturer in the geography department at University College, London. He has worked extensively in Africa and the Middle East on problems of water resource development and environmental degradation. He has recently published a book with Ewan Anderson, *Water Resources and the Arid Realm* (Routledge, 1992), and is currently researching into rural water supplies and drought assessment.

Hazel Barrett is Senior Lecturer in development geography at Coventry University. Her major research interests are agricultural production, gender and population issues in the developing world. Recent work includes a study of food production and marketing in West Africa and regional inequality in South Asia. She is also engaged in a number of joint research projects on women and rural development in West Africa, fertility behaviour and environmental change in sub-Saharan Africa (both with Angela Browne) and the impact of trade liberalization on African farmers (with Tony Binns and Angela Browne).

J. A. (Tony) Binns graduated in geography from the University of Sheffield and gained his MA and Ph.D. in African Studies from the University of Birmingham. He is currently Senior Lecturer in geography in the School of African and Asian Studies at the University of Sussex, where he has taught since 1976. He has had extensive field experience in Africa and has taught at the University of Sierra Leone, Bayero University, Kano, Nigeria, and the universities of Bophuthatswana and Witwatersrand in South Africa. He has published widely on African food production systems in books and academic journals, most recently *Tropical Africa* (Routledge, 1994). He is currently engaged in research (with Kim Geheb) on the interface between farming and fishing on the Kenyan shores of Lake Victoria, and on the impact of trade liberalization on African farmers (with Hazel Barrett and Angela Browne). He is President of the Geographical Association 1994–95.

Steve Brace studied geography in the School of African and Asian Studies at the University of Sussex and then taught geography and humanities in a west London comprehensive school. He subsequently joined ACTIONAID in London as Education Officer and has travelled widely through Africa and Asia visiting development projects. Information gathered from these visits has been used to produce several award-winning education resource packs which are now widely used in British schools.

John Briggs is Senior Lecturer in geography, and currently Head of Department, in the Department of Geography and Topographic Science at the University of Glasgow. Having graduated in geography from the School of Oriental and African Studies in London, he then successfully completed his Ph.D. at the University of Swansea on farmers' responses to planned agricultural development in Sudan. Before coming to

Glasgow, he taught at the Swaziland campus of the University of Botswana, Lesotho and Swaziland and at the University of Dar es Salaam in Tanzania. He has conducted extensive research and published widely on rural, agricultural and environmental problems and issues in Africa, primarily in Tanzania, Sudan and Egypt.

Angela Browne is Principal Lecturer in African Studies at Coventry University. She has a special interest in rural development, including village technologies, sustainability and women's issues. She is currently working on the changing roles of non-governmental organizations, and has joint research projects with Hazel Barrett on women and rural development in West Africa, and fertility behaviour and environmental change in sub-Saharan Africa, and with Hazel Barrett and Tony Binns on the impact of trade liberalization on African farmers.

Reginald Cline-Cole graduated in geography from the universities of Sierra Leone and Bordeaux. He is currently Lecturer in African geography at the Centre of West African Studies, University of Birmingham. He has previously taught at Bayero University, Kano, Nigeria and Moi University, Kenya. His research and publishing have been on fuelwood and forestry, resource appraisal and environment–development relationships.

James Drummond studied at the universities of Glasgow and Witwatersrand in Johannesburg, and has taught in the Geography Department at the University of Bophuthatswana in Mafikeng since 1984. He has published extensively on aspects of rural development in Bophuthatswana, as well as on the political geography of this former 'bantustan'. His present research is examining water resource conflict in the North-west Province, and analysing agricultural restructuring in the 'new' South Africa.

Jennifer Elliott is a Senior Lecturer in geography at Staffordshire University. She has also been an Honorary Research Associate and Lecturer in the Department of Geography at the University of

Zimbabwe. She is currently researching and writing on aspects of the environmental and social impacts of the resettlement programme in Zimbabwe, and has recently published a book, *An Introduction to Sustainable Development* (Routledge, 1993).

James Fairhead is a social anthropologist and Research Fellow at the School of Oriental and African Studies, University of London. He has worked extensively in Africa on the social and technical aspects of agro-ecological knowledge. His most recent research, with Melissa Leach, has examined environmental change and policy in the forest–savanna transition zone of West Africa.

Kim Geheb graduated in geography from the School of African and Asian Studies at the University of Sussex. He is currently undertaking field research in Kenya for his doctorate, 'The sustainability of renewable resources: an investigation into the structure of the fisheries industry in the Kenyan sector of Lake Victoria'.

Don Harrison is Save the Children's Education Officer for Scotland. He has worked as an Education Adviser for Oxfam and has taught in Cameroon, England, Malaysia and Malawi. He is a member of the Geographical Association's International Committee and has published a number of books and resource packs for schools.

Ced Hesse graduated in geography from the School of African and Asian Studies at the University of Sussex, since when he has had extensive field experience in the savanna–sahel region of West Africa. He has worked for Oxfam in Mali and Burkina Faso and was one of the founding co-ordinators of the Arid Lands Information Network, formerly an Oxfam project, but now an independent NGO, based in Dakar, Senegal.

Graham Hollier is an economic geographer with research interests in African rural development, agricultural and marketing systems, and the wider problems of Third World development, on which he has written articles in professional journals and contributed to a number of textbooks. He is currently a Lecturer in the Department of Geography at the University of Strathclyde, Glasgow, having previously held teaching posts at the universities of Leeds and Sussex.

Melissa Leach is a geographer/social anthropologist and Fellow at the Institute of Development Studies at the University of Sussex, Brighton. She specializes in environmental aspects of rural development and gender issues in resource management, mainly in West Africa. Her recent research, with James Fairhead, has also explored the knowledge informing environmental policy processes in Guinea's forest–savanna transition zone, West Africa.

Hamish Main is Senior Lecturer in geography at Staffordshire University, having previously lectured at Bayero University, Kano, Nigeria and the University of Birmingham. He has recently co-edited a book, *Environment and Housing in Third World Cities*, published by Wiley. He is currently undertaking a research project on water supply and sanitation in Calcutta.

Charles Mather gained his Ph.D. from Queen's University, Kingston, Canada, which was based on fieldwork undertaken in South Africa. He has lectured in geography at the University of Bophuthatswana, and from January 1995 he has been a Lecturer in geography at the University of the Witwatersrand, Johannesburg. His recent research and publications have focused on the historical geography of rural transformation and the contemporary restructuring of agriculture in South Africa.

Robin Mearns is a Fellow of the Institute of Development Studies at the University of Sussex. A geographer by training, his research and teaching are concerned with environmental aspects of rural development. He has field experience in Papua New Guinea, East and Horn of Africa, Mongolia and Central Asia, and he has carried out research into land policy and tenure (especially pastoral land tenure), pastoral institutions, common property resource management, social forestry, agroforestry and poverty–environment interactions.

Michael Mortimore is a Research Associate of the Overseas Development Institute in London. He was Professor of geography at Bayero University, Kano, Nigeria from 1979–1986, having previously worked at Ahmadu Bello University, Zaria, Nigeria from 1962. Since 1986 he has carried out a variety of commissioned research projects and consultancies. His recent books include; *Adapting to Drought: farmers, famines and desertification in West Africa* (Cambridge University Press, 1989) and (with Mary Tiffen and Francis Gichuki), *More people, less erosion: environmental recovery in Kenya* (Wiley, 1994).

Garrett Nagle is currently Head of Geography at St Edward's School, Oxford. He has had field experience in Southern Africa, and obtained his doctorate, 'Malnutrition in the Zwelitsha area of Ciskei', from Hertford College, University of Oxford. He has had several articles published in academic journals.

Kevin Phillips-Howard graduated in human ecology and then took his D.Phil. in environmental studies at the University of Ulster. He has taught in a number of universities including the University of Port Harcourt, Nigeria, the University of Wisconsin, Madison, USA, and the University of Juba, Sudan. Until recently he was a Research Fellow on the University of Durham Jos Plateau Environmental Resources Development Programme, based in Jos, Nigeria. He is currently Professor of geography at the University of Transkei, South Africa.

R. E. (Gina) Porter taught for 10 years in Nigeria in the universities of Maiduguri, Ibadan and Lagos. She currently lectures in the Department of Geography at the University of Durham. Her research and writing have focused on rural marketing and contract farming in Africa.

Ian Scoones is a Fellow of the Institute of Development Studies at the University of Sussex and was formerly a research associate in the Sustainable Agriculture and Drylands Programmes at the International Institute for Environment and Development (IIED) in London. He is an agricultural ecologist with an interest in resource management issues in dryland Africa. His recent work has focused on range and livestock management in Zimbabwe. He has edited two books on the subject: *Range Ecology at Disequilibrium: new models of natural variability and pastoral adaptation in African savannas*, and *Living with Uncertainty: new directions for pastoral development in Africa*.

Mary Tiffen retired as Senior Research Fellow at the Overseas Development Institute, London in 1984. She has been engaged in rural socio-economic research, teaching and consultancy in Africa and the Middle East since the 1960s. Her interests are in agricultural change, including irrigation, shifting cultivation and plantations. Her books include *More people, less erosion: environmental recovery in Kenya* (with Michael Mortimore and Francis Gichuki) (Wiley, 1994) and *The Enterprising Peasant: economic development in Gombe Emirate, North Eastern State, Nigeria, 1900–1968* (HMSO, 1976).

Coleen H. Vogel is a Lecturer in the Department of Geography and Environmental Studies at the University of the Witwatersrand, Johannesburg. She teaches courses on climatology, environmental studies and environmental education. She is currently completing her doctorate on drought in South Africa. She has been involved with the Drought Forum and is an active member of the South African Disaster Relief Association.

Lovemore M. Zinyama is Professor of geography at the University of Zimbabwe, Harare, where he has been teaching since 1979. He was educated at the University of Zimbabwe, where he obtained his Ph.D. as well as at the School of Development Studies at the University of East Anglia, UK. He has written extensively on rural development and agricultural change in the small-scale farming sector in Zimbabwe.

Acknowledgements

It has on the whole been a stimulating and pleasurable experience putting together this book. Some 26 authors were invited to contribute to the collection, and between them they have researched and written the 24 studies which are now presented here. Most, though by no means all, of us are geographers, and together we come from no fewer than 16 universities and 6 research institutes and non-governmental organizations. Many of us have worked together at various times and in various places in the past, and this project has provided us with a long overdue opportunity both to renew friendships and familiarity with each others' work, and to collaborate once again. Together we share a strong commitment to in-depth study and a greater understanding of Africa, which we hope in some way, however small, might lead to an improvement in the shamefully low living standards of a large proportion of Africa's people.

I would like to thank my colleagues for their strong commitment to this project and for their efficiency in dealing with my many requests during the production process. Iain Stevenson at John Wiley has been encouraging and helpful throughout, from discussing with me my early ideas to delivering the final product. At the University of Sussex I am grateful to Jane Surry for her invaluable secretarial assistance. I am also particularly indebted to Susan Rowland, our cartographer, whose work has excelled yet further with her new technology. I would, most of all, like to thank my wife, Margaret, and children Sarah and Joseph, for their patience and understanding. I think after two excursions with me to Africa they are gradually beginning to share my fascination with the continent and its people.

Tony Binns
Hove, Sussex
August 1994

Introduction

Tony Binns

The people–environment debate is long-running, but has developed spectacularly in the last decade, moving up national and international agendas, largely because of growing concern with such macro-processes as the human impact on global climatic change. The Rio 'Earth Summit' in June 1992, more correctly known as 'The United Nations Conference on Environment and Development' (UNCED), provided an international forum for discussion of these global issues. The printed output from Rio was immense—five major agreements, including 'Agenda 21', which alone has 40 chapters. The key question one might ask, as indeed after other such international gatherings, is 'Will all the talk and print now be followed by some positive action?' There is much scepticism about, particularly in the light of major North–South disputes in the Rio negotiations. It seems very likely that 'The resulting North–South apartheid reflected in the agreements will remain a central problem in attempts to promote sustainable development' (RIIA, 1993, p. xiii). While recognizing the great importance of studying and debating such global issues, it is important that evidence to further inform the people–environment debate is gathered from a spectrum of different scales, ranging from global to continental to national, regional and local, and at the micro-scale considering the household, which is the key decision-making, producing and consuming unit in most societies.

This book is concerned with people–environment relationships in the African continent, and most of the studies presented here examine issues at the local or regional level. For many years I have felt there was a need to gather together in one volume a collection of up-to-date empirical studies concerning relationships between people and environment in Africa. The mass media so often portray Africa as a dismal, gloomy and unhappy place, plagued with civil war, drought, famine and poverty. Africa's people are frequently accused of degrading their environment. The supposedly advancing Sahara Desert, so it is claimed, is caused by overgrazing and burning land in the Sahel, while deforestation is blamed on Africans chopping down trees indiscriminately for fuelwood. In sharp contrast, the travel companies, desperate to sell their 'exotic' package holidays, present images of Africa with palm-fringed beaches, teeming wildlife and quaint, traditional peoples untouched by the modern world. As anyone who knows Africa well would agree, both sets of images are grossly distorted and dangerously misleading. It seems, therefore, that the challenge for academics and teachers is to work towards presenting, as far as possible, accurate images and data which will inform detailed and rational evaluation of a range of issues and problems.

This is indeed the modest aim of this book. In July 1993 I invited a group of academics and development workers from Africa and Britain to write a series of short case studies based on their own research and fieldwork, focusing on the relationships between people and environment. I had an impressively positive response from my colleagues, many of them sharing my view that such a collection was long overdue. The majority of the writers would be content to be referred to as

People and Environment in Africa. Edited by Tony Binns
©1995 John Wiley & Sons Ltd

'geographers'. But even the few non-geographers in the team would, I feel sure, share a strong empathy with the long-standing tradition within the discipline of research and teaching about the people–environment interface.

As a research student at the Centre of West African Studies in Birmingham over 20 years ago, I remember making frequent use of a valuable collection of papers edited by Mansell Prothero, entitled *People and Land in Africa South of the Sahara* (Prothero, 1972). Many of the studies included in that book are, I believe, excellent examples of the strong and enduring geographical tradition of detailed fieldwork and meticulous data gathering. I still, on occasions, refer to Prothero's collection, and I am pleased that one of the contributors to that book, Michael Mortimore, has also written for this present volume.

I was also introduced as a student to the widely respected work of Ester Boserup, a Danish economist, whose important book, *The Conditions of Agricultural Growth* (Boserup, 1965, 1993), must have received more citations in articles and books on people–environment relationships than just about any other. That Boserup's book is still so highly regarded 30 years after it was originally published, was strong justification for it being republished in 1993. Boserup's simple message, which effectively counters doom-laden neo-Malthusian predictions, has two key elements: firstly, that changes and improvements often occur from *within* agricultural communities, introduced by the indigenous people themselves, not necessarily with any outside interference; and secondly, that technical, economic and social changes are unlikely to take place unless the community concerned is exposed to the pressure of population growth, which may actually be the main stimulus to agrarian change. As Robert Chambers comments in the foreword to the 1993 edition of Boserup's book, 'Whatever the qualifications to this Boserupian thesis, it has proved powerful and sustainable as a source of insight and debate, and has been reinforced by further evidence.'

Indeed, there is now a wealth of literature available which supports, exemplifies and expands Boserup's assertions. Some of the work which I have personally found most stimulating includes that of Polly Hill, and her detailed investigations in Ghana, northern Nigeria and south India (Hill, 1963, 1970, 1972, 1977, 1982). Michael Mortimore's work on northern Nigeria, which has been more or less continuous since the mid-1960s, and his recent work on Machakos, Kenya (see Chapter 7 in this volume), reveal spontaneous adaptations and innovations by farmers in the face of population pressure and harsh physical environments (Mortimore, 1967, 1989; Mortimore (with Tiffen and Gichuki), 1994). Paul Richards and Robert Chambers have also made valuable contributions to the literature on people–environment relationships in Africa. Richards has studied adaptation and innovation in West African food production systems, while Chambers has questioned standard data collection methodologies and proposed new approaches to understanding livelihood systems (Richards, 1985, 1986; Chambers, 1983, 1993; Chambers *et al.*, 1989). Chambers has also played a key role since the early 1980s in emphasizing the importance of seasonality in livelihood systems. In tropical regions with pronounced wet and dry seasons, climatic regimes can have a profound effect on food production and other activities of rural poor people, having implications, for example, for their labour inputs, health and nutrition (Chambers *et al.*, 1981).

My own first field research in Africa, in Sierra Leone in 1974, did much to reinforce my personal commitment to the views expressed by such writers. In Sierra Leone's Eastern Province, in close proximity to the burgeoning settlements of the diamond-mining region, I found many entrepreneurial farmers (Polly Hill would probably call them 'rural capitalists'), who were energetically increasing the quantity and variety of food crops they produced to sell to the growing non-farming population. These farmers showed a good awareness of temporal and spatial price variations and market opportunities, and were investing their sales' earnings in improving their homes, paying school fees and medical bills and planting coffee, cocoa and citrus trees (Binns, 1982). Later, on regular field visits to Morocco, I was impressed with the intricate terraced and irrigated farming systems in the High Atlas Mountains, where farmers also demonstrated a detailed understanding of both the physical and economic environment, and had elaborate institutional arrangements for maintaining the essential water delivery system (Binns and Funnell, 1989). Pastoralists too display a detailed knowledge of environment and a degree of flexibility in their livelihood systems, which is so necessary in the unpredictable arid and semi-arid environments in which they operate. In northern Nigeria, for example, I found that Fulani pastoralists were well aware of environmental features such as the location of pasture, water, economic trees, wild foods and disease, and they also knew about the pressures which were affecting them, with sprawling towns, market gardening and irrigation schemes, cutting across their traditional pastures and migratory routes (Binns and Mortimore, 1989; Binns, 1994). There is, therefore, as I have experienced myself, much evidence on the ground to support the contention that far from being persistent victims of their environment, African farmers and pastoralists generally have a wealth of environmental knowledge and show great skill in manipulating a range of environmental features to secure a livelihood for their families.

We should, however, exercise some caution and beware of being drawn in by what I might call the 'Merrie Africa' syndrome, where everything that is 'traditional' is seen as good, and development schemes are viewed universally as ogres, designed to destroy all harmony between people and nature. We must not lose sight of the fact that African states and their people are among the poorest in the world, whatever economic and social indicators are used. Furthermore, in the period since independence, which for many African countries was in the early and mid-1960s, the bulk of Africa's people have actually become relatively worse off. Achieving a greater understanding of people–environment relationships should not be merely academic inquisitiveness, but it must ultimately lead to raising human living standards.

The contributions

Some common strands run through the contributions. Firstly, the approach adopted by the writers is generally a positive one, providing a sharp contrast to the 'doom and gloom', often highly negative, images portrayed in the mass media. Secondly, there is strong recognition that Africans by and large understand their environments well, and over centuries have proved their ability to adapt their livelihood systems to cope with sometimes difficult environmental conditions. Thirdly, we would all probably agree that if we are to avoid repeated failures of one development project after the other, such as has happened all too frequently in the past, future development planning must be based upon a detailed understanding of what is there now and should fully appreciate the intricacies, strengths and weaknesses of indigenous livelihood systems and the aspirations of the people involved. Detailed empirical studies, such as those presented here, are therefore an essential prerequisite for effective development planning.

The studies have been divided into four roughly equal groups. There were many possible permutations in their arrangement, but in the end it was felt that a regionally based structure was probably the most appropriate. So, the collection opens with five general papers, which are then followed by six studies from North, East and Central Africa, seven from West Africa and six from Southern Africa.

Bill Adams in Chapter 1, 'Wetlands and floodplain development in dryland Africa', examines a type of environment which has a strategic importance for sustainable development that is out of all proportion to its size. The present utilization of wetlands and floodplains for agriculture, grazing and fishing is reviewed, and then the impact of various types of development on these areas is considered. The impact of dams has been particularly significant, it is argued,

3

because knowledge on the part of engineers, economists and other planners about the ecology and human use of Africa's wetlands remains limited. There is urgent need for better environmental appraisal of proposed projects to identify the likely costs and benefits.

In Chapter 2, 'Policies for pastoralists: new directions for pastoral development in Africa', Ian Scoones examines the confusion surrounding the concept of 'carrying capacity' in relation to pastoralism. In the past there has been much emphasis placed on 'fixed' carrying capacity, but in reality livestock numbers and a variety of environmental factors, most notably rainfall, vary considerably through time and space. Livestock herders frequently adopt a flexible and opportunistic approach to herd management. Future development strategies must, therefore, also be flexible and based upon a good understanding of existing herd management strategies, utilizing the wealth of local knowledge which pastoralists have.

Hazel Barrett and Angela Browne in 'Gender, environment and development in sub-Saharan Africa' (Chapter 3), recognize the multiple roles played by African women, many of which involve environmental management. Two popular theoretical perspectives on gender are criticized for underestimating the complexities of particular situations and the interaction between men and women in social reproduction and income generation. Women's various roles are outlined and the important point is made that women rarely have control over the most important environmental resource, land. There is a need to place gender roles and environmental management in the international, national, regional, as well as household context, to help identify appropriate future synergistic policies. For example, improving female education could impact not only on fertility, health, nutrition, agricultural productivity and poverty, but also result in improved environmental management and conservation.

Chapter 4 by Steve Brace, 'Participatory rural appraisal—a significant step forward in understanding relationships between poor people

and their environments', provides an intriguing non-governmental organization (NGO) approach to collecting more accurate and relevent data from rural communities, including eliciting from indigenous people what they regard as the key priorities for improving their living standards. Participatory Rural Appraisal (PRA) has gained much momentum and considerable respect in recent years, not least through the energetic work of Robert Chambers. Steve Brace draws his examples mainly from West Africa, but the methodology, which encourages local people to draw their own trend lines, seasonal calendars, transects and matrices, has widespread applicability. PRA, it is argued, brings a development organization much closer to the needs of poor communities and engenders a spirit of partnership and collaboration.

In Chapter 5, Hamish Main examines 'The effects of urbanization on rural environments in Africa'. This is a thought-provoking and in places controversial essay, relating in different ways to many issues contained in other contributions in this volume. By 2020, Main suggests, the population of sub-Saharan Africa will, for the first time, be predominantly urban. He considers various linkages between rural and urban areas and reviews aspects such as the 'circulation' of population, the production of commodities in rural areas for urban populations—such as grains, vegetables and woodfuel—and the increasing scale of urban pollution on rural hinterlands.

Following the five general introductory papers, the remaining contributions in the collection take the form of detailed and more local case studies, focusing on different aspects of the people—environment interface. The material presented here is in all cases based upon detailed empirical work undertaken by the authors.

The first group of studies is drawn from North, East and Central Africa, and opens (Chapter 6) with John Briggs's investigation from Egypt, 'Environmental resources: their use and management by the bedouin of the Nubian Desert of southern Egypt'. The location of Wadi Allaqi is hyper-arid, but with the completion of the Aswan High Dam in the early 1970s, the resource base was drastically modified and the potential for exploitation and development was soon recognized by hitherto nomadic bedouin groups. In this fragile and marginal environment, water is the critical natural resource, to which the bedouin have adapted a range of livelihood production systems such as sheep-herding, charcoal production, small-scale cultivation, camel-herding and medicinal plant collection. The study reveals a fascinating picture of adaptation to physical and economic environments in the context of an overall strategy which is geared to minimizing risk. The bedouin livelihood systems of Wadi Allaqi, developed over a 15-year period, clearly demonstrate a positive understanding of, and empathy with, the natural environment.

Chapter 7, by Michael Mortimore and Mary Tiffen, 'Population and environment in time perspective: the Machakos story', focuses on Machakos district in south-eastern Kenya and covers the 60-year period 1930–1990. Machakos is portrayed as a region with variable rainfall, poor soils and rapid population growth. However, the local Akamba farmers have worked hard to construct terraces, and conservation has become an accepted part of good farming. No fewer than 76 different production technologies have been introduced, giving much greater flexibility to farming systems in this risky environment. Akamba farmers have also responded well to market opportunities, producing coffee for export and fruit and vegetables for the food canning industry. Through hard work and innovation, food crop production per person has actually kept up with population growth. Contrary to gloomy predictions in the 1930s, the Akamba of Machakos have put land degradation into reverse, conserved and improved their trees, invested in their farms and sustained an improvement in overall productivity. This important study effectively counters Malthusian concerns and gives much weight to Ester Boserup's hypothesis that 'innovation is mothered by necessity'.

Also based in Kenya, and like the previous chapter taking a historical perspective, Kim Geheb in Chapter 8 examines the pressures facing small-scale fishing activity in Lake Victoria—'Exploring people–environment relationships: the changing nature of the small-scale fishery in the Kenyan sector of Lake Victoria'. Some 85% of Kenya's fish supply comes from Lake Victoria and most of this is landed by 25 000–30 000 small-scale fishermen. Geheb examines the fishing activity in the pre-colonial, colonial and post-colonial periods. He shows how the once tightly controlled access to fishing with careful management of resources by the indigenous Luo, has been transformed into a 'free for all', resulting in declining catches, increasing commercialization and absentee ownership of fishing boats and tackle. The situation has been further exacerbated by a range of ecological problems, caused by such factors as the introduction of exotic fish species (including the voracious predator, the Nile perch), and increasing pollution leading to eutrophication. It is argued that the future sustainability of fishing activity in Lake Victoria will ultimately depend on greater control over access, and possibly the reintroduction of communal fishing grounds and resource management such as existed in pre-colonial times.

Robin Mearns draws his evidence in Chapter 9 from Kenya, Sudan and Ethiopia in his study of access to and control over woodfuel—'Institutions and natural resource management: access to and control over woodfuel in East Africa'. The emphasis in this chapter is placed on the importance of institutions, in which there has been much recent interest in development studies. Mearns suggests that interventions aimed at alleviating rural energy problems often require indirect approaches which are situated in the wider context of people's livelihood systems. For example, in parts of western Kenya it is often suggested there is a woodfuel 'crisis', yet there may be an abundance of standing trees and shrubs. Closer examination of rural communities, however, reveals that while it is women who are responsible for providing household fuel, they may be prevented from gaining access to, and effective control over, wood for use as fuel because men plant and own the trees. Mearns advocates a move away from neo-Malthusian approaches which focus on the physical scarcity of natural resources, towards a greater appreciation of the institutional arrangements than underpin people's natural resource management practices.

Mary Tiffen's study in Chapter 10, 'The impact of the 1991–1992 drought on environment and people in Zambia', produces some useful findings. After considering the magnitude of the drought, Tiffen systematically examines its impact on water resources, natural vegetation, crop production, domestic livestock, fisheries, wildlife, soils and people. Zambia decided to mangage drought relief through NGOs, including local churches, which generally seemed to work well. The drought did, however, have some significant effects on individuals, rural households and communities. For example, child malnutrition became more common. Inequality among village families increased, depending on such factors as access to credit and the level of disposal of family assets, such as livestock and vegetables, which had to be sold to buy food. Women's workload increased with greater distances covered in searching for water, and their income-generating activities, such as beer brewing and the sale of vegetables, suffered a decline. On a more positive note, Tiffen shows how the drought resulted in a strengthening of community solidarity and village institutions, with the formation of drought committees. More interest was also shown in crop diversification to reduce future risk, and in soil conservation measures.

Living standards and health care in rural Malawi are the subject of Chapter 11 by Don Harrison—'Evaluating living standards in rural Malawi: the experience of a non-government development agency'. Harrison examines the recent work of Save the Children (UK), in obtaining valuable data on food security and health issues, which can then be incorporated into development planning strategies. Food security risk mapping is one data collection method used, which takes stock of a number of variables such as population distribution, landholding and subsistence and cash crop production. Areas and populations can then be ranked according to the severity of the effects of drought and levels of food

shortage, and the most vulnerable can be targeted for assistance. NGOs, such as Save the Children (UK), are engaged in ongoing analysis of how people use their local environments and adapt their everyday living and food supply strategies to changing features such as climate and population.

The following seven chapters are concerned with West Africa and the first of these (Chapter 12), written by Clive Agnew, focuses on the Sahel—'Desertification, drought and development in the Sahel'. Agnew examines the highly controversial issue of desertification in this marginal and vulnerable region, where there have been numerous media reports about the advancing Sahara Desert. From carefully evaluating the available evidence, he suggests that the link between climatic change, drought and desertification is far from proven. A major problem is undoubtedly the semantic confusion surrounding terms such as desertification, drought, desiccation and land degradation. Agnew believes it is too easy to blame the physical environment, and there is a need for more in-depth studies of human livelihood systems, which do show a remarkable degree of resilience. Much of the confusion, he argues, is due to poor monitoring of human and environmental conditions and the treatment of the Sahel as a homogeneous entity, which it certainly is not.

In Chapter 13, Ced Hesse also looks at the savanna/sahel region of West Africa, in a study which takes up Agnew's call for more detailed monitoring. In this chapter Hesse considers livestock marketing in Mali—'Livestock market data as an early warning indicator of stress in the pastoral economy'. In the search for early warning indicators of impending stress in livelihood systems, Hesse poses the question, 'Can livestock market data be uses as an early warning indicator of stress in pastoral economies?' He sifts through some fascinating information relating to marketing trends at Douentza in Mali between 1980 and 1986, examining seasonal and long-term fluctuations in prices and numbers of animals sold. He concludes that such data might be used to confirm retrospectively favourable and unfavourable environmental conditions, but they fail to provide the fine and consistent detail needed if they are to be used as an early warning indicator. The study provokes thought on the validity of early warning indicators and the problems of acquiring reliable longitudinal data, and suggests that there is more scope for further work and refinement of data collection techniques in relation to pastoral systems.

James Fairhead and Melissa Leach in Chapter 14 consider the forest–savanna transition zone in Guinea—'Local agro-ecological management and forest–savanna transitions: the case of Kissidougou, Guinea'. There has been a long-standing ecological debate about the vegetation 'mosaics' in the forest–savanna transition zone in various parts of West Africa. One view suggests that shifting cultivation and burning have transformed forest into savanna, while others believe the mosaics are a more stable vegetation pattern reflecting variable local edaphic factors. However, relatively little attention has been given to the role of indigenous people in managing the environment and in encouraging the formation of forest vegetation within a savanna landscape. In Kissidougou, Guinea, forest islands now surround some 800 villages, and their formation has been actively encouraged by local people, who believe that the forest provides: protection from wind, heat and fire; valuable forest products and shelter for economic tree crops; and an element of security and secrecy for ritual activity. A comparison of air photographs from different points in time, together with documentary sources and oral histories, reveal an increase in forest cover during this century, contrary to the views of many policy-makers. Fairhead and Leach conclude that these forest islands are products of careful management and not the last relics of a once great forest.

Continuing with the theme of forestry, but moving eastwards to northern Nigeria, Reginald Cline-Cole in Chapter 15 portrays a similar picture of careful indigenous forest management—'Livelihood, sustainable development and indigenous forestry in dryland Nigeria'. Cline-Cole firstly considers the concept of 'sustainable development', and the importance of trees and

forestry as a source of savings, food, employment and income. He advocates a stronger focus on the complex linkages between populations, resources, environment and development (PRED). Trees and tree products are an important element in the rural landscape and economy of semi-arid northern Nigeria. The area around the city of Kano is intensively settled and cultivated, and in the 25 years from 1965 to 1990 the area under cultivation has doubled. However, air photographs show that in some parts of the Kano close-settled zone tree numbers have actually increased through indigenous management practices. Cline-Cole believes that future studies of dryland forestry must address inhabitants' livelihood concerns in these resource-poor and ecologically vulnerable areas, as well as evaluating the sustainability of these environments. These two sets of concerns, he argues, are inextricably linked in indigenous forestry management.

Kevin Phillips-Howard's study (Chapter 16) of indigenous management of soil fertility, is also located in northern Nigeria, but on the distinctive upland region of the Jos Plateau—'Soil and fertilizer use among small-scale farmers on the Jos Plateau, Nigeria'. Land reclaimed from tin mining is intensively prepared and cultivated, and there has been a significant expansion of the cultivated area through the painstaking construction of terraces. Farmers build up and maintain the fertility of their soil through elaborate combinations of ash, inorganic and organic fertilizers. They have their own criteria for distinguishing different types of fertilizer and have developed a detailed knowledge of their individual and collective properties. Meanwhile, the extension service continues to promote the use of inorganic fertilizer, which is either scarcely available or is supplied too late. Phillips-Howard suggests that extension officers could learn much from farmers. Extension services need to be reorientated and made more relevant to farmers' circumstances, working in partnership with farmers to strengthen existing practices and further improve farm production.

A historical investigation of trade and marketing in Borno, north-eastern Nigeria, is the subject of Gina Porter's study in Chapter 17—'Adapting to environment and market: trade and marketing in northern Nigeria'. The author uses field research and colonial archives to chart the spatial pattern of local and long-distance trade in Borno over the last century. Pre-colonial trans-Saharan trade routes once provided vital linkages in a long-established ecologically based long-distance trade between forest, savanna, sahel and desert. In Borno, a dry, marginal and once inaccessible region within Nigeria, environmental factors have been influential in the past as they are still today. Problems with water supply, for example, is a recurring theme and migration during the long dry season is another long-established feature. For the local population, mobility and multiple occupations and activities remain important coping and risk aversion mechanisms in this difficult environment.

The final study from West Africa (Chapter 18), written by Graham Hollier, also examines rural marketing, in this case in the Bamenda Highlands of Cameroon—'Ecological diversity and its impact on rural marketing channels in the Bamenda Highlands, Cameroon'. In this region there is a flourishing rural trading network linking a number of different ecological zones. Important periodic markets have developed in the last century as collection points for local produce and more recently as magnets for bulk-buying for urban centres. In an area of only 18 000 km², no fewer than over 300 market places are functioning. Hollier considers the marketing arrangements for palm oil, cassava/gari and maize, each the product of a different ecological zone. He reveals a remarkably resilient network of traditional periodic markets and the movement of large quantities of foodstuffs between different ecological zones.

The final group of papers contains studies undertaken in Southern Africa. The first (Chapter 19) by Lovemore Zinyama, examines the agricultural sector and smallholder farming in post-independent Zimbabwe—'Sustainability of smallholder food production systems in Southern Africa: the case of Zimbabwe'. The key question which Zinyama asks is, 'How can the social well-being of the rural population be improved, given that the poor lack economic alternatives to the current excessive exploitation of their natural resource base?' Zimbabwe's land reform programme, introduced as a top priority after independence in 1980, has transformed the country's communal farming sector, such that peasant farmers have produced a steadily increasing share of the national agricultural output. However, major inequalities persist, with the best ecological areas still being used for large-scale commercial farming. The black communal areas remain the poorest and their inhabitants most vulnerable. Structural adjustment policies, implemented from 1990, involving cuts in government expenditure and retrenchment, have increased both poverty and pressure upon low quality, often marginal, farmland. In fact poverty and environmental degradation are closely intertwined and should, Zinyama argues, be seen as one complex crisis. He concludes that progress since independence in raising agricultural production in the peasant sector has been highly skewed, both socially and spatially, and is not likely to provide for long-term sustainable development.

Jennifer Elliott's study (Chapter 20) is also on Zimbabwe, and effectively complements Zinyama's study in the previous chapter. Her focus is on land reform and distribution in Zimbabwe since 1980—'Government policies and the population–environment interface: land reform and distribution in Zimbabwe'. Elliott considers the gross inequalities in landholding which existed at independence, when only 7000 white farmers controlled 47% of total farmland, whereas 700 000 black farmers had only 49% of the land, much of it poor quality. A programme of land reform and resettlement was introduced as a key element of the new government's commitment to a socialist future, with the slogan 'growth with equity'. The study examines the impact of the land reform programme on population–environment relationships, and includes a detailed discussion of the use, collection and management of woodland resources in two resettlement scheme areas.

Chapter 21 by Charles Mather, is an intriguing historical account of black 'squatters' and white farmers in north-eastern South Africa—'Environment as weapon: land, labour and African "squatters" in rural South Africa'. Using archival materials, Mather recounts how the struggle for land and labour in the Barberton district of eastern Transvaal, South Africa, interacted with broader environmental and conservation issues. In the late 1930s white farmers complained that black 'squatters' in the district were eroding fragile soils, destroying trees and killing wild animals, with the implication that if these areas became more overcrowded the land would be irreparably damaged for future white settlers. In reality, however, much of the environmental damage was caused by white settlers, who were progressively colonizing, subdividing and overstocking land. Under the apartheid regime, the white farmers' false allegations of damage by black 'squatters' were used as a weapon to evict and burn the homes of hundreds of black families by the early 1950s.

Also from South Africa, James Drummond's study (Chapter 22) of Dinokana, in the former 'independent' black homeland of Bophuthatswana (now North West Province), again reveals the impact of apartheid policies—'Development and change: irrigation and agricultural production in Dinokana village, North-west Province, South Africa'. Irrigated farming in the village and environs of Dinokana was introduced by the first missionaries, including David Livingstone, in the 1840s. The indigenous Hurutshe people responded well to the opportunity to produce and sell a wide range of irrigated crops. This highly productive system, fed by local spring water, thrived until 1957, the year when the National Party required women to carry passes, a measure which was strongly resisted in Dinokana. Many were detained and life and agricultural production were severely dislocated. The situation was further compounded by drought, tighter border controls following Botswana's independence in 1966, and in particular, with the forced movement in 1969 of over 13 000 black 'squatters' from white farms in Transvaal to a new settlement at Welbedacht, a short distance from Dinokana. The new settlement required large quantities of Dinokana's water, which had a severe effect on agriculture. Drummond charts the collapse of a once highly productive irrigated agricultural system and stresses the importance of understanding the historical context in appreciating present-day people–environment relationships.

Coleen Vogel's study (Chapter 23) is also mainly located in the former Bophuthatswana, and examines the official and local responses to drought in South Africa and in the semi-arid environment of the Tswana people—'People and drought in South Africa: reaction and mitigation'. Vogel shows that droughts are endemic features in South Africa, and while there has been considerable investigation into climatic factors leading to drought, relatively little attention has been directed towards the impact of drought on the rural poor. There has been much debate in South Africa about drought relief policy and the need for this to be both more pro-active and also broader-based. At last, with political change, there seems to be general recognition of the need to locate drought relief within a broader rural development context which includes black farmers and the rural poor. There is an urgent need for more detailed examination and understanding of drought-coping strategies at the local level and the various factors which might affect these strategies. A 10-year study (1982–1992) of two Tswana villages in north-western South Africa has revealed some changes in drought-coping strategies. Most notably has been the decline of community support structures and collective coping strategies. Support from local leaders and chiefs has been replaced by state support. Long-term migration is no longer popular, with many people preferring to 'sit-out' the drought in the hope that food aid will come. In conclusion, Vogel argues for further empirical studies to understand how poor rural people cope with environmental stress.

In the final study of the collection (Chapter 24), Garrett Nagle investigates health and health care in another former 'homeland', Ciskei, in south-eastern South Africa—'Health and health care in the "new" South Africa'. Institutionalized

9

inequality, which was a deeply entrenched feature of apartheid South Africa, and was manifested in residential segregation, as well as in separate education and health policies, is likely to take a long time to change with the presidency of Nelson Mandela and the birth of the 'new' South Africa. Nagle examines health care in Ciskei, a small, impoverished and overcrowded former black homeland. Water and sanitation are frequently intermittent or altogether absent. Child malnutrition is widespread and infant mortality is high. Such hospitals and clinics that do exist are often rudimentary and lacking in basic amenities, medicines and qualified staff. However, despite the generally poor facilities, health services in Ciskei do reach a large number of people and have some positive impact on their health status. In the future Nagle sees little cause for optimism in improving health care in this and other similar regions in South Africa, simply because the new regime has so many urgent priorities and there are limited funds available. As he concludes, prospects for health and health care in the 'new' South Africa are on the one hand exciting, but on the other, frightening.

References

Binns, J. A. (Tony) (1982) Agricultural change in Sierra Leone, *Geography*, 67(2), 113–125.

Binns, Tony (1994) *Tropical Africa*, Routledge, London.

Binns, J. A. (Tony) and Funnell, D. C. (1989) Irrigation and rural development in Morocco, *Land Use Policy*, 6(1), 43–52.

Binns, J. A. (Tony) and Mortimore, M. (1989) Ecology, time and development in Kano State, Nigeria, pp. 359–380 in K. Swindell, J. Baba and M. Mortimore (eds), *Inequality and Development: some Third World perspectives*, Macmillan, London.

Boserup, E. (1965 and 1993) *The Conditions of Agricultural Growth*, Allen & Unwin. (Republished in 1993 in paperback, by Earthscan Publications, London.)

Chambers, R. (1983) *Rural Development—putting the last first*, Longman, London.

Chambers, R. (1993) *Challenging the Professions: frontiers for rural development*, Intermediate Technology Publications, London.

Chambers, R., Longhurst, R. and Pacey, A. (eds) (1981) *Seasonal Dimensions to Rural Poverty*, Frances Pinter, London.

Chambers, R., Pacey, A. and Thrupp, L. A. (eds) (1989) *Farmer First: farmer innovation and agricultural research*, Intermediate Technology Publications, London.

Hill, P. (1963) *The Migrant Cocoa Farmers of Southern Ghana*, Cambridge University Press, Cambridge.

Hill, P. (1970) *Studies in Rural Capitalism in West Africa*, Cambridge University Press, Cambridge.

Hill, P. (1972) *Rural Hausa: a village and a setting*, Cambridge University Press, Cambridge.

Hill, P. (1977) *Population, Prosperity and Poverty: rural Kano, 1900 and 1970*, Cambridge University Press, Cambridge.

Hill, P. (1982) *Dry Grain Farming Families*, Cambridge University Press, Cambridge.

Mortimore, M. (1967) Land and population pressure in the Kano Close-Settled Zone, *The Advancement of Science*, 23, 677–688. Reprinted in Prothero (ed.) (1972, pp. 60–70).

Mortimore, M. (1989) *Adapting to Drought*, Cambridge University Press, Cambridge.

Mortimore, M. with Tiffen, M. and Gichuki F. (1994) *More People, Less Erosion: environmental recovery in Kenya*, John Wiley, Chichester.

Prothero, R. M. (ed.) (1972) *People and Land in Africa South of the Sahara*, Oxford University Press, Oxford.

Richards, P. (1985) *Indigenous Agricultural Revolution*, Hutchinson, London.

Richards, P. (1986) *Coping with Hunger*, Allen & Unwin, London.

RIIA (Royal Institute of International Affairs) (1993) *The 'Earth Summit' Agreements: a guide and assessment*, Earthscan, London.

Section I
General issues

Farmer planting swamp rice in Sierra Leone. (Photograph: Tony Binns)

1

Wetlands and floodplain development in dryland Africa

W. M. Adams

Introduction

Wetlands, recognized internationally under the Ramsar Convention signed in 1971, are increasingly being identified as key environments in terms of sustainable development planning (Dugan, 1990; Adams, 1992), and they provide a range of resources for human use. Wetland flooding can contribute to acquifer recharge and flood control (delaying and lowering the peak of flood flows), and also supplies a range of goods, such as water supplies, forage and hunting resources, wood resources, grazing, fish and agricultural produce. Furthermore, a single wetland may produce a number of these outputs at the same time, or serve different communities in different ways through the year.

There are various different wetland environments in Africa (Figure 1.1). Among the most widespread are river floodplains (on all scales from small features only 1 km wide to the vast floodplains of the major rivers, for example those of the Zambezi and Senegal rivers). In places there are larger inland deltas and lacustrine wetlands, notably the Okavango in Botswana and the Sudd in Sudan, Lake Chad and the Niger Inland Delta. Other important categories of wetland include coastal and coastal delta environments (for example the deltas of the Tana, Rufiji, Senegal or Niger rivers, the Basse Casamance or the Banc d'Arguin in Mauritania), freshwater swamps (for example in eastern Zaire), and lakes (Hughes in press, Hughes and Hughes, 1992). This chapter concentrates primarily on floodplain wetland environments, and how people make use of them.

Floodplain wetlands

Seasonal rainfall patterns in Africa are complex, but many of Africa's rivers have a marked seasonal regime, with high discharges and extensive flooding in the wet season and low flows and withdrawal of floodwaters in the dry season. In the upper reaches of a river floodplains tend to be narrower, and there is a more peaked hydrograph. Downstream, floodplains are larger and more complex and floods tend to be slower to rise, and to end later than they do upstream. On the Niger River, for example, the flood peak takes over 100 days to travel the 1760 km from Koulikoro to Malanville (Welcomme, 1979).

People and Environment in Africa. Edited by Tony Binns
©1995 John Wiley & Sons Ltd

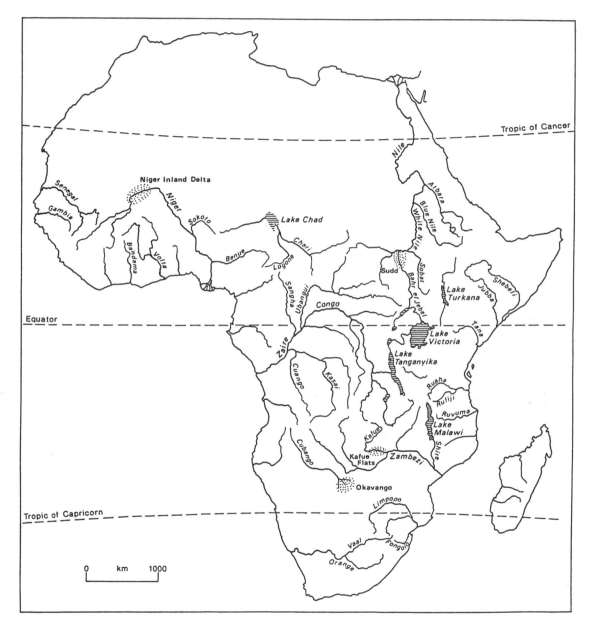

Figure 1.1 *Major wetlands and river systems in sub-Saharan Africa*

The seasonal variation in the extent of inundation in African floodplains is large. The floodplain of the Senegal River (in Senegal and Mauritania) shrinks from some 5000 km² in flood to 500 km² in the dry season. The Niger Inland Delta (in Mali) extends to 20 000–30 000 km² in the flood season, shrinking to 4000 km² at low water. The Logone-Chari system in Cameroon is extremely complex, with extensive fringing floodplains, as well as extensive flooding where the water enters Lake

Chad (the Yaérés Delta). The total area flooded at its peak is about 90 000 km², of which only 7% remains wet at low water.

In geomorphological terms, floodplains are complex, and topography and sedimentary characteristics are very variable. So too are flooding conditions, with some parts inundated for only short periods, or left dry in low-flood years, while other areas flood for many months. Local rainfall can be important in flooding backswamp areas and pools, particularly early in the flood season when it can be important for the timing of agricultural or grazing activity, or in areas such as the Basse Casamance (southern Senegal) which are influenced by brackish or salt water.

Direct economic benefits of African floodplain wetlands include the direct production of food or fibre, both for export and subsistence. The Niger Inland Delta in Mali, for example, supports some 550 000 people, and in the dry season provides grazing for about 1 million cattle and 1 million sheep and goats. There are some 80 000 fishermen, and the delta supports some 17 000 ha of rice, half the total area of rice in Mali (Moorehead, 1988). However, within semi-arid Africa, wetlands have a strategic importance out of all proportion to their size, because economic activities within the wetland are integrated closely with those in surrounding drylands. Integration of valley and upland environments is one of the three basic features of indigenous agriculture in West Africa, with physical management of soil and the practice of intercropping (Richards, 1983). Pastoralists also use wetlands seasonally, concentrating on to seasonally flooded land as surrounding rangelands dry out. In this situation, a relatively small area of wetland provides support for grazing at critical times of the year, and supports this activity through the rest of the year over a much larger area. For example, the Peul of the central Senegal Valley move away from the floodplain with their livestock in the wet season, but come back to farm when the floodwaters recede from the valley in the dry season (Léricollais and Schmitz, 1984).

Floodplain agriculture

The most economically important use of floodplain wetlands in Africa is agriculture (Kimmage and Adams, 1992). In many instances continuous cropping is possible in floodplain environments, without the fallowing which is so widely necessary in drylands. Floodplain wetlands are highly productive in ecological terms compared with the drylands which surround them. The availability of floodwaters extends the growing season of crops and wild plants, and the deposition of silt and other solid material carried by rivers, and the dissolved load of the floodwater contribute to soil fertility. This fertilizing effect can be considerable. The Logone-Chari River, for example, loses 20–60% of its suspended load and 15–35% of its dissolved load when it inundates its floodplain in Cameroon.

Floodplain cultivation often involves simple forms of irrigation. These range from simple adaptation to natural flood patterns in floodplains or inland deltas to systems of complete water control such as the shadoof gardens of Nigeria or Sudan (Adams, 1992; cf. Rodgers and Svendsen, 1992). Data on indigenous irrigation in Africa are poor, but an FAO survey (FAO, 1986) suggested that in 1982 almost half the irrigated area in sub-Saharan Africa lay in the 'small-scale and traditional' sector (2.38 million ha out of a total of 5.02 million ha, 47%). Much, although by no means all, of this irrigation takes place in association with wetlands. The simplest forms of indigenous irrigation involve cropping on rising and falling floods in floodplains, swamps and deltas. Flood cropping embraces a number of distinct practices, including farming on the rising flood (*crue* in French) or on the falling flood (*décrue*). This is particularly well developed in the Niger Inland Delta in Mali although it occurs widely in West Africa. There are also farming systems which involve defence against salt water in coastal environments, for example on the coast of Guinea or Senegal. *Crue* cultivation involves planting before the flood arrives, and harvesting either after the flood has fallen, or from boats. *Décrue* agriculture involves the use of residual soil moisture left by retreating floods. Farmers can judge the likely duration of water and soil moisture in these areas, and plant crops accordingly, sometimes building banks to retain water in pools.

The high productivity of floodplain agriculture is matched by risk, because to some degree the extent and duration of flooding are unpredictable. Floodplain farmers deal with risk in several ways. First, they often have a detailed appreciation of the variation in land types in the floodplain and experience of past patterns of flooding. The Marba of the middle Logone Valley in Cameroon, for example, recognize and name a whole range of different land types on the basis of soil colour or texture or vegetation cover, and for each expect a distinct flood regime (Seignobos, 1984). Second, floodplain farmers are often skilled in selecting crops and crop varieties to plant together in the same field that have different tolerance to flooding and different ecological requirements. In this way the farmer increases the chance of a reasonable harvest whatever the flood level and duration. In the Sokoto Valley in Nigeria, for example, rice varieties which need a lot of flooding are commonly mixed with a variety of red-seeded sorghum which is flood-tolerant, but performs best if only flooded for a short period (Adams, 1986). Third, floodplain farmers spread risk by exploiting environments outside as well as inside wetlands. In Sierra Leone farmers spread risk and deal with bottlenecks in labour demand by integrating the cultivation of swamp rice and dryland crops (Richards, 1985, 1986). Short-duration rices are planted on river terraces and lower slope soils which retain water, using residual soil moisture and wet-season runoff. Medium-duration rices are grown under rainfall on well-drained upland soils, and long-duration varieties are grown in valley swamps or watercourses growing (if they survive) in deeper water. The fourth way in which floodplain farmers deal with risk is to spread their options into different economic activities. Often, floodplain 'farmers' are also fishermen, herders or dryland cultivators; sometimes all three. Flexibility is therefore a key ingredient of success in indigenous production systems.

Floodwater farming is found in most major African floodplains, and is particularly extensive in West Africa. It is important for example in the floodplains of the Logone-Chari system in Cameroon (Seignobos, 1984), the Sokoto and Hadejia floodplains of Nigeria (Adams, 1986, 1992) and in the floodplain of the River Senegal (Léricollais and Schmitz, 1984; Boutillier and Schmitz, 1987). However, probably the most extensive area of flood-related cropping in Africa is in the Niger Inland Delta (Gallais, 1967; Harlan and Pasquerau, 1969; Scudder, 1980). Agriculture involves both flood cropping of sorghum and rice, with rainfed bullrush millet on unflooded land, and in places small gardens are irrigated from wells.

Such irrigation from shallow wells is quite widespread in Africa, for example in the *dambos* of Zimbabwe (Turner, 1986; Bell and Roberts, 1991). In parts of West Africa, for example, the seasonally damp land (*fadama*) of floodplains in northern Nigeria (Turner, 1984a; Adams, 1986), shadoofs have long been used. In northern Nigeria these were rapidly replaced with small motor-powered pumps in the 1980s.

Grazing and fishing in floodplain wetlands

Many wetlands provide important pastoral resources in Africa, often providing key areas of dry-season grazing and hence sustaining grazing systems over large areas of surrounding drylands (Scoones, 1991). A number of African wetlands on seasonal rivers are characterized by extensive seasonal grasslands which provide important grazing resources for pastoral groups. Seasonal movements by pastoralists into floodplains in the dry season can involve very large numbers of animals. In the dry season the Kafue Flats in Zambia, for example, support about 0.25 million head of cattle, while other surveys record 0.15 million cattle on the Shire marshes in Malawi, 0.3 million in the floodplain of the Gambia River and 0.8 million in the Sudd in Sudan (Welcomme, 1979; Bingham, 1982; Howell *et al.*, 1988).

In the Niger Inland Delta in Mali there are about half a million people, including farmers, fishing people and two groups of pastoralists (Moorehead, 1988). The delta floods after the end of the rains, between October and December, and at this time the delta is extensively used for grazing. Fulani pastoralists are resident in the delta, and Tamasheq move in during the dry season. As the rains begin the Fulani leave the floodplain to graze their livestock in rainfed savanna grasslands away from the flood. As grazing resources and surface water supplies run out, the Fulani move back into the delta floodplains and graze livestock on the pastures emerging from the floodwaters. By March their stock are grazing the dry lake beds in the north of the delta, particularly on the wetland grass *bourgou* (*Echinochloa stagnina*) (Moorehead, 1988; Skinner, 1992).

The third main element of economic use of African floodplains is fish production. The life-cycle of many fish species is linked to seasonal flood regimes (Welcomme, 1979). The inundated floodplain is rich in nutrients, and there is rapid growth of aquatic vegetation and a bloom of micro-organisms and growth in invertebrate numbers. This provides plentiful food for fish, and in many species reproduction is timed so that they spawn when rivers are in flood, with the result that young fish grow rapidly. As the floods recede, both adult and young fish of many species move back to the main river channel, and eventually to standing pools where they survive through the dry season. There is significant predation both from fishing people and animal predators at this time of year.

The FAO estimate that there are over 60 000 fishermen on the Niger River (50 000 fishermen in the Niger Inland Delta, plus another 6000 on the River Niger in Niger and Nigeria, and 5000 on the Benue), and that together they produce 120 000 tonnes of fish per year, of which 75% comes from the Niger Inland Delta (Welcomme, 1979). Much remains to be learned about fish biology and ecology, and about floodplain fisheries, but the high productivity of floodplain wetlands is obvious, as are the close links between that productivity and the flood regime.

The impact of the development of floodplains

Floodplain wetlands represent important productive resources in many African countries faced with rising population and considerable poverty, and must have a key role to play in development. However, it is vital that the development programmes and projects in these areas are sustainable. Within the literature on sustainable development there is an emerging consensus that sustainable development should be 'directly concerned with increasing the living standards of the poor' (Barbier, 1987, p. 103), and it must address intergenerational equity and the extent to which costs and benefits of development are unequally borne by different people (Pearce *et al.*, 1988). Sustainable development must involve making sensible and effective use of natural ecosystems, such that the benefits derived from them are optimized over long periods.

Past attempts to develop African floodplains have often proved far from sustainable. The attractiveness to development planners of apparent seasonal 'excess' of water in annual floods, and of 'wastage' of water in wetlands, and the juxtaposition of relatively fertile soils and plentiful water resources, have led to attempts at river control that have had serious adverse environmental impacts on riverine wetlands (e.g. Scudder, 1980; Adams and Hughes, 1986; Adams, 1992). Most of the major African rivers have been dammed in at least one place, and their flows are controlled. Some have multiple dams. The Zambezi system, for example, is dammed on the Kafue at the Kafue Gorge Dam and at Itezhi-Tezhi Dam, and on the Zambezi itself there are dams at Kariba and at Cabora Bassa.

River control and transformation of flooding patterns have serious implications for floodplain ecology. In the lower reaches of the Tana River in Kenya a narrow strip of evergreen floodplain forest is maintained by flood-recharged groundwater in an area otherwise too dry for more than Sahelian savanna vegetation (Hughes, 1984). Dam construction, particularly the closure of the Masinga Dam in 1982, has reduced the size of the largest floods, and it is predicted that in the long run the forest will cease to replace itself. Similar ecological impacts are predicted as a result of the construction of the Turkwel Gorge Dam in northern Kenya (Adams, 1989). The impacts of dams on larger floodplain wetland areas can be more complex. On the Kafue River in Zambia the Itezhi-Tezhi Dam upstream of the Kafue Flats formed a large reservoir of 5700 million m^3 (Howard and Williams, 1982). A study of flood extent using 1981 satellite data showed fairly complex impacts on the extent of flooding, with some areas wetter than before, but a reduction in the duration of floods and erratic fluctuations in water levels in the dry season (Turner, 1984b).

River control can disrupt floodplain agriculture. In the Benue floodplain in Nigeria, for example, the reduction in flooding caused by the Lagdo Dam had a significant impact on flood-recession farming of sorghum. In the dry years of the mid-1980s, the reduction in cultivated area was 50% (Drijver and Marchand, 1985), and there was disruption of production over a wider area because of the unpredictability in timing and height of flooding. The Bakolori Dam on the Sokoto River in Nigeria had similar impacts on floodplain agriculture. Closure of the dam affected the timing of flooding downstream, and reduced both its extent and depth. Rice cultivation in the wet season became more risky than before, and there were areas too dry for rice and yet too easily water-logged by rainstorms to support dryland crops such as millet. More land was left uncultivated in the wet season and there was a reduction in the number of fields growing rice. There was also a major decline in dry-season flood-recession farming and shadoof irrigation (Adams, 1985).

Possibly the most serious single river engineering project in terms of its potential impacts is the Jonglei Canal in southern Sudan. The Sudd region consists of a vast area of permanent swamp (covering some 18 000 km^2) and seasonal wetlands (an additional 11 000 km^2) flooded by the White Nile. In addition to the swamps proper, there are extensive areas of grassland flooded by the river (*toich*), grassland flooded from local runoff and floodplain forest (Howell *et al.*, 1988).

The Sudd region contains 200 000–400 000 people. Most of them are Dinka and Nuer, who are primarily pastoralists. There are some 0.8 million cattle and perhaps 0.2 million goats and sheep in the area, plus about half a million wild grazing animals, including 0.36 million *tiang*, a large wetland antelope (Howell *et al.*, 1988). Flooding of grasslands begins with local rains in April, followed by the flooding caused by the rising level of the Nile. Livestock are moved from rainfed grasslands to lower areas as the floods recede. The wild *tiang* also migrate in response to flood patterns.

Almost half of the flow in the White Nile entering the southern end of the Sudd (about 50 billion m^3) is lost in its passage through the area, and planners have for many decades been attracted by the notion of building a canal to bypass the Sudd and thus provide more water for irrigation in Egypt and northern Sudan (Collins, 1990). The Jonglei Canal was designed to be 360 km long and to carry 20 million m^3 of water per day. Construction began in 1978, but work has been halted since the early 1980s by civil war. It is not therefore possible to do more than predict its ecological and socio-economic impacts, particularly because there has been considerable variation in the flow of the White Nile in recent decades. However, attempts to simulate the effects of the canal suggest a decline in the area of permanent swamp of between 32 and 43%, and in seasonal swamp of between 11 and 32% (Howell *et al.*, 1988). Clearly, if it were finished, the Jonglei Canal would bring about a substantial reduction in flooding in the Sudd, and ecological and socio-economic impacts over large areas.

Changes in annual flow regimes brought about by dams can have significant impacts on fish populations, and indeed a number of studies have shown this to be the case. Work on the Niger River downstream of the Kainji Dam in the 1960s showed that catch sizes fell and there were changes in the composition of the fish population (Lowe-McConnell, 1985). Similarly, in the Sokoto Valley of Nigeria, fishermen complained of reduced catches following closure of the Bakolori Dam in the late 1970s, and a number had taken to travelling hundreds of kilometres to fish elsewhere, for example at Lake Chad. It is predicted that the Diama Barrage on the River Senegal, built to prevent incursion of salt water during periods of low river flow, will cause the loss of some 7000 tonnes of shrimps and fish in the Senegal Delta. There are likely to be much larger reductions in fish catch (about 360 000 tonnes) in the middle floodplain of the Senegal due to the flood-control effects of the Manantali Dam and the development of dyked irrigation schemes. These losses are almost three times the predicted gains from new fish resources in reservoirs within the basin (Drijver and Marchand, 1985).

Clearly development projects can have a significant impact on floodplain environments. Very often these impacts are predominantly negative. They are particularly severe because knowledge on the part of engineers, economists and other planners about the ecology and human use of wetlands in Africa remains limited. To many planners, wetland environments still look under-utilized and in need of intensive development. There are considerable pressures for such development, from both national governments and international agencies. Standard techniques of environmental and economic appraisal have not in the recent past proved very effective in predicting environmental and economic impacts on wetlands and their people (Adams, 1990, 1992).

Conclusion

The substantial development of African flood-plains, and other wetland areas, is not only dependent on, but demands new approaches to, specific development projects. It is also liable to be affected by wider patterns of economic, political and social change. Floodplain resources are valuable, and as this is more widely recognized there can be fierce competition for them between different groups of people, both between those who have long had access to some of the resources of the floodplain, and between these groups and newcomers such as

urban businessmen interested in acquiring land for agriculture. Under the pressure of competition, the sustainable features of existing production systems can all too easily break down. For example, in the middle Senegal Valley there has traditionally been an elegant partitioning of floodplain resources between pastoralists, farmers and fishing people in space and time (Boutillier and Schmitz, 1987). Flooded clay basins are used by fishermen in the floods, then by agriculturalists to grow *décrue* sorghum, then finally by pastoralists in the dry season. In the rains, herders move away from the river to graze their herds in the surrounding bushland, and the fishermen take over again. This annual cycle is both symbiotic (with cattle consuming crop residues and leaving dung) and also interdependent economically (with trade in livestock products and grain), not simply within the floodplain itself, but also with the drylands outside (Boutillier and Schmitz, 1987). Unfortunately, increasing competition for resources and growing external political and economic pressures are changing these systems of shared access to floodplain resources. Production systems in the Senegal Valley are threatened by the construction of the Manantali Dam upstream (Boutillier and Schmitz, 1987), and associated irrigation development has led to conflict between farmers and herders, and eventually serious ethnic violence between Senegal and Mauritania (Horowitz, 1989). Similar conflicts about shrinking floodplain resources are emerging in other areas, for example in northern Nigeria (Kimmage, 1991).

Whether responding to major externally imposed projects or more generalized impacts of socio-economic, political or environmental change, it is clear that the sustainable development of African floodplains is important, and is likely to require new thinking and more innovative policy. In particular, there is a need for better environmental appraisal of proposed development projects, more careful consideration of costs as well as benefits and attention to issues of equity in terms of who bears them.

There may also be potential for quite new approaches to river basin development, particularly the use of dams to release artificial controlled floods to support agriculture, fishing and grazing in the downstream floodplain (Scudder, 1980, 1991). This would reduce the unpredictability in flooding which currently contributes to the risks of floodplain farming, without demanding a wholesale shift to formal irrigation. This flood release would also draw down the level of water in the reservoir itself, revealing an extensive area of damp land every year that could be used for irrigation or grazing. Existing production downstream could be maintained or enhanced by appropriate measures (e.g. provision of credit and extension advice, better roads and simple irrigation, and small technology). This controlled flood release approach has been tried on the Pongolo River in Natal in South Africa (Scudder, 1991), and on the Senegal River between 1988 and 1990 (Salem-Murdock and Horowitz, 1991). Controlled flood releases could convert single-purpose dams (e.g. for hydroelectric power generation) into multipurpose projects that work with and not against nature.

Technically this idea of controlled floods is demanding, since it requires both an understanding of downstream floodplain hydrology, effective real-time monitoring systems and an ability to make effective decisions and releases. However, such an approach is not intrinsically more complex than the projects conventionally designed in the past. The existing economic importance of wetlands in Africa, and their potential for much greater contributions to national and local economies in the future, make it vital that they are sensitively and intelligently managed. No form of development of these environments will be successful without a thorough understanding of the dynamics of these environments and the ways in which people relate to them. This is true, of course, of other environments, but in the case of wetlands the benefits of a thorough understanding of the relations between people and environment are potentially very great, just as the costs of ignoring these relations are both serious and (perhaps fortunately), increasingly obvious.

References

Adams, W. M. (1985) The downstream impacts of dam construction: a case study from Nigeria, *Transactions of the Institute of British Geographers*, NS 10, 292–302.

Adams, W. M. (1986) Traditional agriculture and water use in the Sokoto Valley, Nigeria, *Geographical Journal*, 152, 30–43.

Adams, W. M. (1989) Dam construction and the degradation of floodplain forest on the Turkwel River, Kenya, *Land Degradation and Rehabilitation*, 1, 189–198.

Adams, W. M. (1990) *Green Development: environment and sustainability in the Third World*, Routledge, London.

Adams, W. M. (1992) *Wasting the Rain: rivers, people and planning in Africa*, Earthscan, London.

Adams, W. M. and Hughes, F. M. R. (1986) The environmental effects of dam construction in tropical Africa: impacts and planning procedures, *Geoforum*, 17(3), 403–410.

Barbier, E. B. (1987) The concept of sustainable economic development, *Environmental Conservation*, 14, 101–110.

Bell, M. and Roberts, N. (1991) The political ecology of dambo soil and water resources in Malawi, *Transactions of the Institute of British Geographers*, NS 16, 301–318.

Bingham, M. G. (1982) The livestock potential of the Kafue Flats, pp. 95–103 in G. W. Howard and G. J. Williams (eds), *Proceedings of the National Seminar on Environment and Change: the consequences of the hydroelectric power development on the utilization of the Kafue Flats, Lusaka, April 1978*, Kafue Basin Research Committee, University of Zambia, Lusaka.

Boutillier, J-L. and Schmitz, J. (1987) Gestion traditionnelle des terres (système de décrue/système pluvial) et transition vers l'irrigation, *Cahiers Sciences Humaines*, 23, 533–554.

Collins, R. O. (1990) *The Waters of the Nile: hydropolitics and the Jonglei Canal 1900–1988*, Clarendon Press, Oxford.

Drijver, C. A. and Marchand, M. (1985) *Taming the Floods: environmental aspects of floodplain development in Africa*, Centre for Environmental Studies, University of Leiden.

Dugan, P. J. (ed.) (1990) *Wetland Conservation: a review of current issues and required action*, International Union for the Conservation of Nature and Natural Resources, Gland, Switzerland.

FAO (1986) *Irrigation in Africa South of the Sahara*, Food and Agriculture Organization Investment Centre Technical Paper No. 5, Rome.

Gallais, J. (1967) *La Délta Intérieure du Niger: étude de geographie régionale*, IFAN, Dakar.

Harlan, J. R. and Pasquerau, J. (1969) Décrue agriculture in Mali, *Economic Botany*, 23, 70–74.

Horowitz, M. M. (1989) Victims of development, *Development Anthropology Network*, 7(2), 1–8.

Howard, G. W. and Williams, G. J. (eds) (1982) *Proceedings of the National Seminar on Environment and Change: the consequences of the hydroelectric power development on the utilization of the Kafue Flats, Lusaka, April 1978*, Kafue Basin Research Committee, University of Zambia, Lusaka.

Howell, P. M., Lock, M., and Cobb, S. (eds) (1988) *The Jonglei Canal: impact and opportunity*, Cambridge University Press, Cambridge.

Hughes, F. M. R. (1984) A comment on the impact of development schemes on the floodplain forests on the Tana River of Kenya, *Geographical Journal*, 150, 230–244.

Hughes, F. M. R. (in press) Wetland environments, in W. M. Adams, A. S. Goudie and A. Orme (eds), *The Physical Geography of Africa*, Oxford University Press, Oxford.

Hughes, R. H. and Hughes, J. S. (1992) *A Directory of African Wetlands*, IUCN, Gland, Switzerland and Cambridge, UK/UNEP, Nairobi, Kenya/WCMC, Cambridge.

Kimmage, K. (1991) Small scale irrigation initiatives: the problems of equity and sustainability, *Applied Geography*, 11, 5–20.

Kimmage, K. and Adams, W. M. (1992) Wetland agricultural production and river basin development in the Hadejia-Jama'are valley, Nigeria, *Geographical Journal*, 158, 1–12.

Léricollais, A. and Schmitz, J. (1984) 'La Calabasse et la Houe': techniques et outils des cultures de décrue dans la vallée du Senegal, *Cahiers ORSTOM Série Sciences Humaines*, 20(3–4), 427–452.

Lowe-McConnell, R. H. (1985) The biology of the river systems with particular reference to the fishes, pp. 101–140 in A. T. Grove (ed.), *The Niger and its Neighbours: environment, history, hydrobiology, human use and health hazards of the major West African rivers*, Balkema, Rotterdam.

Moorehead, R. (1988) Access to resources in the Niger Inland Delta, Mali, pp. 27–39 in J. Seeley and W. M. Adams (eds), *Environmental Issues in African Development Planning*, African Studies Centre Cambridge, Cambridge African Monographs 9.

Pearce, D. W., Barbier, E. B. and Markandya, A. (1988) Environmental economics and decision-making in sub-Saharan Africa. IIED–UCL London Environmental Economics Centre, London (LEEC paper 80-01).

Richards, P. (1983) Farming systems and agrarian change in West Africa, *Progress in Human Geography*, 7(1), 1–39.

Richards, P. (1985) *Indigenous Agricultural Revolution*, Hutchinson, London.

Richards, P. (1986) *Coping with Hunger: hazard and experiment in a West African rice-farming system*, Allen & Unwin, Hemel Hempstead.

Rodgers, C. and Svendsen, M. (1992) Defining irrigation: what is and isn't, *ICID Bulletin*, 41(1), 61–72.

Salem-Murdock, M. and Horowitz, M. M. (1991) Monitoring development in the Senegal river basin, *Development Anthropology Network*, 9(1), 8–15.

Scoones, I. (1991) Wetlands in drylands: key resources for agricultural and pastoral production in Africa, *Ambio*, 20, 366–371.

Scudder, T. (1980) River basin development and local initiative in Savanna environments, pp. 383–405 in D. R. Harris (ed.), *Human Ecology in Savanna Environments*, Academic Press, London.

Scudder, T. (1991) The need and justification for maintaining transboundary flood regimes: the Africa case, *Natural Resources Journal*, 31(1), 75–107.

Seignobos, C. (1984) Instruments aratoires du Tchad Méridional et du Nord-Cameroun, *Cahiers ORSTOM Série Sciences Humaines* 20(3–4), 537–573.

Skinner, J. (1992) Conservation in the Inner Niger Delta in Mali: the interdependence of ecological and socio-economic research, pp. 41–48 in E. Maltby, P. J. Dugan and J. C. Lefeuve (eds), *Conservation and Development: the sustainable use of wetland resources*, IUCN, Gland, Switzerland.

Turner, B. L. (1984a) Changing land-use patterns in the fadamas of northern Nigeria, pp. 140–170 in E. P. Scott (ed.), *Life Before the Drought*, Allen & Unwin, Hemel Hempstead.

Turner, B. L. (1984b) The effect of dam construction on the flooding of the Kafue Flats, pp. 1–9 in W. L. Handlos and G. J. Williams (eds), *Development on the Kafue Flats: the last five years*, Kafue Basin Research Committee, University of Zambia, Lusaka.

Turner, B. L. (1986) The importance of dambos in African agriculture, *Land Use Policy*, 3, 343–347.

Welcomme, R. L. (1979) *Fisheries Ecology of Floodplain Rivers*, Longman, London.

2

Policies for pastoralists: new directions for pastoral development in Africa

Ian Scoones

Introduction

Pastoralists are people who make a living primarily, although not exclusively, from livestock. They make up around 15% of the total population of arid and semi-arid areas of East and West Africa (NOPA, 1992). Around 60% of all ruminant livestock in Africa are found in these dry zones, owned and managed by pastoralists, farmers, traders and urban dwellers alike (Winrock, 1992). The total value of livestock products from these areas is estimated at around 25% of the total agricultural output (USDA, 1990). Although often marginalized from mainstream economic and political life, dryland environments of Africa are nevertheless important economically as areas supporting the livelihoods of many people.

This chapter explores the implications of recent thinking in range ecology for future directions of pastoral development in Africa. The first part of the chapter illustrates that the concept of carrying capacity is not as simple as is sometimes assumed. Most dry rangelands in Africa are characterized by high levels of spatial and temporal variability in production. These are non-equilibrium systems where static concepts such as carrying capacity have little utility.

The second part of the chapter examines the implications of this rethinking of range ecology and explores the requirements for ensuring effective, opportunistic management in variable environments. Approaches to such issues as land tenure, institutional capacity, social welfare interventions and development investments are discussed in the light of recent ecological thinking that emphasizes the need to maintain flexibility, responsiveness and adaptation to uncertain conditions.

Rethinking range ecology

Carrying capacity

The term 'carrying capacity' has caused more confusion than perhaps any other term in applied ecology. The popular notion of carrying capacity has a neat and tidy appeal, with the interaction between population and resources defined by a simple relationship leading to a single, ideal number. Simple models of steady-state relationships can apparently be used to define the magic number. For administrators and managers of resources the task therefore appears simple;

People and Environment in Africa. Edited by Tony Binns
©1995 John Wiley & Sons Ltd

if numbers are above the level, then they must be removed (destocking, culling, marketing, resettlement), if they are below there is no need to worry. But, of course the world is more complex than this. This is the problem with simplistic, popular notions of carrying capacity that have been transferred from mathematical ecology, via applied resource management, to popular parlance in the wider field of the environment and development debate.

Carrying capacity, formally defined, is that point when the rate of growth of a population becomes zero. That is when births plus immigration are equal to deaths plus emigration. This is commonly referred to as the point 'K' in ecological science (Caughley, 1979). However, the application of the concept of carrying capacity in the applied ecological and resource management sciences has resulted in a proliferation of definitions. This has caused many problems, as different people, depending on their disciplinary training, have ended up talking about different things, but using the same term. In livestock development, the ecological definition has been confounded with an economic definition of carrying capacity, that incorporates normative management objectives.

In the pastoral setting, there are different stocking rates appropriate to different forms of pastoral production (Behnke and Scoones, 1993). Three cases can be considered. First, if there is a market for stud animals, ranchers may find it profitable to sell few animals in premium condition raised on abundant forage at very low stocking densities. Alternatively, producers may sell ungraded meat by weight. Such producers will keep stocking densities at an economic carrying capacity level where weight gains are maximized. Finally, subsistence-oriented pastoralists who seek to harvest animal output in the form of live-animal products such as milk, blood, manure, traction and transport do not require high levels of slaughter to meet their production objectives. At some cost to output, health and viability of individual animals, such producers may wish to maintain high levels of aggregate output at high stocking densities, at levels approaching ecological carrying capacity ('K').

Thus in the same area, with the same animal and plant species, a pastoral manager may choose three (or any number of) different carrying capacities. Carrying capacity in this context has adopted a different set of meanings that are less to do with biology, but more to do with normative economic (or aesthetic, cultural, conservation) management decisions. These are not the *ecological* carrying capacity levels of theoretical ecology ('K'), but *economic* carrying capacities.

Three questions are asked by the manager in each case. First, what is the economic (or other) objective of management of this resource? Second, what is the way of ensuring this objective by adjusting animal numbers? And finally, what is the permissible level of environmental change? All of these questions are value judgements. Measuring carrying capacity under these settings is not a mechanical, positivist, scientific procedure; it is a socially, economically and politically constructed decision.

In the search for an acceptable definition of 'carrying capacity', Richard Bell concludes

that the only embracing definition of carrying capacity is: 'That density of animals and plants that allows the manager to get what he wants out of the system.' Thus any specific definition of carrying capacity must be expressed in relation to a particular objective, and it must be defined precisely since there are no 'natural' stability points in such interactive systems that act as foci for self-defining concepts (Bell, 1985, p. 15).

Depending on whether we are talking about per individual animal or per unit area, the chosen stocking rate level will differ (Jones and Sandland, 1974). But the important point is that the appropriate stocking rate for livestock on any rangeland will change, depending on the economic (or other) objectives of the producer(s). So, for instance, stocking rates for sire bull breeding, beef production from steers, pastoral meat, milk, blood systems and agropastoral production where animals are used for service uses (draft power, transport, etc.) will differ (from low to high levels) (Scoones, 1993).

The problem with the application of mainstream range management is that the notion of economic carrying capacity has become firmly linked with ranch beef production systems. The profession has been so dominated by concerns with ranch production, whether in the Americas, Africa or Australia, that the language has been appropriated and so the definition and the measures standardized. Thus when used outside the beef ranch setting, the conventional definition and conventional measures are usually inappropriate (Behnke and Scoones, 1993).

The indicators used to 'measure' carrying capacity in beef ranching systems concentrate on changes in the vegetation. Particular grass species are identified that act as indicators (increaser and decreaser species) to the ranch manager of trend and status of range condition. If a particular grass species starts to increase in prevalence or another one disappears this suggests that the stocking rate is inappropriate and must be adjusted. Range management thus has become the management of beef systems, using assumptions about vegetation succession that are largely inapplicable to the highly variable environmental settings of dry African rangelands.

What may constitute 'range degradation' to a beef rancher may represent beneficial environmental change to another producer pursuing a different economic objective. The problem is that the 'beef paradigm' has become so prevalent, and the indicators and measures used so widely, that, irrespective of economic production system, range degradation is proclaimed on the basis of irrelevant indicators or measures. The confusion over what is and is not environmental degradation and appropriate carrying capacity abounds, especially in Africa. Huge 'desertification control' programmes or drastic destocking policies are instituted on the basis of a hopeless confusion over definition and appropriate measurement (Warren and Khogali, 1992).

Non-equilibrium environments

Even if the confounding of what is assumed to be a fundamental and intrinsic ecological 'fact' with something that is essentially a normative,

economic decision was resolved, seeking an appropriate number (or set of numbers), duly related to the objectives of the producers, may be like seeking the holy grail. The assumption behind the very idea of an equilibrium carrying capacity may be flawed in many settings. The dynamics of many ecological systems are such that equilibrium assumptions do not apply—temporal variability (fluctuations and episodic events), spatial heterogeneity and complex dynamic interactions between species may all mean that non-equilibrium dynamics apply much of the time, especially in dryland areas. In this case, the very notion of carrying capacity becomes meaningless.

If rainfall varies widely between seasons, then a different level of plant and animal population can be expected at each point in time. Under these conditions, where population numbers are primarily affected by external factors (i.e. rainfall levels), there is little opportunity for the population to reach a ceiling of ecological carrying capacity, as a series of crashes and recovery cycles are imposed by the inherent variability of the environment. This may be a common pattern in dryland Africa, or anywhere where system dynamics are externally driven, overriding the influence of internal negative feedback mechanisms. Under such settings, there is no natural 'balance of nature' and no homeostatic mechanism for equilibrium. For instance, in the Turkana region of northern Kenya livestock populations follow a pattern of 'boom and bust' over time with livestock numbers determined by patterns of climate variability. Research has shown that Turkana pastoralists do not overgraze their rangelands as has sometimes been supposed, instead they respond opportunistically to high levels of environmental variability (Ellis and Swift, 1988; Ellis *et al.*, 1993).

Under these conditions, population stability is sought through other means—through shifts in spatial scale and through compensation and substitution strategies. If a pastoral population suffers a local fodder shortfall, conventional equilibrium thinking would recommend a fine-tuning of animal numbers; this in turn would feed back to an increase in plant fodder and a maintenance of population stability. However, if the fodder shortfall has been caused by an external factor (such as an occasional drought), then fine-tuned adjustments may be irrelevant. The options are wider, with the expansion of the spatial scale (movement of animals through transhumance) or temporary local substitutions for the period of crisis (switching between or importation of alternative fodder sources).

Conventional range management, and much of applied ecological science, has always adopted an equilibrium view. Stocking rate (numbers/area/time) adjustments have always concentrated on the changing of animal numbers, rather than seeking management options that manipulated area or time. Pastoralists operating in the non-equilibrium environments of the drylands use the range of strategies, but flexible movement and spatial and temporal adjustments are the key to success. Mark Westoby and colleagues suggest that under non-equilibrium conditions

range management would not see itself as establishing a permanent equilibrium. Rather it would see itself as engaged in a continuing game, the object of which is to seize opportunities and evade hazards, so far as possible. The emphasis would be on timing and flexibility, rather than on establishing a fixed policy (Westoby et al., 1989).

Opportunistic management

In the non-equilibrium environments of dry pastoral areas in Africa, an opportunistic approach to management is required (Sandford, 1982; 1994). This involves efficient tracking, where variable available feed supply is matched with animal numbers. There are a variety of ways this can be achieved:

- Increasing the amount of locally available feed by importing fodder, managing browse trees or improving the productivity of high-value patches within dry rangelands (Bayer and Waters-Bayer, 1994).
- Reducing the amount of feed that animals need by changing watering regimes, reducing parasite loads or by selecting hardy, indigenous breeds (Western and Finch, 1986).

- Moving animals to areas of available fodder. This may involve long transhumant movements, as in the seasonal migrations of herds in the Sahel (Breman and de Wit, 1983), or more localized movement in agropastoral systems (Scoones, 1992).
- Destocking and restocking in response to drought cycles through sale and repurchase, raiding or loaning arrangements (Toulmin, 1994).

These are strategies that have always been followed by pastoralists. In addition, livestock management is usually combined with other ways of sustaining livelihoods, such as crop cultivation and seeking off-farm employment.

However, the ability to survive in dry areas is being constrained and tracking sometimes fails. There is often a shortage of skilled labour to carry out fine-tuned herding of animals. This is affected by changing ownership patterns of pastoral herds, as increasingly herds are owned by 'part-time pastoralists'. For instance, many animals herded by the Il Chamus in Kenya are owned by people resident in towns or cities who have invested in livestock on the rangelands (Little, 1985). Access to grazing land is another major constraint for African pastoralists. Encroachment by crop farmers on to land previously used as key grazing resources is undermining pastoralists' ability to respond flexibly to uncertain environmental conditions. In Tanzania, the establishment of agricultural schemes, the gazetting of national parks or forest reserves and the titling of village lands are also major constraints in some areas for Maasai and Barabaig pastoralists (Lane and Moorehead, 1994).

Policies for pastoralists

In the past, development interventions have limited African pastoralists' ability to survive in dry areas. Development planners were influenced by equilibrium thinking about rangeland areas and have tried to impose rigid and inflexible solutions through top-down, blueprint plans. These have taken many guises, but the notion of a fixed carrying capacity has been centrally important. For instance in Botswana, the development projects of the 1960s and 1970s focused on a ranch management model, where paddocking, rotational grazing and regulated stocking rates were intended to result in increased offtake and reduced environmental impact (White, 1992). Across Africa such projects failed. Research from all parts of Africa has shown that returns per hectare from ranching projects were invariably lower than a flexible opportunistic pastoral system (Abel, 1993; Scoones, 1994).

The failure of past projects in pastoral areas is now well documented. But what are the alternatives? What are the basic elements that would support, rather than hinder, pastoralists' adaptive strategies? One important lesson from the past is that technical interventions are inadequate without consideration of institutional, organizational and wider policy issues. The following sections outline some of the key challenges.

Tenure: rights of access, rights of use

In non-equilibrium environments flexible rights of access to grazing and water resources are required. In pastoral areas there are usually many different and often overlapping rights to resources, with arrangements varying from open access, to communal use, to exclusive use, to privatization. The degree to which it is worthwhile investing in defending and managing a resource will depend on its value. In large tracts of dry areas there are limited levels of tenure control, but in high-value patches more exclusive forms of access may be necessary (Behnke, 1994).

Increasingly such key resources are being privatized or are being expropriated for agricultural use. This has very serious implications, because access to resources such as water points, salt licks or fodder reserves is usually vital for survival during dry periods. The changing access to key resource sites has led to serious conflict in pastoral areas, both between pastoral groups and between pastoralists and farming populations. There is thus an increasing need for conflict

negotiation and arbitration procedures. For instance, in northern Nigeria conflict between Fulani pastoralists and settled agriculturalists has intensified as farmers have increasingly exploited the dry-season grazing areas of wetland areas for small-scale irrigation (Kolawole, 1991).

In order that rights of use can be protected and reasonable access to resource guaranteed, the situation must be recognized in law. In more stable, predictable equilibrium environments tenure can be fairly easily specified. However, in non-equilibrium environments, laws need to assign access rights, particularly to key resource sites, and provide a specified procedural framework for conflict resolution (Vedeld, 1994).

Land access and rights are highly politicized in pastoral areas. In most cases, pastoralists have limited political leverage and are marginalized in national political decisions. Institutional mechanisms for more effective lobbying by pastoral organizations will be a prerequisite for more effective land-use planning that allows for opportunism.

Institutional capacity

In highly variable environments, it is essential to develop solutions at the local level. However, such a local level approach needs to be set within a broader hierarchy of institutions responsible for resource management issues at different levels. For example, certain aspects of pastoral resource management and mobility must be addressed at national and sub-regional levels, particularly in years of drought. The process of institution building at local level is inevitably slow, requiring patience and an explicit recognition of differentiation between people and their divergent interests. Experience from work with pastoral organizations in the Sahel demonstrates the need to start small, working with existing organizations. Different types of group may be appropriate for different tasks; permanent organizations may be formed around regular, common tasks or needs which are widely felt, while *ad hoc* bodies tackle episodic events or more specific interests and activities (Sylla, 1994; Shanmugaratnam *et al.*, 1992).

27

Table 2.1 *New directions for pastoral development in Africa (from Scoones, 1994; Sandford, 1994)*

Area	'Old' thinking	'New' thinking
Objectives	Focus on commodity production: livestock development	Focus on livelihoods: pastoral development
Range management	Open range improvement (legumes, fodder trees, rotations)	Focus on key resources: improvement, rehabilitation, creation
	Paddocking and restrictive movement: fences	Mobility and flexibility: no fences
Planning	Blueprint development planning	Flexible, adaptive planning, with local involvement and a recognition of uncertainty
Drought	'Normal' year development and drought relief separated	Drought 'proofing' and safety net provision integrated
	Focus on production issues in 'normal' years	Focus on tracking: de/restocking supplementary feeding, etc.
Tenure	Fixed tenure regimes: privatization (or exclusive communal)	Flexible tenure: complex mix of overlapping and integrated regimes
	Conflict issues largely ignored	Focus on conflict negotiation, mediation and arbitration
Institutions and administration	Service delivery package through centralized extension services	Pastoral organizations for local management issues
	Extension worker for technical delivery	Extension workers as 'institutional organizers'

While pastoralists tend to be politically marginal in most African countries, they could have greater impact on government policy-making through the establishment of a federation of associations. Such federations could take forward a programme of lobbying government and donors on important issues, such as land tenure (Zeidane, 1993).

Pastoral areas provide a classic setting for decentralization of power and responsibilities to the lowest level consistent with provision of services and maintaining accountability (Swift, 1994). However, the state needs to maintain certain critical functions to resolve conflicts between different resource users, and ensure its decisions are respected. Customary institutions do not necessarily provide fair and effective means for resolution of conflict, particularly where there are many different interests at stake.

When tracking fails: safety nets and contingency plans

Tracking does not always work. Conflict, full-scale war, major food shortages and other crises seriously undermine survival in pastoral areas. For instance, recent years have seen major upheavals in many pastoral areas, such as in Somalia and Sudan. It is therefore important that contingency plans are formulated and safety nets are provided to enable people to survive the crisis period, and to return to normal life afterwards. Such safety nets could include:

- Supporting livestock prices in times of stress;
- Food aid, cash aid, food-for-work;
- Nutritional and veterinary assistance for livestock;
- Providing alternative livelihoods for pastoralists, allowing them to re-enter the pastoral economy later.

Development strategies for pastoral areas

Flexibility is the key to planning for development in pastoral areas. Blueprint planning and imposed solutions do not work. If planners use a mechanistic approach based on single objectives (e.g. red meat production) or simplistic environmental management tools (e.g. carrying capacity), plans will be rejected and pastoral livelihoods potentially undermined. Instead, a more adaptive, process-oriented approach to planning is required that builds from an understanding of existing pastoral management strategies and local knowledge of environment and resources (Korten, 1980; Chambers, 1983).

Table 2.1 summarizes the basic elements of a new approach for pastoral development in Africa, contrasting this with past approaches.

Conclusion

Over the last 30 years, millions of dollars have been spent on elaborate projects in pastoral areas in Africa with few obvious benefits. Many development agencies, including national governments, have now effectively abandoned dryland pastoral areas as 'no hope' zones in favour of so-called 'high potential' areas.

But there are good reasons not to abandon pastoral areas. First, the cost is potentially very high. Many pastoral areas in Africa are characterized by conflict or civil strife, with great human costs borne by pastoral people. National governments and the international community, which bear the monetary costs of insecurity and famine, are also badly affected. These problems will only increase if serious efforts are not made to support development and increase pastoralists' livelihood security.

Second, the reasons for past failures are known, and therefore can be avoided. Failures have been analysed, lessons learnt, and some recent projects have had more success. If the most basic mistake of the past has been to impose equilibrium solutions (such as ranching) on a non-equilibrium environment, then with improved understanding, this type of mistake can be avoided. However, such mistakes will only be avoided if a serious attempt is made to listen to what pastoralists are saying about their needs; if development agencies and governments are willing to learn from their experiences; and if training for professional staff working in pastoral areas is modified to take

account of the complexities of working in a highly variable environment.

Acknowledgements

This chapter draws on work carried out in collaboration with Roy Behnke of the Overseas Development Institute, London and Brian Kerr of the Commonwealth Secretariat. The work has been supported by the Overseas Development Administration (UK) and the World Bank. The ecological arguments that form the basis of the new directions for pastoral development are explored more fully in Behnke *et al.* (1993). The policy issues arising are examined in Scoones (1994).

References

Abel, N. O. J. (1993) Reducing animal numbers on southern African communal range: is it worth it? pp. 173–195 in R. H. Behnke, I. Scoones and C. Kerven (eds), *Range Ecology at Disequilibrium: new models of natural variability and pastoral adaptation in African savannas*, Overseas Development Institute, London.

Bayer, W. and Waters-Bayer, A. (1994) Forage alternatives from range and field: pastoral forage management and improvement in the African drylands, in I. Scoones (ed.), *Living with Uncertainty: new directions in pastoral development in Africa*, Intermediate Technology Publications, London.

Behnke, R. H. (1994) Natural resource management in pastoral Africa, *Development Policy Review*, 12, 5–27.

Behnke, R. H. and Scoones, I. (1993) Rethinking range ecology: implications for rangeland management in Africa, pp. 1–30 in R. H. Behnke, I. Scoones and C. Kerven (eds), *Range Ecology at Disequilibrium: new models of natural variability and pastoral adaptation in African savannas*, London.

Behnke, R. H., Scoones, I. and Kerven, C. (eds) (1993) *Range Ecology at Disequilibrium: new models of natural variability and pastoral adaptation in African savannas*, Overseas Development Institute, London.

Bell, R. H. V. (1985) Carrying capacity and offtake quotas, pp. 147–181 in R. H. V. Bell and E. McShane Caluzi (eds), *Conservation and Wildlife Management in Africa*, US Peace Corps, Washington.

Breman, H. and de Wit, C. (1983) Rangeland productivity and exploitation in the Sahel, *Science*, 221, 1341–1347.

Caughley, G. (1979) What is this thing called carrying capacity? pp. 2–8 in M. S. Boyce and L. D. Hayden-Wing (eds), *North American Elk: ecology, behaviour and management*, University of Wyoming Press, Laramie, Wyoming.

Chambers, R. (1983) *Rural Development: putting the last first*. Longman, London.

Ellis, J. E., Coughenour, M. and Swift, D. M. (1993) Climate variability, ecosystem stability and the implications for range and livestock development, pp. 31–41 in R. H. Behnke, I Scoones and C. Kerven (eds), *Range Ecology at Disequilibrium: new models of natural variability and pastoral adaptation in African savannas*, Overseas Development Institute, London.

Ellis, J. E. and Swift, D. M. (1988) Stability of African pastoral ecosystems: alternative paradigms and implications for development, *Journal of Range Management*, 41(6), 458–459.

Jones, R. J. and Sandland, R. L. (1974) The relation between animal gain and stocking rate: derivation of the relation from the results of grazing trials, *Journal of Agricultural Science*, 83, 335–341.

Kolawole, A. (1991) Economics and management of fadama in northern Nigeria, Part 3a, pp. 1–28 in I. Scoones (ed.), *Wetlands in Drylands: the agroecology of savanna systems in Africa*, International Institute for Environment and Development, London.

Korten, D. C. (1980) Community organization and rural development: a learning process approach, *Public Administration Review*, 20, 480–511.

Lane, C. and Moorehead, R. (1994) New directions in rangeland resource tenure and policy, pp. 116–133 in I. Scoones (ed.), *Living with Uncertainty: new directions in pastoral development in Africa*, Intermediate Technology Publications, London.

Little, P. (1985) Absentee herd owners and part-time pastoralists: the political economy of resource use in northern Kenya, *Human Ecology*, 13, 131–151.

NOPA (1992) *Pastoralists at a Crossroads. Survival and development issues in African pastoralism*, Project for Nomadic Pastoralists in Africa, UNICEF/UNSO, Nairobi.

Sandford, S. (1982) Pastoral strategies and desertification: opportunism and conservatism in dry lands, pp. 61–80. in B. Spooner and H. S. Mann (eds), *Desertification and Development: dryland ecology in social perspective*, Academic Press, London.

Sandford, S. (1994) New directions for pastoral development in Africa: improving the efficiency of opportunism, pp. 174–182 in I. Scoones (ed.), *Living with Uncertainty: new directions in pastoral development in Africa*, Intermediate Technology Publications, London.

Scoones, I. (1992) Coping with drought: responses of herders and livestock in contrasting savanna environments in southern Zimbabwe, *Human Ecology*, 20, 293–314.

Scoones, I. (1993) Economic and ecological carrying capacity: applications to pastoral systems in Zimbabwe, pp. 96–117 in E. Barbier (ed.), *Economics and Ecology: new frontiers and sustainable development*, Chapman and Hall, London.

Scoones, I. (ed.) (1994) *Living with Uncertainty: new directions in pastoral development in Africa*, Intermediate Technology Publications, London.

Shanmugaratnam, N., Vedeld, T., Mossige, A. and Bovin, M. (1992) *Resource Management and Pastoral Institution Building in the West African Sahel*, World Bank Discussion Paper, Africa Technical Department Series No. 175, Washington.

Swift, J. (1994) Dynamic ecological systems and pastoral administration, pp. 153–173 in I. Scoones (ed.), *Living with Uncertainty: new directions in pastoral development in Africa*, Intermediate Technology Publications, London.

Sylla, D. (1994) Pastoral organisations for uncertain environments, pp. 134–152 in I. Scoones (ed.), *Living with Uncertainty: new directions in pastoral development in Africa*, Intermediate Technology Publications, London.

Toulmin, C. (1994) Tracking through drought: options for destocking and restocking, pp. 95–115 in I. Scoones (ed.), *Living with Uncertainty: new directions in pastoral development in Africa*, Intermediate Technology Publications, London.

USDA (1990) *World Agricultural Trends and Indicators, 1970–1989*, Statistical Bulletin 815, US Department of Agriculture, Washington.

Vedeld, T. (1994) *The State and Rangeland Management: creation and erosion of pastoral institutions in Mali*, Dryland Networks Programme Issues Paper No. 46, January, IIED, London.

Warren, A. and Khogali, M. (1992) *Assessment of Desertification and Drought in the Sudano-Sahelian Region 1985–1991*, United Nations Sahelian Office, New York.

Western, D. and Finch, V. (1986) Cattle and pastoralism: survival and production in arid lands, *Human Ecology*, 14, 77–94.

Westoby, M., Walker, B. and Noy-Meir, I. (1989) Opportunistic management of rangelands not at equilibrium, *Journal of Range Management*, 42, 266–274.

White, R. (1992) *Livestock Development and Pastoral Production on Communal Rangelands in Botswana*, Commonwealth Secretariat, London.

Winrock (1992) *Assessment of Animal Agriculture in Sub-Saharan Africa*, Winrock International, Morilton.

Zeidane, M. O. (1993) Pastoral associations: latest evolutions and perspectives, paper presented at the conference on New Directions in African Range Management and Policy, 31 May–4 June, Woburn, UK, IIED, ODI and Commonwealth Secretariat, London.

3

Gender, environment and development in sub-Saharan Africa

Hazel Barrett and Angela Browne

Introduction

The link between environmental stress and the development crisis has been a recurring theme of recent reports and studies on sub-Saharan Africa (Oxfam, 1993; WCED, 1987; World Bank, 1992; Unicef, 1994). One of the underlying themes in the environment/development debate is that of gender, and in particular the multiple roles played by women, many of which involve environmental management (Dankelman and Davidson, 1988; Sen and Grown, 1987). Two competing theoretical perspectives have been put forward for the analysis of gender and the environment: the 'women and environment approach' and 'ecofeminism'. In this chapter these two perspectives will be evaluated and a new approach suggested that takes into account the socio-economic context of the gender–environment interface. The links between women's gender roles and their use of environmental resources will show that women, even more than men, are responsible for environmental management. Examples will be given to illustrate the roles played by women, their impacts on the environment and the changes brought about by the process of development. The many socio-economic disturbances affecting sub-Saharan Africa will also be shown to impact upon gender and environment in diverse and sometimes unpredictable ways.

Theoretical perspectives

Two theoretical perspectives have been particularly evident and influential in the literature and policy framework concerning gender and the environment. The first view grew out of the 'women and development' debate of the 1980s. This view, labelled the 'women and environment approach', emphasizes the important role of women as environmental resource managers, stressing in particular their vulnerability to declines in resource availability. This viewpoint advocates the need to develop environmental programmes directed at assisting women. Such programmes treat men and women separately with women's projects running parallel to and separate from men's programmes. The second approach known as 'ecofeminism' derives from a philosophy of feminism which assumes women have a natural affinity with nature. This contrasts with men's urge to control and manipulate the natural world. This philosophy places the burden of environmental

People and Environment in Africa. Edited by Tony Binns
©1995 John Wiley & Sons Ltd

regeneration and conservation squarely on the shoulders of women, absolving men from environmental responsibilities. Advocates of this view seek respect and support for women's efforts to conserve the environment (Jackson, 1993; Joekes *et al.*, 1994).

However, both these viewpoints can be criticized for underestimating the complexities and inter-actions of men and women in social reproduction and income generation in sub-Saharan Africa. Jackson (1993) and Joekes *et al.* (1994) have both published detailed critiques of these philosophies. The 'women and environment' approach is criticized for *assuming* it is in women's interests to conserve local resources, when often the use of these resources may represent acts of desperation in a situation of increasing poverty. It also ignores the increasing demands on women's time from biological and social reproduction, as well as income generation and community management, which ultimately limit the time that women can spend on environmental conservation and regeneration. This approach also implies that gender roles are fixed, unchanging and universal. This is an assumption which is increasingly being challenged as a result of socio-economic shocks, such as economic restructuring and the AIDS epidemic. There is evidence in the 1990s that men help their womenfolk much more than researchers in the 1980s assumed (Cromwell and Winpenny, 1993; Joekes *et al.*, 1994). The ecofeminist school is also widely criticized for its belief that women have a greater affinity to nature than men, which suggests that affinity to nature is biologically determined. These assumptions are contradictory to feminism and ignore the function of social relations in allocating roles and the fact that women are often subordinate to men (Boserup, 1990). Once again it may be women's status, lack of opportunity outside the household, and poverty, which make them apparently 'closer to nature', not their biological make-up.

Gender roles and the environment

Women in Africa are substantial users of environ-mental resources. Through their roles in production,

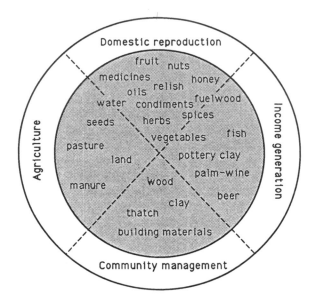

Figure 3.1 *Women's roles and use of environmental resources*

reproduction and community management, women, more so than men, have responsibility for environmental use, for the redistribution of environmental resources and potentially for the destruction or conservation of these resources. Figure 3.1 shows some of the ways in which women's gender roles require them to utilize the natural environment.

Domestic reproduction

In their role as providers for the household, women supply a great variety of produce, including fruits, vegetables, spices, herbs and other relishes, in addition to the major cereal and other subsistence food crops. They are the collectors and carriers of most of the fuelwood and water used in domestic reproduction, often aided by the labour of their children. Recent work by Bryceson and Howe (1993), on rural household transport in Ghana and Tanzania shows the predominance of women as transporters, with women in the Ghana study spending an average of 1000 hours per year on transport activities, more than 300 of this on transporting fuelwood and water. The corresponding figures for men are 350 hours and 25 hours respectively. In Tanzania more than 900 hours per year, out of a total transport time of over 1800 hours, was spent by women in transporting fuel and water. The burden of this work has been highlighted in numerous studies in rural Africa, focusing usually on measurements of time or energy expenditure. The number of trips, distance carried, weight of the loads and time involved reveal a staggering burden for women, with *average* times of 10 hours per week and headloads or backloads of 25 kg being normal.

Over large parts of Africa deforestation, brought about by tree cutting for industrial use, the privatization of previously waste or common land and rapid rates of population increase, has contributed to rural energy shortages and forced women to spend even more time in collecting and transporting fuelwood (Sen and Grown, 1987). Thus, the intersection of macroeconomic and social forces has forced women, because of their gender role as household reproducers, to bear the cost of environmental decline.

Income generation

Many forest products used by women for direct consumption also enter the market economy and play a role, albeit seasonally, in income generation. Edible wild roots, fruits, mushrooms, honey and insects are traded in local markets, with kindling sticks, herbal and medicinal products also important as tradable commodities. In this way, the importance of women as users and distributors of forest products, usually on a small scale and within the local economy, could be claimed by ecofeminists to epitomize the bonds between women and nature. An alternative interpretation is that the selling of 'free' goods from the local environment is a means by which rural women can survive, despite limited access to land or capital resources.

Palm wine and local maize or millet beers are also ubiquitous in the markets and back streets of sub-Saharan Africa. In most communities there is a well-established gender control over these commodities, with men invariably the 'owners' of the trees or crops and women the sellers of the liquor, either in bars or at informal drinking parlours. In the urban areas of Southern and Eastern Africa the 'shebeens' and 'beer gardens' represent a large-scale, highly commoditized (though often illegal) sector of the economy, where women dominate the brewing and selling of the liquor and sometimes the wholesaling and transporting of the main ingredients, maize and sorghum flour (Nelson, 1988).

Domestic pottery production, a task ascribed to women in most of sub-Saharan Africa, is a major localized user of environmental resources. Traditional techniques of pottery making are still important locally in many countries and are as much dependent on a good supply of fuelwood for firing as they are for clays of the required quality. Another income-generating activity widely undertaken by women is drying, smoking and selling fish. In the fisheries industry responsibilities are often clearly delineated on gender lines, with men responsible for catching fish and women for its processing and marketing. In the traditional coastal fishing villages in The Gambia, for example, men go out fishing, women buy the catch on the beach, clean and gut the fish and then headload it to the drying and smoking facilities located on the outskirts of the villages. In response to the deterioration of forest resources in the coastal belt, fuel-efficient smoking ovens have been introduced as part of the government's fisheries development programme.

Community management

Women's role as community managers is becoming increasingly important as the 'efficiency' approach to development under conditions of structural adjustment transfers responsibilities from the state to local communities (Moser, 1989). Villagers now have to find more local resources to build, repair and maintain schools, health posts, watercourses and roads, and women's labour is crucial to the successful implementation of such projects.

In a Kenyan example, Thomas-Slater (1992) found that when there are community-based labour-intensive tasks to be done, it is the women, not the men in the community, who are mobilized by the chiefs and party leaders to undertake them. In The Gambia women are required by the male village elders to clear public refuse sites, sweep the public ways and fill in pot-holes in an attempt to improve the health environment of the village (authors' fieldwork, 1992). As in the Kenyan example, women are notified of the task to be done and the timetable for completing it, and must turn up with the necessary equipment on the designated day. All these activities make inroads into women's time, not only for the labouring task but also in collecting material from the bush and headloading it to the village. The use of women as unpaid labour is consistent with a view that sees women's time as 'elastic' and free, which in turn reflects their subordinate position to men within society. However, in improving the environment of the village, women are also contributing to the productive capabilities of their families and to a more healthy environment in which to carry out their diverse roles.

Agricultural production

Agricultural production is the most important economic activity of women in sub-Saharan Africa, and the most directly dependent on environmental resources. In most countries women constitute over half of the agricultural labour force and in many countries, including The Gambia and Kenya, the figure exceeds 70% (Momsen, 1991). The environment for women's agriculture depends crucially on local practices of access to and rights over land, as well as their access to credit, technology and training. Over much of sub-Saharan Africa communal land-holding and user-rights (usufruct) exist, and women are entitled to cultivate land either through their birthright or more usually through marriage to a village resident. Divisions of land, crops, trees and other resources along gender lines are universal, but are locality and ethnically specific.

For example, in The Gambia Mandinka women have customary rights to rice-land, inherited through the female line and spatially separated from men's land. In some parts of Africa husbands and wives have joint rights to a piece of land, but each 'own' different crops on this land. The most widespread system in sub-Saharan Africa is that women are entitled to land through their husband's family, and the size, location and quality of this land are principally determined by the husband's status, and population pressure.

In much of rural Africa, either as a result of population pressure as in northern Nigeria, or of government policy inherited from the colonial past as in Kenya and Zimbabwe, land reform has promoted individual rights to land. A recurring theme of studies undertaken on the gender implications of this trend is that land is almost always registered in the names of men. In western Kenya, for example, a study of 135 women farmers found that in only 8 cases was the land registered in the woman's name alone, and in the majority of cases the land was registered in the sole name of the women's sons or husbands (Young, 1993). In Zimbabwe it is estimated that to date about 90% of the permits in the resettlement schemes have been allocated to male household 'heads', even if they are absentees; women are eligible to be permit holders only if they are widows (J. Elliott, pers. comm., 1994). This process is also documented for other countries where development projects involve taking over communal land, usually for irrigated schemes. Dey (1985) reports on the experience of irrigated rice projects in five African countries. In all of these women were dispossessed of their customary rights to land and men were registered as the new owners once the irrigation works had been installed. Among the many environmental impacts of these changes, the most significant is the loss of women's specialized knowledge systems that have enabled specific microenvironmental conditions to be exploited. In West African rice farming systems, where women have adapted hundreds of rice varieties over at least two centuries, this will have profound consequences for food production, genetic diversity and the long-term sustainability of these wetland environments (Carney, 1993).

In general, then, African women do not have control over the most important environmental resource, land, and this has significant repercussions on their ability to manage this resource successfully. When to this is added their restricted access to complementary resources such as cash incomes, credit, education and technology, it is hardly surprising that women dominate the 'resource-poor' category of African farmers. Resource-poor farmers often occupy 'marginal' lands that need 'the most infrastructure, management and external inputs if their utilization is not to result in land degradation and environmental destruction' (quoted in Elliott, 1994, p. 69). It is inevitable that women, without these inputs, and often with only their own labour power and that of their children, manage their agricultural land in an increasingly unsustainable way. The imperative for women is food production for immediate needs and this may involve reducing fallow periods, deforestation, reduction in crop diversity and less use of nitrogen-fixing crops. As proponents of the 'women and environment approach', Dankelman and Davidson (1988) highlight the necessity to put rural women at the centre of sustainable development. Through poverty women are contributors to environmental degradation, yet, because of their diverse roles in resource management, are well qualified to *ensure* sustainability, given more gender-aware development.

Gender, environment and the socio-economic context

What is clear is that although in many situations in sub-Saharan Africa women do have primary responsibility for the use and management of natural resources, these roles are affected by a constantly changing socio-economic environment. At the beginning of the 1980s, for example, the nations of sub-Saharan Africa were hit by a number of shocks, including severe droughts, civil strife, economic crises and the AIDS pandemic, all of which continue to impact on gender roles and

the environment. Figure 3.2 illustrates some of the socio-economic changes which should be considered in this context.

Social context

Clearly migration patterns, the status of women and level of welfare provision can have a direct impact on gender roles and hence resource utilization and management. Gender issues associated with land tenure and resource control can also have serious implications for the environment. A number of studies have shown, for example, that tree crops are often regarded as the property of men, thus the planting of trees can result in the loss of user rights by women on fields where trees are planted. In the North Bank Division of The Gambia this resulted in newly planted fruit trees being neglected or destroyed by women in what had traditionally been their vegetable gardens. When questioned the women said they were fearful that men would take over the garden and thus they would lose their usufruct rights to the land (Schroeder, 1993), an example which does not support the ecofeminist point of view.

One of the most significant factors in the environment debate in sub-Saharan Africa is the question of population growth. Africa has the highest fertility rate of any region, with resultant population growth rates in excess of 3.1%. This has fuelled the debate concerning the impact of high population growth rates on the environment (ACTIONAID, 1992). Many, fearing a Malthusian disaster, argue that a decrease in population growth is a top priority in the region. Others including Tiffen *et al.* (1994) take a more Boserupian viewpoint. From fieldwork in Machakos district in Kenya they suggest that a high level of population density is necessary before communities will change their crop intensity and techniques of production, and thus take measures to conserve their environmental resources. In addition to high population fertility, the sub-Saharan region has an increasing number of *de facto* female-headed households, which result from male rural to urban migration and increasing

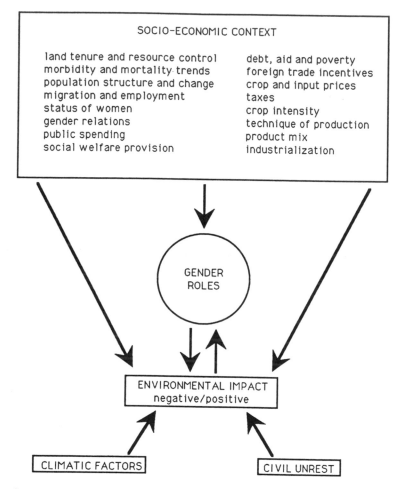

Figure 3.2 *The socio-economic context of gender–environment relationships*

mortality levels associated with AIDS. In some parts of Eastern and Southern Africa it is estimated that over 30% of rural households are female headed. In such households women have to take on a greater responsibility for resource management, while coping with extreme poverty.

Economic context

As a result of economic crises in the 1980s, almost all sub-Saharan African countries have adopted economic adjustment programmes to try to reform their economies. At least 21 countries now have either an International Monetary Fund or World Bank sponsored adjustment policy (Jespersen, 1992). The major components of these policies are demand restraint, 'switching policies' and long-term supply objectives which aim to take African countries from economic crisis to sustained economic growth by the adoption of free-market economic principles. Elson (1991, 1992) argues that demand restraint and switching policies, while affecting all members of society, are more likely to have a negative effect on rural women than on men. Much recent literature on economic adjustment programmes documents the deterioration in rural livelihoods as a result of increases in taxation, reductions in subsidies as well as changes in crop and input prices (see Figure 3.2). The adverse effects on women's workloads of reductions in social services expenditure and switching policies are becoming increasingly more evident (Afshar and Dennis, 1992; Barrett and Browne, 1993a; Geisler, 1992).

By contrast, less is known about how the switch from the non-tradable to tradable sector has impacted on the environment. In most sub-Saharan countries the switch is being achieved by increasing agricultural production for the market, in particular for export. A detailed summary of Malawi's economic reforms and their impact on the environment is given by Cromwell and Winpenny (1993). Here crop and input price reforms have been environmentally damaging by encouraging a switch from maize to the more intensive and erosive crop production systems of cotton and tobacco. The result has been a reduction in the fallow period and a deterioration in soil fertility as farmers attempt to maintain subsistence output while increasing cash crop production.

Further evidence of this switching policy is the dramatic increase in horticultural production for European markets. In some countries, such as Kenya, large agribusinesses dominate this sector and may offer paid employment to women on plantations or estates. Smallholders are also encouraged to grow vegetables on their own land for the export market. Elsewhere communal production in previously non-productive times of the year is favoured. In The Gambia, for example, women's co-operatives are producing okra, aubergines, chilli peppers and green beans for the UK market in the dry season using irrigation. The net result of these changes in crop intensity and methods of production on the environment has been reduced groundwater levels, saline intrusion and leaching as well as reduced soil fertility and erosion (Barrett and Browne, 1991, 1993b).

Conclusion

When considering the relationship between gender and environment, it is imperative to consider theoretical perspectives and the wider socio-economic, political and cultural context as well as spatial variations and temporal changes. Both the World Bank and Unicef now recognize that there are intervening factors which must be considered in the gender–environment equation, which include equitable economic growth coupled with basic education and health services (World Bank, 1994, p. 162). There is an increasing recognition that the situation is further complicated by the international context of aid, trade, finance and debt (see Figure 3.2). It is becoming evident that a new approach is needed, an approach which places gender roles and environmental management in the international, national, regional, as well as household, context. Such an approach could help improve our understanding of gender–environment relationships in sub-Saharan Africa and result in improved environmental management and conservation.

References

ACTIONAID (1992) *Lifestyle Overload? Population and environment in the balance*, Development Report 5, ActionAid, Chard.

Afshar, H. and Dennis, C. (eds) (1992) *Women and Adjustment Policies in the Third World*, Macmillan, Basingstoke.

Barrett, H. R. and Browne, A. W. (1991) Environmental and economic sustainability: women's horticultural production in The Gambia, *Geography*, 76(3), 241–248.

Barrett, H. R. and Browne, A. W. (1993a) Workloads of rural African women: the impact of economic adjustment in sub-Saharan Africa, *Journal of Occupational Science: Australia*, 1(2), 3–10.

Barrett, H. R. and Browne, A. W. (1993b) Horticultural production: the incorporation of sub-Saharan Africa with particular reference to The Gambia, paper presented at a conference, Retail Concentration in the Food Industry and its Implications for Consumers, Producers and the Environment, Science Policy Research Unit, University of Sussex.

Boserup, E. (1990) Population, the status of women, and rural development, pp. 45–60 in G. McNicoll and M. Cain (eds), *Rural Development and Population: institutions and policy*, Oxford University Press, Oxford.

Bryceson, D. F. and Howe, J. (1993) Rural household transport in Africa: reducing the burden on women? *World Development*, 21(11), 1715–1728.

Carney, J. (1993) Converting the wetlands, engendering the environment: the intersection of gender with agrarian change in The Gambia, *Economic Geography*, 69(4), 329–348.

Cromwell, E. and Winpenny, J. (1993) Does economic reform harm the environment? A review of structural adjustment in Malawi, *Journal of International Development*, 5(6), 623–649.

Dankelman, I. and Davidson, J. (1988) *Women and Environment in the Third World*, Earthscan, London.

Dey, J. (1985) Women in African rice farming systems, pp. 419–444 in IRRI *Women in Rice Farming*, Gower, London.

Elliott, J. (1994) *An Introduction to Sustainable Development*, Routledge, London.

Elson, D. (1991) Structural adjustment: its effect on women, pp. 39–53 in T. Wallace and C. March (eds), *Changing Perceptions: writings on gender and development*, Oxfam, Oxford.

Elson, D. (1992) From survival strategies to transformation strategies: women's needs and structural adjustment, pp. 26–48 in L. Beneria and S. Feldman (eds), *Unequal Burden: economic crisis, persistent poverty and women's work*, Westview Press, Boulder.

Geisler, G. (1992) Who is losing out? Structural adjustment, gender and the agricultural sector in Zambia, *Journal of Modern African Studies*, 30, 113–139.

Jackson, C. (1993) Environmentalisms and gender interests in the Third World, *Development and Change*, 24, 649–677.

Jespersen, E. (1992) External shocks, adjustment policies and economic and social performance, pp. 9–50 in G. A. Cornia *et al.* (eds), *Africa's Recovery in the 1990s*, St Martin's Press, New York.

Joekes, S. *et al.* (1994) Gender, environment and population, *Development and Change*, 25, 137–165.

Momsen, J. H. (1991) *Women and Development in the Third World*, Routledge, London.

Moser, C. (1989) Gender planning in the Third World: meeting practical and strategic gender needs, *World Development*, 17(11), 1799–1825.

Nelson, N. (1988) How women and men get by: the sexual division of labour in a Nairobi squatter settlement, pp. 183–203 in J. Gugler (ed.), *The Urbanization of the Third World*, Oxford University Press, Oxford.

Oxfam (1993) *Africa—make or break*, Oxfam, Oxford.

Schroeder, R. A. (1993) Shady practice: gender and the political ecology of resource stabilization in Gambian garden/orchards, *Economic Geography*, 69(4), 349–365.

Sen, G. and Grown, C. (1987) *Development, Crises and Alternative Visions*, Earthscan, London.

Thomas-Slater, B. P. (1992) Politics, class and gender in African resource management: the case of rural Kenya, *Economic Development and Cultural Change*, 40(3), 809–828.

Tiffen, M., Mortimore, M. and Gichuki, F. (1994) *More People, Less Erosion: environmental recovery in Kenya*, John Wiley, Chichester.

Unicef (1994) *State of the World's Children*, Oxford University Press, Oxford.

WCED (World Commission on Environment and Development) (1987) *Our Common Future*, Oxford University Press, Oxford.

World Bank (1992) *World Development Report*, Oxford University Press, Oxford.

World Bank (1994) *Adjustment in Africa*, Oxford University Press, Oxford.

Young, K. (1993) *Planning Development with Women*, Macmillan, London.

4

Participatory rural appraisal—a significant step forward in understanding relationships between poor people and their environments

Steve Brace

The best way to learn about a village is from the people who live there. So the ACTIONAID team sit under a tree in Tempelug (Ghana) with a group of old men, to talk about their past and changes which they have observed in their environment and culture (Griffiths, 1991, p. 4).

Introduction

When ACTIONAID works with poor communities in Africa it recognizes that there is a gap to be bridged between its literate fieldworkers and a poor, usually illiterate, community. How to span this divide, identify peoples' genuine aspirations and then initiate development programmes in which they have a stake, are major issues facing the charity. The charity runs development programmes in 20 countries, including the 10 African nations of The Gambia, Sierra Leone, Ghana, Ethiopia, Uganda, Burundi, Kenya, Somalia, Malawi and Mozambique. Through both long-term development programmes, and also emergency relief, ACTIONAID aims to alleviate poverty in some of the poorest communities in the world.

However, while working with over 2.5 million poor people and spending over £30 million a year, it may seem surprising that sticks and stones are often used to help ACTIONAID decide its development priorities. The use of these basic resources has come about through the growing adoption of *participatory rural appraisal* (PRA) within the charity's work. At its most basic, PRA is a way of involving communities in analysing their lives and providing information about their priorities

People and Environment in Africa. Edited by Tony Binns
©1995 John Wiley & Sons Ltd

for the future. Typically, by working as a group, a community will use locally available materials, such as sticks and stones, to present this information pictorially, using a variety of maps, graphs and tables.

The use of PRA has provided new insights into problems facing African communities. In particular, PRA provides a *window* into the relationship between local people and their environment. For instance, in the Kibwezi area of Kenya's Machakos district there is no single word for *environment*. Nevertheless, subsistence farmers have a good understanding of what pressures there are on their environmental resource base. As one old Kibwezi woman said, what threatens her balance with nature are the 'wild animals of the forest' (Johnson, 1992, p. 6).

As an international organization, ACTIONAID has drawn on its experience of PRA from across Africa, and also Asia. From field staff training, to programme planning and implementation, the following case studies from Africa will identify how PRA has become a valuable technique for a development charity. But first what is PRA?

What is participatory rural appraisal (PRA)?

The constant need for up-to-date and reliable information faces all development charities. During the 1960s and 1970s this need was often met through the use of questionnaire surveys. Vast amounts of quantitative data were collected, and analysed using a range of statistical techniques. However, by the 1980s the major limitations of this approach were becoming apparent. It was increasingly recognized that poor communities do not always conceptualize their lives within the strict limits of a quantitative questionnaire. For example, a group of old men in Sapeliga, northern Ghana, blame environmental degradation on a range of measurable indicators, including: population pressure, erratic rainfall, a lack of fertilizers and also certain qualitative and cultural factors such as 'changing morals and the deviation from indigenous cultural practices . . . [which]

"do not please the God of the land" ' (Griffiths, 1991, p. 4).

There were also concerns that the questions being asked reflected the urban-educated bias of researchers, rather than the actual lives of rural communities. Robert Chambers, in his book, *Rural Development—putting the last first*, presented a critique of traditional research approaches, stressing the need to place poor rural people right at the core of any research (Chambers, 1983). He states, 'questionnaire surveys and statistical analysis limit investigation to what can be asked in interview and what can be counted. The realities of rural deprivation are often missed. The challenge is to question the conventions of academic purity and find better approaches' (Chambers, 1983, p. 199).

As a result of such criticisms of traditional survey methods, a new range of investigational techniques have been devised, including rapid rural appraisal (RRA) from which participatory rural appraisal (PRA) subsequently developed. Researchers using RRA typically spend a few days in a rural setting, often a village, carrying out a range of information-gathering activities. These activities might include semi-structured interviews, drawing maps of the area, transect lines and seasonal calendars. PRA places poor people at the centre of this process, the significant difference from traditional methods being the level of involvement of the local community at the information-gathering stage. Instead of external researchers drawing diagrams and collating information, poor communities now take centre stage. As is shown later in a Gambian context, different groups in a community are asked, using their own local materials, to draw maps of their village, plot trend lines, seasonal calendars, transects and matrices—which fieldworkers will copy. The drawing of these maps and graphs is often characterized by frenetic activity, as different members of the community discuss what important information should be included and where features should be located. However, accommodating many different perspectives within a community PRA allows a wealth of both quantitative and qualitative information to be

Figure 4.1 *Historical transect line for Dobang Kunda, The Gambia. Drawn by the young men of the village showing change in the numbers of compounds and trees from the 1950s to the 1980s (first reproduced in AATG/IIED, 1992, p. 29)*

collected. One example of how this process provides information is shown in Figure 4.1. Here the historical transect lines show how the young men of Dobang Kunda village, The Gambia, identified changes in the number of compounds and tree cover from the 1950s to the 1980s. Sam Joseph, who has trained ACTIONAID staff in PRA, comments,

Rapid rural appraisal is considered more extractive. 'We' (outsiders) interview 'them' (villagers), and use our analysis of the information which we brought away. Participatory rural appraisal moves away from the extractive position and attempts to hand over the initiative . . . to village people. The analysis of information is done in the village with the village people, using their symbols and indicators (quoted in Khan, 1991, p. 2).

Indeed the inventiveness of people in describing their own environment can be seen in

ACTIONAID's work in The Gambia. During PRA exercises in the villages of Ndawen and Dingiraay, 'stones, tin cans, an old shoe, and broken sticks identified important sites such as houses, the seed storage building, the mill, four village wells, the two derelict trucks and the mosque' (Ford *et al.*, 1992, p. 7). Additionally, within matrix exercises people may be asked to mark on a matrix the variety of uses for different crops, such as food, fodder or fuel. Instead of having written representations imposed on them the local people will draw their own symbols to illustrate the different crops. As Khan states,

PRA appears to have achieved a major break-through in building a bridge between the literate and non-literate worlds through the use of creative communication aids. For the first time, means have been developed through which both 'literate' outsiders and 'non literate' villagers are able to share in the systematic identification, collection and collation of information (Khan, 1991, p. 3).

The process of information collection, by being open for all to see, helps to demystify the research process.

PRA also provides an opportunity to run the same exercises with different sections of a community, such as men and women or young and old. One example of how gender differentiation in activities can provide useful information, came to light through ACTIONAID's PRA work in Ghana. In the Chereponi region women's cash is sometimes impounded by their husbands and used for community or family needs. To prevent this from happening women may spend money quickly on their own needs or even hide it. This practice was identified within a PRA exercise, when separate groups of men and women were asked to distribute stones across a matrix to indicate their expenditure. During this exercise some women took some stones off the matrix and held them separately, showing how they hide money for their own use!

Before proceeding to examine case studies of how PRA has been used in the field, it might be useful to summarize the three assumptions underlying PRA:

1. *Local knowledge*. Farmers have knowledge and information, but it needs to be organized.
2. *Local resources*. Villagers have resources, but they need to be mobilized.
3. *Attracting outside help*. Outside resources are available, but they need to be defined in the context of village-identified priorities (Ford *et al.*, 1992, p. 3).

If these assumptions are used as the starting-point for work with poor communities, then it is likely that more accurate information and a clearer direction for future development projects can be achieved.

PRA in action

The relationship between ACTIONAID's fieldworkers and communities in which they work is vital to the success of its development projects. In this respect, the use of PRA has allowed a clearer insight into the problems facing disadvantaged people. Additionally, it has also allowed community groups a greater level of participation in development planning.

These issues are clearly shown in the following case studies of the use of PRA within The Gambia. ACTIONAID has been working in The Gambia since 1979. Following a review in 1991, ACTIONAID-The Gambia (AATG), reorientated its attention from *input* delivery to the *impact* of its work on communities. To support this shift, new operational methods and a staff training programme were introduced. As AATG and the International Institute for Environment and Development (IIED) state, 'to encourage the anticipated shift amongst field workers, a field-based training in PRA was planned. AATG sees the field workers as the catalysts of community-based planning and the backbone of AATGs development work' (AATG/IIED, 1992, p. 2). The following examples identify two stages in the integration of PRA techniques within different areas of AATG's work; first staff training and then programme planning.

A key priority was to enhance the understanding and ability to use PRA techniques among the organization's field workers, and this process has been well documented (AATG/IIED, 1992).

During December 1991 ACTIONAID fieldworkers, working with local communities from the three villages of Dobang Kunda, Misera and Njoren, took part in the PRA training course. Staff were trained to run standard PRA activities with the local community. The feedback from this work showed not only an increase in the fieldworkers' ability to use PRA, but also their greater understanding of the villagers themselves. Indeed, some fieldworkers expressed surprise that:

- villagers can draw maps;
- villagers were very willing to co-operate and spend time on discussion and exercises;
- the villagers could remember village history well;
- villagers will discuss relative wealth;
- villagers give reliable information (AATG/IIED, 1992, p. 9).

Additionally, some of the most important lessons learnt in this training course were demonstrated by feedback from the staff on the evaluation of the PRA training, including such comments as:

(Poor) people can be involved in planning for their future development.
Most people belittle the role of illiterates.
I should not make a lot of assumptions on the side of the villagers.
The ability to get reliable information from the villagers' own point of view about their current situation which could be used to develop strategies for viable intervention projects (AATG/IIED, 1992, p. 10).

A further example shows how some of the lessons learnt in the PRA training were then put into practice. In particular, the experiences highlighted in *Sustaining Development through Community Mobilisation: a case study of participatory rural appraisal in the Gambia*, illustrate how PRA allows a community to play a key role in identifying their priorities for future development and their subsequent implementation. In 1992 ACTIONAID fieldworkers, over a period of a few days, ran PRA in the two villages of Ndawen and Dingiraay, to 'test whether a community-based methodology such as PRA could pass initiatives along to village institutions and introduce projects which community institutions could plan, implement and sustain' (Ford *et al.*, 1992, p. 2).

In their introductory talks to the communities, ACTIONAID workers stressed that PRA was not necessarily going to mean the charity would bring more resources. Instead, it was emphasized that the aim was to help local people to examine how their community could build solidarity and action around their own priorities. Dividing the villages into three groups, older men, older women and younger people, mapping and graphical activities were then carried out. The sketch map of Ndawen village (Figure 4.2), clearly shows how accurate sketch maps of the local area can be drawn by community members. In addition, the changing fortunes of this village, shown in the trend line diagram (Figure 4.3), with regard to population, literacy and education, rainfall and crop production, were identified during PRA. By using the trend lines as a focus for discussion, the community then provided the fieldworkers with explanations for the different trends.

From the information, people were asked to identify the problems they experienced. The following list was drawn up:

- water scarcity
- quality of firewood sources
- poor health
- low farm productivity
- poor animal health
- low literacy
- the labour demands on women
- weak community institutions

The community then moved on to analyse and rank these problems and decide on the various options for addressing them. They quickly focused on the need for water, and viewed the construction of a borehole as the next step to the exclusion of other options. As Ford *et al.* record, 'the borehole was the first, second and third priority for the village' (1992, p. 35). Indeed, information obtained from PRA had shown that many local wells were no longer in use and that women had to draw water from depths of 50 m by hand, which is both time-consuming and arduous.

The borehole option was chosen, even though the community recognized that it might be unwise in terms of costs and future sustainability. As Ford *et al.* state, 'At several points during the ranking discussions, ACTIONAID staff indicated they were sceptical about the village's capacity to purchase fuel, buy spare parts, and maintain the pump. In the full awareness of this information, the villages decided they would like to try' (1992, p. 37).

ACTIONAID had already established that it was not appropriate for it simply to step in and build a tube well, but instead the charity decided to work with local people to produce a six-month community action plan. During this period ACTIONAID would support the community leaders in undertaking feasibility studies into the borehole, and also help them make contact with organizations in The Gambia which specialize in water projects.

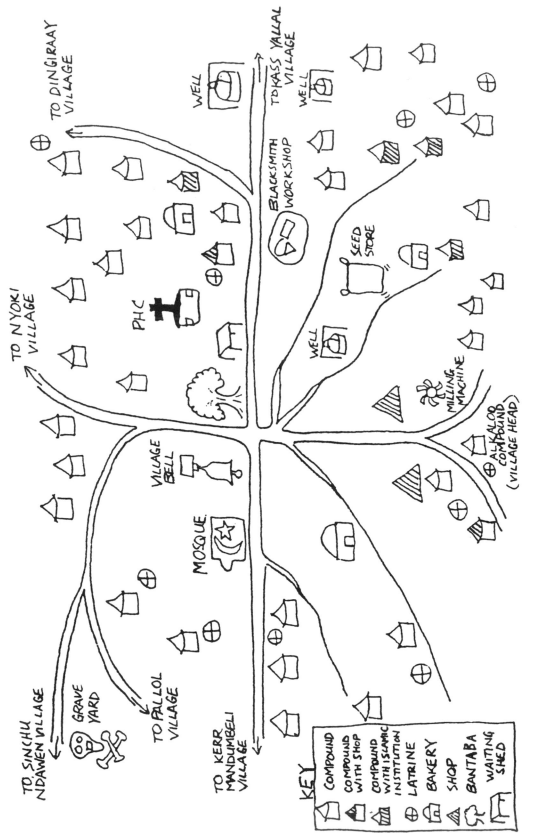

Figure 4.2 *Sketch map of Ndawen village, The Gambia (first reproduced in Ford et al., 1992, p. 9). Note: Bantaba = meeting place; PHC = primary health centre*

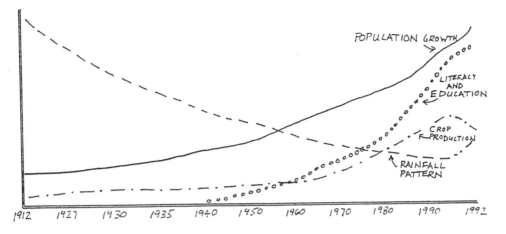

Figure 4.3 *Trend lines for Ndawen village, showing change in population, literacy and education, rainfall and crop production. The explanations resulted through discussing the graph with the community. Explanations: 1912–40, no formal education; 1912–70, enough rainfall due to adequate tree cover; 1912–60, low crop production due to lack of technology and inputs; 1940–80, low education; 1960–90, increased production due to advances in technology and availability of farm inputs; 1970–90, declining rainfall patterns. Source: Ford* et al. *(1992, p. 15)*

Conclusion

It should be recognized that PRA does not provide all the answers needed to support good development practice. However, this approach does bring an organization closer to the needs of poor communities. It is a step forward in evaluating individual and community needs, and better planned and implemented development programmes should result.

As the information from The Gambia has shown, PRA helps to develop a new level of partnership based on collaboration between a community and a development charity's field-workers. As Khan states, 'genuine participation could only take place among equals. Since total equality in a development context was not felt to be feasible when it comes to command over resources, . . . equal participation should be sought at the level of ideas or as a "partnership of minds"' (Khan, 1991, p. 18).

PRA not only allows charities to focus their attention on the priorities communities identify but it also provides benefits within communities themselves. By using PRA, communities can explore the wider opportunities for mobilization to address their problems. PRA diagrams can also be re-examined later, monitoring the progress made by the community—for example, in identifying the number of households whose children have been immunized since the original survey.

Finally, as Ford *et al.* comment, 'PRA is unique in several ways. It helps rural communities to support activities which they design and implement. It strengthens local leadership and institutions. It integrates sectors at the community level related to natural resources management, and helps to build collaboration among development agents external to the community' (Ford *et al.*, 1992, p. 3).

References

ACTIONAID The Gambia (AATG), International Institute for Environment and Development (IIED) (1992) *From Input to Impact: participatory rural appraisal for ACTIONAID The Gambia*, ActionAid, London.

Chambers, R. (1983) *Rural Development—putting the last first*, Longman, Harlow.

Ford, R., Kabutha, C., Mageto, N. and Manneh, K. (1992) *Sustaining Development through Mobilisation: a case study of participatory rural appraisal in the Gambia*, ACTIONAID, The Gambia.

Steve Brace

Griffiths, M. (1991) People and planet in lifestyle overload? *Population and environment in the balance*, p. 4 in V. Johnson (ed), ACTIONAID Development Report No. 5, ACTIONAID, London.

Johnson, V. (1992) What is environment? p. 6 in *Common Cause*, ACTIONAID, London.

Khan, S. (1991) *Participatory Rural Appraisal*, an ACTIONAID discussion paper, ACTIONAID, London.

5

The effects of urbanization on rural environments in Africa

Hamish Main

Introduction

Urbanization, the process by which an increasing proportion of a given population resides in urban rather than rural places, has the potential for positive as well as negative effects on rural environments. It is clear that the period of most rapid urbanization in Africa has coincided with an era of widespread environmental degradation. But this chapter airs the contention that, like many other development processes, urbanization also embodies some of the means by which pressures on environments can be ameliorated and environmental degradation can be averted, halted or even reversed.

Amid the great web of mutually reinforcing processes comprising African development/under-development, however, to separate the effects of urbanization from those of related processes must be to some extent arbitrary. Population redistribution, population growth, commoditization and proletarianization are among the processes that overlap with urbanization in their genesis and in their effects. But some portions of the literature make broad assumptions about the negative environmental impacts of urbanization, without considering the possibility that some of its effects might also be positive (Harrison, 1979;

Eckholm *et al.*, 1984; Timberlake, 1985). As Pearce (1994, p. 28) puts it: 'In environmental demonology, large cities are seen as parasites on the surrounding farmland.' No doubt some aspects of large cities and their growth warrant such a view, but to universalize this demon to the exclusion of the positive impacts of cities and urbanization on rural environments is misleading. Some of these positive features have been indicated by detailed regional examinations (Mortimore, 1972; Cline-Cole *et al.*, 1990; Tiffen *et al.*, 1994) and by recent overviews (Harrison, 1992; Main, 1993).

If, in assessing environmental impacts and their causes, urbanization is to be separated from associated development processes, then the hypothetical question should be considered: if development to current levels of population and consumption per person could have been achieved *without* the urbanization that has occurred, what would have been its likely environmental effects? Such an expansion in rural population and production, if it were feasible, would surely have had far more damaging environmental impacts. It follows that the redistribution of population towards urban residence is on balance a positive process environmentally (as well as socially and

People and Environment in Africa. Edited by Tony Binns
©1995 John Wiley & Sons Ltd

economically). In other words, urbanization tends overall to ameliorate the potentially damaging impacts of development on rural environments. Far more environmental damage is probably caused by the nature of technological change and growth in consumption per person than by either the growth or distribution of population experienced recently in Africa.

This chapter is not directly, then, about the effects of rural environmental changes on urbanization. Nor does it consider the impacts of urbanization upon urban environments, on which a considerable literature has been published with reference to Africa and elsewhere in the Third World (Douglas, 1983; Hardoy *et al.*, 1992; Main and Williams, 1994). The concern here is with urbanization's environmental effects outside the cities, in rural Africa where the effects of urban growth and urban bias in market processes and government policies are likely to be felt all the way from the edge of the capital city to the furthest rural periphery.

Definitions of positive and negative environmental effects are not offered here. But the position is taken, as in Tiffen *et al.* (1994, p. 14), that the replacement of natural vegetation by sustainable farming is a positive development; and by the same token the conversion of rural to urban land uses is not in itself considered to be negative in principle, though there are of course some aspects of urban expansion that do have negative environmental implications.

The chapter proceeds by outlining the broad numerical dynamic of urbanization in Africa, which indicates declining growth rates first in rural population from about the mid-1970s and subsequently in urban population since about the mid-1980s. Attention then turns to the nature of urbanization's environmental effects. Among the processes mediating between urbanization and rural environmental change in Africa, three—each of them having the potential for both positive and negative effects—are pursued:

1. Reducing rural population pressures on land and other environmental resources, as rural population growth rates decline and even in some regions become negative;

2. Rising urban demand for rural resources, as urban population growth and industrialization generate increasing consumption;
3. The spatial concentration of population and production.

The use of examples from around Africa permits a wide variety of material to illustrate the discussion, but the range of places precludes detailed examination of linkages between ubanization and associated development-related processes or between the latter and rural environmental changes.

Urbanization, urban population growth and rural population growth

Every country in mainland Africa recorded increasing levels of urbanization during each 10-year period between 1960 and 1990; temporary declines occurred only in Cape Verde and Mauritius, island states with small populations. Thus the urban proportion of Africa's total population grew quite steadily from 19% in 1960 to 33% in 1990 (World Resources Institute *et al.*, 1988, p. 266). But the period of most rapid growth in the continent's urban population is probably past: the annual increase seems to have peaked at just over 5.0% between 1980 and 1985, soon after rural population growth had peaked at approximately 2.3% per annum in the mid-1970s (see Table 5.1). And only 12 of Africa's 49 countries recorded a higher rate of growth in total urban population in the late 1980s than during either 1965–70 or 1975–80 (World Resources Institute *et al.*, 1988, p. 266).

There are of course major regional differences within these continental data, and several countries display striking variations from the regional norms: very low urbanization levels in western East Africa, Burkina Faso and Ethiopia, for example, and high levels in Cameroon and Zambia, and outside tropical Africa. But overall growth of urban population has been over twice as rapid as that of rural population since the 1950s, and by the end of the 1980s Africa's urban population was growing more rapidly than its

Table 5.1 *Estimated urbanization, urban and rural population in Africa, 1960–90*

Date	Total population		Level of urbanization (%)	Urban population		Rural population	
	Millions	Interim annual growth rate (%)		Millions	Interim annual growth rate (%)	Millions	Interim annual growth rate (%)
1960	281		19	53		228	
		2.4			4.2		2.0
1965	316		21	65		251	
		2.6			4.5		2.1
1970	359		23	81		278	
		2.9			4.7		2.3
1975	414		25	102		312	
		3.0			4.8		2.3
1980	479		27	129		350	
		3.0			5.0		2.2
1985	555		30	165		390	
		3.0			4.9		2.1
1990	642		33	209		433	
		3.1			4.9		2.1
1995 projected	747		36	266		481	
		3.0			4.8		1.9
2000 projected	866		39	337		529	

Source/derived from: World Resources Institute *et al.* (1988, pp. 246, 266; 1992, pp. 246, 264).

rural population not only in terms of growth rate but also in the sheer number of people added to the population. It is predicted that by 2020 sub-Saharan Africa's population will be predominantly urban for the first time (Mink, 1993, p. 29), and that the continent's rural population growth will peter out or become negative a decade or two after that (Harrison, 1992, p. 110).

Clearly it would be misguided to place too much faith in the exactitude of distant projections like these. Considerable variation exists within these continental generalizations between regions where rural population growth is already close to zero and those where it presently remains at as high a level as urban growth; and even the continental estimates might prove badly awry if, for example, the large-scale demographic effects of AIDS are more devastating than now seems probable. Yet it does seem fair to assume that for the foreseeable future most of Africa's population growth will be urban. It is estimated that sub-Saharan Africa's rural population will increase by 50% in the 30 years from 1990, but that urban population increase during the same period will be five times greater (Mink, 1993, p. 30).

Some of the possible environmental implications of fundamental population changes like these are considered in the following sections. But it would be misleading to attach too great a weight to the statistics of population numbers,

growth rates and distributions. Rural population numbers are already declining overall in Latin America and East Asia, with little apparent impact on continuing environmental problems. Increasing rural as well as urban consumption per head of population, and changes in the technologies used in production and consumption, are as a rule more salient elements in the environmental impact equation. This is an important context against which the following evidence should be set.

Declining rural population pressures

As rural population growth rates decline and even in some cases become negative, so the pressures of rural population on land and other environmental resources also reduce. This implies a reduction in the rural environmental degradation arising from rural population pressures, but the association between rural population growth and rural environmental degradation is by no means a direct one. Under some circumstances rural population growth can be a force for environmental sustenance, and it has been argued that this positive impact is in fact more a general rule than an occasional exception (Boserup, 1965). Thus declining rural population growth rates might also be responsible for negative environmental impacts.

Reducing pressures to overproduce

A reduction in rural population pressures on rural environments has long been achieved in various parts of Africa through a strategy of rural–urban mobility from regions with marginal environments. Seasonal circulation from sahel–savanna regions of West Africa, formerly very widespread, is known in Hausa as *cin rani*—literally, 'eating away the dry season'—and this conveys several of the senses in which such labour circulation can benefit rural communities: spending several months away from home, earning money during the dry season when little productive work can be done at home, saving village food stocks and smoothing rural consumption levels through the year, and thereby helping to relieve pressures on the village and its land (Prothero, 1957). The nature of population mobility from marginal rural regions like these has changed considerably during the past 30 years or so, the time spent away from home becoming in increasing numbers of cases longer than a single dry season (i.e. *bida*, rather than *cin rani*) and movements being aimed more towards urban destinations (Abdu, 1982, p. 46). Eventually temporary circulations become permanent migrations (*kaura*); these are even more likely to be urbanward, and the effect of reducing or removing pressures on fragile rural ecosystems is reinforced to the extent that large numbers of new urban residents would otherwise have been rural. For farmers in many parts of Hausaland seeking to accumulate wealth or raise their status, spatial mobility is seen as an alternative to *in situ* options of agricultural intensification or increasing off-farm activities. Thus labour circulation has been more likely from more remote villages with fewer opportunities for these alternatives (Goddard *et al.*, 1975). The major cities coped with vast human influxes from rural Hausaland seeking refuge during the 1972–74 drought without mass starvation or breakdowns in law and order; this is testimony to the ability of an established urban system, and especially of existing rural–urban networks, to reduce dire rural pressures on fragile ecosystems at times of environmental crisis like drought (Mortimore, 1982, pp. 54–55).

Something similar occurred across the West African Sahel in Mauritania, Mali and Niger during the droughts of the 1970s and 1980s, and the impact on cities like Bamako and Niamey and particularly Nouakchott has been greater than on Nigerian cities which are part of a large and complex urban hierarchy. Over a quarter of Abidjan's population now originates from outside Ivory Coast, the great majority from environmentally marginal areas of Burkina Faso and Mali. For many of these people, poor by the standards of Abidjan, rural–urban mobility has been essential for the continued functioning of their home villages. Referring to one such village in Burkina Faso, Harrison (1992, p. 179) writes: 'If all the migrants returned, everyone would starve. Much contemporary migration from marginal areas is of this compulsory nature.'

Loss of rural labour and skills

But rural outmigration can also have negative impacts on rural environments. Those who move from village to city, whether for one dry season or permanently, tend to include a high proportion of the most productive people in a farming community, resulting in labour shortages disproportionate to the numbers involved. While the work identified as most essential in the short term or during the busy season might continue to be done, work producing longer-term benefits or during the dry season tends to suffer: the maintenance of terraces or irrigation channels, the application of manure, and so on. The Ngas people have farmed parts of the south side of the Jos Plateau, on awkward hillside sites, in 'a perfect demonstration of theoretical anti-erosion measures carried out on a wide and successful scale over centuries' (Fairbairn, 1943, p. 190). But circulatory and migratory movements to Jos, Kaduna and other Nigerian cities during the 1970s and 1980s have reduced labour inputs to maintain their terraces and have been a major element in the eventual abandonment of some of their villages and farmlands. The neighbouring Kofyar have also been migrating away from this region, but in most cases to the plains below the escarpment rather than to the cities (Binns, 1994, pp. 72–77). Yet the effect on the areas they have left is much the same. Ecosystem disturbance caused by the abandonment of intensive and sustained farming systems might not represent environmental degradation from a purely physical viewpoint, but it does mean a loss of human ability to adapt to an awkward natural environment.

Negative rural environmental impacts arising from the loss of productive labour have been apparent elsewhere in Africa, as in the labour reserves around the Republic of South Africa, and in Congo where, through unwise environmental management by those who remain in the villages, it is 'probably the main cause of excessive cutting of gallery forests along the river and stream banks in the Plateaux and Pool regions' (Colchester, 1993, p. 171).

Rising urban demand for rural resources

As cities grow, they create additional demand for resources drawn from nearby rural hinterlands and from more distant regions: demand for labour, land and building materials, food, water, energy and other commodities. This demand can generate rural income both directly, through rising prices for growing volumes of rural products, and indirectly through additional opportunities for non-farm income. At the same time the declining ratio of rural to urban population implicit in urbanization means that urban demand for food and other agricultural products is met through rising labour efficiency in overall rural production. From all of this comes a range of potential environmental impacts on rural source regions.

Additional capital and incentive to invest in maintenance of rural environments

A detailed recent study of Machakos in central Kenya has shown how a rural region with severe environmental problems (grassland denudation, soil erosion and gullying) during the colonial period has been restored since about 1960 to environmental sustenance, while human and animal populations have grown rapidly and agricultural production has more than kept pace with population (Chapter 7 and Tiffen *et al.*, 1994). Central within this quiet rural success story has been a range of linkages with urban societies and economies. Considerable rural–urban labour circulation until the 1960s raised money to invest in farms and guard against climatic disaster, but subsequently permanent migrations to the cities and remittances back to rural families became a more prominent source of income diversification for the area. Today the cities are important markets for production in rural Machakos of meat, fruit and vegetables, sand and timber for construction, charcoal and other goods: 'The major influence of the growth of large towns such as Nairobi and Mombasa has been to increase the profitability of farming' (Tiffen *et al.*, 1994, p. 62). Sufficient capital is now invested in terracing and other soil and water conservation measures, in the purchase of equipment and fertilizer and other inputs, to sustain the ecosystem, and outmigration from rural Machakos is declining.

The positive net role of rural–urban mobility, mainly through its generation of additional income for investment in rural environmental maintenance, has been apparent in many African regions besides Kenya. A large literature on the subject about the end of the colonial era examined such effects for example in Tunisia (Clarke, 1957), in Burkina Faso (Skinner, 1965) and elsewhere in West Africa (Berg, 1965); but dissenting voices like Amin (1974), on West Africa, have emphasized that potential gains in available rural capital do not necessarily materialize, and must be measured against the loss of rural labour and skills. More recently Harrison (1992, p. 112) has commented on the positive effects of urban–rural market relations on reforestation in the Kenyan Highlands and in Rwanda during the 1980s.

Increasing urban pressures on rural areas to overproduce

Hundreds of dams have been constructed in Africa during the past 30 years in response to a range of mainly urban needs: to ensure continuous water supply, to generate electricity and to irrigate land for intensive agricultural production. It is now recognized that large dams and reservoirs, and the agricultural projects sustained by them, have caused considerable environmental degradation locally and downstream (Goldsmith and Hildyard, 1984–85; Dixon *et al.*, 1989). Urban demand for rural output also creates pressures on small-scale farmers and pastoralists to intensify their production, and this can lead to overcultivation, overgrazing and overpumping, with a wide variety of potentially damaging environmental effects.

The replacement of traditional staple foods by new staples, especially bread and rice, has been most far-reaching in the cities of many African regions. After Nigeria banned foodstuff imports in 1986, an eightfold increase in the market price of wheat within three years encouraged farmers to grow more wheat. Although ecological conditions are unfavourable, wheat production did expand rapidly in some irrigated areas of northern Nigeria with heavy application of fertilizer (Kimmage, 1991, pp. 478–479). The mechanical clearance of land for wheat cultivation was very damaging to soils in areas like the acacia scrublands of river floodplains in parts of north-eastern Nigeria, where the breakdown of soil structure and sheet erosion combined with rainstorms to create gullying and a rapid reduction in soil fertility and organic matter (Kimmage, 1991, pp. 493–495). A continuation of these processes might have caused the creation of localized dustbowls in areas like these, but this has probably been averted by Nigeria's lifting of the ban on wheat imports in late 1992 and the removal thereby of the strong incentive to grow wheat where it was ecologically unsuitable. An environmental problem has perhaps been resolved at least temporarily at the expense of an economic problem, though this was hardly the main concern of the Nigerian government. But there are many more examples of governments prioritizing economic needs ahead of environmental needs. Many African governments have sought to ensure cheap, reliable food supplies for urban populations: in Zambia, for example, this resulted in rural peasants having to grow maize on marginal land to sell cheaply to the state marketing boards, with the result that their farms' soil was quickly degraded and eroded (Blaikie, 1985, pp. 121–122).

Woodfuel accounts for maybe three-quarters of total energy consumption in sub-Saharan Africa, and urbanization is at the heart of a set of mutually reinforcing processes that encourage its commoditization. Whereas in many regions trees have previously been cultivated by farmers along with their crops, and rural people have accessed woodfuel communally rather than through market processes, rising urban demand for woodfuel tends to encourage traders to 'mine' tree stocks in rural supply zones. The urban poor then become vulnerable to rising woodfuel prices that they cannot afford: many people in Ouagadougou, Niamey and Bujumbura, for example, have been reported as spending 20–30% of their income on cooking fuel (Eckholm *et al.*, 1984, p. 13). Meanwhile deforestation in some rural supply zones lays bare the soil to erosion and possibly extensive environmental degradation. The two woodfuel crises have the potential to exacerbate each other, as higher woodfuel prices in urban markets make it more viable for traders to travel further afield in search of new supplies, while deforestation and market scarcities force urban market prices even higher. Supply zones now extend over 400 km from cities like Kano, Khartoum and Nairobi. Severe depletion of tree stocks within a radius of this magnitude represents considerable potential for environmental degradation. But some reports of resulting desertification and agricultural collapse have been grossly exaggerated. Eckholm *et al.* (1984, p. 28) wrote of 'severe deforestation and the collapse of a sustainable agricultural system' within a 40-km radius of Kano. Cline-Cole *et al.* (1990, pp. 43–55) have shown how in fact the very opposite of this has occurred, as tree numbers around Kano actually increased between 1972 and 1981 and the area's system of agroforestry coped admirably with the 1970s drought, followed by economic inflation and then recession, all accompanied by rising expectations. This rural area around Kano has undoubtedly benefited from its close social and economic links with the nearby city.

Many African cities (including Dakar, Freetown, Khartoum and Lusaka) obtain a high proportion of their energy from charcoal, which is lighter to transport and therefore cheaper than wood and also more compact to burn on the fire. But in terms of wood volume used, charcoal is 40% less efficient than fuelwood. Charcoal-consuming urban dwellers thereby exert a greater demand per head of population on forest resources than do fuelwood-consuming rural people (White, 1989, p. 8), though the rising costs of fuelwood and charcoal for urban consumers have an opposite effect, by discouraging them from using as much as they might otherwise do.

Urban demand for rural land that reduces scarce fertile farmland

Rural land consumed by physical urban growth is as a rule relatively fertile: 'towns usually blossom, not in forests, deserts or swamps, but in the heart of agricultural land' (Harrison, 1992, p. 107). New farmland needed to compensate for this loss to the cities tends to be located in often peripheral areas of less fertile land, where more fertilizer must be applied in order to maintain existing levels of food production. On the other hand, increasing efficiency in agricultural production might mean that a reducing area of land is required to support a given population.

Although the direct transformation of rural land through outward urban expansion affects relatively small areas of land (Satterthwaite, 1991, p. 121), it is likely to be particularly damaging where fertile agricultural land is lost in a region where it is in short supply. For thousands of years Egyptians have understood well the critical need to sustain the thin strip of fertile farmland either side of the River Nile, but between 1950 and 1984 12% of Egypt's farmland was lost to urban sprawl (*Nature*, 1993). Cairo's massive growth in recent decades has made this precious farmland more valuable, as a short-term investment, for building new suburbs than for agriculture. Government regulations designed to protect farmland from construction have proved ineffective in the face of market forces around Cairo, as around so many other African cities.

Urban demand for rural land that degrades rural environments

Rural land is transformed into urban land uses to accommodate both the construction of outward urban expansion and also the infrastructure required by growing cities beyond their built-up areas. Roads that carry additional traffic generated by urban development, and quarries and borrow pits from which building material is taken, consume land that can no longer be used for agriculture and might also cause damaging side-effects such as landslides. Cattle *en route* to urban markets and abattoirs trample land and denude it of grass and shrubs, as around Omdurman (Lewis and Berry, 1988, p. 354). Coal-fired power stations that produce electricity very largely for urban consumers create local air pollution where they are sited. Urban solid waste is disposed of in dumps and landfills at increasing distances from city centres, in the nearby rural periphery or further afield. Waste-disposal sites are sources of air pollution as long as they remain open and, depending on geological conditions, their contents are liable to seep into groundwater even after they have been covered. Dakar's biggest municipal dump, on the rural periphery 15 km from the city centre, is sited between two shallow freshwater lakes which are surrounded by land used for intensive market gardening. People in nearby villages, as well as in new residential development around the dump, draw their water from wells that are now threatened by effluents seeping into groundwater from the dump, which is not covered or managed in any way (White, 1989, p. 8).

Spatial concentration of population and production

Rapid urban growth in Africa since the mid-twentieth century has occurred at the same time as rising urban income and consumption levels and, in many cases, industrial development. These development processes have combined to increase the output of urban pollution much in excess of the rate of growth of urban population. Concentration of population also means concentration of sewage and household refuse. Growth in industrial production means growth in industrial wastes, and the inorganic nature of an increasing proportion of both domestic and industrial wastes gives less scope for natural recycling. At the same time urban overpumping can reduce groundwater recharge, while the quantity of rainwater reaching aquifers under cities is reduced through the spread of concrete and tarmac, so that pollutants entering groundwater are less effectively diluted.

Pollution of water, air and land

Water pollution by domestic sewage and toxic industrial wastes affects both surface water and groundwater, and rural communities are threatened either downstream or where underground water bodies are sufficiently extensive. Over-extraction for urban consumption has caused groundwater pollution in and around Dakar, where salt water has intruded the groundwater of villages along Cap Vert, as well as under the city itself (White, 1989, p. 7).

Only 13% of Africans had sewer connections by the late 1980s, and little of this was treated prior to discharge into rivers and lakes, where it supplemented domestic waste from the large majority of urban populations without sewer connections (Harrison, 1992, p. 196). It is usually difficult to quantify the downstream effects of urban water pollution, but the direct discharge of Alexandria's industrial and domestic effluents into nearby Lake Maryut appears to be the major reason for an 80% decline in fish production during the 1980s and a marked decline in the lake's

popularity as a recreational area for Alexandria's residents (Hamza, 1989, p. 24). Industrial effluent from factories in Port Harcourt has polluted creeks providing domestic water for downstream rural communities (Izeogu, 1989, p. 66). Such problems are suffered by rural communities around dozens of African cities.

Atmospheric pollution often exceeds World Health Organization guideline levels in cities with heavy traffic volumes such as Ibadan, Lagos, Cairo and Nairobi; this is likely to affect nearby rural areas, and can be extended further afield by meteorological conditions like the harmattan wind in West Africa. Urban air pollution has the potential for much wider regional implications for acid deposition and low-level ozone (Faiz, 1992). Large areas of Africa with lateritic soils, containing high levels of acidity, are particularly vulnerable to acid rain produced by industrialization and motorization (Harrison, 1992, p. 208).

Urban generation of materials useful for rural environmental sustenance

One of the best-known instances of economic and environmental symbiosis benefiting both urban and rural parties is furnished by the donkey-borne fuelwood trade in Kano described by Mortimore (1972). The city's energy needs have been met for hundreds of years mainly by fuelwood carried daily from a distance of up to 30 km by donkeys, involving thousands of animals at the height of the trade in the mid-twentieth century. On their return, the donkeys carried loads of nightsoil from the city to manure surrounding village fields. This apparently simple trade performed several important functions. Economically, it exchanged goods and generated income for traders, donkey-owners and -drivers. Environmentally, it disposed of urban waste and maintained the soil fertility on which intensive perennial cultivation in the Kano close-settled zone depended.

The population of metropolitan Kano has grown to well over a million today, the city's wastes have a much higher inorganic content than previously, and the donkey-borne trade is no longer so important. But around the rural periphery of Kano, as around many other African cities, piles of urban refuse are sorted for organic content that can be used to fertilize farmland.

Investment in waste disposal

The concentration of population and of population-generated wastes in urban locations suggests a potential for these wastes to be disposed of in a more cost-effective manner than if population were more dispersed. But the rudimentary nature of waste disposal in most African cities today, and the volume of industrial wastes in many of them, indicate that for the foreseeable future urban waste disposal will be a major problem for both urban and nearby rural environments (Mink, 1993, p. 27).

Conclusion

While it is apparent that urbanization affects rural environments in a wide variety of ways, the intricate manner in which urbanization and associated development processes are interwoven makes it very difficult to isolate the effects of urbanization from those of, say, industrialization or rural–rural mobility. Some tentative conclusions can be drawn from the material presented above, however.

Strong temporal correlations between urban or rural population growth rates and specific environmental changes are not readily apparent in Africa. Close links have been identified in some world regions, including China, between the halting of rural population growth and the halting of net deforestation (Harrison, 1992, pp. 110–111). Although the former might under some circumstances encourage the latter, it is clearly not a sufficient precondition—net deforestation has continued in large regions of South America, for example, long after their population growth rates became negative about the mid-1970s. But Harrison is optimistic that, once appropriate measures such as the ending of state subsidies on

ranching are taken, net afforestation will come about: 'Urbanization could be the saviour of the Amazon' (1992, p. 110)! African evidence in support of this association is, however, patchy: although the reversal of net deforestation during the 1980s in parts of the Maghreb (Mather, 1992, p. 370) approximately coincided with lower rural population growth rates, for example, correlations in other African regions where net deforestation has apparently ceased, like Burundi and Malawi, are unclear.

On the other hand the dynamism of urban–rural relations, and related change in the nature of urban impacts upon rural environments, are evident; in Machakos, for example, declining population mobility and the rise in importance of urban market provisioning have been closely associated with the environmental revitalization of the past thirty years.

Urbanization presents opportunities for rural environmental sustenance, then, as well as dangers of rural environmental degradation. Among the material presented above, such opportunities are more apparent in the increasing urban consumption of rural-produced goods than in the increasing urban production of wastes to be disposed of. Where rural producers are able to supply urban consumers through accessible and effective market systems, the potential exists for capital thereby generated to be invested in rural environmental sustenance. In contrast, pollution of air, water and land is a growing problem for extensive areas within and beyond many of Africa's large cities. This needs to be addressed urgently for the health of rural as well as urban environments and people. The Urban Management Programme of the joint UNDP/World Bank/UNCHS 'brown agenda' approach does address this problem, but few benefits from it are so far evident in and around Africa's cities.

The continent-wide review attempted in this chapter has yielded material indicating a range of positive as well as negative impacts of urbanization upon rural environments. But it has not been possible in the space available to present an in-depth scrutiny of a relatively homogeneous region that might go some way towards separating urbanization's environmental impacts from those of other development processes. A more convincing case for the rural environmental benefits or disadvantages of urbanization would require analysis of a much smaller region, in which such linkages are examined in a more holistic manner, and consideration is given to regional circumstances of physical environment, human culture and the nature of articulation between capitalist and pre-capitalist modes of production.

References

Abdu, S. P. (1982) Dry season migration, pp. 46–47, in: K. Swindell (ed.), *Sokoto State in Maps: an atlas of physical and human resources*, University Press, Ibadan.

Amin, S. (ed.) (1974) *Modern Migrations in Western Africa*, Oxford University Press, London.

Berg, E. J. (1965) The economics of the migrant labor system, pp. 160–181 in H. Kuper (ed.), *Urbanization and migration in West Africa*, University of California Press, Berkeley.

Binns, T. (1994) *Tropical Africa*, Routledge, London.

Blaikie, P. (1985) *The Political Economy of Soil Erosion in Developing Countries*, Longman, Harlow.

Boserup, E. (1965) *The Conditions of Agricultural Growth: the economics of agrarian change under population pressure*, Allen & Unwin, London.

Clarke, J. I. (1957) Emigration from southern Tunisia, *Geography*, 42, 96–104.

Cline-Cole, R. A., Falola, J. A., Main, H. A. C., Mortimore, M. J., Nichol, J. E. and O'Reilly, F. D. (1990) *Wood fuel in Kano*, United Nations University Press, Tokyo.

Colchester, M. (1993) Slave and enclave: towards a political ecology of Equatorial Africa, *The Ecologist* September/October, 23(5), 166–173.

Dixon, J. A., Talbot, L. M. and Le Moigne, G. J-M. (1989) *Dams and the Environment: considerations in World Bank projects*, World Bank Technical Paper No. 110, World Bank, Washington.

Douglas, I. (1983) *The Urban Environment*, Arnold, London.

Eckholm, E., Foley, G., Barnard, G. and Timberlake, L. (1984) *Fuelwood: the energy crisis that won't go away*, Earthscan, London.

Fairbairn, W. A. (1943) Forestry in Plateau Province, *Farm and Forest*, 4(4), 182–192.

Faiz, A. (1992) Motor vehicle emissions in developing countries: relative implications for urban air quality, pp. 175–186 in A. Kreimer and M. Munasinghe (eds)

Environmental Management and Urban Vulnerability, World Bank Discussion Paper No. 168, World Bank, Washington.

Goddard, A. D., Mortimore, M. J. and Norman, D. W. (1975) Some social and economic implications of population growth in rural Hausaland, pp. 321–338 in J. C. Caldwell, N. O. Addo, S. K. Gaisie, A. Igun and P. O. Olusanya (eds). *Population growth and Socio-economic Change in West Africa*, Columbia University Press, New York.

Goldsmith, E. and Hildyard, N. (1984–1985) *The Social and Environmental Effects of Large Dams*, vols 1 and 2, Wadebridge Ecological Centre, Wadebridge.

Hamza, A. (1989) An appraisal of environmental consequences of urban development in Alexandria, Egypt, *Environment and Urbanization*, April, 1(1), 22–30.

Hardoy, J., Mitlin, D. and Satterthwaite, D. (1992) *Environmental Problems in Third World Cities*, Earthscan, London.

Harrison, P. (1979) *Inside the Third World*, Penguin, Harmondsworth.

Harrison, P. (1992) *The Third Revolution: population, environment and a sustainable world*, Penguin, Harmondsworth.

Izeogu, C. V. (1989) Urban development and the environment in Port Harcourt, *Environment and Urbanization*, April, 1(1), 59–68.

Kimmage, K. (1991) The evolution of the 'wheat trap': the Nigerian wheat boom, *Africa*, 61(4), 471–501.

Lewis, L. A. and Berry, L. (1988) *African Environments and Resources*, Unwin Hyman, London.

Main, H. A. C. (1993) Urbanisation, rural environmental degradation and resilience in Africa, pp. 469–485 in A. Mukherjee and V. K. Agnihotri (eds), *Environment and Development: views from the East and the West*, Concept, Delhi.

Main, H. A. C. and Williams, S. W. (eds) (1994) *Environment and Housing in Third World Cities*, Wiley, Chichester.

Mather, A. (1992) The forest transition, *Area*, 24(4), 367–379.

Mink, S. D. (1993) *Poverty, Population and the Environment*, World Bank Discussion Paper No. 189, World Bank, Washington.

Mortimore, M. J. (1972) Some aspects of rural–urban relations in Kano, Nigeria, pp. 871–878 in P. Vennetier (ed.), *La croissance urbaine en Afrique noire et à Madagascar*, Centre Nationale de la Recherche Scientifique, Paris.

Mortimore, M. J. (1982) Framework for population mobility: the perception of opportunities in Nigeria, pp. 50–57 in J. I. Clarke and L. A. Kosinski (eds), *Redistribution of Population in Africa*, Heinemann, London.

Nature (1993) *Mother of the Mega-cities*, BBC2 Television, London.

Pearce, F. (1994) Deserting dogma, *Geographical* January, 66(1), 25–28.

Prothero, R. M. (1957) Migratory labour from north-western Nigeria, *Africa*, 27, 251–261.

Satterthwaite, D. (1991) Urban and industrial environmental policy and management, pp. 119–136 in J. T. Winpenny (ed.), *Development Research: the environmental challenge*, Overseas Development Institute, London.

Skinner, E. P. (1965) Labor migration among the Mossi of the Upper Volta, pp. 60–84 in H. Kuper (ed.), *Urbanization and migration in West Africa*, University of California Press, Berkeley.

Tiffen, M., Mortimore, M. J. and Gikuchi, F. (1994) *More people, less erosion: environmental recovery in Kenya*, Wiley, Chichester.

Timberlake, L. (1985) *Africa in Crisis: the causes, the cures of environmental bankruptcy*, Earthscan, London.

White, R. R. (1989) The influence of environmental and economic factors on the urban crisis, pp. 1–19 in R. E. Stren and R. R. White (eds), *African Cities in Crisis: managing rapid urban growth*, Westview, Boulder.

World Resources Institute/International Institute for Environment and Development/United Nations Environment Programme (1988) *World Resources 1988–89: an assessment of the resource base that supports the global economy*, Basic Books, New York.

World Resources Institute/United Nations Environment Programme/United Nations Development Programme (1992) *World Resources 1992–93: a guide to the global environment*, Oxford University Press, New York.

Section II
North, East and Central Africa

Berber village in the High Atlas mountains, Southern Morocco. (Photograph: Tony Binns)

6

Environmental resources: their use and management by the bedouin of the Nubian Desert of southern Egypt

John Briggs

Introduction

Considerable attention has been paid to the interrelationship of human activity and natural resource use and management in Africa in recent years (Harrison, 1987; Timberlake, 1985; Lewis and Berry, 1988; Omara-Ojungu, 1992; Agnew and Anderson, 1992; Adams, 1990). Perhaps triggered by the Sahel drought of the 1970s, the debate has since broadened to take in issues such as population growth (World Bank, 1992, 1993) and sustainable development (Smith, 1993; Harrison, 1993; Pearce *et al.*, 1990; Ghai and Vivian, 1992; Elliott, 1994). Nevertheless, the central tenet has remained the human–natural environment interface, perhaps more important in Africa than many other parts of the world because of the low technology levels prevalent in much of the continent. Given recent events in Africa, much of the debate has been concerned with resource overuse and abuse, and with the understanding and alleviation of stress conditions. Consequently, the human–natural resource relationship has frequently been portrayed in antagonistic terms, dominated by negative and even hostile perceptions, in which the players may be interpreted as passive victims or,

even worse, villains with no meaningful strategic view of the future. This chapter aims to redress this view by offering an analysis of the ways in which two bedouin groups in the Nubian Desert of southern Egypt manage their livelihood systems to ensure household reproduction, in the context of changing environmental conditions brought about by the creation of Lake Nasser.

Background

Wadi Allaqi, the focus of the study, is located on the east side of Lake Nasser, about 180 km south of Aswan (Figure 6.1). It is situated in a hyper-arid environment, experiencing negligible rainfall, although winter rain may fall to the east in the Red Sea Hills, mainly brought about by orographic influences. Occasionally, there may be sufficient rainfall for a brief period of surface-water flow in Wadi Allaqi. For most of the time, however, the wadi is completely dry at the surface. Before the construction of the High Dam at Aswan, much of Wadi Allaqi lay in the centre of an almost waterless, and hence harsh and unforgiving, natural environment.

People and Environment in Africa. Edited by Tony Binns
©1995 John Wiley & Sons Ltd

Figure 6.1 *Location of Wadi Allaqi, Egypt*

With the completion of the High Dam in 1971, and the subsequent inundation by the High Dam Lake (Lake Nasser in Egypt, Lake Nubia in Sudan), the natural resource base in Wadi Allaqi has been drastically modified. In turn, the subsequent resource opportunities for production have also been substantially changed. By 1978, Wadi Allaqi had been inundated to nearly 100 km of its length. Critically, this has resulted in important groundwater modifications in the area, such that vegetation growth at distances of up to 20 km from the lake shore can now be supported, thus providing a potential grazing resource for livestock. The soil resource base of Wadi Allaqi is also promising, at least in the short term (Briggs *et al.*, 1993). A combination of lake deposits and occasional fluvial deposits has resulted in relatively fertile soils, although there appears to be an enduring problem of nitrogen deficiency, an issue yet to be fully addressed.

Attracted by these new resource opportunities, two bedouin groups have moved into Wadi Allaqi over the last 15 years, settling on the floor of the wadi immediately to the south-east of the lake shore. The Ababda have been resident in the south-eastern Egyptian Desert (the Nubian Desert) for several centuries (Hobbs, 1989), and it is members of three key Ababda families that have chosen to move from the desert areas to the east and into Wadi Allaqi. The three main families, or clans, represented are the Sadanab, Fashekab and Hamadab. In addition, a group of Bishari, mainly from the Al-Mallak clan, have moved into Wadi Allaqi over the same period. Unlike the Ababda, the Bishari do not come traditionally from the Egyptian Desert, but from further south in the Red Sea Hills area of north-east Sudan. However, while the Egypt–Sudan border may have considerable political significance in Cairo and Khartoum, it is of little consequence to the Bishari and offers no barrier to their migratory movements in the desert. At present, there is no marked social or economic tension between the Ababda and Bishari in Wadi Allaqi. This results from the lack of land pressure at the present time, as well as the increasing trend to intermarriage between the two ethnic groups.

Natural resource availability

The critical natural resource for economic activity in the area is water. However, its availability varies throughout any 12-month period, and this, in turn, has a key controlling influence on bedouin production. The two main factors affecting this availability are variations in the water level of Lake Nasser; and the incidence of winter rainfall in the hills to the south and east of Wadi Allaqi.

The level of water in Lake Nasser is, of course, determined by the balance of inflow and outflow. On the one hand, the rate of outflow is readily controllable, and is managed by the Aswan High Dam Authority to satisfy water demands in lower Egypt and the delta, mainly in the summer months. Theoretically, Egypt's water offtake is set at 55.5 billion m^3 of water per year by the 1959 Nile Waters Agreement (Chesworth, 1990). On the other hand, however, the rate of inflow is substantially more problematic, being dependent on the volume of rainfall in the two key catchment areas of the Blue Nile in the Ethiopian Highlands and the White Nile in the Lake Victoria region of East Africa. Of far greater significance is the Blue Nile catchment, as it contributes about 80% of the annual Nile flow. The result is that over a period of years, the mean lake level can vary substantially, reflecting annual variations of rainfall in the catchment areas. In 1978 Lake Nasser reached its record peak of 178 m above sea level (a.s.l.), but by 1988 the level had dropped back to 154 m a.s.l. Since that time, however, the lake has continued to rise again, such that by December 1993 it had reached nearly 175 m a.s.l. Such large differences in lake-level heights are significant in that they translate into large lateral surface-water movements on the eastern side of the lake. In the case of Wadi

Allaqi, the retreat of the water from 178 to 154 m resulted in 35 km of land inundated in 1978 being exposed by 1988, and therefore potentially economically usable.

In addition to the long-term patterns of lake-level change, there are also important changes over a 12-month period. Typically, the lake reaches its minimum annual level in June or July. Thereafter, as the flow from East Africa and Ethiopia reaches the High Dam, the lake fills up. By January, it reaches its maximum level, after which there is a steady drawing off of water for lower Egypt. The result is that there is typically a vertical difference of 6–8 m between minimum and maximum water levels in any one year. This can result in around 10 km of wadi floor being seasonally exposed. Significantly, the soils in the exposed area are resilted and well soaked annually, contributing to their continued relative fertility. Furthermore, even after the surface water has retreated, associated groundwater can still be found, ensuring the regeneration and maintenance of vegetation such as tamarix, acacia and sparse grasses, as well as being available for small-scale irrigation from hand-dug wells of depths of up to 4 m. Although it was the former long-term changes which were responsible for generating the new resource opportunity for attracting bedouin to Wadi Allaqi in the first place, it is the latter short-term changes which form the underlying basis of the present bedouin livelihood systems.

The second key water resource relates to the incidence of rainfall in the hills to the south and east of Wadi Allaqi. Although rainfall is negligible around Wadi Allaqi itself, and, indeed, in the southern Nile Valley generally, there is regular rainfall during the winter period from December to mid-February in the hill areas to the east, and especially towards the Red Sea coast. The main areas where vegetation responds to such rainfall include places such as Gebel Elba and Abraq. Although only low rainfall totals are experienced, around 50 mm annually, it is sufficient to stimulate the growth of potential grazing resources. For much of the rest of the year, the area is practically rainless and consequently offers a difficult environment, apart from in one or two basin areas where groundwater may be found within 5–10 m of the surface.

Livelihood system

It is in this resource context that the bedouin have developed a livelihood system which maximizes the available resource opportunities, but importantly in a managed and sustainable manner. This is absolutely crucial, as the bedouin live in a highly fragile and marginal environment; to be careless in the use of the available natural resources would result only in disaster. Moreover, the bedouin are well aware of this, and hence the management system which operates is environmentally sympathetic.

Figure 6.2 sets out the basic agricultural calendar for Wadi Allaqi, relating the five components of the livelihood system to the months of the year. It is clear that there is a direct relationship between resource availability, in this particular case water availability, and economic activity. This relationship is strongest with regard to sheep-herding, charcoal production and small-scale cultivation; camel-herding and medicinal plant collection are less constrained by seasonal water availability. In any case, both these activities are of secondary importance for most households.

Indeed, in the case of medicinal plant collection, this is practised by only a few households, and then rarely on a systematic scale; usually, medicinal plants are collected as and when necessary to cure a particular ailment prevalent in the household at that time.

Camel-herding is more problematic in the sense that levels of camel ownership vary considerably between households; indeed, it can be argued that this is the key factor in household wealth differentiation among the bedouin. However, there is no difference in the relative seasonal importance of camel-herding. Camels are well adapted to the difficult conditions of the desert and many are allowed to roam freely in and around Wadi Allaqi, grazing off tamarix (preferably young, green shoots which are less salty) and acacia. It is not uncommon for camels to wander in groups in the desert to the east of Wadi Allaqi for extended periods of time, sometimes for up to two to three years. Each bears its owner's brand, minimizing ownership disputes, a system which is not as lax or disorganized as might first seem. Camels tend to move to areas of water and grazing well known to the bedouin. Consequently, if camels are needed by their owner, it is a relatively straightforward task to travel into the desert to find them. More important, however, is the fact that by allowing camels to go off to graze

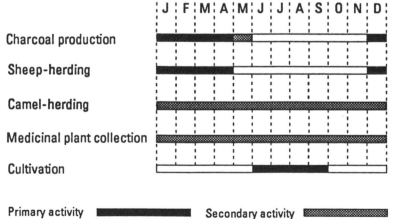

Figure 6.2 *Wadi Allaqi: agricultural calendar*

freely, grazing pressures on vegetation within Wadi Allaqi are much reduced. Moreover, it ensures that the vegetation in the wadi can be allocated more to sheep and goats which do not have the same resilience as camels to a desert existence. Given the fragility and marginality of resources, this makes sound managerial sense.

Both sheep-herding and charcoal production are winter activities, and the extent to which they are undertaken in any one year is strongly related to the incidence of rainfall in the hills to the east. Typically, these activities dominate during the months from December through until March or April. At this time, sheep are taken for grazing into the hills, as these areas may possess sparse grasses and green shrubs stimulated by winter rain. Whereas in the past, whole families may have moved with the animals, this is now rarely the case. Nowadays, perhaps two or three men take the sheep for periods of up to two to three months, leaving the rest of the household in Wadi Allaqi, where there is at least an assured water supply. The creation of Lake Nasser has had a profound impact on the bedouin, in that they have changed from a truly nomadic system to one of semi-nomadism, or, indeed, of transhumance. Significantly, many of the older men reminisce of the 'good old days', but on being pressed few would wish to return to them. Many of the women, interestingly, do not share their spouses' views of the 'good old days', and much prefer the more settled lifestyle of Wadi Allaqi. Indeed, it may well be pressure by women to remain settled in Wadi Allaqi that is an important contributory factor to the decline of true nomadism in the region.

The length of time the sheep are grazed in the hills is entirely dependent on the amount of rainfall experienced during that particular winter season. There is little doubt that this is a crucial part of the livelihood system. Assuming that the winter rain has been adequate, the improved diet for the sheep results in a rise in milk yields, as well as an improvement in the general health status of the sheep. In a good winter season, the sheep build up sufficient reserve, such that when they are brought back to Wadi Allaqi in the early summer, and they are fed with the less nutritious tamarix and dried aquatic weeds from Lake Nasser, milk yields decline less steeply than they otherwise might and physical deterioration of the sheep is slower.

At the same time as this sheep-grazing takes place, the bedouin also take the opportunity to produce charcoal. In the hill areas, there are stocks of acacia, of which *Acacia raddianna* is the preferred species for charcoal production. Harvesting of acacia is a careful and managed process. Only dry or dead wood is used; green and healthy wood is left undisturbed. While tending the sheep, one person can realistically expect to produce up to five sacks of charcoal per month, although it may be fewer if the tree stock is more sparsely distributed, requiring producers to collect material over a wider area. Each sack can be sold for up to LE50 (50 Egyptian pounds) in Aswan, thus giving a potential monthly income per person of up to LE250 (about £50 sterling at 1994 prices).

It is clear that there is strong interrelationship between sheep-herding and charcoal production, and that these activities are at their height during the cooler and hopefully wetter winter months. Furthermore, those households with a greater commitment to livestock transhumance also tend to be those which attach greater importance to charcoal production. This, in turn, reinforces the patterns of household differentiation. Better-off households are in a stronger position to send or take more sheep to the hills for longer periods of time, exploiting the grazing for longer periods, and hence producing higher lambing percentages. Furthermore, producing more charcoal generates more household income, reinforcing the patterns of wealth differentiation between these households and those where sheep-herding and charcoal production are relatively less important in household economic structure, for whatever reasons. In addition, there is little doubt that the present arrangement plays an important role in sustaining the natural resource base of bedouin society. While the sheep are being grazed in the hills, the grazing resources of Wadi Allaqi are allowed a recovery period, thus reducing potential pressures from overuse. Similarly, by ranging over a wide area, pressures on charcoal resources are kept under control. It does, however, raise the question of what the environmental consequences might be of a continuing trend towards even more permanent settlement in Wadi Allaqi, with fewer bedouin taking sheep to the hills in winter. It is already clear that this is steadily becoming less popular among the Allaqi bedouin, with the trend at the moment appearing to be towards greater permanent settlement.

During the summer months, drought and oppressively high temperatures (often approaching 50°C) mean that most people return from the hills to Wadi Allaqi. Cultivation has never been an important bedouin activity, clearly because of the water constraints of the desert. However, inundation by Lake Nasser has created a new opportunity to which the bedouin have responded, although the degree of response varies between households. The exact timing of cultivation differs between years and is largely determined by the rate of lake retreat. However, usually by May or June, most farms are prepared and planted, although further farms may be brought into production later in the summer. By late August or early September, however, the lake starts to rise again, so all cultivation needs to be completed, or in its final stages, by this time to minimize crop losses from inundation.

As the lake water retreats in the early part of the year, the land which is exposed has the twofold advantage of being water-saturated and of having a fresh layer of fertile silt deposited. Furthermore, wells do not have to be dug much more than 2 m in depth for a guaranteed water supply later in the production cycle. The choice of farm location depends on a range of environmental factors. There is a need to balance the desire to minimize the length of period during which well-water might become brackish (as it tends to do as the lake continues to retreat), and to maximize the length of the growing season. A location chosen too early in the summer may result in it eventually having critical water-supply problems if the lake retreats too far. Alternatively, leaving the choice until later in the summer may result in a farm having only a short growing season before being inundated again in late summer. As yet, because of the relatively short period of time over which the

bedouin in Allaqi have been active in cultivation, there is only a relatively limited store of environmental knowledge and experience in terms of water use for cultivation. As this builds up, decisions about farm location will become more accurate and reliable.

Judgements on soil quality also play a part in farm location decisions, and already bedouin are building up a significant microenvironmental knowledge base. There is a recognition that seasonal inundation helps to maintain fertility by resilting, but there is also the view that soils deposited by occasional fluvial action may be equally important. In particular, a runnel is located towards the centre of Wadi Allaqi, and is dominated by sediments deposited after intermittent flow following rain in the hills to the south-east. Similarly, soils found at the junction of tributary wadis with Wadi Allaqi are likewise seen to have a high potential value. There are two reasons for this: firstly, high-quality silts are washed down and deposited in intermittent flood events; and, secondly, these same events flush out salts from the soil. High salt content can be a particular problem in Wadi Allaqi, especially where there is or has been tamarix cover. Tamarix leaf-drop is saline and can be prolific, thus any flushing mechanism, either in the form of lake-water inundation or intermittent fluvial events, is highly beneficial to soil quality. Preferred soil textures are those which are clayey rather than gravelly, while those soils with a reddish tinge are perceived to be salty. Crop cultivation is orientated very much to household consumption with virtually nothing being sold. Food crops dominate, especially tomatoes, water melons, beans, millet and okra, all of which are important in providing variety in the bedouin diet. Despite this greater desire among the bedouin to be involved in cultivation, there is little doubt that it has a substantially lower priority than livestock-herding.

Conclusion

It is clear that the bedouin of this part of the Egyptian Desert manage and use the available natural resources in a sensible and sympathetic manner. This is not, however, simply a reactive response to a harsh and difficult environment, where any mistakes made can have serious consequences for household survival. In this context, it might be seen that the bedouin might adopt a conservative household strategy to ensure that minimum risk is taken, which in turn might suggest that the natural environment is the dominant player. However, the relationship between bedouin and natural environment is more positive and proactive than this. Households have very much developed livelihood strategies which demonstrate a positive understanding of, and empathy with, the natural environment. The discussion has shown that the bedouin not only recognize and manage new natural resource opportunities, as long as they are seen to be of benefit to household production, but also that they are willing and able to accumulate and assess new environmental knowledge.

References

Adams, W. M. (1990) *Green Development: environment and sustainability in the Third World*, Routledge, London.

Agnew, C. and Anderson, E. (1992) *Water Resources in the Arid Realm*, Routledge, London.

Briggs, J. *et al.* (1993) Sustainable development and resource management in marginal environments: natural resources and their use in the Wadi Allaqi region of Egypt, *Applied Geography*, 13, 259–284.

Chesworth, P. (1990) History of water use in Sudan and Egypt, pp. 41–57 in P. P. Howell and J. A. Allan (eds), *The Nile: resource evaluation, resource management, hydropolitics and legal issues*, Royal Geographical Society, London.

Elliott, J. A. (1994) *An Introduction to Sustainable Development: the developing world*, Routledge, London.

Ghai, D. and Vivian, J. M. (eds) (1992) *Grassroots Environmental Action: people's participation in sustainable development*, Routledge, London.

Harrison, P. (1987) *The Greening of Africa: breaking through in the battle for land and food*, Paladin/Grafton Books, London.

Harrison, P. (1993) *The Third Revolution: population, environment and a sustainable world*, Penguin Books, London.

Hobbs, J. J. (1989) *Bedouin Life in the Egyptian Wilderness*, University of Texas Press, Austin.

Lewis, L. A. and Berry, L. (1988) *African Environments and Resources*, Unwin Hyman, Boston.

Omara-Ojungu, P. H. (1992) *Resource Management in Developing Countries*, Longman, Harlow.

Pearce, D. *et al.* (1990) *Sustainable Development: economics and environment in the Third World*, Earthscan Publications, London.

Smith, L. G. (1993) *Impact assessment and sustainable resource management*, Longman, Harlow.

Timberlake, L. (1985) *Africa in Crisis: the causes, the cures of environmental bankruptcy*, Earthscan Publications, London.

World Bank (1992) *Annual Report 1992*, World Bank, Washington, DC.

World Bank (1993) *Annual Report 1993*, World Bank, Washington, DC.

7

Population and environment in time perspective: the Machakos story

Michael Mortimore and Mary Tiffen

Introduction: linkages between population growth and the environment

The linkages between population growth and environmental degradation are controversial. The view, widely held, that rapid population growth is incompatible with sustainable management of the environment is influenced, knowingly or not, by the neo-Malthusian belief that resources are limited. According to literature prepared for the United Nations Conference on Environment and Development (the Rio Earth Summit), 'the number of people an area can support without compromising its ability to do so in the future is known as its population carrying capacity' (UNCED, 1993).

In agricultural terms, each agro-ecological zone is believed to have a carrying capacity which must not be exceeded if environmental equilibrium is to be maintained. In the words of Mustapha Tolba, formerly head of the United Nations Environment Programme, 'when that number is exceeded, the whole piece of land will quickly degenerate from overgrazing or overuse by human beings. Therefore, population pressure is definitely one of the major causes of desertification and the degradation of the land' (Tolba, 1986). According to such a view, degradation threatens to diminish food production, and thereby the human carrying capacity, in a cumulative downward spiral.[1]

More sophisticated estimations of population supporting capacities take account of technological alternatives to the low-input systems that are found in much of the tropical world. A recent study shows that if technology is varied (or levels of inputs increased), the limits rise accordingly (FAO/UNFPA/IIASA, 1984; FAO, 1984). The critical constraint, for practical purposes, is access to technology. However, poverty inhibits investment, and the poor are said to be incapable of conserving their environment: rather, 'poverty forces them to exploit their limited stocks just to survive, leading to overcropping, overgrazing, and overcutting at unsustainable rates. A vicious circle of human need, environmental damage and more poverty ensues' (UNCED, 1993).

A negative view of the effects of population pressure on the environment, which has been underwritten by several UN organizations, the Rio Earth Summit, and influential writers carries great weight in the environmental debate. Nevertheless it is not supported by some well-documented situations in Africa.

One of these, Machakos district of Kenya, is the subject of a recent study of resource management by African smallholders. The study covered the

People and Environment in Africa. Edited by Tony Binns
©1995 John Wiley & Sons Ltd

period 1930–90, which is long enough to control for rainfall variability, and for changes in the political economy. Profiles of change were constructed for all the major environmental and social variables. The linkages in what the World Bank has called the 'population, agriculture and environment nexus' were systematically investigated. The study shows positive, not negative influences of increasing population density on both environmental conservation and productivity.[2]

Characteristics of Machakos district, Kenya

Machakos lies in south-east Kenya (Figure 7.1). Its northernmost point is about 50 km from the capital, Nairobi, from which it stretches some 300 km southwards. Since at least the eighteenth century it has been inhabited by agropastoralists known as the Akamba, who also populated the neighbouring Kitui district. Men looked after the livestock and cleared new land, while women cultivated a small plot for food crops (Lindblom, 1920).

Agro-ecological zones (AEZs) are classified mainly according to rainfall and altitude (which govern temperature). About 9% of the district (the highest areas) are in AEZ II or III, which in Kenya are considered to have high potential for agriculture (see Figure 7.2). Most of it is in AEZ III, which is marginally suited to coffee. About 40% is in AEZ IV, which is moist semi-arid, and 50% is in AEZ V or VI, which is dry semi-arid. In these areas the Akamba keep livestock and grow maize and beans.

Figure 7.1 *Kenya: showing Machakos district*

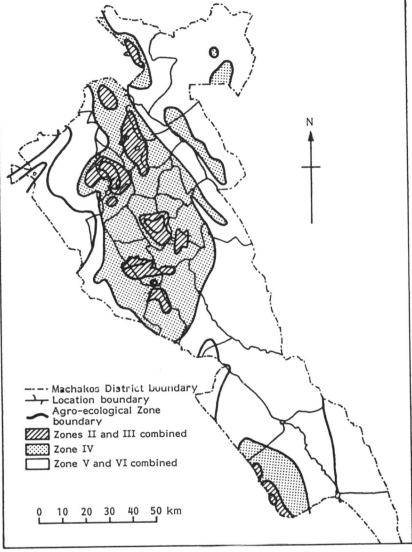

Figure 7.2 *Machakos district, Kenya, showing agro-ecological zones. Source: Tiffen* et al. *(1994, Figure 2.3)*

Most of Machakos district is subject to moisture stress at frequent intervals. The mean annual rainfall is in the range 500–1100 mm. There are two short growing seasons, and in each one, less than half the district receives enough rain to grow a crop of maize as often as 6 seasons out of 10. In the hilly central and northern area lower temperatures combine with more reliable rainfall to provide the most favourable agroclimatic conditions. In the surrounding plains, higher temperatures and variable rainfall greatly increase the level of agricultural risk. No trend is discernible in the rainfall records of the last 100 years. Cycles of 9–11 years in the long rains (March–May) and of 16–22 years in the short rains (October–December) are found in the records since 1957; for Machakos town these are apparent since records began in 1892 (Tiffen *et al.*, 1994, Chapter 3). There is high interannual variability, and sequences of three or more seasonal droughts have occurred.

The soils of the district, except on the wettest hills, tend to be low in fertility (especially carbon, nitrogen and phosphorus) and susceptible to erosion (at rates of 5–15 tonnes of soil per ha per year). These characteristics are explained by long continued cultivation and grazing, and the removal of protective vegetation.

Setting the scene for an ecological disaster

When British rule was imposed on Kenya, the Akamba people were confined in the Ukamba Reserve by the colonial government's Scheduled Areas (White Highlands) policy. Figure 7.3 shows the densely populated reserve area in 1932. It was bounded by European settlers' farms and ranches on the north and west. To the east and south were uninhabited Crown lands, on which the government allowed only grazing, by permit. Thus encircled, the Akamba grew in numbers, and in livestock, while clearing extra land for shifting cultivation of maize and other crops, and chopping down trees for fuel burning and construction of their homes. Despite their protests, the government refused to relax its policy of containment.

During the period 1930–90, the population of Machakos district grew from 238 000 to 1 393 000, and an annual rate of increase of over 3% was maintained from the 1950s until after 1989 (Table 7.1). After 1962, the Akamba were allowed to settle on the semi-arid former Crown lands, and also took over some of the Europeans' farms in government schemes. Thus the land available to them effectively doubled. However, the growth of the population reduced the amount of land available to less than a hectare per person by 1989 (Table 7.1)

This conjunction of rapid population growth with unreliable rainfall, frequent moisture stress, low soil fertility and high erodibility, suggests the likelihood, on the premises outlined above, of population-induced degradation on a grand scale. This was indeed the diagnosis offered in

assessments of the reserve in the 1930s. A disastrous series of droughts (in 1929, 1933, 1934, 1935 and 1939) caused major crop failures, losses of livestock, pest outbreaks, the deterioration of vegetal cover and accelerated erosion. In 1937, Colin Maher, the government's soil conservation officer, wrote despairingly:

The Machakos Reserve is an appalling example of a large area of land which has been subjected to uncoordinated and practically uncontrolled development by natives whose multiplication and the increase of whose stock has been permitted, free from the checks of war and largely from those of disease, under benevolent British rule.

Every phase of misuse of land is vividly and poignantly displayed in this Reserve, the inhabitants of which are rapidly drifting to a state of hopeless and miserable poverty and their land to a parching desert of rocks, stones and sand (Maher, 1937).

No less than eight official visits, reports and recommendations were commissioned between 1929 and 1939, strongly reflecting an official consensus view centred on overstocking, inappropriate cultivation, and deforestation in a reserve thought already to be overpopulated in relation to its carrying capacity. Did events bear out this gloomy prognosis?

Saving the soil or the water?

In the 1930s, there was concern world-wide about soil erosion. As the axioms of soil conservation were being hammered out in the USA, efforts were made to comprehend the scale of the problem in African territories, such as Kenya, Lesotho, South Africa and Nigeria (Bennett, 1939; Hailey, 1938, pp. 1056–1114; Huxley, 1937; Jones 1938; Anderson, 1984). The cause of the problem was generally perceived to be inappropriate native land use.

In 1937, the government established a Soil Conservation Service within the Agricultural Department, under the direction of Maher, with R. O. Barnes particularly responsible for work in Machakos.

One experiment with trash lines of crop residues was to slow down water flow, photographed by R. O. Barnes in 1937 (Figure 7.4). However, this technique was not promoted, since it encouraged the carry-over of pests and diseases. Experimental bench terraces were established near a school in Matungulu location in 1937.

Maher was convinced that a large-scale programme was essential, involving removing people from the worst eroded areas. Elspeth Huxley (1937) shows how the urgency of the situation was believed to justify a coercive solution. The government also made a disastrous attempt partially to destock the reserve of cattle in 1938. The Akamba resisted to the point of demonstrating outside Government House in Nairobi, and engaging the services of a lawyer in London. The government lost credibility and trust. Fears spread among the Akamba that their rights to land, which in custom were established by clearing and cultivation, would be threatened by works done by government tractors or government-paid labour gangs. They reluctantly accepted compulsory labour on terracing and grass-planting two mornings a week. This was enforced by the government-appointed chiefs. One person per household had to be sent; it was often a woman since many of the men were working away.

The bench terrace fell out of favour after Maher visited the USA in 1940, and brought back the 'narrow-based' technique. Attracted by the simplicity and labour economy of the method, he made it the basis of the government's promotion of terrace construction during the next 14 years. In Figure 7.5 (from a sketch made about 1948 to guide administrative officers), the upper sketch shows the narrow-based terrace, created by throwing the soil downhill from a contour ditch. Although easy to construct, the ditch requires desilting each season, or overflowing water breaks the bank and damages the terraces downslope. The lower sketch shows the bench terrace, which the accompanying note recommended only for valuable crops such as tea and coffee (grown by Europeans) or vegetables, because of its high labour requirement. The soil is thrown uphill (which gives it its local name *fanya juu*—throwing upwards) from a levelled area or trench formed along the contour. It tends to become more level over time. The lip must be protected from damage with vegetation, but if this is done it needs only occasional repair. Storm water accumulates at the rear of the terrace, where it can do less damage, instead of at the front, where the structure is least stable.

A post-war expansion of effort seemed urgent after severe food shortages in 1943. The African Land Development Board committed about £1.5 million to land improvement schemes in Machakos district between 1946 and 1962. There was political opposition at the outset, particularly to the use of government machinery, for reasons already given, but the free provision of vast numbers of hand tools was popular among farmers whose poverty seems to have prevented such investments.

A real breakthrough was made in about 1956, when an Akamba officer in the Community Development Department secured the replacement of compulsory work, directed by officials, with a variant of the traditional work party or *mwethya*, by which a person called in neighbours to help with a special project, such as building a hut. The terracing *mwethya* operated under its own leaders, on the farms of its members, who chose the technology. As women predominated, they came to exercise leadership positions in society, almost for the first time. They almost invariably chose *fanya juu*, as the first stage to a bench terrace.

Agricultural officers also began to promote *fanya juu*, particularly after Maher's retirement in 1951. Indeed, benches were compulsory for coffee, which some African farmers were allowed to grow in 1954, under strict supervision. However, some Akamba farmers had already found the bench terrace to be well suited to horticulture, and a 1949 annual report tells of an ex-soldier bringing the technique with him from India for this purpose.

In the 1950s, the arable area protected by terraces grew to over 40 000 ha (Peberdy, 1961). Huxley (1960) called the results a 'Machakos miracle'. Certainly there had been a change of attitude, and much progress. But a hiatus occurred from about 1959. Many narrow-based terraces

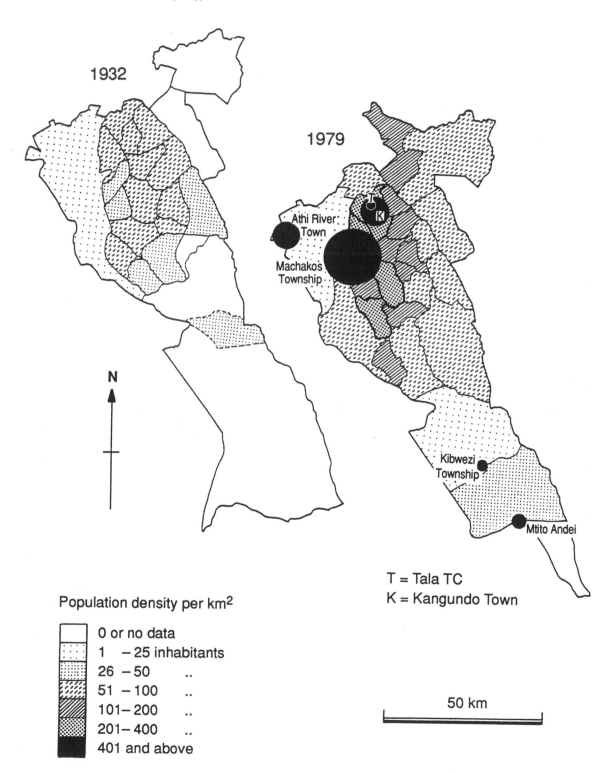

1932

1979

Athi River
Town

Machakos
Township

T = Tala TC

K = Kangundo Town

N

Kibwezi
Township

Mtito Andei

Population density per km²

	0 or no data
	1 – 25 inhabitants
	26 – 50 ..
	51 – 100 ..
	101 – 200 ..
	201 – 400 ..
	401 and above

50 km

Table 7.1 *Growth in the population of Machakos district, 1932–89*

Year	Total population (thousands)	Growth rate (% p.a.)	Average density (ha/person)
1932	240	—	2.66
1948	366	2.68	1.93
1962	566	3.17	1.38
1969	707	3.22	1.92
1979	1023	3.76	1.33
1989	1393	3.09	0.97

Source: Calculated from relevant Kenyan census data. See Tiffen *et al.* (1994).

were allowed to decay, and new building was almost halted. Conservation had been corrupted, in Akamba eyes, by its association with colonial authority, soon to be removed. After independence in 1963, the government switched agricultural staff and resources out of Machakos to districts where good quality former European land was being divided up among African smallholders.

However, accumulated observation had shown farmers that crops do better on terraces. This was confirmed by later analysis (Lindgren, 1988; Holmberg, 1990). It is due to the superior soil moisture on bench terraces, which improves yields in the dry plains and in bad years, even in the wetter hills. A remarkable turn-around seems to have begun from about 1965, accelerating as more and more farmers (and their wives) invested in conservation work on their own and their neighbours' farms (through *mwethya* groups or by hiring labour). A comparison of air photographs shows a relatively small increase in terracing between 1948 and 1961, partly because many narrow-based terraces decayed. The air photographs of 1978 show almost complete terracing of arable in the long-settled areas, despite the lack of any large-scale government assistance since 1961. In one location in AEZ IV, Masii, about

13% of arable land was terraced by 1948, 29% by 1961 and 100% by 1978 (Figure 7.6).[3]

Severe droughts of 1972–76 prompted new donor-assisted programmes for soil conservation. These got under way in 1978, when the Swedish International Development Agency (SIDA) began providing tools, food aid and supervision for soil conservation in part of northern Machakos. The Catholic diocese, supported by some NGOs, also began a food aid programme. In the same year, the Machakos Integrated Development Project (MIDP) was established, running under European Community support till 1988. Its soil conservation component organized terracing by farmers on a catchment basis, particularly in the areas of newer settlement, where farmers had not yet been able to accumulate their own resources for the task. Almost all terraces are now of the *fanya juu* or bench terrace type.

In the 1980s, over 4500 km of terraces were constructed each year with donor or agency support (compared with a peak of about 5000 km in the 1950s). But air surveys show that the total was much larger—8500 km each year between 1981 and 1985 (Ecosystems, 1985/86 Tables 2.14, 2.15). Thus about half of the effort was provided, unassisted, by the farmers themselves, even at that time, when interventions peaked. By 1985, 54% of the district's arable land was considered to be adequately conserved, and in hilly areas, no less than 83%. The dramatic impact of conservation work is shown in Figures 7.7 and 7.8. Terrace construction continues unabated in the 1990s. Conservation is now an accepted part of good farming. Under low and variable rainfall, saving moisture is at least as important as saving the soil itself.

A farming revolution

Change in Machakos was multi-faceted. Technical innovation was not restricted to soil and water

Figure 7.3 *Population density, Machakos district: (a) 1932; (b) 1979. Source: Tiffen et al. (1994, Figure 4.3). Note: The 1932 count was for tax purposes, but was unusually thorough, as it was to provide data for the Kenya Land Commission the following year. Akamba living on the European ranchlands were counted, but figures are not available for the population of parts of the then Thika district, to the north, which were incorporated in the district after 1962. The Crown lands to the west and east were virtually uninhabited, although a few hundred herdsmen were probably utilizing them seasonally. The 1979 map is based on the census of that year*

Figure 7.4 *The first photographic record of soil conservation work in Machakos—trash lines laid along the contour in a field near Muisini, 1937 (Photo: R. O. Barnes, reproduced by permission of Kenya National Archives)*

conservation (in which techniques other than those discussed here were also used—see Gichuki, 1991 and Tiffen *et al.*, 1993). An inventory of production technologies in Machakos identified 76 that were either introduced from outside the district or whose use was significantly extended during the period of the study (Mortimore and Wellard, 1992). They included 35 field and horticultural crops, 5 tillage technologies and 6 methods of soil fertility management. The technical options available to farmers were thereby extended, adding flexibility to the farming system. Such flexibility is a great advantage in a risky environment.

Making money from farming

In the 1930s, capital was mostly locked up in livestock, and occasional sales provided needed cash. From cultivating maize, beans and pigeon peas for subsistence, farmers have since moved into marketing crops. The most successful of these, until its price fell in the 1980s, was coffee. Some Akamba learnt to grow it while employed on European coffee farms, but in 1938 the government expressly forbade 'native' coffee growing in order to protect the European producers' interests. After the overturning of this ban in 1954, strict rules were enforced in the growing, processing and

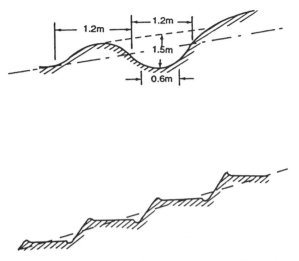

Figure 7.5 *Terracing techniques, as sketched in the late 1940s: Upper: narrow-based terrace; Lower: bench terrace. Source: Kenya National Archives, DC/MKS/8/5 [Touring notes] Reconditioning (reproduced in Tiffen et al., 1994, Figure 11.5)*

marketing of coffee. African producers successfully achieved high grades. Coffee was an attractive component of rehabilitation programmes, since it was profitable and had to be grown on terraces. Coffee output increased spectacularly in the 'boom' of the later 1970s (see Figure 7.9). It generated investment funds, and supported improved living standards, in the sub-humid zone. This had spill-over effects in the drier areas, through the demand of coffee-growing farmers for agricultural labour, for food and livestock products in which they might no longer be self-sufficient, and for a whole range of consumer goods, housing improvements and services. By 1982–83 over 40% of rural incomes in Machakos district were being generated by non-farm businesses and wages (Kenya CBS, 1988).

In contrast to coffee, cotton, which is rec-ommended for the drier areas, was not a success in the long term. Its price was only rarely high enough to compensate for its tendency to compete with the food crops for labour and capital, and the profit margins were reduced by marketing inefficiencies. Three attempts to promote cotton—in the 1930s, 1960s and 1978–84—ran into the sand. Output limped along (see Figure 7.9), and in

1991 the closed ginnery at Makueni offered silent testimony of failure.

Both coffee and cotton were sold to monopsonist parastatal marketing boards and required govern-ment support in extension and supervision, and in supervising officially sponsored co-operatives for input provision, processing and grading. By contrast, expanded growing of a great variety of perennial and annual fruit and vegetables was closely linked with the growth of Kenya's canning industry, the Nairobi and Mombasa retail markets, and exports of fresh vegetables by air. Itinerant Asian buyers, firms operating contract-buying and enterprising Akamba, as individual traders or in formal co-operatives or informal groups, have all played a role. A generally high value per hectare facilitated the skilful exploitation of wet micro-environments, even in the driest areas, and the development of technologies such as micro-irrigation and the cultivation of bananas in pits. Fruit production is attractive to women farmers, as trees do not compete with food crops (for which they often have the main responsibility).

Akamba farmers have adapted rather well to the opportunities provided by the market. No amount of promotion can succeed without incentives. But given these, innovation in both production and marketing aspects is commonplace. Meanwhile, livestock sales, on which they depended for market income in the 1930s, have steadily declined.

Achieving food sufficiency

The staple food of the Akamba is white maize. The shortness of the two growing seasons, and the high probability of drought, call for varieties that either resist drought or escape it by maturing quickly. In the 1960s, the government's local research station began a search for drought-escaping varieties that culminated in the release of Katumani Composite B (KCB) maize in 1968.

The new maize was promoted by the extension service, and it was steadily, if unspectacularly, adopted by the farmers. Various surveys suggest that from two-thirds to three-quarters use it, but

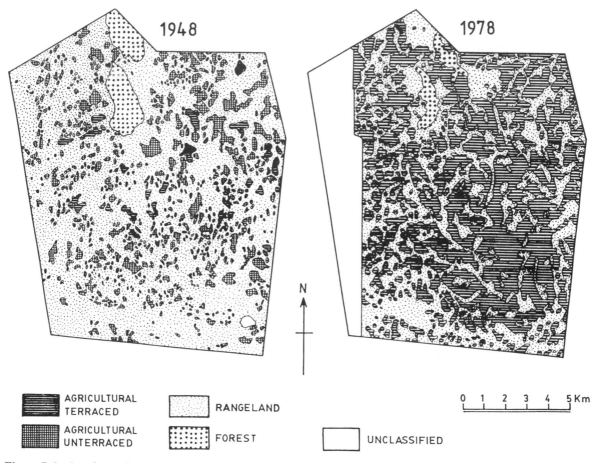

Figure 7.6 *Land-use change in Masii, 1948–78 (based on air photo interpretation). Source: Tiffen* et al. *(1994, Figure 5.3)*

it is not known how much of the maize area is planted to it, nor what proportion of output it contributes. Of 40 farmers interviewed in five locations in 1990, only a third said they used it exclusively, and another third used it together with local and hybrid varieties.

This was no 'green revolution'. The ambivalent response has, however, an explanation. Given the unpredictable rainfall, farmers need to keep their options open. Their local varieties, though slower to mature, are more resistant to drought, and hybrids do better in wetter sites. KCB is liked because, in combination with other varieties, it strengthens this flexibility rather than undermines it. Some farmers cross-pollinate it with their

local varieties, further enhancing their adaptive choice.

With and without KCB, food crop production per person kept up with population growth from 1930 to 1987 although imported foods remained necessary after a series of bad seasons. The district's dependence on imported food in the period 1974–85 was less than in 1942–62 (8 kg per person annually compared with 17), notwithstanding major droughts in both periods (see Tiffen *et al.*, 1994, pp. 40–41 and 81). Food output per person in 1984 (after three seasonal droughts) was slightly higher than in 1960–61 (after two seasons with drought, and one with floods).

Figure 7.7 *A degraded hillside (upper), photographed in 1937, has been transformed into terraced fields in 1991 (lower). The woodland has not degraded and erosion has been reduced*

Figure 7.8 *A grassed slope of more than 25°, with patches of cultivation, photographed in 1937 (upper), has been transformed into terraced fields, woodlots and farmsteads in 1991 (lower)*

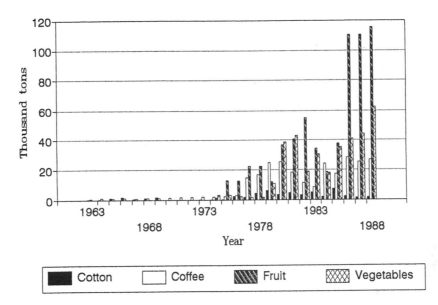

Figure 7.9 *Recorded output of market crops (in thousand tons). Source: Derived from official agricultural reports, as shown in Mbogoh (1992). See also Tiffen et al. (1994, Figure 6.4(b)). Note: Sales of livestock and livestock products (not shown) fluctuated throughout the period. Farmers in the drier areas sell substantial amounts of maize and pulses, but this trade is unrecorded. Much horticultural trade is probably unrecorded*

Faster tillage

In view of the reputation then enjoyed by the Akamba for resistance to change, it is surprising that the ox-plough, introduced to the district as early as 1910, had spread to about 600 (or 3%) of the district's households by the 1930s (*Kenya Land Commission Report*, 1934). Farmers trained their own cattle, and ploughs were cheap (about equivalent to the price of a cow in 1940); furthermore the technology was being tested and developed on nearby European farms where some Akamba worked. Ownership greatly increased the area a farmer could cultivate, and enabled him to sell maize or cotton. Its adoption called for the cessation of shifting cultivation, and facilitated the adoption of row planting and better weeding, in place of broadcasting seed.

After the Second World War, ex-soldiers who had seen ploughs in India returned with the capital to buy their own. Proceeds from trade and employment outside the district were also invested in ploughs. The government made ox-ploughs the basis of a new farming system imposed on a supervised settlement at Makueni location. The government, and traders, provided some credit. Coffee (after 1954), horticulture and cotton (in some years) generated investment funds. Adoption accelerated in the 1960s and was more or less complete by the 1980s. Surveys found 62% or more of farmers owning a plough, the remainder being too poor, or having fields too small and steep for its use.

The plough proved to be both a durable and a flexible technology. The first ones in use were adapted to opening new land, with teams of six or eight oxen. Farmers later selected a lighter, two-oxen instrument suitable for work on small, terraced, permanent fields. The Victory mouldboard plough, though much criticized on technical grounds, is used everywhere, and for several operations—primary ploughing, seed-bed preparation and inter-row weeding—and attempts to promote its replacement by a more expensive tool-bar have failed. It saves labour, and is also used by women (Figure 7.10). The 'oxenization' of Akamba agriculture was, in a

Figure 7.10 *Alice Mulandi and her plough at Makaveti. Her well-built grain store derives from a technology introduced under ALDEV*

measure, a triumph of capitalization in a capital-poor, risk-prone and low productive farming system.

Fertilizing the soil

Shifting cultivation used to rely on long fallows for replenishing the soil. In the 1930s, there was very little systematic manuring. But the fertility of arable land, as measured by yields, was low. The Agricultural Department favoured farmyard manure over inorganic fertilizers. It also, unsuccessfully, promoted composting. It was not until the 1950s that manuring became widespread, in the northern sub-humid areas. By this time, arable fields were fixed, and cultivated every year. The silent spread of this practice can be judged from the fact that by the 1980s, 9 out of 10 farmers were doing it, in both wetter and drier areas (ADEC, 1986). Now, most arable land is cultivated twice a year—in both rainy seasons—and composting is being adopted by small farmers with few livestock.

By contrast, the use made of inorganic fertilizers is minimal, the bulk of it on coffee. Manure is made in the *boma* (stall or pen) and supplemented with trash and waste. The amount applied depends on how many livestock there are, and how much labour and transport are available when needed. Every farmer knows that, under present technical and economic conditions, sustaining output depends on the use made of *boma* manure (Probert *et al.*, 1992). Few can afford inorganic fertilizers in quantity.

Feeding the livestock

At the beginning of our period (the 1930s), Akamba women cultivated food crops at home, while their men used to take the livestock away to common grazing lands for several months of the year. However, common grazing land vanished as it was transformed into new farms. After about 1960 settlement on Crown lands could no longer be restrained, and thousands of families moved into them. Each household must now keep its animals within the bounds of the family farm, or obtain permission to use another family's land, often in return for some rent or service. More than 60% of the cattle, sheep and goats are stall-fed or tethered for a part or all of the year (ADEC, 1986). When in the *boma*, cut fodder and residues are brought to them, which requires additional labour. Fodder grass is grown on terrace banks. These changes are most advanced in the sub-humid zone. A third of the livestock are grazed all the time, mostly in the dry semi-arid zone. The effort required to maintain livestock is making grade or crossbred cattle popular (estimated to number about 9% of the total in 1983 and to have grown rapidly since), whose milk yields and value are superior to those of the native zebu, though their increased health risks call for frequent dipping.

Farming the trees

From the 1920s, the Forest Department believed that reafforestation was necessary to arrest environmental desiccation, and supply the growing need for domestic fuel and construction timber (Mortimore, 1992). For several decades the department struggled, under-resourced, to reserve and replant hilltop forests. In 1984, however, estimates of household fuel requirements put the need for new plantations at 226 000 ha (15 times the area of gazetted forest reserves!) (Mung'ala and Openshaw, 1984). The destruction of surviving natural woodland seemed an imminent possibility.

But sites photographed in 1937 and 1991 showed little sign of woodland degradation (Figures 7.7 and 7.8). A fuel shortage has failed to develop on the expected scale and the district does not import wood or charcoal in significant quantities. Indeed it exports some. Part of the explanation for this expert miscalculation lay in ignoring the use made of dead wood, farm trash, branch wood from farm trees, and hedge cuttings, for domestic fires. The other part lay in failing to appreciate a major area of innovative practice: the planting, protection and systematic harvesting of trees. Forest policy in the 1980s was shifting towards farm forestry promotion, but in this it was following, not driving, farmers.

Tree densities on farmland in one location, Mbiuni, averaged over 34 per ha (14 when bananas are excluded) by 1982. Furthermore, the smaller the farm, the greater the density (Gielen, 1982). The range of trees planted includes both exotic and indigenous, both fruit and timber species. Akamba women generally manage fruit trees, while the men look after the timber trees (Rocheleau, 1990). Owners of grazing land manage the regeneration of woody vegetation, which is used for timber, fuel, browse, honey production, edible and medicinal products (Tiffen *et al.* 1993).

Producing more with less

These were some of the features of a revolution in farming wrought in unpromising circumstances. What was the driving force behind these changes?

The growth of population had two important outcomes: the subdivision of a man's landholdings among all his sons, according to Akamba custom, and the increasing scarcity of land as former communal grazing and Crown land became new private farms.

As holdings shrank in size, the arable proportion rose, leaving less and less land for grazing (as is apparent from Figure 7.6, for Masii) while the cultivated area per person stagnated. Table 7.2 shows how the percentage of arable land increases from the older settled areas to the new, and from the wetter to the drier areas.

These changes created the imperative for intensification. By intensification we mean the application

Table 7.2 *Increases in the cultivated area, 1948–78, in five study areas (%)*

Area	1948 Population density/km^2	Cultivated area	1978 Population density/km^2	Cultivated area
1	123	35.3	261	80.7
2	97	13.6	199	54.2
3	75	23.4	138	50.9
4	2	1.2	53	30.1
5	0	0	<25	19.8

Note: The sequence 1–5 denotes a range from wetter to drier ecology and from older to recently settled areas. The study areas are as follows: 1, Kangundo/Matungulu/Mbiuni; 2, Kalama/Mbooni; 3, Masii; 4, Makueni; 5, Ngwata.
Source: Rostom and Mortimore (1991).

Table 7.3 *Large and small farms in Mwala, 1980*

	Quartile 1	2	3	4
Farm size (ha)	1.3	3.2	7.5	17.8
Cropped area (%)	77	50	25	18
Cash inputs per cultivated ha	331	191	167	135
Livestock units per ha	3.5	1.9	1.3	0.7
Net farm income per ha	1619	611	272	154
Non-farm income per family	3529	1503	1811	2628

Source: Rukandema *et al.* (1981) and our calculations. A livestock unit is one mature head of cattle or five sheep or goats. Cash figures are in Kenya shillings.

of increasing amounts of labour and capital per ha to raise crop yields. Crop–livestock integration is intrinsic to this process in dryland farming systems in Africa (McIntire *et al.*, 1992; Tiffen *et al.*, 1993; Mortimore and Turner, 1993). It was driven by the needs for draft energy on the farm, for fodder (the stalks of maize and haulms of beans, for example), for manure and milk.

Two changes—to intensive livestock feeding systems, and to permanent manured fields, often under plough cultivation—were pivotal in this transformation, whose outcome was an increasingly efficient system of nutrient cycling through plants, animals and soil. The changes could not have occurred without security of title. Akamba custom had already recognized individuals rights in land, including the right of sale, in the older settled areas by the 1930s. Security has been reinforced by statutory registration of title, a slow legal process which began in Machakos in 1968 and has still not covered all areas.

Equally important were sources of investment capital. This was not only required for terraces and ploughs. To clear and cultivate new land, build hedges or plant trees requires labour which often has to be hired, as well as tools and expertise. The off-farm incomes earned by Akamba men inside and outside the district have contributed for decades to agricultural investment. Such incomes are often high in households with small farms, and there is little evidence that investment per ha falls

where farmers are poorly resourced in land (see Table 7.3).

The outcome of this process of intensification was an increase in the value of output per square kilometre (at constant prices) from 1930 to 1987 (Figure 7.11). This was calculated by taking output data for the only three available years before 1974 (1930, 1957 and 1961), selecting two later years which were climatically average (1977 and 1987), and converting all the values into maize equivalent at 1957 prices. The year 1957 was an unusually good one and 1961, as already noted, unusually bad, hence the upward trend was interrupted. The trend continued despite the additions of large areas of the more arid types of land in 1962. Output per capita closely reflected this curve.[4]

We conclude that, contrary to the expectations expressed in the 1930s, the Akamba of Machakos have put land degradation into reverse, conserved and improved their trees, invested in their farms, and sustained an improvement in overall productivity.

Facilitating change

It is not possible here to do more than mention the social and institutional factors that facilitated these changes (Tiffen *et al.*, 1994; Bahemuka and Tiffen, 1992). The extended family in which wives and cattle were highly valued evolved towards a nuclear unit characterized by closer

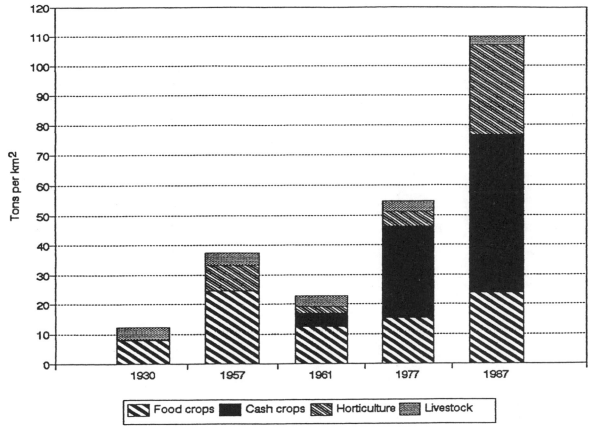

Figure 7.11 *Output per km² in constant 1957 maize prices. Source: Tiffen et al. (1994, Figure 6.4b)*

partnership between a man and (one) wife. Longer working hours are called for in intensive farming (Figure 7.12) but families faced an inadequate labour supply, with children often remaining at school until the age of 20, and one adult usually having a non-farm occupation. The old division of labour between the sexes has been abandoned to create a more flexible family labour force, which may be supplemented by hired labour or by collective effort through the *mwethya* groups. *Mwethya* is used for many community assets, and for rotational labour between the farms of neighbours as well as contributing to terracing. Women's leadership and participation are crucial to many of these groups.

Local leadership has evolved from a system of chiefs, obliged to collaborate with the colonial administration and not always respected for that,

into a more diversified system, in which churches, political parties, co-operatives and other group provide means to influence decisions reached at higher levels and to obtain access to resources.

The missions, the schools, markets and travel facilitated formal education, the acquisition of technical knowledge, and experimental attitudes, of which there is abundant anecdotal evidence. Education gave access to employment outside the district, which in return brought investment funds back to house and farm.

Government attempts to influence the course of change relied too much, particularly but not only in the colonial period, on coercive or directive methods. Yet among the many techniques tried, with varying success, experience was gained which stood the Akamba in good stead when, after independence, they came to believe that they

Figure 7.12 *A young woman takes a moment off to attend to her children while she works with her husband at planting onions. Taken just before nightfall, this photograph exemplifies the long working hours that intensive farming requires, and the change in gender roles in agriculture*

were more in control of their own resources and destiny.

The question that needs be asked is whether the achievements in Machakos were due to disproportionate investments of public funds. In the period 1947–62, 32% of the expenditures of the African Land Development Board in Kenya were committed to the district. Yet much of this was lost, for example in subsidizing terraces that were not maintained. The most lasting effects of the ALDEV programme included 300 small dams, the Makueni resettlement scheme, better farming promotion and tsetse fly control. More recently, the considerable expenditures of the Machakos Integrated Development Programme in the early 1980s did not exceed the average (on a per capita basis) for Kenya's semi-arid lands as a whole. The greater part of these went into the improvement of domestic water supply.

Our conclusion is that, particularly since independence, the government's main role in the transformation of Machakos was to pursue an open market path to economic development, provide national economic infrastructure, support individual title to land, and promote channels for learning and communicating new or adapted knowledge.

No miracle in Machakos?

What happened in Machakos did not contravene the laws of nature, as the Malthusian paradigm would express them, but rather grew logically from a conjunction of increasing population density, market growth and a generally supportive economic environment. The technological changes we have described, in conservation and production, cannot be adequately understood as exogenous, as mere accidents that gave breathing space on a remorseless progression towards irreversible environmental degradation and poverty. Rather, as argued long ago by Ester Boserup and more recently by Julian Simon, they were mothered by necessity (Boserup, 1965; Simon, 1986). Technological change was an endogenous process, in which multiple sources and channels were employed, involving selection and adaptation by farmers.

Increasing population density is found, then, to have positive effects. The increasing scarcity (value) of land promoted investment, both in conservation and in yield-enhancing improvements. The integration of crop and livestock production improved the efficiency of nutrient cycling, and thereby the sustainability of the farming system.

The Machakos experience offers an alternative to the Malthusian models of the relations between population growth and environmental degradation. Elsewhere in Africa, there are more documented cases of positive associations, though it would be foolish to ignore the differences (Turner *et al.*, 1993).

Successful intensification under rising densities has certain preconditions. These are peace and security, for trade and investment, and a marketing and tenure system in which economic benefits are shared by many, rather than monopolized by a few. Degradation may occur, as it did in Machakos, when a change from a long fallowing system is first needed, but when population densities or other conditions are not conducive. Normally, as population grows, so do the opportunities for specialization and trade (Boserup, 1965). To the stick of necessity the market adds the carrot of incentives and resources for investment in new technologies.

In the past, development planners tried to transform farming systems that were seen as inefficient and technically conservative. In fact, they are changing themselves, as studying them in time perspective shows, and there is scope for supporting positive change with appropriate policies. The guiding principle must be to go with the grain of historical change. This means

encouraging investment, by encouraging trade and by improving farm-gate prices (for example, by improving roads and by avoiding heavy taxation of agricultural products). There is also a need to protect investment when crises (e.g. famines) threaten to force households to sell their assets. Increasing the technical options available to local resource users in a risky environment is one of the most productive avenues to pursue, by encouraging endogenous experimentation, by increasing information through general education as well as agricultural extension, and by creating new avenues for technological development and transfer.

Acknowledgements

The study was financed by grants from the World Bank, the Rockefeller Foundation and the Overseas Development Administration of the United Kingdom. It was sponsored in Kenya by the Ministry of Reclamation and Development of Arid, Semi-arid Areas and Wastelands. It was carried out by the Overseas Development Institute, London in association with the University of Nairobi. An earlier different version of this chapter appeared in *Environment*, 36/8, October 1994, 10–21, 28–32; this chapter appears with the agreement of Heldref Publications, Washington DC.

Notes

1. The definition of desertification adopted in 1977 gave a major role to management, and only a minor one to climate change. That bias has recently been corrected. See UNEP (1993).
2. For results see Tiffen *et al.* (1994), English *et al.* (1994) and a series of ODI working papers *Environmental Change and Dryland management in Machakos District, Kenya*, Numbers 53–59 and 62–63, published by the Overseas Development Institute, London in 1991 and 1992. The latter contain the detailed results of the field studies carried out with researchers from the University of Nairobi.
3. Five sample areas, with four sets of three photographs, 1948, 1961 and 1978, and one set of two, 1961 and 1978 are given in Rostom and Mortimore (1991). Of course, 100% arable terracing does not necessarily mean that terraces were adequate in spacing or maintenance.
4. Tiffen *et al.* (1994, pp. 92–96) also present calculations based on changing price relatives.

References

ADEC (African Development and Economic Consultants) (1986) *Machakos Integrated Development Programme Socio-economic Survey. Final Report*, Ministry of Planning and National Development, Nairobi and Machakos.

Anderson, D. M. (1984) Depression, dust bowl, demography and drought: the colonial state and soil conservation in East Africa during the 1930s, *African Affairs*, 83(332), 321–343.

Bahemuka, J. M. and Tiffen, M. (1992) Akamba institutions and development, 1930–90, in M. Tiffen (ed.), *Environmental Change and Dryland Management in Machakos District, Kenya, 1930–90: Institutional Profile*, Working Paper 62, Overseas Development Institute, London.

Barnes, R. O. (1937) *Soil Erosion, Ukamba Reserve*, report to the Department of Agriculture, Kenya National Archives, DC/MKS/16a/29/1, Nairobi.

Bennett, H. H. (1939) *Soil Conservation*, McGraw-Hill, New York.

Boserup, E. (1965) *The Conditions of Agricultural Growth*, Allen & Unwin, London. (Reprinted 1993 by Earthscan, London.)

Ecosystems (1985/86) *Baseline Survey of Machakos District, 1985*. Vol. 4: *Land Use Changes in Machakos District 1981–85*, Ecosystems Ltd, Nairobi.

English, J., Tiffen, M. and Mortimore, M. (1994) *Land Resource Management in Machakos District, Kenya 1930–1990*, World Bank Environment Paper No. 5, the World Bank, Washington, DC.

FAO (1984) *Land, Food and People. FAO Economic and Social Development Series 30*, Food and Agriculture Organization of the United Nations, Rome.

FAO/UNFPA/IIASA (1984) *Potential Population Supporting Capacities of Lands in the Developing World*, Food and Agriculture Organization of the United Nations, Rome.

Gichuki, F. N. (1991) *Environmental Change and Dryland Management in Machakos District, Kenya 1930–90. Conservation profile*, ODI Working Paper 56, Overseas Development Institute, London.

Gielen, H. (1982) *Report on an Agroforestry Survey in Three Villages of Northern Machakos, Kenya*, Wageningen Agricultural University, Netherlands/ International Council for Agroforestry Research, Nairobi.

Hailey, Lord (1938) *An African Survey. A Study of Problems Arising in Africa South of the Sahara*, Oxford University Press.

Holmberg, G. (1990) An economic evaluation of soil conservation in Kitui District, Kenya, J. A. Dixon, D. E. Jones and P. B. Sherman (eds), *Drylands Management, Economic Case Studies*, Earthscan, London.

Huxley, E. (1937) The menace of soil erosion, *Journal of the Royal African Society*, 36, 357–370.

Huxley, E. (1960) *A new earth*, pp. 188–203. London.

Jaetzold, R. and Schmidt, H. (1983) *Farm Management Handbook of Kenya*, vol. 2: *Natural Conditions and Farm Management Information*, Part IIC: East Kenya (Eastern and Coast Provinces), Ministry of Agriculture, Nairobi.

Jones, B. (1938) Desiccation and the West African colonies, *The Geographical Journal*, 91/5, 401–423.

Kenya Land Commission Report (1934) 3 vols, Her Majesty's Stationery Office, London.

Kenya CBS (1988) *Economic Survey*, Central Bureau of Statistics, Ministry of Finance and Planning, Nairobi.

Lambert, H. E. (1945) *A Note on Native Land Problems in the Machakos District with Particular Reference to Reconditioning*, DC/MKS/7/1, Kenya National Archives, Nairobi.

Lindblom, K. G. (1920) *The Akamba of British East Africa*, Appelborgs Boktrycheri Aktieborg, Uppsala.

Lindgren, B. M. (1988) *Machakos Report 1988: Economic Evaluation of a Soil Conservation Project in Machakos District, Kenya*, Ministry of Agriculture, Nairobi.

McIntire, J., Bourzat, D. and Pingali, P. (1992) *Crop–livestock Interactions in Sub-Saharan Africa*, The World Bank, Washington, DC.

Maher, C. (1937) Soil erosion and land utilisation in the Ukamba Reserve (Machakos), report to the Department of Agriculture, Mss Afr.S.755, Rhodes House Library, Oxford.

Mbogoh, S. G. (1992) Crop production, in M. Tiffen (ed.), *Environmental Change and Dryland Management in Machakos District, Kenya, 1930–90: Production profile*, Working Paper 55, Overseas Development Institute, London.

Mortimore, M. (1992) *Environmental Change and Dryland Management in Machakos District, Kenya, 1930–90: Tree management*, Working Paper 63, Overseas Development Institute, London.

Mortimore, M. and Turner, B. (1993) *Crop–livestock Farming Systems in the Semi-arid Zone of Sub-Saharan Africa. Ordering diversity and understanding change*, Network Paper 46, Agricultural Administration (Research and Extension) Network, Overseas Development Institute, London.

Mortimore, M. and Wellard, K. (1992) *Environmental Change and Dryland Management in Machakos District, Kenya, 1930–90. Profile of technological change*, ODI Working Paper 57, Overseas Development Institute, London.

Mung'ala, P. and Openshaw, K. (1984) Estimation of present and future demand for woodfuel in Machakos District, Kenya, C. Barnes, J. Ensminger and P. O'Keefe (eds), *Wood, Energy and Households: perspectives on rural Kenya*, Beijer Institute/Scandinavian Institute of African Studies, Stockholm/Uppsala.

Owako, F. N. (1969) *The Machakos problem. A study of some aspects of the agrarian problems of Machakos District of Kenya*, Ph.D. thesis, University of London.

Peberdy, J. (1961) Notes on some economic aspects of Machakos District, mimeo, Report for Ministry of Agriculture, Nairobi, Kenya.

Probert, M. E., Okalebo, J. R., Simpson, J. R. and Jones, R. K. (1992) The role of boma manure for improving soil fertility, pp. 63–70 in M. E. Probert (ed.), *A Search for Strategies for Sustainable Dryland Cropping in Semi-arid Eastern Kenya. ACIAR Proceedings No. 41*, Australian Centre for International Agriculture Research, Canberra.

Rocheleau, D. (1990) Gender, ecology and the science of survival: stories and lessons from Kenya, *Agriculture and Human Values*, 8(11), 156–164.

Rostom, R. S. and Mortimore, M. (1991) *Environmental Change and Dryland Management in Machakos District, Kenya, 1930–90: Land use profile*, Working Paper 58, Institute of Overseas Development, London.

Rukandema, M., Mavua, J. K. and Audi, P. O. (1981) *The Farming System of Lowland Machakos, Kenya: farm survey results from Mwala*, Farming Systems Economic Research Programme Technical Report (Kenya) 1, Ministry of Agriculture, Nairobi.

Simon, J. L. (1986) *Theory of Population and Economic Growth*, Basil Blackwell, Oxford.

Tiffen, M., Mortimore, M. and Ackello-Ogutu, A. C. (1993) *From Agro-pastoralism to Mixed Farming: the evolution of farming systems in Machakos, Kenya, 1930–1990*, Network Paper 45, Agricultural Administration (Research and Extension) Network, Overseas Development Institute, London.

Tiffen, M., Mortimore, M. and Gichuki, F. (1994) *More People, Less Erosion. Environmental recovery in Kenya*, John Wiley, Chichester.

Tolba, M. (1986) Desertification, *World Meteorological Organisation Bulletin*, 35, 17–22.

Turner, B. L., Hyden, G. and Kates, R. (eds) (1993) *Population Growth and Agricultural Change in Africa*, University Press of Florida, Gainesville.

UNCED (United Nations Conference on Environment and Development) (1993) *Earth Summit in Focus, No. 6*. Reproduced in *The Courier*—Africa–Caribbean–Pacific–European Union, No. 144, 1994, 52–54.

UNEP (United Nations Environment Programme) (1993) Good news in the fight against desertification, *Desertification Control Bulletin*, 22, 3–4.

8

Exploring people–environment relationships: the changing nature of the small-scale fishery in the Kenyan sector of Lake Victoria

Kim Geheb

Introduction

Straddling the Equator, Lake Victoria is the largest lake in Africa, and is part of the territory of three countries: Kenya, Tanzania and Uganda. This chapter focuses on change in the Kenyan sector which, despite being the smallest portion of the lake (6% of the total surface or 4100 km^2), is the most heavily fished and commercialized. Most of the Kenyan sector lies within the Nyanza Gulf (see Figure 8.1). On the gulf's eastern shore is Kisumu, the administrative centre for the region, and location of a number of industrial fish processing plants. A wide savanna plain surrounds this sector of the lake, stretching some 10 km from the water's edge to the Mau Escarpment. This region is more suitable for cattle-herding than farming, although small-scale subsistence farming is carried out.

Lake Victoria provides 85% of Kenya's fish (World Bank *et al.*, 1991), and most, if not all of this fish is landed by small-scale fishermen. An estimated 25 000–35 000 fishermen derive

livelihoods from the lake (Ochieng' Okatch, 1992; Ogutu, 1992). If subsidiary activities are included, such as fish trading and transporting, beach-side bars, cafés and hotels, the number of people who rely on the fishery multiplies considerably; for example, the ratio of fish-traders to fishermen is thought to be as high as 3 : 1 (Ogutu, 1992).

For the purposes of this chapter, a 'small-scale' activity is one where the amount of capital required to start fishing is generally small, and includes anything from a simple fishing line to a whole boat complete with nets and crew. Furthermore, small-scale fishing is also 'labour-intensive', relying on labour rather than labour-saving technology. On the other hand, 'large-scale' activity involves much greater investment, such as in trawlers (forbidden in Kenya waters since 1989), large fish-processing plants and a high technological intensity employing relatively little labour.

Because fishing in Lake Victoria is dominated by small-scale fishermen, it is important to understand changes within this group *vis-à-vis* changes in the lake, and to understand how the

People and Environment in Africa. Edited by Tony Binns
©1995 John Wiley & Sons Ltd

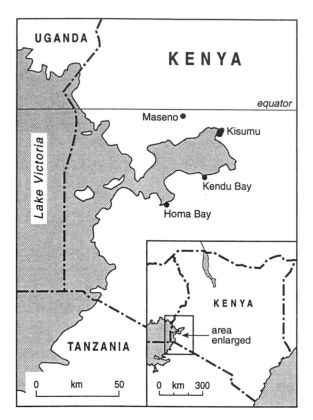

Figure 8.1 *The Kenyan shores of Lake Victoria*

In this chapter, we consider access to Lake Victoria's fishery through three periods of time: the pre-colonial period (around 1850 to 1900); the colonial period (1900–62) and the post-independence period (1963 to the present). The chapter examines how access has changed over time and how this has affected both the lakeside communities and the resource base on which they rely.

The pre-colonial fishery

The people who live on the shores of the Kenyan sector of Lake Victoria are mainly Luo, who claim common origin from Sudan (Ogot, 1967). Their society is arranged around 'clans', which identify with a common ancestor or ancestors, normally individuals who proved themselves to be great leaders or warriors during the Luo migration from southern Sudan to Kenya in the sixteenth century. Within each clan are 'sub-clans'. Although many sub-clans can live side by side in the same clan, they are identified primarily from the kind of economic activity they undertake. Thus, sub-clans can be identified by cattle-herding, agriculture and, for those with lakeside territory, fishing.

Each clan had territory, and for those with lakeside territory, this extended into the lake. This marine territory was bounded on either side by the territory of neighbouring clans and extended to the furthest point in the lake that the clan's boats could go. It was forbidden for members of one clan to fish in their neighbour's waters.

Fishing was considered a highly skilled activity, entailing a detailed knowledge of fish and their migratory habits, the manufacture and use of nets and traps, and an understanding of seasonal variations in the movement of fish species. Considerable strength and stamina were required as fishing could be both dangerous (crocodiles were especially feared) and extremely hard work. As a consequence, people born into fishing sub-clans often could not fish until they reached a certain, 'mature' age. For example, in the Wasiko sub-clan of the Kasagam clan, this age was 15, but it could be different in other clans.

one affects the other. The nature of the relationship between the small-scale fishery and the lake has changed over time, and it is this change which is the focus of this chapter. The approach adopted here is from the perspective of changes in 'access'. Access implies the relative ease by which a person or a group of people can exploit a resource, in this case the fish of Lake Victoria. Thus, at one extreme, we have 'open access', where exploitation is unregulated by any mechanism, such as legal institutions of government, or cultural institutions within an ethnic group. In areas where there are high levels of poverty, rapid population growth and few job opportunities, open-access resources often suffer considerably from over-exploitation.

At the other extreme we have 'restricted access' to a resource, where both the level and nature of resource exploitation are controlled and access is difficult to gain.

It was not possible for people from non-fishing clans to start fishing, which meant that fishing was excluded to all except those who had the good fortune to have been born or married into a fishing sub-clan. As a result, the practice of fishing was exclusive to a small, well-defined group of people. Fish was, however, available to all within and beyond the clan through a barter system involving exchange in vegetables and cattle products. Indeed, the size of the market appears to have been restricted only by transportation problems and, given that fishing sub-clans were fairly small, a physical inability to catch enough fish.

Thus in the pre-colonial period, the key features of fishing were:

1. Access was restricted through territorial rules and regulations enforced and accepted by Luo society as a whole. This served to limit how many people could use the lake, and confined them to using specific areas on the lake.
2. The fishing 'effort' was regulated: the *effort* is the total number of people involved in fishing. Effort was controlled by restricting numbers of people who could fish (only members of fishing sub-clans), when they could fish (traditional age limits on involvement in fishing) and also important fishing skills and the physical strength needed to be acquired before one could start fishing.
3. Resource responsibility: users were 'responsible' for the waters they fished. Because these waters belonged to the clan, it was their responsibility to ensure that people from other clans did not fish in their territory; to ensure that only certain people could fish; and to ensure that the fishery continued to be productive despite seasonal variations in yield. This responsibility was embedded in the community.

Given that individual communities tended to operate in the interests of the whole clan, then regulations were not only easier to enforce, but easy to monitor. As such, this mechanism was 'self-regulating'. These regulations were the product of community traditions and culture, and did not set out to directly conserve fish. Indirectly, however,

these regulations did act to preserve the resource base in such a way that it was consistently productive. Thus, by way of their own customs and traditions, some kind of steady equilibrium was created between fishing communities and their fisheries resource base. The colonial period was to alter this equilibrium considerably.

The colonial fishery

The arrival of the railway at Kisumu from Nairobi and Mombasa in 1901 signalled the start of profound economic changes in the region. These changes involved:

1. Market changes: In the pre-colonial fishery, the market was limited because of difficulties in transportation, restricted effort and relatively low demand, which indirectly helped to conserve the fishery. However, with the arrival of the British and the railway, the market area and demand increased dramatically and there was a corresponding increase in fishing intensity.
2. The cash-based economy: The colonial government forced Kenyans into a cash-based economy through the imposition of taxes. In order to pay these taxes, fishermen had to create a marketable surplus to generate cash.
3. Population increases, through improved medical care and in-migration to the lake region, combined with a lack of other employment opportunities, also served to increase the intensity of fishing activity.
4. The introduction of new and more efficient fishing technologies, for example the gill-net in 1905 and the beach seine soon afterwards, resulted in greatly increased catches in response to the increased demand. Furthermore, these new fishing technologies were easier to use and made fishing accessible to all, and the earlier restrictions governing the use and manufacture of traditional gears no longer applied.
5. Changes in other aspects of the colonial economy also had repercussions, particularly in agriculture: the rise of tea, sugar and cotton plantations in the highlands of western Kenya,

for example, forced many off the land. In the absence of alternative employment, many sought incomes in fishing, further increasing the numbers involved.

Thus, with a desire for cash incomes and with the effects of wider markets, new technologies and population growth, the fishing effort expanded considerably. The search for surplus fish to sell also brought the customary restricted access mechanisms under considerable pressure. The effect of these changes soon became evident. For example, tilapia catches within the Nyanza Gulf at the turn of the century were as high as 25 fish per net (Garrod, 1961) but by 1920, catches were down to 7 per net and by 1940 were only 2 per net (Graham, 1929; Beverton, 1959).

As the customary restricted access mechanisms crumbled, a 'regulatory vacuum' appeared. In an effort to remedy this, the British administration sought, in the 1940s, to regulate fishing activity through restrictions on net mesh sizes. Thus, any mesh size below 5 inches (12.5 cm) was declared illegal. The colonial government also introduced a closed season from 1 April to 31 August when fishing for 'small' fish was prohibited.

However, these efforts failed on two counts. Firstly, the Lake Victoria Fisheries Service (LVFS), established in 1947 to implement and enforce these regulations, was undermanned and poorly equipped to ensure lake-wide monitoring. Secondly, because the legal mesh sizes and the closed season forced fishermen to fish only for large fish (over 5 inches in width), the stock of large fish was rapidly depleted. As a result, fishermen turned to using illegal mesh sizes and ignored the closed season, so concentrating on juvenile fish. Although this meant that the fish tonnage increased only nominally, it did mean that the total number of fish caught increased markedly. Because fish were sold in numbers and not by weight, profits, therefore, initially rose. Seeing the potential for increased profits, more people entered the fishery in an attempt to get a 'slice of the cake'.

However, the reproductive capacity of the fish did not correspond to the increases in fishermen. As such, the potential profit to be generated by the fishery remained largely unchanged, and as the numbers of fishermen increased, so the profit had to be shared among more and more people. Under these conditions, the incomes of individual fishermen dropped (Mann, 1969). This meant that in order for an individual fisherman to maintain the same level of profit, he had to fish for longer hours and often with even smaller mesh sizes. Thus, with fishing effort levels increasing and longer hours worked, the fishery came under further pressure with the result that by the end of the 1950s, the fishery appeared close to collapse. However, in the absence of alternative employment opportunities, the fishing effort continued to increase and fishermen often failed to earn more than subsistence levels of income. Furthermore, with the increased effort and concentration on catching juvenile fish, the market was saturated. Desperate to see their fish sold, fishermen lost their power to communicate prices to the market, and instead had to accept the prices they were offered. As a result, fishermen became 'price takers' and not 'price makers' (Oduor-Otieno *et al.*, 1978). Furthermore, small-scale, open-access fisheries, while often easy to enter, are difficult to exit if no alternative employment opportunities appear (Panayotou, 1982).

Thus, a 'vicious circle' developed whereby the fishery gained in fishermen every time small increases in profit occurred, but there were no corresponding increases in either resource base or the potential amount of income that could be gained from it. As more and more fishermen entered the fishery, the profit to each individual grew less until such a point that no profits were gained and fishermen only managed to maintain subsistence levels of production. At this stage, the rate of entry into the fishery would slow down and the fishery would stabilize for a short period of time. However, the moment there was a small increase in profits (for example, when there were seasonal increases in fish), then the rate of entry would increase again. Thus, changes in profit margins only served to affect the rate at which fishermen joined the industry and failed to reduce the total amount of fishermen in the effort. In the absence of alternative employment opportunities, fishermen could not leave the fishery even if they wanted to.

Under this pressure, customary fishing regulations were further eroded and fishing pressure was maintained at high levels. This feature was to prove a constant problem in the fishery. Given the futility of the mesh-size regulations, the Kenyan colonial government repealed these laws in 1961 (Mann, 1969).

In the light of these problems, the following important changes were evident:

1. In the drive to gain surplus yields, high levels of competition arose between fishermen. Any respect held for territorial waters was rapidly eroded, and the last signs of territorial rights in the Kenyan sector of Lake Victoria had disappeared by 1960.
2. The lack of alternative employment opportunities helped to exacerbate this competition, and, combined with high levels of in-migration, led to the virtual collapse of almost all customary practices that served to restrict the fishing effort.
3. The introduction of new fishing technologies served to make fishing easier and more accessible to all. The degree of 'exclusiveness' associated with fishing in the pre-colonial period disappeared, further hampering attempts to control effort. Furthermore, in the absence of alternative employment, fishing became a 'safety net', providing a livelihood to those who otherwise had no income.
4. Increases in effort and competition between individual fishermen also led to the breakdown of customary community relationships, exacerbating the ability of both colonial and clan administrators to regulate effort.
5. Finally, and perhaps most crucially, the responsibility for managing the resources of the lake moved away from lakeside communities to more centralized control in Nairobi. The regulations imposed by early colonial administrators were out of touch with the serious socioeconomic conditions in which lakeside peoples had to operate. British attempts to regulate the fishery failed, with the consequence that the size of the fishing effort and the practices used went unregulated, effectively turning Lake Victoria into an open-access fishery, where neither formal regulations nor diminishing yields served to regulate increased effort.

At the dawn of Kenya's independence in 1963, the deficiencies in the official regulations were becoming increasingly clear, and in a last effort to improve yields, the British introduced exotic fish species into the lake. Between 1950 and 1962, six exotic species of tilapia were introduced, together with a voracious predator, the Nile perch, in 1954 (Coulter *et al.*, 1986). The effect of these introductions have proved to be dramatic and potentially disastrous during the post-colonial period.

The post-colonial fishery

The newly independent Kenyan government inherited a largely unregulated fishery from the British. Early efforts to control the fishing effort, on the same lines as the colonial government, were equally futile in the face of continually increasing numbers of fishermen. In 1973 there were an estimated 12 000 fishermen, but this figure increased to around 33 000 in 1983, a growth of 63% in just 10 years (Ochieng'-Okatch, 1992). This period also witnessed profound changes within the fishing community itself.

Changes in the ownership of the means of production

In the pre-colonial fishery the fisherman was largely in control of the physical apparatus and knowledge required for catching fish. In other words, the fisherman controlled his own 'means of production', owning his traps, nets and the knowledge of how and where to use them. Furthermore, the materials needed for manufacturing traps, such as papyrus, were readily and freely available. As such, the fisherman could control the way in which he caught fish, the methods he used, and the means by which he disposed of his catch. This level of independence served to provide the fisherman and his family with a good degree of control over their economic security. The position of the fisherman within the community and clan served to further reinforce this control, but also provided other benefits. For example, should the fisherman become ill, then the community would provide extra labour to ensure that his catch would be procured on that day. The community was also the means by which the fisherman could dispose of his fish in exchange for goods such as vegetables, meat and other products. Thus, the clan also played the role of a 'safety net' in times of difficulty or when various needs arose. Clans were regarded as extended families, and it was the responsibility of the clan, and particularly the sub-clan, to maintain the well-being of its members. It ensured that the fishermen could on the one hand control their own means of production, while also providing a supportive framework through which this could be achieved.

This pre-colonial framework has changed considerably in the post-colonial period. At present, control over the means of production is expensive and is determined by the capacity to invest in the three most important components in the production process: labour, boats and nets. If these three components are controlled, then the chances of catching more fish are greater. As a consequence, access to fish becomes determined by the capacity to invest in the means of production. Low investment in the means of production, such as a single fishing line, would normally yield correspondingly low catches. However, investment in a boat, crew and several nets allows much greater access to the fish and greater mobility across the lake to more productive fishing grounds. The cost of owning a single boat, nets and paying a crew's wages can be prohibitive and in 1988 was as high as Kshs. 45 000 (Feb. 1994: 100 Kenya shillings ≈ £1) (Ogutu, 1992), depending on the size of the boat. The greater the investment in the means of production, the greater the opportunity for larger catches and a greater surplus.

Given the prohibitive cost of controlling boats, nets and crews, the fishery has attracted outside interests with higher investment potential. Thus, people with non-fishing backgrounds have become increasingly responsible for the means of production. Boats are often owned by people who have little or no contact with the fishery, other than a desire to achieve rapid profit. These people are often Nairobi-based business people and politicians, and it is estimated that as many as 50% of the boats in the Kenyan sector of Lake Victoria are now owned by people who do not themselves work on them (N. Odero, former Director of the Fisheries Department, Nairobi, interview 12 and 13 September 1993).

Thus, because the greater part of this ownership is now from outside the fishery, the community is no longer responsible for its own means of production, nor can it afford to be. Thus, access is now determined primarily by the *capacity to invest*.

Divisions of labour

The second important change has been the creation of greater 'divisions of labour'. In the pre-colonial fishery, every fisherman controlled his own means of production. Because of this, there was little or no emphasis on the control of labour, and whatever extra labour a fisherman needed was provided by the community. Thus, for example, when hauling in large papyrus nets (*gogo*), at least 16 men were required, and these were provided by the community. In return, the fisherman would help with the hauling of other *gogo*. However, because control over the means of production has now moved away from the community and its members, the necessity for controlling labour has increased, and this has given rise to greater divisions of labour. Indeed, these labour divisions are indicative of the change in control over the means of production.

Within the present production process, certain hierarchical 'levels' have appeared, with clear divisions between the people working in each of the levels (Figure 8.2).

At the top of the hierarchy is the boat owner, who may, as we have seen, be an 'absentee' boat owner (Figure 8.2(a)). An absentee boat owner

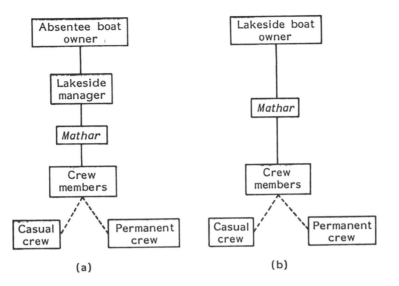

Figure 8.2 *Divisions of labour for: (a) absentee boat owners; (b) lakeside boat owners*

may often employ a lakeside manager (Harris, 1992), who in turn employs, for each boat, a *mathar*, a boat skipper who is normally a fisherman of considerable experience. The *mathar*, in turn, may employ crew on a casual daily basis, or alternatively be in charge of a permanent crew which rarely changes. Thus there are clear 'levels' in a chain of command. The lower down the chain of command, the less an individual's control over the means of production and the less their income. For example, crew members may earn as little as Kshs. 750 per month, while boat owners may earn as much as Kshs. 80 000 per month, depending on how many boats he/she owns (Ogutu, 1992). Boat owners will normally get half the value of the catch, while the remainder is divided between maintenance of the boat(s) and nets and wages for the crew.

Absentee boat owners commonly have several sources of income and are rarely seen at the landing beaches. However, there are some boat owners who do frequent the beaches (lakeside boat owners), playing the role of both manager and boat owner. These people rarely own more than three boats and often have relatives among their crew members. However, divisions of labour are also evident within this arrangement (Figure 8.2(b)).

Regardless of the type of boat owner, the labour division has taken the responsibility for the lake's resources away from local communities and has placed it in the hands of a small and élite group of people. These labour divisions are not restricted solely to the catching of fish, but are also evident in marketing. Typically, labour divisions in marketing would be as follows:

1. Fishermen sell their fish directly to women fish traders (illegally) on the beach or to their beach co-operative society. Women traders then sell their fish, either in a processed form (fried, dried or smoked) or fresh, to other fish traders located further away from the beach, or directly to consumers. Much of the fish sold in this fashion consists of local delicacies, such as lung fish, various species of catfish, small sardine-like fish (*Rastrineobola argentea*), as well as the commercially important tilapia species.

2. Fishermen are supposed to sell all their fish through the beach co-operative society. If they do, the co-operative society can then sell fish either directly to consumers or to fish distributors who visit the beaches with refrigerated trucks and take the fish to markets such as Nairobi and Mombasa. Most of the fish

disposed of in this way is either Nile perch or tilapia, and may be sold directly to distributors in these markets, or to large-scale industrial fish filleters. Many filleters send their own trucks to the lake's beaches.

3. Virtually all the fish processed by industrial filleters is Nile perch. Apart from fillets, the Nile perch yields fish 'swim bladders', suitable for the production of beer finings and traditional medicines in the Far East. Its skin may be processed for use as shoe-leather, although this is still rare. The remaining waste carcasses may be processed into fish-meal, or dumped outside the factories and sold to local vendors who fry and sell them. The disposal of carcasses in this fashion is common in Kisumu. Most, if not all, Nile perch fillets are exported to outlets in Europe, Israel and Australia.

These different marketing levels also indicate the loss of control by fishing communities over their markets. The capacity to invest is now a deciding factor in both the size and success of markets, and the higher the investment, the higher the potential profits. The processing of fish requires considerable investment, as does the capacity to export this produce to Europe and beyond. High levels of investment are also required in the form of suitable vehicles and refrigeration facilities to distribute fish to intra-country markets.

As a consequence, fishing communities are becoming increasingly restricted in their exploitation of both the fishery's resource base and markets by investment in capacity. These restrictions serve to maintain the vicious circle through their impact on income, and do not contribute to solving the problem of increasing effort. Indeed, because these restrictions contribute to the erosion of customary resource relations, they serve to maintain the open-access status of the lake, thereby exacerbating the problem of effort increases. The investment dilemma further serves to isolate fishing communities in a low power and income environment where options for survival are limited. Within this vicious circle, fishermen remain the specialist elements in a far greater

production process over which they now have little or no control.

Under these conditions, one of the few options that fishermen feel are open to them is to increase their effort in an attempt to increase catches and income. Indeed, because fishermen's incomes are so low, few fishermen can afford to use legally sized meshes, for fear of procuring no catch. However, these efforts only serve to undermine the resource base and the sustainability of the lake as a whole, particularly when coupled with continually increasing numbers of fishermen.

The economic well-being of fishermen is further complicated by a lake-wide ecological crisis.

Ecological problems

With rapid industrial and agricultural development in the lake's drainage basin, pollution levels appear to be on the increase, particularly through pesticide use on agricultural land (Bugenyi and Balirwa, 1989), which is contributing to eutrophication and the increased incidence of oxgyen-using algal blooms (Ochumba and Kibaara, 1989). Coupled with this, the introduction of exotic fish species in the 1950s has severely affected the lake's ecology. The arguments concerning this change concentrate on two factors.

Firstly, the Nile perch. During the early 1950s, as yields declined through overfishing, it was argued that the Nile perch ought to be introduced and that it would feed off the commercially unimportant *Haplochromis* species group, and so improve the economic viability of the lake (Anderson, 1961). Since its introduction, the Nile perch has systematically destroyed the *Haplochromis* species group. Whereas prior to its introduction the *Haplochromis* species group constituted some 80% of the fish biomass, it is at present thought to constitute less than 1% of the fish biomass. This reduction is thought to be directly attributable to predation by the Nile perch, leading to the extinction of some 200 species of *Haplochromis* (Witte *et al.*, 1992). The results of this mass extinction are likely to be far-reaching and severe. The *Haplochromis* species group is believed to have played an important role in ensuring that nutrients and oxygen were constantly brought back in to solution (termed 'mixing'). Without *Haplochromis*, severe levels of deoxygenation have occurred in the lake, as evidenced by the increasing frequency of mass fish deaths, mainly Nile perch (Kaufman, 1992). Without its preferred food being readily available, the Nile perch has now changed its diet to include the commercially important 'omena' (*Rastrineobola argentea*), the freshwater shrimp (*Cardina nilotica*) and even its own young (Achieng, 1990).

Secondly, the introduction of exotic tilapia species has led to competition between the exotic and indigenous species for lake environments which they both prefer and share. This ecological competition is thought to have contributed to the extinction from the lake of one indigenous tilapia, *Oreochromis esculenta*. The other indigenous tilapia species, *O. variabilis*, is now rare and unusual in catches.

As a consequence of these ecological changes and exacerbated by high demand, fishing activity has concentrated on just three main species: the exotic Nile perch, the indigenous *omena* and the exotic tilapia, *O. niloticus*. Although other species continue to be fished, these are currently the three most important commercial species. The effects of this pressure are seen in the decreasing average size of fish landed. Fish filleters in Kisumu now regularly accept Nile perch as small as 800 g (adult Nile perch can weigh as much as 200 kg), and Fisheries Department officers on the fish landings agree that in the past five years the average size of individual tilapia landed has decreased considerably.

Post-independence regulatory efforts

Present government efforts to regulate the fishery are based on the 1989 Fisheries Act, and concentrate on the prohibition of certain mesh sizes, fishing methods and closed seasons for certain species. These efforts have, however, failed for the following reasons:

1. Regulations are strict and penalties severe, but the regulations also fail to take into account the socio-economic conditions of fishermen. Fisheries Department 'scouts' are aware of these conditions and find it hard to implement these regulations.

2. Corruption on the fishing beaches is rife. Given that a single net can be the income basis for an entire family, the potential for bribery is high. Rather than risk not fishing for some days, or having to buy prohibitively expensive nets, fishermen gladly bribe fisheries officers. Bribes range from Kshs. 500 to 1000 for the return of a seized net, to 'soda' bribes, where fishermen buy Fisheries scouts soft drinks to keep them amiable. Indeed, beach leaders and even co-operatives play active roles in arranging graft for their members. Bribery is so great that it may now be considered a legitimate cost for fishermen.

3. The control of mesh sizes is ineffective for a number of reasons. Mesh-size restrictions cover two types of nets: mosquito seines and gill-nets. The former are fine-meshed nets used for the capture of *omena* and the legal minimum is 10 mm. Gill-nets which are larger-meshed nets used for the capture of bigger species, have a legal minimum mesh size of 5 inches (12.5 cm). However, it is unlikely that fishermen will catch only *omena* in mosquito seines, and any other fish taken are considered to be 'accidental catches' by fisheries officers. There is little to stop fishermen using these nets for species other than *omena*, and Nile perch of less than 30 g are frequently caught. Gill-nets of the legal size do not, fishermen claim, yield good catches because there are too few legally sized fish in the lake. As a consequence, illegal mesh sizes are common. Furthermore, because these mesh-size restrictions cover only Lake Victoria, the manufacture and sale of nets of less than 5 inches for use in other water bodies is permitted.

4. There is one closed season from 1 April to 31 August, which covers only *omena*. However, *omena* fishing is carried out at night when Fisheries Department officers are off duty.

Omena are then sold to fish traders before the officers come on duty. Furthermore, there is no prohibition covering the sale of *omena* during the closed season, so marketing channels remain open and profitable.

5. Finally, the 1989 Fisheries Act does not prohibit entry into the fishery. Provided one has a licence to fish, anyone can fish anywhere and at any time. While the Fisheries Department tries to limit effort through restricting sales of licences and boat registrations, there is little they can do to ensure that all have licences and registered boats. Undermanned, underfunded and without the use of sophisticated monitoring technology—each district Fisheries Department is assigned only one boat with an outboard engine—the capacity for effective regulation is minimal.

As a result of these problems, the regulation of fishing activities on Lake Victoria is minimal and the lake can effectively be considered to be 'open access', with no restrictions on access or fishing practice. Furthermore, present-day fisheries regulations also suffer from the same problems as colonial regulations, in that they fail to consider the socio-economic context in which fishermen operate. Trapped between a resource base that is diminishing because of ecological upheaval and overfishing, and lost control over marketing, labour ownership and the means of production, fishermen today just cannot afford to ease fishing pressure and use legal mesh sizes. With a tonne of Nile perch worth some Kshs. 30 000, and a tonne of tilapia worth Kshs. 50 000 in 1994 (regardless of the size of individual fish), the incentives for illegal fishing practices are high, even including the use of explosives for fishing.

Conclusion

Most fishermen in the Kenyan sector of Lake Victoria fully understand the regulations and the consequences of fishing pressure on the sustainability of both the lake and their own futures. However, because of the vicious circle in which they are now trapped, fishermen are forced to exploit the lake such that it may not be able to sustain current levels of productivity for much longer. Fishermen are caught between problems within the lake—diminishing catches and an ecological crisis—and broader concerns related to their loss of control over factors integral to the production process. Trapped in this position, fishing communities have become increasingly vulnerable with regard to both their economy and their resource base, and, given this vulnerability, the incentives to risk regulatory infringements are considerable, despite possible legal repercussions.

Regulation efforts have not been successful, it is suggested here, largely because they have failed to take into account this vulnerability. Furthermore, it would appear that regulations have consistently failed to address the crucial problem of the increasing numbers of fishermen. This problem caused colonial regulations to fail, and continues to hamper efforts to regulate the fishery today. Given the pressures that currently face the lake, one option that might be considered is the reintroduction of communal fishing grounds. Under such a strategy, the potential for increasing the control that fishing communities have over their resource base would improve, as might their standing *vis-à-vis* markets. Such a development may encourage the fishery to be self-regulating, cheap and requiring little technology or paid manpower. Ecological conditions could improve if fishermen were to make their own marine territories more attractive to fish and were provided with the legal means to prosecute those who, for example, pollute it. Furthermore, the reintroduction of territorial rights for fishing communities might be more compatible with the social, economic and cultural conditions in which the Luo live. Crucially, it could also provide the most effective means by which entry into fishing could be regulated without state intervention. Under these circumstances, the resource base would be effectively placed back into the hands of the local Luo people who would then become responsible for its maintenance, security and future sustainability.

Acknowledgements

This chapter is based on initial data from current research. The author is grateful for comments made by Peter Ochumba (Kenya Marine and Fisheries Research Institute, Kisumu) and the Editor on earlier drafts.

References

Achieng, A. P. (1990) The impact of the introduction of the Nile perch, *Lates niloticus* (L.), on the fisheries of Lake Victoria, *Journal of Fish Biology*, 37, Suppl. A, 17–23.

Anderson, A. M. (1961) Further observations concerning the proposed introduction of Nile perch into Lake Victoria, *East African Agricultural and Forestry Journal*, XXVI(4), 195–201.

Beverton, R. J. H. (1959) A report on the state of the Lake Victoria fisheries, mimeo, Fisheries Laboratory, Lowestoft.

Bugenyi, F. W. B. and Balirwa, J. S. (1989) Human intervention in the natural processes of the Lake Victoria ecosystem: the problem, pp. 311–340, in J. Salanki and S. Herodek (eds), *Conservation and Management of Lakes, Biological Symposium of Hungary*, Vol. 38, Akedemiai Kiado, Budapest.

Coulter, G. W., Allanson, B. R., Bruton, M. N., Greenwood, P. H., Hart, R. C., Jackson, P. B. N. and Ribbink, A. J. (1986) Unique qualities and special problems of the Great African Lakes, *Environmental Biology of Fishes*, 17(3), 161–183.

Garrod, D. J. (1961) The history of the fishing industry of Lake Victoria, East African, in relation to the expansion of marketing facilities, *East African Agricultural and Forestry Journal*, XXVII(2), 95–99.

Graham, M. (1929) *A Report on the Fishing Survey of Lake Victoria 1927–1928 and Appendices*, Crown Agents for the Colonies, London.

Harris, C. K. (1992) *Distributional and redistributional impacts of Lake Victoria fisheries introductions*, paper prepared for presentation at the Symposium on the Impact of Species Changes in African Lakes, 27–31 March 1992, Imperial College of Science, Technology and Medicine, London, UK, Draft 23/3/92.

Kaufman, L. (1992) Catastrophic change in species-rich freshwater ecosystems: the lessons of Lake Victoria, *BioScience*, 42(11), 846–858.

Mann, M. J. (1969) A resumé of the evolution of the Tilapia fisheries up to the year 1960, *EAFFRO Annual Report 1969*, Appendix B, pp. 21–27, East African Freshwater Fisheries Research Organization, Jinja, Uganda.

Ochieng'-Okatch, J. I. (1992) The development of Lake Victoria fisheries (Kenya) to date and priority areas for future research, pp. 107–111, in G. E. M. Ogutu (ed.), *Artisanal Fisheries of Lake Victoria, Kenya: options for management, production and marketing*, Proceedings of the Artisanal Fisheries (Kenya) Workshop, Kisumu, 24–26 November 1988, Shirikon Publishers for the Artisanal Fisheries (Kenya) Project, Nairobi.

Ochumba, P. B. O. and Kibaara, D. I. (1989) Observations of blue–green algal blooms in the open waters of Lake Victoria, Kenya, *African Journal of Ecology*, 27, 23–34.

Oduor-Otieno, M. L., Karisa, R. S., Odiambo, J. O. O. and Ryan, T. C. I. (1978) *A Study of the Supply Function for Fish in the Kenya Waters of Lake Victoria and on the Kenya Coast*, IDS Working Paper No. 346, Institute of Development Studies, University of Nairobi, Nairobi.

Ogot, B. A. (1967) *History of the Southern Luo*, Vol. 1, *Migration and Settlement, 1500–1900*, East African Publishing House, Nairobi.

Ogutu, G. E. M. (ed.) (1992) *Artisanal Fisheries of Lake Victoria, Kenya: options for management, production and marketing*, Proceedings of the Artisanal Fisheries (Kenya) Workshop, Kisumu, 24–26 November 1988, Shirikon Publishers for the Artisanal Fisheries (Kenya) Project, Nairobi.

Panayotou, T. (1982) *Management Concepts for Small-scale Fisheries: economic and social aspects*, FAO Fisheries Technical Paper No. 228, FAO, Rome.

Witte, F., Goldschmidt, A., Goudswaard, P. C., Ligtvoet, W., van Oijen, M. J. P. and Wanink, J. H. (1992) Species extinction and concomitant ecological changes in Lake Victoria, *Netherlands Journal of Zoology*, 42(2–3), Ch. 26, pp. 214–232.

World Bank/UNDP/CEC/FAO (1991) *Fisheries and Aquaculture Research Capabilities and Needs in Africa: studies of Kenya, Malawi, Mozambique, Zimbabwe, Mauritania, Morocco and Senegal*, World Bank Technical Paper No. 149, Fisheries Series, World Bank, Washington, DC.

9

Institutions and natural resource management: access to and control over woodfuel in East Africa

Robin Mearns

Introduction

The early 1990s have been marked by a growing recognition of the importance of institutions in development theory and practice in general, and in understanding the relationships between people and their environments in particular (McNicoll and Cain, 1990; de Janvry *et al.*, 1993). Institutions are understood here as regularized patterns of behaviour between individuals and groups in society, or 'complexes of norms, rules and behaviors that serve a collective purpose' (de Janvry *et al.*, 1993, p. 566).[1] Attention is increasingly being paid to the institutional constraints and potentials at local, national and international levels that combine to shape the ways different groups of people gain access to and control over natural resources, and in so doing manipulate their local environments with various intended and unintended consequences (Blaikie and Brookfield, 1987; Leach and Mearns, 1991; Thrupp, 1993).

This more socially articulated view of people–environment relations shares much in common with the 'entitlements approach' of Amartya Sen, originally developed to help explain the incidence of famine and hunger even in situations where there is food available (Sen, 1981, 1984; Drèze and Sen, 1989). The central elements of this approach have been summarized as 'analysis of effective legitimate command, and its various channels and determinants, including attention to the rules and institutions that control access, and to the distinctive positions and vulnerabilities of different groups' (Gasper, 1993, p. 690).

Take the case of household energy. The household sector accounts for 50–95% of total energy consumption in sub-Saharan African economies, in contrast with the world's industrialized economies in which the household share is usually around 25–30%. The highest proportions are found in the poorest countries such as Tanzania and Ethiopia, in which households rely almost exclusively on biomass sources, including woodfuels (fuelwood and charcoal), crop residues and animal dung. Within the household sector, levels of energy use and the mix of fuels vary widely from place to place, depending on climate and altitude; the nature of local farming systems; household size and income; the availability and cost of 'modern' substitutes such as kerosene, and end-use technologies; and cultural factors such as diet, cooking habits, and the use of fires as a social focus.

People and Environment in Africa. Edited by Tony Binns
©1995 John Wiley & Sons Ltd

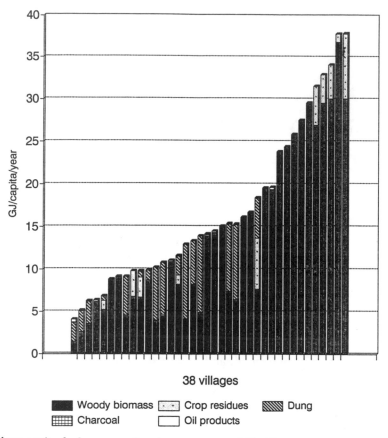

Figure 9.1 *Annual per capita fuel consumption from a survey of 38 villages in Ethiopia. Source: CESEN (1986)*

Figure 9.1 illustrates this local diversity, using data from a survey of 38 villages in Ethiopia. Total annual energy consumption varies from 4 to 38 gigajoules (GJ)[2] per person. The mix of fuels also varies: dung accounts for over half of all energy consumed in some villages but none in others, while crop residues are significant in just a few villages.

The 'woodfuel crisis' has come to be regarded as the archetypal environmental problem in developing countries (Agarwal, 1986). But the nature of the problem is widely misunderstood and its extent overgeneralized, largely as a result of the type of analysis conventionally used in its identification (Leach and Mearns, 1988; Dewees, 1989). The usual approach is to compare total woodfuel demand, based on estimates of average per capita consumption, with standing stocks and

annual growth of trees. A woodfuel supply shortfall is typically identified of, for example, 70% for Sudan, or 150% for Ethiopia (Anderson, 1987). Since consumption has to be met from somewhere, it is assumed that it is made up by cutting into tree stocks. The shortfall is then projected into the future, usually in direct proportion to population growth. As consumption rises and trees are felled, the annual growth falls, the shortfall grows and tree stocks are inexorably depleted. Woodfuel demand is therefore assumed to be the prime cause of deforestation (Anderson and Fishwick, 1984), in turn contributing to accelerated soil erosion and 'downward spirals' of environmental degradation (Durning, 1989).

What is wrong with this analysis and why does it matter? There are at least four serious flaws in the approach. First, as Figure 9.1 illustrates, woodfuel consumption patterns defy generaliz-ation. Second, the data on which the analysis rests are generally very poor. Third, it is unrealistic to assume that consumption will continue to rise in line with population, even while supplies dwindle to vanishing point. As scarcity worsens and wood prices or the labour costs of gathering fuels increase, people are likely to respond in various ways, whether by planting trees, using fuel more economically, switching to more abundant fuels such as crop residues, or intensifying efforts to encourage the natural regeneration of woody vegetation. Fourth, and most fundamental, it is agricultural land clearance and not woodfuel consumption that is the principal cause of deforestation in sub-Saharan Africa.

As a consequence of these analytical errors, the conventional analysis leads to the wrong conclusions and inappropriate development policies and projects. By focusing narrowly on defores-tation as an energy-related issue, the analysis projects on to people an 'environmental problem' which they may themselves perceive very differently or not at all. Furthermore, what outsiders believe are the apparently obvious solutions—namely, planting trees to increase fuel supply, and/or introducing technology (improved cooking stoves and charcoal kilns) for improving energy con-version efficiency so as to reduce demand—may themselves impose substantial additional costs on people. In reality, people face competing priorities besides household energy, and woody vegetation itself is managed to serve multiple purposes in addition to or in preference over household fuel, including building timber and poles, fruit production, shade, and/or animal fodder. Inter-ventions aimed at alleviating rural 'energy' problems therefore require indirect approaches, situated in the wider context of people's livelihood systems. The policy implications of this alternative analysis are not our main concern here, but are considered elsewhere (Leach and Mearns, 1988).

The alternative analysis considered in this chapter is motivated by a concern to move beyond the neo-Malthusian view represented in popular images of the people–environment interface in Africa that is by and large fixated with population

increase and natural resource depletion and degra-dation. What is missing from the conventional analysis of the 'woodfuel crisis' is an appreciation of the institutional arrangements that underpin people's natural resource management practices. It is these institutional dimensions that explain how it is, for example, that there can still be a 'woodfuel crisis' in parts of western Kenya, even where there is an abundance of standing trees and shrubs, because women whose socially assigned responsibility it is to provide household fuel are prevented from gaining access to and effective control over wood for use as fuel.

From physical scarcity to 'institutional scarcity'

A wide range of institutional arrangements are potentially relevant for understanding the issue of effective legitimate command over wood for use as household fuel. They include rules of land and tree tenure and the ways they operate in practice; the structure of labour markets; family and kinship systems; gender relations; community organization; and local government administration, including issues of public finance and the operation of the legal system. For the remainder of this chapter, a few examples from East and the Horn of Africa are used to illustrate how such issues structure access to and control over woodfuel, paying particular attention to gendered rights and responsibilities, and to the availability of labour.

Gendered rights and responsibilities

Consider the following example. Kisii and Kakamega districts of western Kenya are high potential agricultural areas with population den-sities rising to over 300 farm households per km^2. Annual rainfall totals are around 1000–2000 mm (Figure 9.2). Farming systems are based on maize/beans food intercrops, with dairy cattle in some areas, and various cash crops including coffee, tea, pyrethrum, bananas and sugar. Various configurations of planted woody biomass

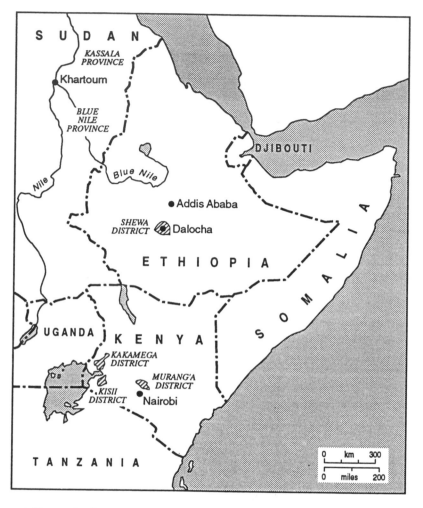

Figure 9.2 *East and Horn of Africa*

are an integral part of most of the farming systems in the region, including woodlots, hedges and other boundary plantings, windrows, and trees in fields, and make up around 5–15% of total land cover (see Figures 9.3–9.5). Adult men are frequently absent from farm households to seek wage labour in Kakamega, Kisumu, Nairobi and other towns and cities. Such migration for work occurs especially where farms are small and subdivided by inheritance and population densities are correspondingly high (Bradley, 1991).

Figure 9.6 shows the relationship between farm size and woody vegetation cover for 11 subregions of Kakamega district. Contrary to what one might

expect, as farm size declines and population density increases, tree cover actually rises. Moreover, the share of the trees and shrubs that are planted is greater on smaller farms and in areas of higher population density. These findings, matched by data for Kisii district, seem to contradict much of the conventional thinking on population-led deforestation. But it would be wrong to jump to easy conclusions with regard to the existence or otherwise of a 'woodfuel crisis' in this case.

Calculations from data for Kegoye sub-location in Kakamega district reveal that, despite a ground cover of woody vegetation of 29%, there is still an average woodfuel deficit from trees on farms of

Figure 9.3 *Metembe sub-location, in the southern tea zone of Kisii district, Kenya (Robin Mearns, May 1988)*

roughly 633 kg per year per homestead, given what is known about the end uses to which various types of woody vegetation are put (Bradley, 1991, p. 199).[3] This is in spite of the fact that a very high proportion of the land is covered by woodlots of *Eucalyptus saligna*, managed by coppicing, from which an estimated 33% of woody biomass is available for use as fuel on a turnover of around five years (see Figure 9.5). The major part of production from these woodlots is made up of building poles for sale. If all of this wood could be used for household fuel, the annual woodfuel deficit would be insignificant.

What explains the lack of access to available wood for use as household fuel? Rights and responsibilities with respect to trees and land in Kisii and Kakamega districts are subject to strong gender differences (Chavangi, 1987; Wisner, 1987). Socially assigned roles are such that it is

women's responsibility to provide household fuel as part of the day-to-day running of the household. At the same time, they have very little effective access to wood from planted trees on farms, and as natural trees and shrubs have dwindled, women have been forced to meet household energy needs from crop residues such as maize stalks, low-grade twigs and purchased fuelwood.

Tree-planting is dominated by men, and control over the uses to which planted trees are put is also exercised largely by men. Trees in woodlots in particular are managed as cash crops under male control. Rights to trees are not separated from rights to land, which accrue exclusively to men. By tradition, tree-planting on land that is not one's own is regarded as evidence of intention to claim ownership of the land. Men's ownership of trees 'has been effectively sustained through well manipulated cultural taboos' (Bradley, 1991,

Figure 9.4 *Joseph Mwamba in field of maize intercropped with* Calliandra *sp. trees (in seed at time of photo), Metembe sub-location, Kisii district, Kenya (Robin Mearns, May 1988)*

p. 206), including the beliefs that a woman who plants a tree will become barren, or that her husband will die, or that she is directly challenging his supremacy in the household, which could result in divorce. In each of these instances, a substantial loss of social status would befall the woman.

Figure 9.5 *Woodlot of Eucalyptus (*E. saligna*), first established in 1929 and managed by coppicing, Kegoye sub-location, Kakamega district, Kenya (Robin Mearns, May 1988)*

Other taboos against women planting trees are specific to wood used for house construction, or for ritual purposes.

There are some exceptions to this picture of male control over trees. Various indigenous tree species that are not thought of as 'proper' trees, owing to their shrubby growth, have been effectively adopted by women as sources of fuelwood, since men are uninterested in them owing to their low value for other purposes. These include *Sesbania sesban*, which is deliberately cultivated on fallow land for its soil fertility-enhancing qualities, and *Tithonia diversifolia*, a quick-growing hedge species (Leach and Mearns, 1988, p. 145; Dewees, 1989, p. 1164).

Although they remain powerful, in spite of the countervailing influences of religion and education, the nature and strength of these gendered rights

and responsibilities vary between societies and according to household circumstances, and are susceptible to change over time by a process of bargaining between household members and other relatives. Gender divisions of labour, and cultural taboos around female participation in tree cultivation, are stronger among the Luyia of Kakamega district than in Gusii and Kisii society. Women who are effectively heads of household—when their husbands are absent as wage labourers in urban areas—have a greater degree of freedom in gaining access to and control over household resources and decision-making. They may circumvent cultural restrictions to tree-planting by persuading their sons, or hired male labour, to plant trees for them, often without their husband's knowledge. Older women appear to be more successful than younger women in such activities,

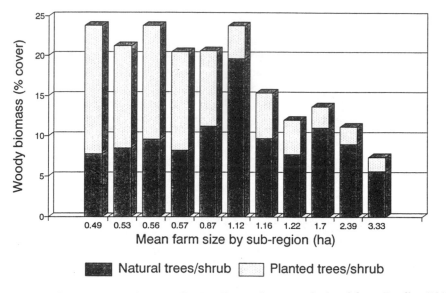

Figure 9.6 *Farm size and tree cover, Kakamega district, Kenya. Source: calculated from Bradley (1991, Table. 4.5, p. 135)*

as well as in negotiating greater effective legitimate command over household resources and decisions, including the uses to which on-farm trees may be put.

Availability of labour

Conventional analysis of the 'woodfuel crisis' suggests that physical scarcity is the key issue to address. Two of the most commonly used indicators of woodfuel scarcity are the time taken to gather fuelwood in rural areas, and rising prices in urban woodfuel markets. These too, however, are often better explained with reference to the broader institutional arrangements that determine whether or not people have access to and control over wood for use as household fuel. Most important among these are labour constraints.

Take the case of woodfuel markets and charcoal prices in Khartoum, Sudan. On the conventional analysis, it is assumed that woodfuel prices will rise as forest stocks are depleted and transport distances from the city to the main woodfuel source areas lengthen. Figure 9.7 shows the observed prices of charcoal in Khartoum's markets

for the period 1976–86. Far from the secular rising trend suggested by conventional analysis, the reality is one of sharply fluctuating prices, both within and between years, but with no indication of long-term price increase.

On closer inspection, these price dynamics turn out to reflect more the availability of labour than the relative physical scarcity of wood. Khartoum's charcoal markets show a high degree of vertical integration, with most production, transport, distribution and sale controlled by a few entrepreneurs. This keeps overheads low, and enables them to maintain their profit margins even in the face of increasing physical scarcity. Virtually all charcoal is hauled on a return trip basis, as a pick-up load on the way back to the city, so transport costs account for only 20–25% of the final retail price, a much lower figure than for many other African cities (Leach and Mearns, 1988). Consequently labour costs are relatively more significant, and typically account for a fifth of the delivered price of charcoal.

Agricultural labour and labour for charcoal burning are very close substitutes, since charcoal burning is a seasonal activity carried out by small farmers and seasonal migrants to supplement farm

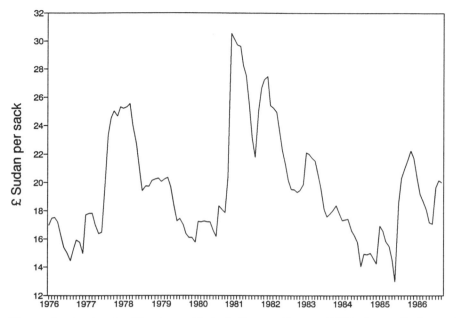

Figure 9.7 *Charcoal price trends, Khartoum (Sudan). Source: Dewees (1987, Appendix 1, pp. 195–7). Note: Constant prices are derived from current prices using the low-income consumer price index for Khartoum (September 1986 = 1.00). Price per sack is adjusted for changes in sack weight over the period, and normalized based on September 1986 sack weights*

incomes. Owing to the greater demand for agricultural labour, the price of farm labour dictates the wage of charcoal burners (El Faki Ali, 1985). As a result, charcoal prices are highest when demand for agricultural labour is highest, such as during years when there have been particularly good harvests. As Dewees has shown (Dewees, 1987), charcoal prices showed peaks during the 1977 and 1981 harvests, but bottomed out during the 1984 drought (see Figure 9.7). Other institutional factors also contribute to charcoal price dynamics. For example, the petroleum price increase of 1979 is likely to have contributed to the charcoal price peak in 1981, owing to scarcities of truck fuel and bottled gas. These pushed up transport costs at the same time as charcoal demand increased from urban consumers unable to afford bottled gas. This does not mean that there is not a growing physical scarcity of wood in Sudan's Blue Nile and Kassala provinces, from which about 80% of Khartoum's charcoal supply comes, but does suggest that pricing trends are a poor indicator of the extent of such scarcities.

In Murang'a district, another densely populated, high-potential agricultural area of Kenya, tree-cultivation practices have been shown to be closely related to changing supplies of and demands for household labour (Dewees, 1991, 1993). Woodlots of black wattle (*Acacia mearnsii*) are more likely to be established as households age and family labour becomes scarce, and are more likely to be cleared when labour is more available to cultivate the holding. In households with an older age structure, in which adult children and male heads of household are frequently absent and engaged in formal sector employment, woodlots are an efficient way to use available land, since they demand little labour and have low capital and recurrent costs. The cultivation of other cash crops such as coffee and tea would yield higher returns to land, but this option is not open to labour-constrained households. Neither would they be likely to sell or rent out their land, since there are high social costs to selling inherited land; and the potential uses of rented land are limited, since coffee or tea—as the primary cash crops in the

111

area that would generate sufficient returns to pay rent—are permanent crops which would jeopardize the original landholder's rights to the land under customary rules of tenure.

By contrast with the Luyia of Kakamega district, there is little evidence of strong cultural restrictions over women planting trees among the Kikuyu of Murang'a district (Dewees, 1993, p. 30). However, gender differences remain evident in the decision to establish or to clear woodlots. Woodlots are more likely to be established by households headed by women whose husbands are absent in formal sector employment. One reason for this pattern is suggested to be related to labour supervision. Where household labour is inadequate for cultivating a holding, so that labour needs to be hired to help with cultivation or harvesting, norms of behaviour in Kikuyu society make male labour more responsive to male supervision. Where male household heads are absent, 'the establishment of a woodlot which requires little supervision frees the rest of the household from this responsibility' (Dewees, 1993, p. 31).

Finally, consider wood gathering. This is one of the labour tasks that in East Africa tends to be socially assigned to women. There is compelling evidence from time budget studies for rural women that the time spent gathering fuelwood can vary greatly from one week or season to the next depending on agricultural and other labour demands. In Germama peasant association, near Dalocha in Ethiopia's southern Shewa province, for example, women of poorer households spend many hours a day gathering fuelwood during the 'hungry' season, the season of the main rains (*kiremt*) around June–August, just before harvesting (McCracken and Mearns, 1989). The main criterion used by these households in regarding themselves as 'poor' is their inability to meet annual household food requirements from their own production. During the hungry season, when the previous year's grain stocks have been depleted, women from these households engage in various trading activities to raise cash with which to purchase food grains in the market. Much of the fuelwood gathered during the hungry season is not for their own household use but for

sale. A time-use survey carried out soon after the harvest would find women spending much less time gathering fuelwood.

This example shows that the time spent in fuelwood gathering is a weak measure of physical scarcity of wood. It is often minor even in 'wood scarce' areas compared with the time spent drawing water or preparing food, and may not be perceived as a problem by local women. In other areas, the time taken to gather fuelwood may well be high and increasing, and regarded as a serious problem. This may be a result of growing physical scarcity of wood, or of institutional factors such as gendered differences in effective legitimate command over wood. But in such cases, the real 'crisis' is one of women's and family welfare (Cecelski, 1984; Tinker, 1987). The effects may be seen in the worsening nutritional status of children within the household, or in declining agricultural production (Khumar and Hotchkiss, 1988).

Conclusion

The intention of this chapter has been to shift the relative weight of emphasis in thinking about the relationship between people and environment in Africa, with specific reference to the 'woodfuel crisis' in East and the Horn of Africa, away from the physical scarcity of natural resources and towards institutional issues. This is not to deny that there are serious and growing problems of availability of woody vegetation in many parts of Africa, nor that high prices for woodfuels have serious consequences for many poorer urban and rural households. But we need to recognize that the 'woodfuel crisis' takes on a very different character in different places, and for different groups of people in the same place. These differences between groups of people in their ability to secure effective legitimate command over wood for use as household fuel are explained by institutional factors.

Rather than viewing natural resource availability and biophysical yields as the limiting factors in rural development, it is often more appropriate, and more positive, to regard institutions as being the true scarce resource. They are 'scarce' in the sense that institutions that would assist in achieving some desired outcome—in this case secure access to and control over wood for use as household fuel—are absent, or that the existing set of institutional arrangements are somehow rigid or inappropriate for achieving the desired outcome. Rather than exhorting people to plant trees for fuel, this suggests an alternative approach to easing household energy constraints as part and parcel of broader livelihood systems. It might include, for example, tackling the issue of gendered cultural restrictions over tree-cultivation practices, as the Kenya Woodfuel Development Programme has done, by means of a sensitive extension programme with both men and women; or seeking to improve the structure of urban woodfuel markets in places where there is scope for reducing transport costs. In search of pragmatic solutions to 'environmental problems', attention should be directed towards understanding local people's own conceptions of the problem, and needs to shift away from natural resources themselves and towards the humanly devised institutions that—for better or worse— surround their management.

Acknowledgements

This chapter draws principally on research originally carried out with funding from the Royal Norwegian Ministry for Development Co-operation under the auspices of the International Institute for Environment and Development, London. This updated version has been made possible with research programme funding from the UK Overseas Development Administration to the Institute of Development Studies. The opinions and conclusions presented here are those of the author alone.

Notes

1. Organizations are usually a manifestation of, but are not synonymous with, institutions. Not all institutions have an organizational manifestation, e.g. marriage, money, the law; and some organizations are not institutions, e.g. a particular grassroots organization.
2. The joule (J) is the standard unit of energy, work and heat in the SI system; 1 gigajoule (GJ) = 10^9 joules.

3. These calculations were made from data collected under the Kenya Woodfuel Development Programme, and assume a daily per capita woodfuel consumption requirement for Kisii and Kakamega districts of 0.79 kg. The detailed wood production and access assumptions underlying the calculations are given in Bradley (1991, Chapter 6). Kegoye sublocation of Kakamega district has a very high population density of 913 persons per km^2.

References

Agarwal, B. (1986) *Cold Hearths and Barren Slopes: the woodfuel crisis in the Third World*, Zed Books, London.

Anderson, D. (1987) *The Economics of Afforestation: a case study in Africa*, Johns Hopkins University Press for the World Bank, Baltimore and London.

Anderson, D. and Fishwick, R. (1984) *Fuelwood Consumption and Deforestation in African Countries*, Staff Working Papers 704, the World Bank, Washington, DC.

Blaikie, P. and Brookfield, H. (1987) *Land Degradation and Society*, Methuen, London and New York.

Bradley, P. N. (1991) *Woodfuel, Women and Woodlots*, Volume 1, Macmillan, London and Basingstoke.

Cecelski, E. (1984) *The Rural Energy Crisis, Women's Work and Family Welfare: perspectives and approaches to action*, International Labour Organization, Geneva.

CESEN (1986) *The Rural/Urban Household Energy Survey*, Technical Report No. 7, CESEN (for the Ministry of Mines and Energy, Ethiopia, May), Genoa, Italy.

Chavangi, N. A. (1987) Agroforestry potentials and land tenure issues in western Kenya, pp. 193–200 in J. B. Raintree (ed.), *Land, Trees and Tenure*, International Council for Research in Agroforestry and Land Tenure Center, Nairobi and Madison.

de Janvry, A., Sadoulet, E., *et al.* (1993) State, market, and civil organisations: new theories, new practices, and their implications for rural development, special section of *World Development*, 21(4), 565–689.

Dewees, P. A. (1987) *Consultant's Report on Charcoal and Gum Arabic Markets and Market Dynamics in Sudan*, Joint UNDP/World Bank Energy Sector Management Assistance Programme, Washington, DC.

Dewees, P. A. (1989) The woodfuel crisis reconsidered: observations on the dynamics of abundance and scarcity, *World Development*, 17(8), 1159–1172.

Dewees, P. A. (1991) The impact of capital and labour availability on smallholder tree growing in Kenya, unpublished Ph.D. thesis, University of Oxford.

Dewees, P. A. (1993). *Trees, Land, and Labor*, World Bank Environment Department Papers 4, the World Bank, Washington, DC.

Drèze, J. and Sen, A. (1989) *Hunger and Public Action*, Clarendon Press, Oxford.

Durning, A. B. (1989) *Poverty and the Environment: reversing the downward spiral*, Worldwatch Papers 92. Worldwatch Institute, Washington, DC.

El Faki Ali, G. (1985) *Charcoal Marketing and Production Economics in Blue Nile*, National Council for Research (Energy Research Council), Khartoum.

Gasper, D. (1993) Entitlements analysis: relating concepts and contexts, *Development and Change*, 24, 679–718.

Khumar, S. K. and Hotchkiss, D. (1988) *Consequences of Deforestation for Women's Time Allocation, Agricultural Production, and Nutrition in Hill Areas of Nepal*, IFPRI Research Reports 69, International Food Policy Research Institute, Washington, DC.

Leach, G. and Mearns, R. (1988) *Beyond the Woodfuel Crisis: people, land and trees in Africa*, Earthscan Publications, London.

Leach, M. and Mearns, R. (1991) *Poverty and Environment in Developing Countries: an overview study*, Economic and Social Research Council, Global Environmental Change Programme, Swindon.

McCracken, J. and Mearns, R. (ed.) (1989) *ActionAid in Local Partnership: an Experiment with Rapid Rural Appraisal in Ethiopia*, ActionAid-Ethiopia and International Institute for Environment and Development, Addis Ababa and London.

McNicoll, G. and Cain, M. (ed.) (1990) *Rural Development and Population: institutions and policy*, Oxford University Press and the Population Council, Oxford and New York.

Sen, A. (1981) *Poverty and Famines: an essay on entitlement and deprivation*, Clarendon Press, Oxford.

Sen, A. (1984) *Resources, Values and Development*, Clarendon Press, Oxford.

Thrupp, L. A. (1993) Political ecology of sustainable rural development: dynamics of social and natural resource degradation, pp. 47–73 in P. Allen (ed.). *Food for the Future: conditions and contradictions of sustainability*, John Wiley & Sons, London and New York.

Tinker, I. (1987) The real rural energy crisis: women's time, *Energy Journal*, 8, 125–146.

Wisner, B. (1987) Rural energy and poverty in Kenya and Lesotho: all roads lead to ruin, *IDS Bulletin*, 18(1), 23–29.

10

The impact of the 1991-92 drought on environment and people in Zambia

Mary Tiffen

Introduction

Rainfall in Zambia (Figure 10.1) reduces in quantity and reliability as one goes from the north to the south. Figure 10.2 shows the 30-year mean and the rainfall in 1991-92 and 1992-93 for three stations, each typical of the main climatic zones in Zambia. The three heaviest rainfall months are December, January and February, when Ndola in the north normally receives 250-300 mm per month; Chipata in Eastern Province and the middle section of the country 225-250 mm per month and Livingstone, in Southern Province and the most arid zone, 140-160 mm per month. Southern Province and parts of the central, eastern and western areas of the country suffered from the 1991-92 drought which hit a great part of Southern Africa.

While the drought had a severe effect on human welfare and the economy of the country, the vegetation and wildlife, adapted over centuries to climatic variations, 'bounced back' following the good rains of 1992-93. Human systems, however, particularly in the rural areas, will take longer to make a full recovery, partly because the drought took place when the economy was at a very low point and the political system was in the throes of change.

Disentangling the effects of drought and other factors

Only 58% of Zambia's population of just under 9 million lived in rural areas in 1990 (Zambia, CSO, 1990). Figure 10.3 shows there is a substantial mining and manufacturing sector. The impact of the drought was felt above all by farm families, because most urban people continued to receive their usual incomes, and, thanks to food imports, could continue to buy food.

The rural population increased by a million between the 1980 and 1990 census, when the stagnant urban and mining areas ceased to attract incomers. Over most of the country population density is less than 10 per km^2; only a few rural districts exceed 30 per km^2. This makes marketing costly, and provides no incentive to husband the land resource. There are pockets of high density, and the recent rapid growth of rural population has led to much clearing of the natural vegetation to create arable fields, and to build houses. Larger villages tend to be surrounded by treeless areas, as people still find it easier to walk a few kilometres to fetch wood in the bush than to plant trees near their homes and protect them from village livestock.

The 1991-92 drought hit Zambia when it was in the midst of an economic and political transition.

People and Environment in Africa. Edited by Tony Binns
©1995 John Wiley & Sons Ltd

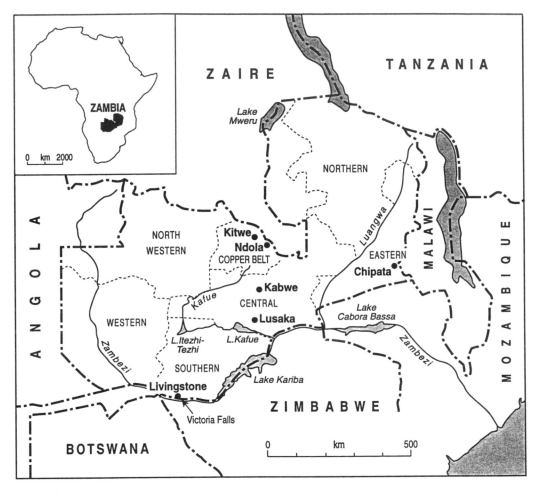

Figure 10.1 *Zambia*

Copper and cobalt revenues were long used by government to promote industrialization, and subsidize maize production. The maize price was fixed on a pan-territorial basis, making it the most profitable crop even in remote parts of the country, where, on the basis of transport costs, the production of a diverse range of crops to meet local needs would have been both economically more logical, and a safer strategy to meet local food needs in face of varying rainfall. Most farmers instead monocropped hybrid maize which gives high yields if combined with chemical fertilizer (which was also subsidized). They sold this as soon as they could, and bought back subsidized maize meal during the year. Maize often travelled long distances both from and to rural areas. The state-managed marketing system was characterized by gross inefficiencies. Despite the subsidies, a 1969–72 survey showed about 23% of children aged 0–4 suffered from moderate to severe malnutrition, and malnutrition indicators increased in the 1980s.

As maize production varied with the rains, the government had sometimes to arrange substantial imports, and at other times expensive storage. However, averaging out years, Zambia was self-sufficient in maize. The Southern and Eastern provinces, with the highest rural populations and most affected by the drought, were normally

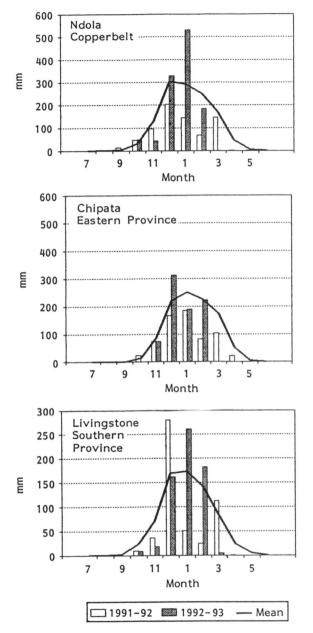

Figure 10.2 *Rainfall 1991–92, 1992–93 (till February 1993) and 30-year mean. Source: Data from Meteorological Department*

surplus areas, while the north and west were generally deficit areas (FAO, 1991, p. 19).

Figure 10.3 shows that in the decade 1982–91 there was almost no growth in gross domestic product, so incomes per head were actually falling. The government reacted slowly to the collapse of copper prices in 1974–75, and the continued lower levels since. Growing food subsidies in the face of declining mining revenues constantly reduced money available for other government services, where, as usual, the personnel element was protected at the cost of funding for operation and maintenance. There was a continuous decline in the quality of government services, notably in the water sector and rural roads, but also in agriculture, veterinary services, health, education, etc. Budget deficits led to 'high and accelerating rates of inflation, which reached 125% in 1989 and fell to 93% in 1991' (IFAD, 1993, p. 6). By this time, some structural adjustment policies had been introduced, in a rather stop–go fashion.

On 31 October 1991 the Movement for Multiparty Democracy (MMD) won a landslide victory, displacing Kenneth Kaunda and his United National Independence Party. The new government favoured liberalization of the economy, increased reliance on the private sector, devolution of many functions to elected local authorities and the encouragement of community self-help. However, the new local authorities were only being elected when the drought set in, and had neither established a new revenue basis nor begun to take over the provision of local services. People had been accustomed to relying on central government even for the simplest things, so that many wells and boreholes in rural areas were not functioning, because the community felt no responsibility, even to replace a bucket or rope, and the government had no funds for maintenance. While in the best of circumstances a new economic framework relying more on market forces would have led to short-term disruptions and suffering by the groups most reliant on subsidy, before it began to stimulate effective responses, its introduction unfortunately coincided with the worst drought in living memory.

About 80% of the cattle are held by small-scale farmers. About half the national cattle herd is in Southern Province. A traditional coping strategy in the case of bad years is to sell livestock. Unfortunately, Southern Province was affected by

117

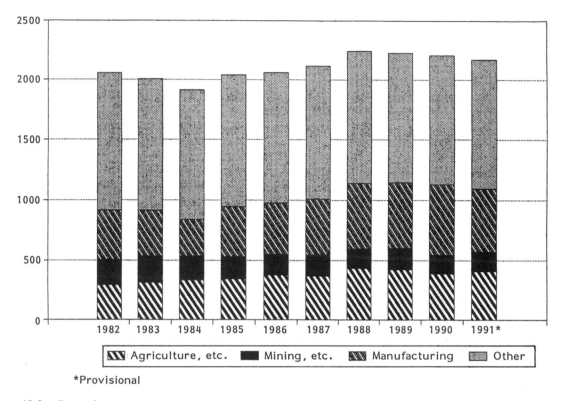

Figure 10.3 *Gross domestic product by activity, at 1977 constant prices. Source: Zambia, CSO (1992)*

an epidemic of virulent East Coast fever or theileriosis, which started in the late 1980s. Many families lost cattle before or in the early stages of the drought, leaving them with no reserve.

Another negative factor was the spread of AIDS. AIDS cases tend to cluster in families, who then suffer both loss of adult labour, and an increased burden for the care of orphans and invalids (Foster, 1993).

The nature of the drought and its impact

The total amount of rainfall in 1991–92 was not unprecedentedly low. Figure 10.4, for a station in Southern Province, shows similar low totals in the 1920s as well as illustrating that unreliability is characteristic. Figure 10.2 shows the problem lay in exceptionally low rainfall in January and February. This ruined the 1992 hybrid maize crop,

which had not been planted till December 1991, since farmers awaited the usual late delivery of seed by the official co-operatives. However, it also affected local varieties of maize, sorghum and pulses, which require a long season to mature.

The rainfall gap had different effects on water resources, natural vegetation, wildlife, crops and domestic livestock, and there were different rates of recovery after the good rains of 1992–93.

Impact on water sources

Effects in 1992

The drought came at the end of a dry decade, as can be seen from Figure 10.4. Therefore, large reservoirs such as Lake Kariba were already low. River flow at Hook Bridge, on the Kafue River above the first regulatory dam, was the lowest recorded since 1905–6 (although nearly paralleled

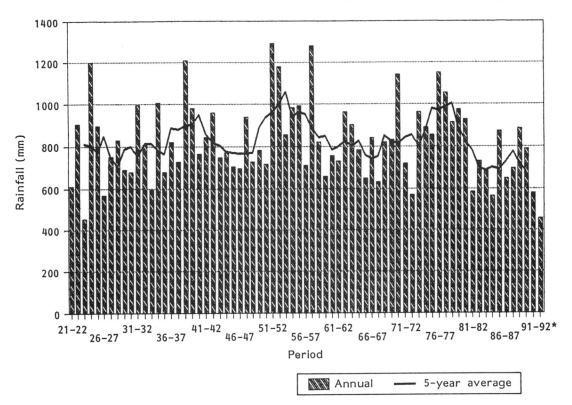

Figure 10.4 *Annual and 5-year average rain, 1921–22 to 1991–92, Monze, Zambia. Source: Data supplied to S. Foster (Foster, 1993). Note: asterisk refers to incomplete data*

by two low years in the 1920s). The Zambezi was similarly affected. Figure 10.5 gives some impression of what this meant in terms of water missing from normal inflows into the reservoirs.

The Zambezi flows are stored in Kariba (in so far as Zambia is concerned) and the Kafue in the Itezhi-Tezhi. These reservoirs enable power generation to continue throughout the year at Victoria Falls and the Kafue Gorge stations respectively. The low inflows from the rivers put the Kariba reservoir at a dangerously low level in December 1992, leading to power rationing and load shedding between October 1992 and February 1993. This was the main drought impact felt by industry and urban consumers.

Normally, the Itezhi-Tezhi dam is managed to release 300 m³/s in March into the Kafue Flats, an important wetland and grazing area in Southern

Province. In March 1992 only 96 m³/s came into the reservoir, and the management released 120 m³/s, thus very slightly moderating the drought impact on the wetlands.

Smaller streams, small dams and wetland areas in the valleys (*dambos*) dried up early, reducing water for human consumption, for livestock use, and vegetable production. Access to safe drinking water was exacerbated by the fact that 4000 boreholes and wells were already out of action, due to missing spare parts.

Most of the small towns in Southern Province, and some densely populated rural areas, are served by larger dams, which can retain more than a year's supply. These prevented a disaster. People in Eastern Province were more dependent on streams and shallow wells, and more people had to trek long distances to get water.

119

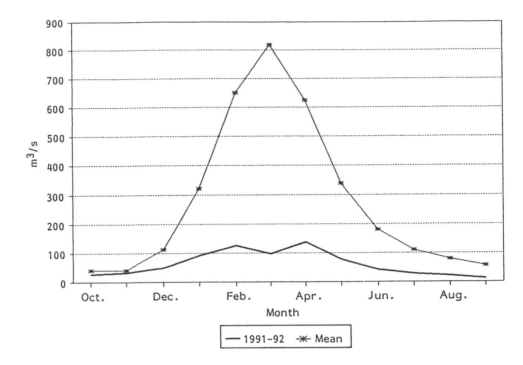

Figure 10.5 *Flows on Kafue River at Hook Bridge (m³/s)*

Recovery in 1993

The heavy rains of 1992–39 refilled the Itezhi-Tezhi reservoir. There was so much water coming in that much more water had to be released than usual, and the Flats were flooded in 1993 to a greater extent and depth than in the past decade (see Tiffen and Mulele, 1994 for details). The Kariba reservoir recovered to its level in 1990. However, it will take at least three more good rains to recover to levels common in the 1970s. It has been dangerously low twice in recent years. Many small dams overfilled and some broke in Southern Province. Farmers were able to cultivate *dambo* land again, and in some places there was indeed a glut of vegetables.

Impact on natural vegetation

Large areas are kept as national parks, forest reserves, and land leased to large-scale commercial farmers or parastatals, or are urban areas. On the remaining land families have rights of control while the land is under cultivation. Land under fallow can be used by anyone for grazing or for the collection of wild plants. If fallowed for several years it becomes woodland again. Grazing land merges into woodland. As trees become older and thicker, their canopy discourages grass regeneration.

There has been no long-term monitoring of the productivity of the range and woodland, so it is difficult to quantify the impact of the drought. Change in their productivity is a constant process, affected by the level of human and livestock use, varying populations of elephants and other wild herbivores, and seasonal rainfall.

Some woodland sites in Central Province were being monitored during 1991 and 1992 in connection with a study on the effects of charcoal burning. In the opinion of the researcher (E. N. Chidumayo, University of Zambia) the impact of the drought was minor. Peak biomass was lower in 1992 than in 1991, but the difference was not statistically significant, due to large standard deviations. The vegetation is already adapted to intervals without rain, and total rainfall was within 70% of the average. The level of nutrients in the soil remained higher than usual because there was less leaching by rain. To an unknown extent this may have counterbalanced the effects of water stress on growth.

Villagers interviewed in Southern Province felt there had been no marked effect on local grazing, particularly as stock had been reduced by disease. Many grasses are tuberous, and can withstand drought. In some areas cattle were moved earlier than usual to the Kafue Flats, or to the lake shore, for access to water.

Trees, with their deeper roots, were affected later, in the dry season, because the deep soil moisture was not recharged. In Lusaka Province many lost leaves in April–May, rather than in September, as normal. In Southern Province, new growth started later than usual. Die-back on ridges in Kalomo district was observed (Middleton, 1993).

Impact on vegetation after the 1992–93 rains

Observation suggests that grass cover is now good. Any impact created by more cattle than usual on the Kafue Flats was mitigated by the much larger flooding than usual in 1993. While some tree seedlings may have died in the drought, this will have given more room for others to develop, and will not, therefore, have a long-term negative impact. Villagers in Southern Province in August 1993 said that the main trees valued for wild fruit were looking as if they would bear well.

Indirect effects of the drought on woodland

It was widely reported that more people engaged in charcoal burning and woodfuel sales to generate income to replace lost earnings from crops. Demand for rural woodfuel and for urban charcoal is on a steady upward trend due to increase in population and formation of new households, but demand is unlikely to have surged greatly in 1991–92. In rural areas, people would need to replace the maize cobs and stalks which normally form part of the household fuel resource. Charcoal use may have increased slightly among the urban population due to electricity cuts. Dealers may have stockpiled. If average price fell after discounting inflation, some urban families may have increased their use of charcoal. Nevertheless, it is difficult to imagine that demand for charcoal would have doubled compared with 1991–92.

If we assume that charcoal production doubled, the impact would still be limited. Most of Zambia is covered by forest and woodland and in the mid-1980s, the National Resources Department estimated the annual loss of woodland in Zambia to be 0.5% per annum (Monö, 1993). Most of this loss occurs through the increase in urban areas and through clearing for cultivation. In central Zambia, only 2.5% of the annual loss is due to charcoal production. If charcoal burning doubles, it will still only account for 5% of an annual woodland loss of 0.5%. The effects of charcoal burning are also temporary. Some of Chidumayo's study sites had been cleared 29 years previously and showed no long-term effect. The reduction in canopy and increase in light occasioned by cutting for charcoal stimulates seedling shoot growth once an adequate root system has been established.

Woodfuel cutting normally has little environmental effect, as people take branches and trees regrow. Cutting for building poles around settlements has more effect, and clearing for cultivation even more, but this is an effect of population growth, not of drought. There is no evidence, one way or the other, as to whether the drought led to more bush fires. Chidumayo's study areas experienced burning which was little different from previous years. He observed that the moisture content of the grass was less than in the previous season, but this was to an extent buffered by the fact that there was slightly less grass. However, young, planted trees did suffer, particularly those aged four years or less.

Impact on crops

The 1992 situation

Table 10.1 shows crop production in the year before the drought, during the drought year, and

Table 10.1 *Production of some important crops, 1990–91 to 1992–93, in tons*

Crop	1990–91	1991–92	%*	1992–93
Maize	1 095 908	483 492	44	1 597 767
Sorghum	20 957	13 007	62	35 448
Irrigated wheat	53 601	54 490	102	69 286
Mixed beans	14 123	20 401	144	23 534
Groundnuts	28 188	20 504	73	42 301
Soyabeans	27 713	7 006	25	28 026

*1991–92 as % of 1990–91.
Source: Zambia MAFF (1992) for 1990–91. MAFF and CSO (1993) for 1991–92 and 1992–93.

the year after, with the return of good rains. Maize production in 1990–91 was about average for the dry decade of the 1980s, but half the amount obtained in the good years of 1988 and 1989. Production in 1991–92 was less than half the 1990–91 figure.

Less rain produced better crops than normal in the northern areas where crops often suffer leaching of nutrients by excessive rain. By contrast, 85% of crop areas in Southern Province, 67% in Lusaka Province, 61% in Western Province, 37% in Eastern Province and 51% in Central Province were affected by drought losses (Zambia, MAFF and CSO, 1993).

Government-distributed hybrid maize, received and planted late, died. Many Zambian farmers plant first some local open-pollinated maize varieties, preferred for family use because of their taste and good storage qualities. However, most have a long maturity time, and despite being planted relatively early, they were caught by the cessation of the rains. Farmers were therefore left without either their normal food supply, or next year's seed supply. They also lost groundnuts, beans, cowpeas and other seeds important for a varied and balanced diet.

Degree of recovery by August 1993

Thanks to the good rains in 1992–93, and the distribution of maize seed as part of the relief programme, many farmers had a good harvest, as demonstrated by the production figures for 1992–93 in Table 10.1. Nationally, the main problems in 1993 were connected with marketing and storage, not shortage. However, some farmers had poor crops, for reasons discussed later.

Impact on domestic livestock

Livestock statistics are notoriously unreliable. Reports from surveys and anecdotal evidence suggest an increase in sales, mainly because farmers were in urgent need of cash, only partly because they feared losses. The Veterinary Department thought that forced sales were reduced once yellow maize and food for work became available.

Generally, grazing resources remained adequate, because the stock population had already been reduced by disease. Domestic livestock had to be trekked further to obtain water. This stressed them, and left them more susceptible to disease, particularly to the epidemic of East Coast fever which was already raging. However, the government, as one of its responses to the drought, abolished the charge for dipping and the drought also directly brought about a temporary reduction in the tick population, which assisted in bringing the disease under control.

Generally, ARPT (Adaptive Research Planning Team) surveys found that the condition of the remaining cattle was not too bad in October 1992. This is what we should expect, given the limited impact of the drought on pasture and browse, and the mobility of smallholder cattle which can be moved to water.

The combined effect of losses from disease and sales was a shortage of draft animals, although farmers sold off first their small stock, and protected their cattle as long as they could. Families also lost the milk supply they normally enjoy in the wet season.

Fisheries

There are two main types of fishing in Zambia: lake fishing, especially in Lake Kariba and Lake Itezhi-Tezhi, and swamp fishing.

In Lake Kariba, *kapenta*—a small, sardine-type fish—is caught by large commercial fishermen, and bream is caught inshore by small fishermen.

When rain in the catchment area and inflows are low, so are nutrient levels and fish numbers. Recorded catches in 1991–92 went down slightly on the Zimbabwe side, up slightly on the Zambia side. Statistics are unreliable, as fishermen evade registration and payment of licence charges for their boats and fish traders evade checkpoints and collection of dues. In recent years there has been an increase in the number of small traders who sell dried fish and a reduction in the number of large, more easily registered traders operating refrigerated lorries.

The low and fast-diminishing water levels in swamps and smaller lakes, ponds and streams made it easier to catch fish. The number of fishermen increased, as people attempted to compensate for the failure of their crops. High fish catches of breeding adults in 1992 may affect fish numbers in 1993 and subsequent years. However, juveniles grow faster when there is reduced competition for nutrients, and the good rains of 1992–93 increased nutrient inflows into lakes and swamps. The long-term impact of the drought is difficult to estimate.

Wildlife

The drought had a limited, temporary effect on wildlife. It led to some deaths, mainly due to water shortage, especially among hippo. Land-based herbivores were stressed, but most survived, and there is evidence of increased breeding since. Poaching may have increased temporarily, but department officials are not conscious of any area where this caused a noticeable reduction in any species, although they are not in a position to produce hard data.

Impact on soils

In areas that have been farmed for a long time farmers have noticed a fall in fertility, but this is not due to the drought. However, the drought made some farmers more conscious of the need to conserve soil and water resources. The heavy rains of 1992–93, falling on bare soil, caused more than usual gullying.

The drought's impact on people

Overall organization of relief

Zambia decided to manage its drought relief largely through NGOs, including local churches. Lead NGOs were appointed in each area to co-ordinate efforts, and to work through committees of local people in the organization of food relief and Food for Work (FFW) programmes. The new government was distrustful of the civil service it had inherited, and the new local authorities were not yet operational. The general opinion was that the operation went remarkably smoothly, and that aid reached the right people (Tiffen and Mulele, 1994).

The national-level organization of maize imports, the involvement of donors, the redistribution of maize to the provinces, and the assessment of seed requirements for recovery also went well, with only the minor difficulties to be expected in a programme of its size. The failure of the rains was realized early in February and led to immediate purchases of grain and solicitation of aid funds. The early ordering of imports meant that the towns felt no acute shortages. Very few deaths occurred. Rural people recognized this to be the result of the programme. As women farmers in Southern Province said, in droughts 'On our own we would die. Government must help.' However, despite the relief operation's title, Programme against Malnutrition (PAM), malnutrition did occur, and was still increasing in 1993. The water programme was hampered by the poor original state of facilities, the lack of any community organizations to manage them, and shortages of funds.

Nutritional and health impacts

Although the successful distribution of maize prevented deaths from famine, there was an increase in children underweight for their age (an indicator of longer-term food insufficiency, in quantity or quality, unlike weight for height), which continued, or even increased, after the 1992–93 harvest was in. Although the CSO weight for age statistics are taken from a limited sample of mother and child welfare clinics, they probably reflect a real problem (Tiffen and Mulele,1994), the cause of which is not immediately clear. High energy and protein supplements (HEPS) were distributed to vulnerable families attending health clinics. However for a long time there had been a lack of balance in the diet of pregnant and nursing mothers, and children who were being weaned, since many of the relishes accompanying the maize staple have been lacking. These include legumes and vegetables, good sources of important amino acids, vitamins and minerals. What livestock and vegetables rural people had were sold to purchase the more essential maize, before FFW programmes began. Hunting and fishing, legal or not, were undertaken to generate cash. Rural families, when asked, identified the need for non-maize foods as part of the relief programme. Thus, in an Oxfam report on community meetings in Nyimba district, Eastern Province, in April 1992, food requirements were stated as being: 'Maize, beans, *kapenta*, groundnuts for adults. Sugar, milk, soya beans and HEPS for children and those that are malnourished'. In our own and ARPT interviews, in both Southern and Eastern Province, farmers emphasized their need for legume seeds.

Some gathered fruits, vegetables and insects are always used in the diet, and their use probably expanded, though some wild trees provided less fruit than usual in the drought. Some gathered foods were sold, to generate cash (Gender Studies Unit, 1993). In a drought, desperate people will range further afield to find wild foods, but the cost in energy expenditure will be high in relation to the calorific benefit. The denser the population, the more scarce will wild foods be.

Asset sales

The drought stripped many rural families of their assets. For most, the harvests they had expected to make at the end of the 1991–92 season were a major part of their usual income, expected to end the shortages and hardship that frequently precede the harvest. Unlike urban families and rural civil servants, they probably lost 30–100% of their income in kind and cash, depending on the variety of income sources which they had. Problems started with the loss of green maize from their early planted local maize crop in March or April 1992 and continued for a year until the next harvest. Although some were able to earn a little money from activities like charcoal manufacture and fishing, this was more possible for those living near roads and urban centres (and hence observable by outsiders) and less feasible for those in more distant communities.

The consequences, as one group of women farmers explained, was they had to sell whatever they had in order to buy maize before the relief yellow maize started arriving in June 1992. They sold the vegetables that still remained in the *dambos* and their chickens, goats, pigs and such cattle as had not died from disease. They ended the year, naturally, with no cash saved either to buy fertilizer or to replace the seed they would normally have retained.

Recovery from such asset loss can be hastened by credit, and the government arranged for 1991–92 debts to be forgiven or rolled over. However, many families were ineligible for official credit, because they owed money from previous years. Credit was also in short supply because lending organizations had financial problems in the inflationary situation, or were disorganized by the new marketing situation.

The difference credit made was illustrated by two women farmers in Siakachamatanga village, Southern Province. Both had received 10 kg of hybrid maize seed under the recovery programme. The first had also obtained a loan for fertilizer, and had been able to buy another 10 kg of seed. As a result, she had harvested some 110 bags of maize, and had put 66 bags in the family store and sold 54. This family would have enough to eat during the year, and was well on the way to recovery. However, only 6 of the 13 women farmers in the group interviewed had got loans. A farmer without a loan, unable to obtain fertilizer, harvested only six bags from 10 kg seed. (Poorer farmers without loans are often also those without oxen, who plant late.) Those who had a good harvest would have cash to buy fertilizer next year, but the rest would still be struggling. Fertilizer is recognized as important. A farmer interviewed by ARPT in March 1993 said that without fertilizer he would remain in patched clothes. In some of the drier areas people were given improved sorghum seed instead of hybrid maize, the former not needing fertilizer. However, supplies of seed were limited owing to water supply difficulties on the government farm that was producing an irrigated crop.

Long-term social effects

Negative effects

Some families were left with insufficient income and food to carry them through to the harvest of 1993–94, because they lacked draft power or access to credit in 1992–93. Others did well, and had begun to restore their assets. The likely long-term effect of the drought is, therefore, an increase in inequality among village families.

Some families received assistance from urban relatives during the drought, but this seems to have been exceptional. Indeed, some observers thought that family relationships were put under acute strain, when rural families visited urban relatives and were made unwelcome. Urban families were suffering the effects of inflation, and in some cases, from short-time working due to electricity cuts, and may themselves have been in genuine difficulty.

The drought probably increased women's workloads more than men's. The Gender Studies Unit (1993) found that more women were involved in FFW programmes than men, in all districts except Mongu, Western Province (where the type of work, on irrigation canals, was traditionally done by males). In addition, women retained their responsibility for water collection, which became a more time-consuming and tiring job during the drought, owing to greater distances to the collection point, and long queues and waits once there. Many other gathering activities are also regarded as traditionally female activities, but it was noted that in Katete and Luangwa districts, in Eastern Province, men were also involved, and seemed also to be equally involved in all agricultural activities. Of course, there was a reduction in harvesting work, but when the rain began again, there was a double workload, on the family fields in the morning and on FFW in the afternoons.

One reason for less male participation in FFW was that most of the extra income-earning activities, such as cattle sales, fishing, charcoal manufacture, basket and mat manufacture, were undertaken by men. Men are also more often able to find casual work. In some cases, as the owners of assets such as draft oxen and carts, their contribution to FFW programmes was in transportation, rather than labouring.

Women's income-generating activities, such as beer-brewing and sale of vegetables, were reduced as the drought set in. Female-headed households were those most likely to have to reduce the number of meals per day, and absenteeism from school was more prevalent among their children, due to difficulties with costs and the need to call on them for assistance.

School absenteeism increased, which was often, teachers said, because of hunger. In other cases, children were needed to assist in income generation (mainly boys) or water-carrying, etc. (mainly girls). There was no marked difference between the sexes in rates of absenteeism; it varied according to local circumstances.

Positive effects

The drought has strengthened village institutions, through the formation of drought committees under the PAM programme. These committees generally assisted in deciding which activity to undertake under the FFW programme, which led to the repair of roads, wells, dams, latrines and school buildings. Local people realized they could themselves organize improvements. People were proud of what they managed to achieve, and there was at least some hope that the new facilities would be looked after, especially where, as in the case of water, some training in maintenance was being organized.

The involvement of NGOs, both foreign-aided and locally based, led to a greater appreciation of how they can work together with government. In both agriculture and water, for example, government officers now provide technical advice, if NGOs or local communities provide funds for transport and other needs. However, there is a danger that people think free food is a necessary element in a community programme.

While community solidarity in working together for community facilities has probably been stimulated, the extent of people's willingness and ability to help the poorer members of their own community should not be exaggerated. A suggestion made to women farmers that those who had done well in 1992–93 might be able to help those who had poor harvests was not well received!

The drought also changed attitudes to crop diversification. While farmers still appreciate the qualities of hybrid maize, particularly in conjunction with fertilizer, they are also much more conscious of the dangers of over-reliance on this one crop. ARPT surveys and government extension officers have remarked on the greater interest being shown in new sorghum varieties, legumes and roots such as cassava and sweet potato. The problem is access to seed or planting material.

Farmers may become more interested in storing greater amounts of maize and other crops on farm, under a liberalized marketing system, in the hope of getting higher prices later, but this will require them to invest in improved storage structures. In August 1993 the marketing system was still in confusion and future responses could not be judged.

Farmers also seem to have become more interested in soil conservation measures. This is in the context of their greater appreciation of the need to improve yields with less reliance on fertilizer, now that the latter has become more expensive, and given the credit difficulties. However, there is still little interest in new methods of grazing management, or control of wood collection, or planting woodlots. Generally, it is still thought that grazing and fuelwood can and should be obtained by free access to uncultivated land, controlled by nobody. Land control is becoming an issue in some areas, but more for cultivation rights than for grazing. This is due to growing population pressure in some areas, rather than the drought.

Conclusion

The 1991–92 drought in Zambia resulted in the impoverishment of many rural people, forcing them to dispose of important assets such as livestock and seed stocks. The need for seeds was met in part by the PAM programme, but the prolonged shortage of legumes, together with other dietary deficiencies, were the main causes of an increase in malnutrition. Those farmers who managed to obtain credit and retain their oxen, have been able to make a good recovery. However, others who received no credit will again face difficulty before the next harvest. There has been a notable increase in inequality within village society. However, the drought has also had some more positive effects. The way the FFW programmes were organized and the food distributed, has strengthened village-level organization and has often left communities with some improved facilities. There is also now a greater awareness of the need to diversify crops and to further develop various soil conservation methods. It is to be hoped that lessons learned from this study of the effects of the 1991–92 drought will be incorporated into future development strategies, so that the impact of future droughts on poor rural people can be ameliorated.

Acknowledgements

This chapter is a summary of a report prepared, with Mr M. R. Mulele, Director of Agriculture, Department of Agriculture, Lusaka, Republic of Zambia for the IUCN, the World Conservation Union, and published as Mary Tiffen and M. R. Mulele (1994) *The Environmental Impact of the 1991–2 Drought on Zambia*, IUCN: Gland, Switzerland, and Lusaka, Zambia, with the financial assistance of IRISH AID. Permission to reproduce material and diagrams is gratefully acknowledged.

References

Note: ARPT (Adaptive Research Planning Team) reports referred to are on file in the Mount Makulu Research Station of the Ministry of Agriculture Forest and Fisheries and are listed in Tiffen and Mulele (1994).

FAO (1991) *Zambia. Comprehensive Agricultural Development and Food Security Programme*, Rome.

Foster, S. D. (1993) Maize production, drought and AIDS in Monze District, Zambia, *Health Policy and Plannihg*, 8, 342–354.

Gender Studies Unit, University of Zambia (1993) *Coping Strategies of Women during the 1992 Drought and the Impact of Relief Programmes on the Position of Women*, Lusaka.

IFAD (International Fund for Agriculture and Development) (1993) *General Identification Report (Southern Province, Zambia)*, Vols I–IV, Report 0425-ZA.

Middleton, T. (1993) Drought—wildlife vs cattle, *Kobus*, March, Lusaka.

Monö, R. (1993) *Environmental Profile Zambia. A study for SIDA*, Lusaka.

Tiffen, M. and Mulele, M. R. (1994) *The Environmental Impact of the 1991–2 Drought on Zambia*, IUCN, Gland, Switzerland.

Zambia, Republic of, CSO (1990) *1990 Census of Population, Housing and Agriculture*, Lusaka.

Zambia, Republic of, CSO (1992) *Country Profile*, Lusaka.

Zambia, Republic of, MAFF and CSO (1993) *Final Crop Forecasts, 1992/93 Season*, Lusaka.

11

Evaluating living standards in rural Malawi: the experience of a non-government development agency

Don Harrison

Introduction

This chapter aims to show how a non-government development agency operates at a range of levels from daily decision-making to long-term strategic planning. Working together with families in their communities involves the need for an ongoing analysis of how people use their local environments and adapt their everyday living and food supply strategies to climatic and population changes. In this way interactions between people and the rural environment can hopefully be evaluated in order to plan effective development action. The example is from Save the Children (UK), one of the many Save the Children organizations currently working in Southern Africa (and referred to in this chapter simply as 'Save the Children').

Among images which Save the Children could present of its project work in Mchinji, a small town close to Malawi's western frontier with Zambia (Figure 11.1), might be a woman in the hospital compound winnowing maize for the evening meal. Or an alternative image could be of the maps and files inside the primary health care unit, containing records of nutritional status and incidences of disease in the district. Such images might be used to convey to the public in Europe how and why an external aid agency uses donated funds for 'development' work related to food and health in Africa. The aid processes behind the images are complex, involving a range of strategies to understand and respond to the key issues in local economies and societies. Since any place is unique in time and space, this chapter aims to examine strategies for assessing food and health issues in Mchinji, in the context of an infinitely shifting set of local variables. Although the acquisition of data adds much to understanding and decision-making, it can never create a truly complete picture of a particular place and its people.

Evaluating food security in Malawi

In order to monitor food requirements and availability at the national level, the Malawian Ministry of Agriculture regularly surveys crop returns. This provides baseline data which can be measured against calorie requirements, in order to provide a measure of nutritional status for each district in the country. In times of drought, as in 1991–92, these figures can be used to create a map

People and Environment in Africa. Edited by Tony Binns
©1995 John Wiley & Sons Ltd

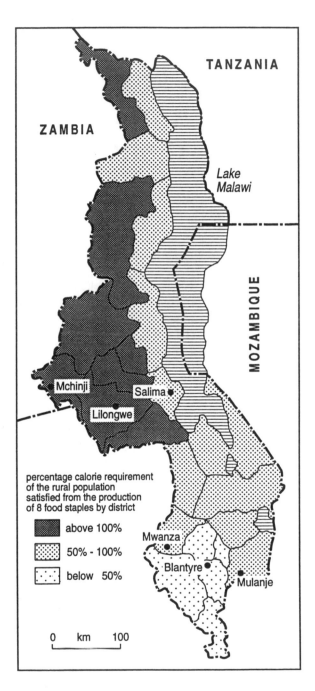

TANZANIA

ZAMBIA

Lake
Malawi

MOZAMBIQUE

Mchinji
Salima
Lilongwe

percentage calorie requirement
of the rural population
satisfied from the production
of 8 food staples by district

above 100%

50% - 100%

below 50%

Mwanza

Blantyre
Mulanje

0   km   100

Figure 11.1 *Food balances in Malawi after the 1989 harvest. Source: Ministry of Agriculture, third crop estimates, 1988/89*

of where supplementary maize bought from neighbouring countries might be targeted. Figure 11.1 maps the actual calories produced from eight staple crops (maize, cassava, rice, millet, sorghum, groundnuts, pulses, sweet potatoes) in relation to a minimum calorie requirement for the rural population of 2200 calories per person per day (1989 figures). Areas most vulnerable to food insecurity in Malawi are shown to be the hotter low-lying areas along the Shire River in the south, where it is more difficult to produce a range of crops for consumption and sale. The maize- and tobacco-producing plain of the Central Region is shown to be the most food sufficient area (MacAskill, 1993).

Experience from other studies shows that people living in areas of high vulnerability may often cope with times of hardship better than people in lower-risk areas, probably because they have a greater variety of coping strategies. A key problem for development agencies is finding a reliable way of evaluating such coping strategies in order to build up a more accurate map for targeting food relief in times of shortage. Vaughan's research (Vaughan, 1987), on official and individual responses to famine conditions in the lower Shire during the 1940s, has highlighted the gender-distinctive nature of relief strategies, where British colonial concepts of welfare assumed male-headed household structures, and applied Eurocentric models to the colonial periphery without seeking to modify them in response to local circumstances. At that time, many Malawian males were working away from home, either on other people's land or in South African mines. This trend continues to the present day in Malawi, such that 30% of rural households are headed by women.

In analyzing responses to the 1992 drought, Allen (1993) hints at the varied strategies used by Malawians to find sources of extra income. In one example, single-parent families are shown leaving their land to work in the tea estates around Mount Mulanje, even though the women and children earned wages as low as 50% of the male wage for casual work during the tea harvest. Allen asks about the existence of other forms of support for such disadvantaged groups: 'Do the social ties between these people and Malawians elsewhere open up an economic safety-net in bad times? What other possibilities for food exist which are largely "hidden" to the outsider?' (Allen, 1993). Clearly an attempt to map food production in relation to estimated calorie requirements, cannot by itself provide a measure of the detailed local understanding and responses to drought situations.

Living standards in Mchinji district

Mchinji district is a predominantly maize- and groundnut-producing area in Malawi's Central Region. The district has a variety of agro-ecological zones, ranging from the Kasungu Plain in the north to the upper Bua Plain in the south, and to the Mchinji Hills in the west along the frontier with Zambia. Most of Mchinji district has an annual rainfall range of 762–1016 mm, with the area of the Mchinji Hills, where the main town of Mchinji is situated, having an annual rainfall range of 890–1270 mm (figures from Mkomba, 1993a). Temperatures in the plateau areas of Malawi range from a mean 15–18°C in July to 22–25°C in November, before the rains start. The rainy season usually lasts until March or April, when the principal maize harvest takes place.

The national food vulnerability mapping exercise shows Mchinji district to be a middle-risk area, generally food sufficient unless the rains finish too early. Yet, considering other indicators, the district appears less 'developed', or at least lower in welfare status, than other districts of Malawi. For example, Mchinji has an infant mortality rate of 185 per 1000 births, which compares unfavourably with Malawi's national average of 135 (1982 figures), reflecting the poverty of the district in a generally poor country.

Save the Children signed an agreement with the Malawian Ministry of Health to support primary health care work in Mchinji district during the period 1991–96. Subsequently, on account of already undertaking health work in the district, the Ministry of Agriculture asked Save the Children to assist with maize distribution during the drought of 1992. The outcome to date of Save the Children's

aid and development activities is a series of reports and surveys, which together add much to our understanding of people's daily lives in Mchinji district and indicate how nutrition and health might be improved. However, the available documentation is unfortunately difficult to integrate as different methodologies and indicators have been used. At district level the process of mapping food needs and responses to environmental factors proves complex. The closer an external agency works with people in their communities—one of the stated aims of Save the Children—the more detailed the social and cultural factors which have to be evaluated.

One outcome of the food relief operation in Mchinji district was the commissioning of a baseline document for food security risk mapping, carried out by a senior member of the Ministry of Agriculture during 1993. A parallel baseline document was prepared for the lake-shore Salima district, where Save the Children had also assisted with the distribution of supplementary food during the 1992 drought (Mkomba, 1993a,b). These surveys attempt to measure population distribution, landholdings, subsistence and cash crop production for each extension planning area (EPA) of the two districts—the EPAs corresponding to traditional authorities, the standard subdistrict divisions. The purpose of such a survey is for 'ranking areas and populations according to the severity of the effects of the drought and assessing areas of chronic food shortages'. By scoring each variable according to how it affects household food security, a table can be produced which ranks EPAs by magnitude of insecurity (Table 11.1). The table shows Chioshya EPA (which is close to Mchinji town) as most at risk and Mkanda EPA (in the northern Kasungu Plain) as least at risk. At one level these results reflect the more fertile tobacco-producing land in the north of the district which provides more possibility for cash crop incomes.

Whereas these conclusions may well be obvious without such a survey, the risk-mapping process helps to indicate the complexity of the variables which need to be taken into account when attempting to produce a measure of people's

Table 11.1 *Ranking of extension planning areas (EPAs) in Mchinji District by magnitude of food insecurity (source: Mkomba, Ben, 1993a)*

Variable	Extension planning areas					
	Mkanda	Kalulu	Mikundi	Chioshya	Mlonyeni	Msitu
Registered population	2	3	4	6	1	5
Total average crop kcals	1	3	6	4	5	2
1992 total crop kcals	1	3	2	6	5	4
Average food crop production	1	4	6	2	5	3
1992 food crop production	1	3	2	5	4	6
Average cash crop production	5	1	2	4	6	3
1992 cash crop production	2	6	1	4	5	3
% Farmers using credit	5	6	1	6	1	4
% Credit repayment	1	6	4	5	4	1
% Area improved maize	5	3	1	6	2	4
Total score	24	38	29	48	38	35
Overall rank	6	2	5	1	3	4

Key: For each variable in each area: 1 = best security position; 6 = worst security position. For the final ranking: 1 = area most at risk; 6 = area least at risk.

vulnerability to environmental and other factors. The survey summary states that 'although Mchinji District is on average a food surplus district, some EPAs are more vulnerable than others' with the further need to research the roles in drought situations played by 'crop diversification in reducing the risk of total crop failure' and 'non farm sources of food supplies' (Mkomba, 1993a). In other words, such baseline analysis provides a crude, but potentially useful, measure of food security in local areas which can then form a basis for long-term strategic planning. In drawing up an overall country strategy, Save the Children can utilize these results to facilitate the identification of districts which might be targeted for external interventions in health, water provision or agricultural development. The two reports recognize the unreliability of the variables measured. Population statistics, for example, vary widely from the official census figures of 1987, to those registered for food relief in 1992. Cash crop production figures, as a measure of potentially available food, are also difficult to calculate on any realistic basis. Furthermore, the conversion of income into kilocalories is based on a fixed exchange rate for the value of cash crops, but such values are constantly changing with market price fluctuations.

Health care and the impact of refugees

Despite data unreliability, the baseline survey of Mchinji district does clearly reveal a picture of families with small landholdings averaging 2 ha, coping in a drought situation with a variety of strategies. These strategies range from the sale of cash crops, to providing labour on other people's land, to temporary migration to towns to find other kinds of employment. A family may use a mixture of coping strategies in order to maintain the family's survival on the land until the next fruitful harvest. A more detailed understanding of how communities make daily decisions about their living standards can be gained from the primary health care survey carried out in Mavwere traditional authority (Msitu EPA) of Mchinji district (Dimond, 1992). This survey, based on interviews undertaken by health workers in the area, clearly highlights the differences between the 40 000 indigenous Malawians and the 20 000 Mozambican refugees who were living at the time in four camp areas. As the refugee camps were provided with protected wells and better sanitation than the local population (Table 11.2), 70% of Malawian families, compared with 46% of Mozambican families, were assessed as being at risk of ill health. Studies of the ecological effects

Table 11.2 *Water sources in Mavwere Traditional Authority (source: Dimond, 1992)*

| | Dry season (%) | | Wet season (%) | |
	Malawians	Mozambicans	Malawians	Mozambicans
Protected well	30	54	27.5	57.5
Unprotected well	59	41	62.5	41
River/stream	11	5	10	1.5

of a rapidly growing refugee population along Malawi's frontier areas with Mozambique have indicated intensified land use and deforestation:

By affecting Malawian agricultural practices the presence of refugees has also made an indirect ecological impact. In the Chifunga area of Mwanza, for example, refugee labour has been used by Malawians to increase the area under cultivation, leading to deforestation and reduced grazing and wild resource access. . . . Furthermore, in most areas the replacement of Malawian wage labour by refugees has led former Malawian wage labourers to intensify production on their own small-holdings (WFP, 1989, p. 99).

Mchinji district experienced relatively less refugee influx than other districts in Malawi's Southern Region, and unfortunately no comparable survey into ecological effects has been carried out there. However, the rate of deforestation is an item of daily conversation in Mchinji. What can be concluded from the Mavwere health survey is that the Mozambican refugees did affect local economies in one important way, by attracting aid investment through the office of the United Nations High Commissioner for Refugees which improved access to clean water. As the refugee population gradually moves back into Mozambique with the cessation of hostilities, the greater number of protected wells remains an important benefit to the local Malawian population.

Work at the people–environment interface

In supporting a multi-sectoral primary health care programme in Mchinji district, Save the Children aims to train local health personnel within a sustainable development programme. Diagnostic surveys form one part of a process of identifying and trying to measure strategies for achieving better health. The Save the Children supported programme in Mchinji is run by a team of professional staff who are based at the primary health care unit in the district hospital in Mchinji and who work closely with government health officials based at the hospital. Team members are involved in a wide outreach programme which involves travelling by Land-rover or motor cycle to remote rural areas of the district. Regular meetings are held with staff at local health centres to strengthen their planning and evaluation of health care strategies. Such close support at community level must be one of the key factors in the eradication of outbreaks of cholera in the district since the 1992 drought. Discussions in local health centres may focus on apparently trivial, yet sensitive, issues such as the most suitable dress for women health surveillance assistants, when only male bicycles are currently available to facilitate their village outreach work!

Some members of the primary health care team are involved in health-focused programmes like working with traditional birth attendants and running an AIDS awareness programme, while others specialize in supporting water and community development initiatives. Encouraging local committees to maintain their water pumps properly is as much part of preventive health care as sitting with a traditional chief to discuss how to plant more trees in the village. In the latter case, the community development worker in the team can facilitate this by requesting seedlings from the forestry officer and arranging transport. Through such a wide range of initiatives, this example of an externally funded development project has helped families towards better health, by achieving greater control over their environment. Local people perceive, through daily contact with aid workers (Malawian and expatriate), how these outsiders are working for their interests. Such locally gained, personal—even anecdotal—knowledge adds to an understanding of processes of development, although it is evidently often much harder to analyse than crop yield surveys and large-scale movements of refugees. Save the Children would hope to combine community-gained insights with external assessments when planning future development interventions.

Conclusion

Fieldwork for this chapter was carried out during a Save the Children study visit in March 1994, which also aimed at establishing school links. Malawian school students were invited to express their views about food and health, agriculture and urbanization to share with school students in Scotland. In an African country like Malawi, where half the population is under 15 years of age, it might be argued that more attention should be given to the insights and issues of concern that young people have when planning future development strategies. This is perhaps an area where international Save the Children organizations, whose mission involves helping to improve children's rights, can bring fresh insights to collaborative programmes with government departments. Through extensive experience of working for children, their families and their communities, Save the Children has tried to

develop integrated, multi-sectoral approaches. It is likely that the Mchinji primary health initiative, planned and executed closely with the Malawian Ministry of Health, will be extended to other districts in the country which are regarded as priority areas. Evaluating the complex relationships between people and environment in drought-prone areas is one important strand in deciding where and how to operate development projects. This chapter has considered a part of the learning process of one non-government development agency, in building upon a basis of people's own knowledge and controls over their environment.

References

Allen, Penny (1993) *First Steps towards an Understanding of Rural Economy in Malawi*, SCF(UK), London.

Dimond, Caroline (1992) *Mavwere Primary Health Care Survey*, SCF(UK), Mchinji.

MacAskill, Jane (1993) *Food Security in Malawi*, SCF(UK), Lilongwe.

Mkomba, Ben (1993a) *Mchinji District Baseline Document for Food Security Risk Mapping*, SCF(UK), Lilongwe.

Mkomba, Ben (1993b) *Salima District Baseline Document for Food Security Risk Mapping*, SCF(UK), Lilongwe.

Vaughan, Megan (1987) *The Story of an African Famine: gender and famine in 20th Century Malawi*, Cambridge University Press, Cambridge.

WFP (World Food Programme) (1989) *Food Provisioning amongst Mozambican Refugees in Malawi: a study of aid, livelihood and development*, Refugee Studies Programme, Oxford.

Section III
West Africa

Huts and granaries in a village on the Jos Plateau, Nigeria. (Photograph: Tony Binns)

12

Desertification, drought and development in the Sahel

C. T. Agnew

Introduction

Drought and desertification threaten agricultural production world-wide, in both developing and developed nations. In the 1980s drought affected most parts of the globe from Australia to Latin America, reducing food production and farm incomes. More recently in 1992–93, Southern Africa has experienced food production shortfalls rivalling those in Ethiopia and Sudan during 1984–85 (Collins, 1993); and Donald Wilhite (1993) has just reported that drought will again plague the western United States in 1994. The UNEP (1992) has produced alarming statistics on the threat of desertification: 70% of the world's drylands used for agriculture are believed to have been affected by land degradation, one-sixth of the world's population is threatened by desertification, and each year 6 million ha of land is lost to production worth US$42.3 billion (1990 prices). Some 20% (1 billion ha) of the world's dryland area is believed to be experiencing some form of soil degradation. The area where terrain is not reclaimable (extreme degradation) or requires major engineering works (strong degradation) is estimated to cover 0.138 billion hectares or 14% of the total degraded land.

Agenda 21 (UNCED, 1992) paid particular attention to these environmental problems. In Chapter 12, 'Managing fragile ecosystems: combating desertification and drought', the following recommendations were adopted:

1. Strengthening the knowledge base and developing information and monitoring systems for regions prone to desertification and drought, including the economic and social aspects of these ecosystems;
2. Implementing soil conservation measures;
3. Eradicating poverty;
4. Improving anti-desertification planning;
5. Developing drought preparedness and drought relief schemes, including self-help arrangements and programmes to cope with environmental refugees;
6. Encouraging and promoting popular participation and environmental education.

Toulmin (1993) notes that negotiations are under way to agree a convention to combat desertification, based on Agenda 21, for Africa in 1994 and for Asia and Latin America in 1995. Recent signs are that progress will not be rapid, which is not surprising given that the estimated cost

People and Environment in Africa. Edited by Tony Binns
©1995 John Wiley & Sons Ltd

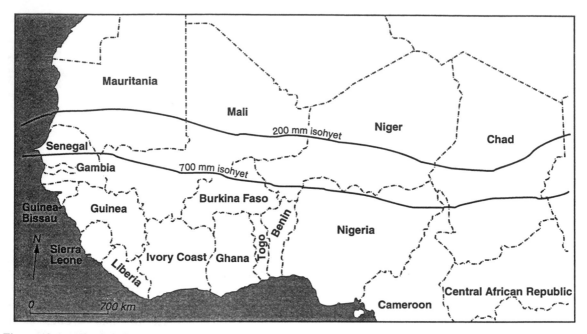

Figure 12.1 *The Sahel region, lying south of the Sahara between the 200 and 700 mm annual isohyets*

(UNCED, 1992) of tackling drought and desertification globally is $9 billion.

The Sahel

The Sahelian region of Africa, lying on the southern borders of the Sahara Desert and often extended eastwards to include Ethiopia and Somalia (Figure 12.1), has been the recipient of world attention due to reports over at least the last 30 years of drought, desertification and famine (Figure 12.2). Between 1965 and 1983 the population in the Sahel doubled, with a fivefold increase occurring in urban areas (Reardon, 1993). Although food production rose generally (at 2% per annum for millet and sorghum), it has not been able to keep pace with population increases of around 3% per annum (Table 12.1).

Most of the population in these countries are reliant on some form of agropastoral food production and are therefore dependent on the vagaries of the environment. Three major droughts have occurred in the Sahel this century, during the 1910s, 1940s and 1970s (Nicholson and Palao, 1993). The last is of most concern because it appears to have heralded the onset of even drier conditions. Sir Crispen Tickell (1986), as head of the Overseas Development Administration (UK), wrote about acute drought affecting the Sahel since 1968 and this view is endorsed by many climatologists (Druyan, 1989; Hulme and Kelly, 1993). Cooke *et al.* (1993) note that increasing aridity has been evident for the last 5000 years (with wet periods in the sixteenth and seventeenth centuries and again late in the nineteenth century). Figure 12.3 shows the persistent downward trend in rainfall across the Sahel since the 1960s with corresponding diminution in River Senegal discharges. UNEP (1992) identified large areas experiencing severe soil degradation (Figure 12.4) and Pritchard (1990, p. 246) describes the situation as:

The desert is extending partly because of recurring cycles of drought, but also because of man . . . over the last 50 years the Sahara has advanced to cover one million square kilometres . . . an area equal to Mali . . . in the Sudan deserts have advanced 100 km in 17 years and the present rate of advance is about 6 km a year.

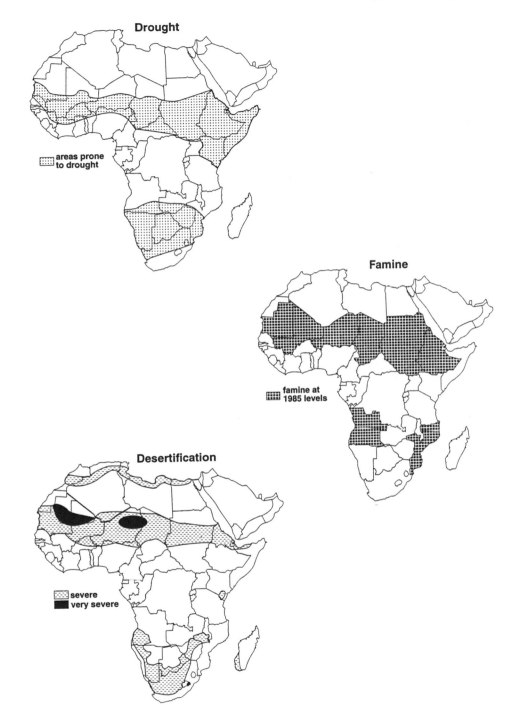

Figure 12.2 *Coincidental areas of famine, drought and desertification across the Sahel, adapted from Thomas (1993). Reproduced by permission of* The Geographical Journal

Table 12.1 *Food production in the Sahel (1979–81 average: 1988 comparison)*

Production	Total production (%)	Per capita (%)
Ethiopia	+5	−9
Mali	+22	−3
Niger	+24	−2
Senegal	+19	−3
Sudan	+26	−1

Source: *FAO Production Year Book 1988*, and *Quarterly Bulletin of Statistics*, Number 1, 1990.

A telex from the Sahel to Unicef in 1973 reported that governments had been overwhelmed and the desert was advancing in drought-stricken regions. At this time drought-related deaths were estimated around 100 000 (Copans, 1983) with massive destruction of livestock herds, particularly cattle. During the 1980s media attention moved to eastern parts of the region, with famine in Ethiopia and Sudan. Druyan (1989) suggests that by the end of the decade the cumulative impact of drought had resulted in the deaths of hundreds of thousands of people with millions more displaced. Reports

of environmental degradation have continued to appear for all parts of the Sahel and Odingo (1992, p. 6) describes the area: 'after a 20 year series of droughts, the Sudano-Sahelian region remained the most permanently vulnerable area and desertification had adversely affected the well being of some 80–85% of the population of the region'.

The Sahel is then facing both human tragedy and an environmental disaster, the causes of which have been blamed on both bungled development attempts and natural environmental changes.

Physical causes of environmental degradation

Hulme and Kelly (1993) show that the areal extent of the Sahara, based on satellite imagery, fluctuated markedly during the 1980s, and that 83% of the variation could be explained by rainfall. Climate change is an obvious mechanism which is intensifying drought and desertification in the Sahel, which has been reviewed by Druyan (1989), Hulme and Kelly (1993) and Rasmusson (1987).

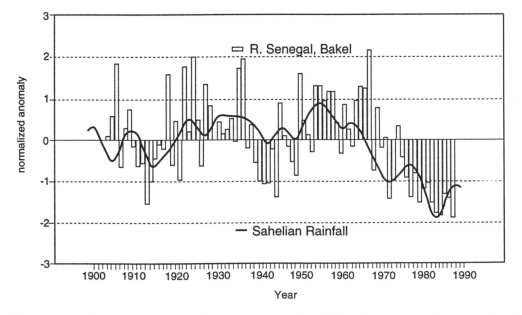

Figure 12.3 *Normalized departures from the long-term mean ($(x − x^t)/s^t$), where x is the observed value, x^t is the mean over period of observations t, and s^t is the standard deviation over period t), of annual discharges of the River Senegal at Bakel and Sahelian rainfall (after UNEP, 1992)*

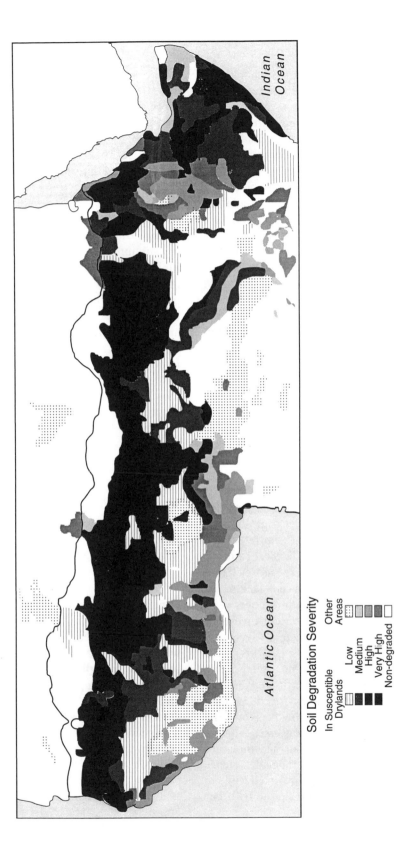

Indian Ocean

Atlantic Ocean

Soil Degradation Severity

In Susceptible Drylands	Other Areas
Low	
Medium	
High	
Very High	
Non-degraded	

Figure 12.4 *Soil degradation in the Sahel region, adapted from UNEP (1992). Reproduced by permission of Edward Arnold (Publishers) Ltd*

All consider local feedbacks through changes to land surfaces, alongside global alterations of atmospheric circulations. Sea surface temperatures in the Atlantic have been correlated with Sahelian rainfall and the recent period of desiccation appears related to lower ocean temperatures north of the Equator. The cause of these temperature differences is unproven, but they may be due to global warming or a natural change in circulation patterns. Global circulation models (GCMs) have not been able to model regional rainfall reliably in the Sahel, although it is suggested that some of the recent decline in precipitation could be attributed to global warming. However, this alone does not explain the rainfall pattern over the last 20 years. GCMs are not yet capable of saying whether recent desiccation is the result of human activity, nor whether rainfall will continue to decline or not.

Much attention has been paid to more local influences on climate. The belief that overgrazing could increase albedos, hence inducing drought, was suggested by several writers in the early 1970s including Otterman (1974) and Charney and Stone (1974). Their explanation concerned energy budget alterations through removal of vegetation cover leading to lower temperatures and hence reduced rainfall. Middleton (1991) has monitored increased atmospheric dust over the Sahel and suggests that this could also produce more stable atmospheric conditions leading to lower rainfall. The albedo explanation, however, ignores latent heat fluxes and advection; evidence is lacking on widespread removal of vegetation cover and significant albedo changes; and recent investigations suggest temperatures have actually increased in desertified areas. The IUCN (1989), for example, refute the notion that overgrazing around wells has removed vegetation cover over large areas and the importation of dung may actually improve vegetation growth. None the less, climate modelling has suggested that a feedback exists between land surface moisture regimes and convective rainfall in the Sahel. Hence vegetation removal may contribute to a decline in rainfall when the latter has been caused by other factors.

The link between climate change, drought and desertification is therefore far from proven, especially given the potential confusion over the meanings of these terms. For instance, Cardy (1993, p. 5) notes that in 1991 the UNEP took desertification to be: 'land degradation in arid, semi-arid and dry subhumid areas resulting mainly from *human activities*', i.e. excluding secular climate change. A year later at the Earth Summit (UNCED, 1992) the definition of desertification became: 'land degradation in arid, semi-arid and dry subhumid areas resulting from various factors including *climatic variations and human activities*'.

However, these definitions fail to distinguish between the expansion of existing deserts (the most appropriate meaning of desertification according to Warren and Agnew, 1988), and the impoverishment of the soil environment through human activities (land degradation) which occurs mostly away from desert margins. Furthermore, Warren and Khogali (1992) make the distinction between:

drought	moisture supplied below average for short periods of 1–2 years
desiccation	process of aridization lasting decades
land degradation	a persistent decrease in the productivity of vegetation and soils

Drought is generally seen to be an abnormal reduction in water availability, and should not then be confused with desiccation (or aridity) which involves a longer-term decline in moisture supplies. Drought may trigger off land degradation, but is not a prime cause. Conversely, Hulme and Kelly (1993, p. 39) state: 'In the light of current empirical and modelling evidence, then, it appears that desertification is not, in itself, a primary cause of recent desiccation in the Sahel.'

Apart from water shortages, desertification can result from a multitude of human activities that ultimately remove vegetation cover and impoverish soils. The UNEP (1992) list overgrazing, deforestation, fuelwood collection and agricultural intensification. The physical processes involved, for example soil salinization, wind erosion and surface runoff, are discussed in Mainguet (1991) and Grainger (1990). However, the underlying causes are too often ignored. For example, Toulmin (1993) includes land tenure, levels of debt and inappropriate technologies as causes of desertification. In addition, the monitoring of changes over time has not received sufficient attention, while a focus on vegetation removal has ignored the importance of the underlying soil (Warren and Agnew, 1988). There is then much debate over the fundamental causes of environmental degradation, while some have begun to question the evidence that drought and desertification are widespread (Agnew and Warren, 1993).

How reliable is the evidence of environmental degradation?

Care should be taken when reviewing evidence of environmental degradation in the Sahel for four reasons:

1. The Sahelian environment is semi-arid and inherently variable spatially and temporally. Identifying change and trends is then risky.
2. The data base is poor, despite attempts in the 1970s to improve agroclimatological information, the development of drought warning systems and the increasing use of remote sensing.
3. The resilience (ability to recover after a shock) of ecosystems and food production systems is often ignored. A natural environment may be impoverished in some respect, for example soil fertility or vegetation cover, but if it can recover is it then degraded? That is, we need to distinguish between temporary and permanent degradation, and determine over what time period this is assessed. In drylands this is particularly difficult because ecosystems may remain dormant or recover slowly due to the lack of water (Binns, 1990).

4. Institutional facts (see Warren and Agnew, 1988), which may lead to the promotion of evidence on environmental degradation through the need to highlight an environmental problem or through self-interest. For example, Winifred Ewing (SNP) announced to the European Parliament that aid must go to the Sahel because the desert was advancing at 8 km a year (see below for a criticism of this claim). In 1984 the President of Niger urged his countrymen to join in the fight aganst the Sahara and used this environmental threat to shelve plans to liberalize the political system: 'we cannot talk politics on an empty stomach'.

Many writers refer to the threat of the advancing Sahara noted by Stebbing in 1935. Various rates of advance have been postulated in the intervening years, but how is the edge of the desert demarcated? Lamprey (1975), working in Sudan, delineated the desert edge in 1958 using rainfall and associated vegetation growth and then compared this with an aerial survey in 1975. The result is of questionable reliability, given the prevailing drought conditions in the 1970s and the comparison of two such different measures of the desert boundary. Ahlcrona's (1988) studies in the same area have cast further doubt on the spreading desert theory in the Sudan and this scepticism has been noted by the media. A recent article in *New Scientist* (12/12/1992) by Fred Pearce referred to the 'mirage of the shifting sands', while Nigel Hawkes (*The Times*, 23/1/1992) suggested : 'The sun is setting on the creeping desert theory'. Thomas (1993, p. 323) is equally emphatic: 'the concept of an advancing desert front, used to infer desertification and the spread of the Sahara is incorrect'.

But why focus on the desert edge anyway? Few people inhabit this hyper-arid region, and the more productive agricultural areas to the south are much more prone to environmental degradation with higher rainfall and greater population pressure. But even here the data collected on desertification are speculative. Warren and Agnew (1988) criticize the method of data collection employed by the United Nations Plan of Action to Combat Desertification (created 1977) to produce numerous statistics—e.g. each year 21 million ha of once productive soil are reduced by desertification to a level of zero or negative productivity. The reasons for this criticism are that the data are based upon a questionnaire carried out in 1982, the analysis treated large areas as experiencing similar conditions, the prevailing low rainfall was not taken into account, and the 'snap-shot' approach failed to determine whether degradation was temporary or permanent, i.e. long-term averages were not sought.

The exercise to map the extent of desertification has recently been repeated (UNEP, 1992), by the International Soil Reference and Information Centre, on the basis of questionnaires completed by 250 soil experts from all over the world. They recorded information on the degree of soil degradation, its extent, type, cause and rate. The need to take account of the persistence of desertification was then acknowledged; unfortunately the data concerning rates of change were omitted from the data set because of the ambiguity of replies. But do the published maps and statistics provide an objective analysis of the problem or do they merely reinforce existing perceptions? How much faith can we place in these mapped boundaries based on questionnaire replies?

Drought also needs to be more carefully scrutinized. Gordon (1993) saw drought as being concerned only with rainfall, while Druyan (1989) considered solely climatological causes. Yet a drought is caused by a shortage of water, which can occur either as a result of a reduction in supply, an increase in demand or both. Most analyses of drought in the Sahel only consider rainfall, i.e. a meteorological drought. This is a statistical exercise that establishes what is abnormal and then identifies drought when rainfall is below this amount. Figure 12.5 reveals that Sahelian rainfall stations have not all displayed a uniform decline since the 1960s. The horizontal lines in this figure indicate rainfall at 80% of the mean which can be taken as a drought threshold. These data show the variability of

drought occasions. Agnew (1990) has indicated the spatial variability of meteorological drought, but such analysis ignores two fundamental problems.

Firstly, in such a variable environment how can 'normal' be established? For example, Figure 12.3 shows that flows in the River Senegal have been persistently below the long-term average (1904–87) since the 1970s. If the average is calculated (Figure 12.6) between 1970 and 1987 a different interpretation may be reached, with an above-average wetter period followed by a return to 'normal' flows in the 1970s and 1980s. The dilemma faced with such a poor data base across the Sahel is how to establish a suitable time period over which to compute comparable averages and departures from them.

Secondly, there is no universal definition of drought (Agnew, 1989) but definitions abound for meteorological (rainfall), hydrological (surface flows, lake levels and groundwater levels) and agricultural (crop and livestock water supplies) droughts. It is unlikely that human activities in the Sahel have evolved around average conditions. It is more likely that extreme events are significant and that each land-use system has developed its own complex strategies in response. Investigations of drought need to accept that different human activities will have different drought tolerances. Given the same rainfall, maize drought is more likely than a millet drought because of the different crop water requirements. Hence, a switch from millet to maize could increase the incidence of drought, even without a change in climate. Agricultural drought could then result from land-use changes, exacerbated by meteorological drought. Investigations of water supplies for millet growth have suggested that 'agricultural drought' is not as frequent as claimed in southern parts of the Sahel, but is prevalent further north in the marginal lands where 'meteorological drought' has been reported (Agnew, 1991a; Bley et al., 1991). That is, agricultural drought is occurring because of occupation of marginal lands for cultivation, possibly through population pressure, a point discussed below.

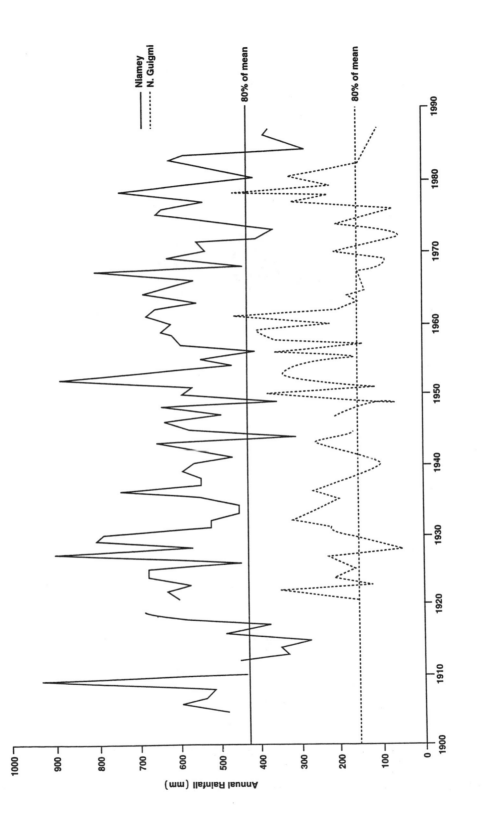

Figure 12.5 *Rainfall at two stations in Niger with 80% mean annual rainfall plotted as a drought threshold*

145

Development and mismanagement

The recent experiences of Ethiopia and Sudan have suggested that environmental constraints are not the sole influence on human activities in the Sahel, with political instability, warfare and economic disruption of equal significance (Agnew and O'Connor, 1991). It has been noted by many that it is all too easy to blame the physical environment in marginal lands (Agnew, 1991b;

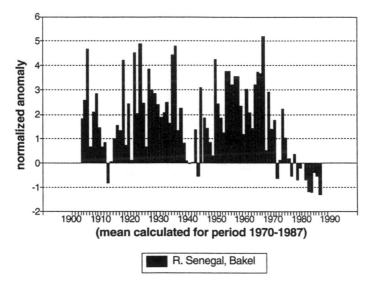

Figure 12.6 *Normalized departures ((x − x^t)/s^t), where* t *is the time period 1970–87), of River Senegal discharges at Bakel*

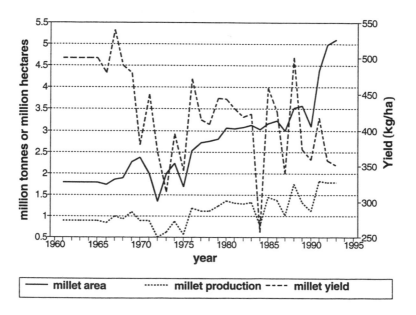

Figure 12.7 *Millet production and yields in Niger. Source: annual publication of* FAO Quarterly Bulletin of Statistics

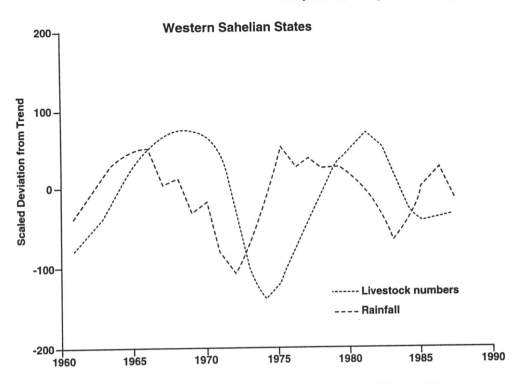

Figure 12.8 *Changes in livestock numbers and rainfall in the Sahel, after IUCN (1989)*

Garcia, 1981; Glantz, 1987; Gritzner, 1988; Wijkman and Timberlake, 1985). The Sahelian economies have increasingly been exposed to the outside world and this has had effects beyond those caused by 20 years of below-average rainfall.

Most Sahelian countries can be listed among the 20 poorest nations of the world. The total amount of debt is smaller than that faced by Latin American countries, e.g. Brazil and Mexico (Grove, 1990), but it is still a serious impediment to development. Warren and Khogali (1992) report that many Sahelian countries have debts greater than their GDP, and that in 1986 the IMF took out US$ 1 billion more than it put into Africa. Between 1980 and 1985 only Senegal, Chad and Somalia experienced economic growth greater than 3%, and most of the Sahel suffered a decline. Sahelian states have tried to improve their economic growth through developing cash crops and livestock herds and by adopting irrigation. The drilling of deep boreholes and improvements in veterinary care, following good rainfall in the

1960s, led (it is believed) to significant overstocking of the rangelands. Franke and Chasin (1980) see the adoption of cash crops at the expense of food crops as a major reason for the impoverishment of soils and the increase in famine. Timberlake (1985) notes that this has been recognized by Sahelian governments, who acknowledge the need for self-sufficiency in food supplies, yet very little aid has gone into such programmes.

The general decline in crop yields since the 1970s can be seen for Niger in Figure 12.7, and the effects of drought in the early 1970s and 1980s are apparent. Agricultural production has, however, increased in the Sahel over the last 20 years, mostly through increasing areas under cultivation (Reardon, 1993). Figure 12.8 shows that livestock herds have been affected by rainfall but following droughts in the 1970s and 1980s herds were re-established. Swift (1984) examined livestock herds in Niger following drought, and found that pastoral survival strategies, particularly migration, enabled herds to be maintained. Claims that agricultural and livestock production systems have been overwhelmed are often gross exaggerations. Clearly, environmental constraints do affect agricultural activities, and fluctuations in production are to be expected. But a more significant environmental threat would appear to be posed by population growth. Reardon expressed concern that the potential for increasing production of staple crops such as millet and sorghum is now poor as most of the usable land is already cultivated. Decline in yields is therefore related to falling soil fertility, due to shortening fallow periods, and the increasing use of marginal lands. With expanding human populations, the goal of self-sufficiency appears over-optimistic.

Conclusion

Drought, desertification and development are closely bound together. Population growth and attempts to improve agricultural production have increased pressures on the land. Increasing use of marginal lands and intensification of agriculture have worsened soil conditions and may have increased the occurrence of agricultural droughts. Desertification in turn may affect rainfall and has focused international attention on the need to achieve sustainable development in these marginal lands. With such complex linkages, and causal factors operating at local, regional and international levels, embracing both environmental and economic systems, it is no wonder that confusion abounds. This confusion is exacerbated by the poor monitoring of environmental conditions and the treatment of the Sahel as a homogeneous entity. It is not. The Sahel extends some 6000 km west to east (an equivalent distance is London to Khartoum), encompassing many cultures, agricultural activities and environments. We would do well to remember the words of Gilbert White: 'No two points of the arid zone are alike in all respects . . . generalities about arid lands are to be approached with . . . caution' (in Kates and Burton, 1986, p. 127). This has been reiterated more recently by Nicholson and Palao (1993,

p. 386) who commented that 'the entire Sahel cannot be treated as homogeneous with respect to rainfall variability' and they proceeded to identify three distinct regions: West coast, Sahel, and Guinea coast on the basis of rainfall trends and variability.

It is also useful to distinguish between an *environmental change* (concerning monitoring and analysing physical systems) and an *environmental problem*. The latter concerns the impacts of the environment upon people, and the impacts of people upon the environment. An 'environmental problem' is thus a cultural construct, and cannot be divorced from the particular human activity system under investigation. We are increasingly aware that drought and desertification affect humans in a variety of ways and the threshold at which environmental problems occur differs. We need to know more about the changing relationships between people and their environment in the Sahel. After a century of study by Western scholars we still know surprisingly little about this region and its peoples.

References

Agnew, C. T. (1989) Sahel drought, meterological or agricultural? *International Journal of Climatology*, 9, 371–382.

Agnew, C. T. (1990) Spatial aspects of drought in the Sahel, *Journal of Arid Environments*, 18, 279–293.

Agnew, C. T. (1991a) Evaluation of a soil water balance model for the analysis of agricultural drought in the Sahel, pp. 583–592 in M. V. K. Sivakumar *et al.* (eds), *Proceedings of Workshop on Soil Water Balance in the Sudano Sahelian zone*, 18–23 February, IAHS Publication 199, Wallingford.

Agnew, C. T. (1991b) Disaster in the arid realm, pp. 56–79 in F. Slater (ed.), *Societies, Choices and Environments*, Collins Educational, London.

Agnew, C. T. and O'Connor, A. M. (1991) The meteorological scapegoat, *Geographical Analysis*, Sept., 1–4.

Agnew, C. T. and Warren, A. (1993) The sand trap, pp. 517–525 in J. Hatton and P. B. Plouffe (eds), *The Culture of Science*, Macmillan, New York.

Ahlcrona, E. (1988) The impact of climate and man on land transformation in central Sudan, *Applications of Remote Sensing*, Meddelanden fran Lunds Universitets Geografiska Institutioner, Avhandlinger, 103, 140 pp.

Binns, T. (1990) Is desertification a myth? *Geography*, 75, 106–113.

Bley, J., Ploeg, R. R., Sivakumar, M. V. K. and Allison, B. E. (1991) A risk probability map for millet production in southwest Niger, pp. 571–581 in M. V. K. Sivakumar *et al.* (eds), *Proceedings of Workshop on Soil Water Balance in the Sudano Sahelian zone*, 18–23 February, IAHS Publication 199, Wallingford.

Cardy, F. (1993) Desertification—a fresh approach, *Desertification Control Bulletin*, 22, 4–8.

Charney, J. and Stone, P. (1974) Drought in the Sahel: biogeophysical feedback mechanism, *Science*, 187, 434–435.

Collins, C. (1993) Famine defeated, *African Recovery*, 9, 1–12.

Cooke, R. U., Warren, A. and Goudie, A. (1993) *Desert Geomorphology*, UCL Press, London.

Copans, J. (1983) The Sahelian drought: social science and the political economy for underdevelopment, pp. 83–97 in K. Hewitt (ed.), *Interpretations of Calamity*, Allen & Unwin, London.

Druyan, L. M. (1989) Advances in the study of sub-saharan drought, *International Journal of Climatology*, 9, 77–90.

Franke, F. and Chasin, B. (1980) *Seeds of Famine*, Allanheld, Osman & Co., New Jersey.

Garcia, R. V. (1981) *Drought and Man:* Volume 1: *Nature Pleads Not Guilty*, Pergamon, Oxford, 300 pp.

Glantz, M. (ed.) (1987) *Drought and Hunger in Africa*, Cambridge University Press.

Gordon, A. H. (1993) The random nature of drought: mathematical and physical causes, *International Journal of Climatology*, 13, 497–507.

Grainger, A. (1990) *The Threatening Desert*, Earthscan, London.

Gritzner, J. A. (1988) *The West African Sahel: human agency and environmental change*, Geography Research Paper 226, University of Chicago.

Grove, A. T. (1990) *The Changing Geography of Africa*, Oxford University Press.

Hulme, M. and Kelly, M. (1993) Desertification and climate change, *Environment*, 35(6), 5–11, 39–45.

IUCN (International Union for Conservation of Nature) (1989) *Sahel Studies*, IUCN, Nairobi.

Kates, R. W. and Burton, I. (eds) (1986) *Geography, Resources and Environment: the selected writings of Gilbert White*, University of Chicago Press.

Lamprey, H. F. (1975) *Report on the Desert Encroachment Reconnaissance in Northern Sudan*, UNESCO/UNEP Consultant Report, Paris.

Mainguet, M. (1991) *Desertification: natural background and human mismanagement*, Springer-Verlag, Berlin.

Middleton, N. (1991) *Desertification*, Oxford University Press.

Nicholson, S. E. and Palao, I. M. (1993) A re-evaluation of rainfall variability in the Sahel, *International Journal of Climatology*, 13, 371–389.

Odingo, R. S. (1992) Implementation of the plan of action to combat desertification (PACD) 1978–1991, *Desertification Control Bulletin*, 21, 6–14.

Otterman, J. (1974) Baring high albedo soils by overgrazing, *Science*, 186, 531–533.

Pritchard, J. M. (1990) *Africa*, Longman, Harlow.

Rasmusson, E. M. (1987) Global climate change and variability: effects on drought and desertification in Africa, pp. 3–22 in M. Glantz (ed.), *Drought and Hunger in Africa*, Cambridge University Press.

Reardon, T. (1993) Cereals demand in the Sahel and potential impacts of regional cereals protection, *World Development*, 21(1), 17–35.

Swift, J. (1984) *Pastoral Development in Central Niger*, Report of the Niger Range and Livestock Project, Ministère du Developpement Rural, Niger.

Thomas, D. G. (1993) Sandstorm in a teacup? Understanding desertification, *Geographical Journal*, 159(3), 318–331.

Tickell, C. (1986) Drought in Africa: impact and response, *Overseas Development*, 102, 10.

Timberlake, L. (1985) *Africa in Crisis*, Earthscan, London.

Toulmin, C. (1993) *Combating Desertification: setting the agenda for a global convention*, International Institute for Environment and Development Paper 42, London.

UNCED (United Nations Conference on Environment and Development) (1992) *Earth Summit, Rio de Janeiro*, Regency Press, London.

UNEP (United Nations Environment Programme) (1992) *World Atlas of Desertification*, Edward Arnold, London, 69 pp.

Warren, A. and Agnew, C. (1988) *An Assessment of Desertification and Land Degradation in Arid and Semi Arid Areas*, International Institute for Environment and Development, Paper 2, 30 pp.

Warren, A. and Khogali, M. (1992) *Assessment of Desertification and Drought in the Sudano-Sahelian Region 1985–1991*, UNSO, New York.

Wijkman, A. and Timberlake, L. (1985) Is the African drought an act of God or of Man? *Ecologist*, 15(1/2), 9–18.

Wilhite, D. (1993) Editorial, *Drought Network News*, 6(1) 1–4.

13

Livestock market data as an early warning indicator of stress in the pastoral economy[1]

Ced Hesse

Introduction

Two observations can be drawn about the 1983–84 famine in the Sahel. First, pastoral people were the major victims. Second, conventional early warning systems used by governments and international agencies failed to trigger the desired responses, either in sufficient time or with the necessary spatial precision, to avert the crisis (see de Waal; Walker, 1989 for a description of early warning systems, their objectives and failings). This failure had especially severe consequences for pastoral groups.

There are two reasons explaining the marginalization of the pastoral sector within government and international agency early warning systems. First, these early warning systems focused on the monitoring of rainfall and the evolution of the agricultural season, with only limited attention paid to production determinants of the pastoral sector (e.g. condition of livestock, availability of pasture and water). Second, these early warning systems only addressed one aspect of food acquisition, that of agricultural production. They failed to take into account, on the one hand, other

social, political and economic factors related to food acquisition (food prices and availability, purchasing power, employment opportunities, capital resources) which are of equal, if not greater, importance in the chain of events leading to famine; and on the other hand, those populations who rely to a great extent on systems of barter or market exchange for the acquisition of food which they themselves do not produce.

Following the drought of the mid-1980s, a number of aid and research organizations in Mali (the Famine Early Warning System funded by USAID, the SCF/UK-funded Suivi Alimentaire Delta-Seno project, Oxfam) invested in the business of predicting famines before they occur. Their approach lay in monitoring, in addition to meteorological and agro-meteorological conditions, certain economic, social and nutritional phenomena—cereal and animal prices, livestock supply and demand profiles, population movements, sale of capital assets, malnutrition and the consumption of famine foods. It was argued that the inclusion of socio-economic data would serve as proxy indicators of stress not only in advance of the crisis, but also with sufficient

People and Environment in Africa. Edited by Tony Binns
©1995 John Wiley & Sons Ltd

spatial precision to allow more timely and well-targeted intervention. It was further argued that much of these data were already available, since it was routinely collected by the government ministries of agriculture, health, animal husbandry, etc.

The aim of this chapter is to test whether one of these proxy indicators, livestock market data, can be used as an early warning indicator of stress in the pastoral economies of the Sahel. Data collected by ODEM (Opération de Développement d'Elevage dans la Région de Mopti) livestock agents at Douentza market over 1980–86, the period covering the most recent drought, are used to test this hypothesis. Douentza is an important

market town in northern Mali (Figure 13.1) attracting international livestock traders from Niger, Nigeria, Burkina Faso and Ivory Coast. A series of economic and political disturbances during 1984 (Nigeria closing its frontiers, the European Union dumping subsidized beef in Ivory Coast and a border dispute with Burkina Faso) diminished the presence of these traders.

The analysis addresses three questions of importance concerning the validity of an early warning system using livestock market data as one of its indicators:

1. Is it possible by collecting and analysing livestock market data to recognize both normal

Figure 13.1 *Mali*

2. Is it possible to identify well-defined moments of change or 'break-points' between changing livestock marketing patterns? Sudden deviations from the norm are of great interest since they could represent useful early warning of changing conditions and thus act as triggers for action.

3. Do moments of sudden change or 'break-points' in fact announce a sustained deviation from a previous trend sufficiently in advance of the former reaching its conclusion? This is crucial to proving the worth of an early warning indicator, and its ability to give advance warning of an impending crisis.

The theory: stages in the evolution of a pastoral famine

One indicator of stress in a pastoral economy is believed to be the behaviour of the livestock market. The market represents to herders the major medium through which they can acquire cereals which they themselves do not necessarily produce, in return for selling livestock and livestock products such as milk, hides, etc. Herders are therefore vulnerable to fluctuating terms of exchange between the livestock products they offer and the food products they desire. In good years, the terms of trade between livestock and cereal are to the herders' advantage, but this situation is rapidly reversed under conditions of drought.

Jeremy Swift (n.d.) has argued that there are three stages to a pastoral famine which can affect market behaviour, though these stages are in turn complicated by seasonal price movements.

Stage one: Pre-famine

Poor rains lead to low crop and pasture production, thus raising post-harvest cereal prices as farmers conserve limited stocks. Since cereals are costly and livestock prices depressed, herders have to sell more animals then usual to acquire grain. In the first year of drought, however, most herders would have sufficient animals to maintain their optimum sales strategy of selling mature steers (castrated males)—the category of animal most commonly destined for sale.

Stage two: famine

Poor rains continue, resulting in further bad harvests and poor pasture yields, reduced milk production, low rates of animal reproduction and increased livestock deaths. Consequently, grain prices continue to rise while livestock prices plunge. Herders, whose dependence on cereals has increased due to reduced milk availability, are having to sell more animals at lower prices to obtain a fixed quantity of grain. Sahelian herd structures, however, are unable to cope with these increased sales, especially with the added constraint of increased livestock deaths. Herders, therefore, are forced into distress sales of younger and younger males, young females, and eventually reproductive stock, as their herds are progressively depleted. Markets are flooded with animals, often in poor condition, and, since supply far exceeds demand, livestock prices finally collapse, thus destroying herders' purchasing power and their ability to buy food.

Stage three: Post-famine

Good rains result in better crop and pasture production. Cereal prices drop and livestock prices rise sharply as animals, in short supply and better condition, are in great demand. The price of reproductive female stock is especially high as herders seek to reconstitute their herds. Those herders with surviving animals are able to profit from high livestock prices and low cereal prices to purchase the grain they need with a minimum of animal sales, thus further limiting livestock supply. Those herders with few or no animals continue to experience difficulty in procuring food and thus remain vulnerable to droughts for many years.

The above hypothesis indicates six changes in livestock marketing patterns during the early, late and post-drought periods. These changes can serve as early warning indicators.

1. *During the drought*
   (a) An increase in the number of animals presented for sale which rises sharply when stress becomes acute.
   (b) The age and sex composition of animals presented for sale changes from steers to younger and younger males, and, as conditions worsen, to young females and finally reproductive stock.
   (c) Animal prices drop and then collapse.
   (d) The ratio of animals presented for sale to actual sales increases, and then accelerates as the market is flooded and sellers fail to find buyers.
2. *Post-drought*
   (a) Animal prices rise sharply especially for reproductive stock.
   (b) There is a drop in the number of animals presented for sale, especially reproductive stock.

Predictable seasonal marketing profiles

In normal, drought-free years Sahelian livestock marketing profiles follow seasonal trends. These need to be understood before analysing the effects of drought on marketing trends.

Price profiles

Animal prices typically follow the following seasonal trends in drought-free years.

Post-harvest/cold season (October–March)

Livestock prices rise after the harvest in October and peak at the end of the cold season in February/March. This is for several reasons:

● Animals have benefitted from the improved environmental conditions during the rainy season.
● Farmers are able to invest money from surplus grain sales in the purchase of livestock.
● Livestock merchants from large urban centres and other countries profit from the good environmental conditions and buy livestock, driving them to more profitable markets.
● Cereal prices are low and thus herders are not forced to liquidate their animals for the purchase of food.

Hot and rainy season April—September

Livestock prices fall during the hot season and then stabilize during the rains for the following reasons:

● Environmental conditions deteriorate, thus impairing animal health and body weight which discourages investment by potential buyers. This is particularly acute at the onset of the rains when animals, weak after the rigours of the dry season, are especially susceptible to the diseases and illnesses that abound at this time of the year.
● During the hot season herders increasingly need to sell their animals to purchase food, but since cereals are expensive and potential investors scarce, livestock prices decline as sellers fail to find willing buyers.
● During the rains, as herders' milk supply increases and herds undertake wet season transhumance which distances them from market centres, the supply of livestock on the market declines, thus discouraging investors and thereby maintaining low animal prices.
● During the rains, and especially the 'hungry season' (July–September), when food supplies are short before the harvest, potential investors (farmers, traders) often lack the resources or time to buy livestock.

Figure 13.2 depicts hypothetical livestock price profile based on the above observations.

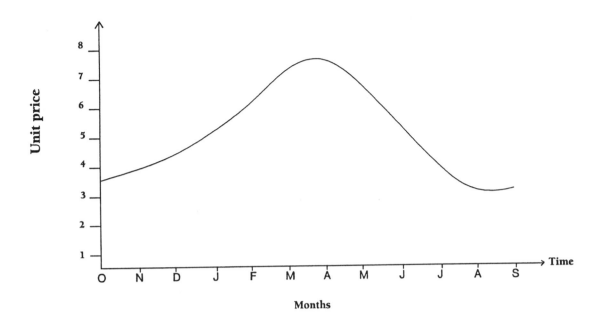

Figure 13.2 *Hypothetical livestock price profile in 'normal' years*

Monitoring changes to 'normal' seasonal prices and supply and demand profiles could, in theory, provide evidence of abnormal conditions such as drought.

Supply and demand profiles

In order to be able to interpret the data correctly, seasonal shifts in livestock availability have to be understood. Under 'normal' drought-free conditions, the following seasonal livestock supply and demand profiles might be anticipated.

Post-harvest/cold season (October–March)

The number of livestock presented and sold gradually increases, with actual sales representing a high proportion of the number of animals presented. This is for several reasons:

● Herders profit from high livestock prices and low cereal prices to sell one or two prime animals to cover household subsistence needs. Livestock supply is thus fairly controlled.

● Potential investors wish to purchase animals due to their good condition, and to profit from the environmental conditions which will allow their transport. Livestock demand is thus high.

Hot season (April–June)

The supply of livestock rises while demand decreases. The main reasons are as follows:

● As milk availability declines, so herders become increasingly dependent on cereals for their food, and are thus obliged to sell animals.

● Potential investors either lack the resources or are not prepared to risk purchasing animals during this critical period of the year.

Rainy season (July–September)

The supply of livestock declines for several reasons:

● As milk production increases with the improved environmental conditions, herders are less obliged to sell livestock to purchase food.

155

- Herders start wet season transhumance which distances them from market centres.
- Potential investors often need all the available resources to face the 'hungry season'.

Figure 13.3 portrays a hypothetical livestock supply and demand profile during normal years based on the above observations.

The data base

Data available to test whether Malian pastoralists showed the expected responses to drought are of two kinds:

1. The average monthly price of heifers and steers in CFA francs (roughly £1 to 500 CFA) sold at Douentza market between April 1980 and October 1986.
2. The average number of cattle presented and sold at Douentza market between January 1980 and October 1986. Unfortunately, the ODEM monthly livestock reports do not break down the supply and demand of livestock by age/sex categories.

The importance of this data base is that it spans the years of the most recent Sahelian drought, and the following two seasons of relatively good rainfall in 1985 and 1986.

Observed marketing trends

Price profiles

Figure 13.4 shows the average monthly price in CFA francs of heifers and steers at Douentza market from April 1980 to October 1986. The price profiles of both categories of livestock generally follow a similar pattern, although greater seasonal variations in the price of steers may be observed. Figure 13.4 reveals two trends: an interannual pattern and a seasonal pattern (i.e. intra-annual).

Interannual

Both livestock categories show a price increase during 1981 and peaking in April 1982, when prices of heifers and steers had risen to the extent

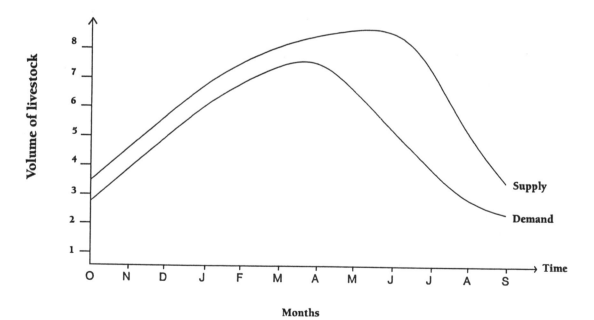

Figure 13.3 *Hypothetical livestock supply and demand profile in 'normal' years*

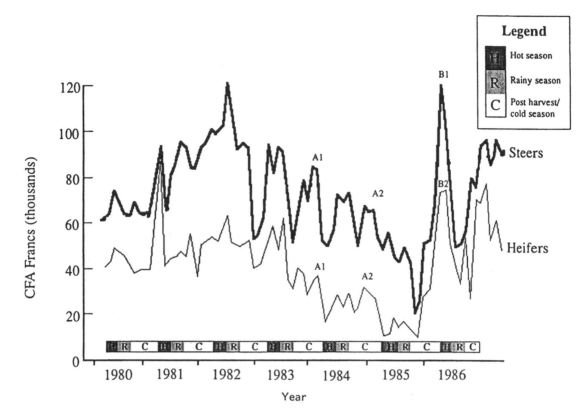

Figure 13.4 *Douentza livestock market 1980–86, monthly price of heifers and steers*

of 50 and 80% respectively. Prices then underwent a gradual, but marked, decline from May 1982 until May/June 1985 (three years)—the value of heifers and steers fell over this period by 82 and 80% respectively. Livestock prices then rapidly increased during 1985, and to a lesser extent in 1986, to regain their 1981 values.

The long-term price trend indicates a pre-drought period of high animal prices followed by a significant decrease in livestock value during the drought years of 1982–1984, and then a price revival with the better rains of 1985 and 1986.

Seasonal

From 1981 to the hot season of 1983, the prices of livestock generally followed anticipated seasonal trends. The price trend for heifers and steers, from March 1983 to June 1985, underwent a gradual

but prolonged decline. This period corresponds to the drought years of 1983–84, thus indicating that livestock prices are sensitive to changing environmental conditions, which is further reinforced by the rapid rise in the value of livestock following the improved wet season of 1985.

However, subsequent fluctuations in the price of livestock from October/November 1985 to June/July 1986 are unexpected. One would have anticipated high prices, particularly for reproductive stock, as a result of improved environmental conditions, and an increased demand for livestock.

Furthermore, there are several instances of unusual seasonal price trends among steers, in particular between March 1983 and May 1985. For instance, prices rose between May 1983 and October 1983, and then plunged from

October 1983 to December 1983. More significantly, the price of steers began to fall from September 1984 until May 1985—a period of the year when prices should normally rise.

With the advantage of hindsight, Figure 13.4 does indicate the passage and end of the 1983–85 drought. The figure shows, on the one hand, the rapid depression of livestock value from the hot season of 1983, through 1984 and the dry season of 1985; and, on the other hand, the sharp price rises during the rainy season of 1985 which announced the end of the drought period.

Figure 13.4, furthermore, suggests break-points (represented as points A1 and A2) when livestock price patterns deviated to follow an unexpected trend. Points A1 and A2 show a marked decline in the price of livestock at the start of the cold season in October/November 1983 and 1984, respectively, when under 'normal' conditions a price increase would have been expected. In retrospect, these points could be regarded as specific indicators giving an early warning of deteriorating conditions. This theory, however, does not hold true if point B1 is considered, because the latter announces a similar depression in livestock price, also during the cold season, but following what is considered to have been a good rainy season.

The extent to which these livestock price data either could have been used to give an early warning of drought, or be exploited as baseline data for the future early warning of stress in the pastoral economy is questionable. In theory, it could have been possible to announce unusual price trends in the cold season of 1983 and 1984 (points A1 and A2), and thereby give up to six months' early warning of a collapse of livestock prices. However, since these price trends were preceded by equally unusual price patterns in the rainy season of 1983 and 1984, when livestock prices suddenly rose in what was considered to be the worse drought in the Sahel since records began, the question has to be asked whether at the time any credence would have been given to this data?

Supply and demand profiles

Figure 13.5 depicts the average monthly number of cattle presented and sold at Douentza market from January 1980 to October 1986. The supply and demand profiles can be examined both at a general interannual level, and at a more specific seasonal level.

Interannual trends

If the great seasonal variations in the number of animals presented and sold are disregarded, it is possible to identify two marketing trends. First, a gradual increase in the number of animals presented for sale with a corresponding decline in actual animal sales from late 1981 till the hot season of 1985. Second, a marked decline in the number of livestock presented for sale, with a corresponding increase in the number of animals bought, from the hot season of 1985 until the end of the rains in 1986.

This pattern corroborates the theory that as environmental conditions worsen so herders seek to sell their animals, but fail to find buyers. And as conditions improve, the number of animals presented for sale decreases, while demand increases.

Seasonal trends

When livestock supply and demand trends are analysed on a more detailed seasonal level it is more difficult to establish consistent patterns. Table 13.1 presents a summary of the seasonal patterns of livestock supply and demand interpreted in the light of the hypothetical trends outlined above.

In summary, the supply and demand profiles, although indicating in general the passage and end of a series of drought years, do not give a very clear and definite image of seasonal trends. Therefore, while such data might be used to confirm retrospectively favourable and unfavourable environmental conditions, they fail to provide the fine and consistent detail needed if they are to be used as an early warning indicator.

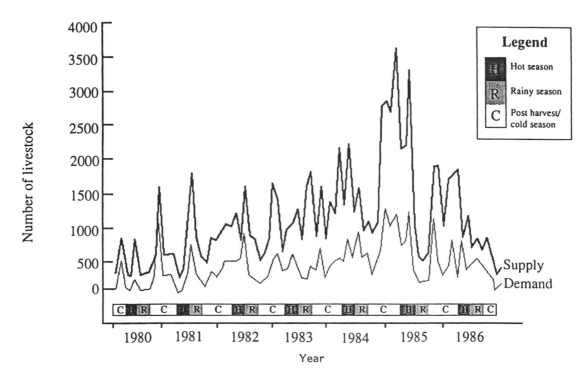

Figure 13.5 *Douentza livestock market 1980–86, monthly supply and demand of livestock*

Rather the data tend to confirm known conditions than to provide an early warning of deteriorating conditions to come.

Conclusion

The data presented and analysed in this chapter do not give a clear and consistent image of livestock marketing patterns. Although general interannual trends do seem to indicate anticipated livestock marketing profiles under 'normal' and drought conditions, it is more difficult to identify consistent seasonal patterns. Furthermore, due to great seasonal fluctuations in marketing trends it has not been possible to identify well-defined and consistent moments of change, or break-points, which herald sustained deviations from a previously established pattern.

Explanations may be advanced for this failure. First, that aggregate livestock marketing data are not sufficiently sensitive to identify early signs of stress, and that it is only when the problem is well established that it becomes apparent at the market-place. If this is the case then livestock marketing data can only be used to confirm existing conditions, and cannot serve as an early warning indicator of stress in pastoral economies.

Second, that the quality of the data is suspect, and bears little resemblance to actual livestock marketing characteristics. If this is the case then the premise that early warning systems can be based on existing data sets need to be reviewed closely.

Third, that the market at Douentza is not a major centre of exchange for herders and, therefore, would fail to identify conditions of stress in the pastoral economy.

The main purpose of this chapter has been to use the Douentza example to provoke thought and comment on the question of validity of early warning indicators. It seems obvious that one

Table 13.1 *Seasonal pattern of livestock supply and demand profiles at Douentza market (January to October 1986)*

Season	Supply and demand profile
1. 1980 rainy season	Supply and demand rise sharply with actual sales accounting for most presentations. This is an unusual pattern for a non-drought year
2. 1980/81 cold season	Supply and demand drop. This is unusual for a non-drought year
3. 1981 hot season	Supply and demand rose sharply although relative sales decline. This is an unexpected trend in a 'normal' year
4. 1981 rainy season	Supply and demand diminish which, although premature, is an anticipated trend in a 'normal' year
5. 1981/82 late rains/ cold season	Supply and demand rise progressively over the cold season to peak in April, and although relative sales especially during the cold season are low, it is an expected trend for a 'normal' year
6. 1982 hot season/early rains	Supply and demand drop. Under 'normal' conditions, demands should diminish and supply continue at a high level for a few more months
7. 1982 rainy season	Contrary to expectations, supply rises sharply while demand, as expected, drops slightly
8. 1982/83 cold season	Supply and to a lesser extent demand rises as expected
9. 1983 hot season	There is a sharp increase in supply with a comparative decline in the number of sales which is to be anticipated in 'normal' years. The magnitude of the difference between presentations and actual sales might be indicative of the drought conditions of 1983
10. 1983/4 cold season	Supply of livestock rises sharply while demand is comparatively low. Low demand is unusual for normal years, but might be indicative of a drought year
11. 1984 hot season/ early rains	Supply decreases rapidly while demand shows a comparative increase. This is an unusual trend to witness in what is considered to be the second year of the drought
12. 1984/85 rainy and cold seasons	Very sharp supply increase with a marked comparative demand decline. This is an anticipated trend for a drought year
13. 1985 hot season	Very sharp supply decline with relative demand increase. Under drought conditions a sustained livestock supply with limited demand would be anticipated
14. 1985 rains/early cold season	Increased supply and demand. While an increased demand is to be expected following the good rains of 1985, one would expect a corresponding decline in number of livestock presented for sale
15. 1986 cold, hot and rainy seasons	Gradual decline of livestock supply with high relative demand. This is in keeping with supply and demand trends following a drought

cannot interpret livestock marketing data in relation to broader trends without a high-quality database, and a detailed knowledge of the internal mechanisms of local marketing conditions. It is also important to recognize the role that national and international economics play in determining local marketing conditions. During the drought, for example, Niger prohibited movements of grain into eastern Mali; Nigeria closed its border in 1984; Ivory Coast switched its beef imports from Sahelian countries to subsidized EU and Argentine produce; and there was a war between Burkina Faso and Mali in 1985. Any of these external factors may well have influenced marketing behaviour in a significant, but unknown, way. Furthermore, there are still many outstanding questions regarding how to ensure given indicators are indeed valid. For example, how easy is it to collect good quality data and how long can money be spent on its collection during non-drought years when they do not serve to indicate deteriorating conditions necessitating an emergency response? Just how much of an early warning can they give? And just how sensitive are they in identifying moments of stress which are not drought induced? One is forced to conclude that much work is required in learning how to acquire and interpret early warning indicators of stress in the pastoral economy.

Note

1. This chapter is adapted from a paper originally presented at the Oxfam Arid Lands Management workshop, Cotonou, Benin (23–27 March 1987),

and subsequently published as an ODI Pastoral Development Network paper, August 1987.

References

Curry, B. *Famine Forecasting: fourteen fallacies*, undated discussion paper, Oxford Food Studies Group, Oxford.

Cutler, P. (1985) *The Use of Socio-economic and Social Information in Famine Prediction and Response*, Report to the ODA, No. R3779.

De Waal, A. (1988) Famine early warning systems and the use of socio-economic data, *Disasters*, 12, 81–91.

Swift, J. *Notes on a Sahelian Pastoral Famine Early Warning System*, undated discussion paper.

Walker, P. (1989) *Famine early warning systems: victims and destitution*, Earthscan Publications Ltd., London.

14

Local agro-ecological management and forest–savanna transitions: the case of Kissidougou, Guinea

James Fairhead and Melissa Leach

Introduction

West Africa's forest–savanna transition zone, lying between the Guinea savanna zone to the north and the tropical humid forest zone to the south, presents a striking picture of dense semi-deciduous rainforest patches in an otherwise generally grassy savanna landscape. There has been considerable ecological debate as to this vegetation mosaic's origins and evolution. In Kissidougou prefecture of Guinea (Figure 14.1) this issue is more than academic, since interpretations of forest–savanna transitions orientate attitudes towards local land use and policies designed to influence it.

One view, predominant among Kissidougou's policy-makers, considers the patches of forest found as islands around villages and strips of streamside gallery forest to be relics of an original, and formerly much more extensive, dense humid forest cover (e.g. Aubréville, 1949). It is suggested that inhabitants have progressively converted forest to 'derived' savanna by their shifting cultivation and fire-setting practices. Climate[1] and the presence of humid forest

species and associations are taken as indicative of high forest potential and hence of its past existence.

Many ecologists would now dispute this view, considering the forest–savanna mosaic as a more stable vegetation pattern principally reflecting edaphic differences: in a zone climatically marginal for forest, only certain soils and sites can support it (e.g. Morgan and Moss, 1965). This view presents local agro-ecological practices less as destructive and more as adaptive, working with and conserving the diversity of vegetation types in the mosaic. This second argument, for vegetation stability, has itself been modified for the West African region in the light of evidence of forest advance into savanna, the lagging legacy of long-term climatic rehumidification (Avenard *et al.*, 1974).[2] But while assorted ecological processes are found to mediate this effect of climate change on forest–savanna boundary dynamics—such as changing termite activity, soil conditions and fire patterns (e.g. papers in Furley *et al.*, 1992)—no attention has been given to the possible role of inhabitants' management practices in forest advance.[3]

People and Environment in Africa. Edited by Tony Binns
©1995 John Wiley & Sons Ltd

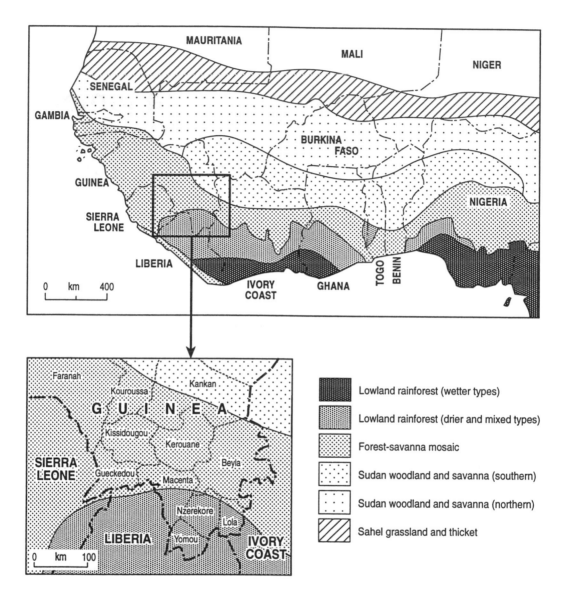

Figure 14.1 *Kissidougou prefecture in the forest–savanna mosaic zone of West Africa. Based on the UNESCO/ AEFTAT/UNSO vegetation map of Africa*

This chapter examines how people work with and manage processes involving soil, fire, grazing, grass and tree species in meeting their livelihood needs, encouraging the formation of forest vegetation in savanna. In Kissidougou prefecture, this applies to both the establishment of high forest patches, and the upgrading of savanna fallows to secondary forest ones (cf. Fairhead and Leach *et al.*, 1992; Leach and Fairhead, 1993).

Forest islands

Far from being relics of a past forest cover, the forest islands which surround Kissidougou's 800 or so villages have been encouraged to form in savanna by their inhabitants. These forests provide villagers with protection from bush fires, high winds and excessive heat; with convenient sources of forest products; with shelter for tree crops; with military defence and with secrecy for ritual activity. Kissi and Kuranko elders describe how their ancestors encouraged forest patch formation around settlements which had been founded either in savanna or beside gallery forests. This same process is at work today around recently established villages, and the growth of forest islands can be seen when comparing modern air photographs with those from 1952 (Figure 14.2).

Forest island development is encouraged more or less deliberately in the course of everyday life,

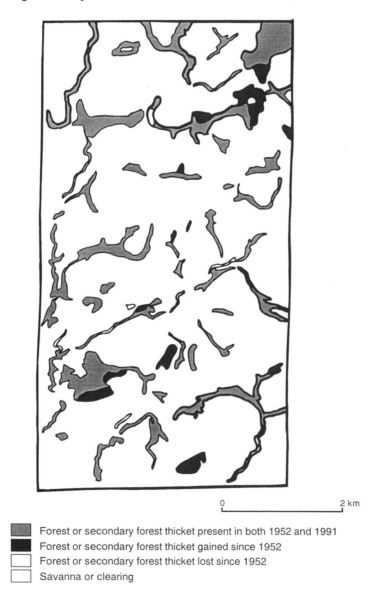

0   2 km

▨ Forest or secondary forest thicket present in both 1952 and 1991
■ Forest or secondary forest thicket gained since 1952
☐ Forest or secondary forest thicket lost since 1952
☐ Savanna or clearing

Figure 14.2 *Comparison of 1952 and 1991 aerial photographs to show the formation of forest islands, north-east Kissidougou*

occasionally by tree planting, but principally by creating the fire and soil conditions which favour forest development. Villagers prevent annual savanna fires destroying their settlement by creating a fire-break, through everyday activities which reduce the quantity of inflammable grasses on the village margins. They collect thatch and fencing grass there, and tether their cattle, whose grazing diminishes grass levels, during the farming season. They burn grasses which remain there early in the dry season, further reducing the fuel available for more threatening late-season fires. Thus protected, village-edge areas develop dense semi-deciduous moist forest vegetation over the years and as the island of forest expands, grass collection and grazing are gradually moved further out.

Farmers have sometimes encouraged forest establishment by regularly cultivating the margins, which, they explain, 'opens' and 'matures' the soil there. This improves water infiltration and storage, and creates soils in which trees more easily establish and grow. Sometimes cultivation is for only a single year which has less impact on the soil, but which nevertheless favours tree development. This is by temporarily eliminating flammable grasses, improving the seedbed and tree germination and seedling survival. It also multiplies the number of existing trees which can coppice or which can develop as suckers from damaged roots. The fertilization of village-edge soils by the deposition of human and animal faeces, as well as ash and household waste, further encourages forest development.

When necessary, villagers deliberately accelerate forest island formation and expansion by transplanting seedlings or cuttings of 'forest-initiating' trees. Such fast-growing, relatively fire-resistant trees enable subsequent forest regeneration in their shade. In the past, silk cotton trees (*Ceiba pentandra*) were frequently used, often to help fortify villages whether as gate posts or living stockades. Villagers would train these trees either to grow high as look-out posts (by clipping their lateral branches and by fertilizing them), or to branch densely for rapid concealment and island development (by cutting the tree's

'head', or apical meristem). Certain villages had several rings of these trees. Today, villagers initiating forest islands usually use mango trees and certain exotics.

Forest islands become a convenient source of gathered products from forest species which provide ropes, basketry materials, building poles, seeds, nuts, medicines and dead wood for fuel. And villagers enrich and extend their forests by planting economically useful species such as kola, bananas or fruit trees which, for reasons of microclimate or fire, cannot grow in savanna. Indeed, during the 1950s when coffee was a profitable cash crop, forest islands were extended and their canopies selectively thinned to house villagers' smallholder plantations. Currently, forest islands are again changing in quality— although not necessarily diminishing in size or integrity—as larger trees are felled for the commercial timber market.

As forest islands are associated with settlements, there is a positive relationship between population growth and high forest cover; more villages mean more forest islands. This relationship is modified, however, by changes in population distribution and settlement patterns. During the nineteenth century (and perhaps earlier), settlement numbers increased under prevailing conditions of warfare and migration, leaving a pattern of parent villages surrounded by small dependent settlements, each developing their own forest islands. In contrast, population growth during the twentieth century has been accommodated mainly through the growth of existing settlements, and indeed some consolidation of them. Thus the multiplication of forest islands in the nineteenth century has not been replicated in the twentieth century despite population increase.

Since it is normally everyday activities which promote forest island growth around an inhabited village, village abandonment can precipitate forest island loss. Villages may be abandoned or shift site for reasons such as settlement consolidation, shortage of space or water, social problems, illness, or to be nearer roads. And while uninhabited forest islands are sometimes maintained for their economic trees and for their ritual significance, people tend to shift their attention to the developing forest island around their new settlement, and may convert the old one partly or wholly to agricultural use to take advantage of the highly fertile soils beneath it. Thus forest islands come and go in relation to the dynamics of settlement.

Between the islands

Comparison of air photographs, documentary sources and oral histories shows that woody cover on the upland slopes and plateaux between Kissidougou's forest islands has generally increased during this century, and not declined as policy-makers have supposed. The nature and extent of this vary: in many parts of the north and east of the prefecture, grass savannas have become more densely wooded with relatively fire-resistant savanna tree species and greater numbers of oil palms. In the south and south-east, large areas of savanna have ceded entirely to bush fallows of secondary forest thicket. These transitions are also confirmed by changes in everyday resource use which indicate vegetation change: for example, the introduction of tree felling in agricultural operations, increased availability of preferred fuelwood species, changes in the materials used in roofing and thatching, changing patterns of palm oil trade with a switch from import to export in certain localities, changing patterns of bird nesting, distribution and control, and changes in termite species and the availability of edible fungi associated with them. The transitions to greater woody cover reflect, in part, the ways that inhabitants work with ecological processes, and changes in their management of farming, grazing and fire in the context of changing socio-economic conditions.

Nowadays, villagers grow much of their rice in the inland valley swamps. Nevertheless, farmers also cultivate rainfed rice, peanuts, cassava and fonio[4] on upland areas which have either secondary forest thicket or savanna fallows. Where fallows cleared for farming are secondary forest thicket—either in riparian galleries or on

uplands—this tends to re-establish after cultivation. A 'mature' forest fallow, once under-brushed, felled, burned and cleared, provides a relatively fertile, weed-free site for sowing rice and a variety of intercrops. Farmers often cultivate parts of the site for a second year with lightly mounded peanuts or cassava, but they then leave it fallow until the forest regenerates and 'matures' once more: when, in local perspective, it will suppress weeds and provide sufficient fertility for the following rice crop. As the fallow should not be too laborious to fell with hand tools, a period of 8–12 years is generally ideal. While farmers suggest that forest regeneration from seed, coppice and cut roots can be delayed by a second year crop, and while flammable grasses sometimes invade during the first two or three years, their experience is that the soil conditions usually ensure eventual forest re-establishment. Where necessary, farmers protect young fallow regeneration from fire, and accelerate regeneration by conserving adjacent patches of uncleared forest as sources of seed and shade.

Where uplands are savanna, farming possibilities are more varied, but tend to fall into either short- or long-term farming sequences involving rice, fonio, cassava, peanuts and other root crops. In short-term sequences, once the savanna trees are felled and the grass is burned and uprooted, the site is cropped for one to three years with rice or cassava as a fallow-breaking crop, and then left fallow for five years or more. While short-term farming of rice in savanna induces little change in subsequent vegetation, a single crop of cassava can enhance tree density. Cultivation for rice only scratches the soil surface and the rice is harvested before the dry season, but cassava, in contrast, is planted in deeply cultivated mounds and lasts in the ground for a year. Deeper cultivation not only encourages tree-sucker development, as suggested earlier, but also alters grass species composition more effectively, and this and the longer maturation reduce fire risk for a full season.

In long-term sequences, farmers use gardening techniques (mounding and incorporating weeds and crop residues) and manure from tethered cattle to maintain soil fertility for five or more years, rotating peanuts, cassava, fonio and other garden crops. When such sequences are begun in savanna, they can enable subsequent fallows to develop secondary forest fallow thicket cover. This, farmers suggest, is because gardening has enduring effects on soil structure, soil-water relations and grass composition, and hence on fire. New trees rapidly establish on the site, and gain some fire protection from the improved water-holding capacity of the ripened soils, and from the heavily grazed post-cultivation grasses which burn less. While long-term garden cropping used to be confined to the gardens around villages and wet-season farm camps, these sequences have become more prevalent since the 1950s, especially as women who find this a convenient labour and land-use pattern have used it to increase their independent peanut and cassava production to meet heightened food and cash needs. Nowadays, farmers congregate on areas of improved land, and move in unison between such areas, leaving them fallowed in turn; fallows which in time develop a cover of secondary forest thicket.

Cattle—of the trypanosomiasis-resistant Ndama variety—also have a major impact on upland vegetation. Just as around forest islands, their concentrated grazing on inter-island savannas can create conditions in which forest comes to dominate over savanna (cf. Boutrais, 1992). Farmers observe this where large numbers of cattle congregate, and those seeking improved bush fallow may target cattle grazing for this purpose. Depleted by disease and war at the turn of the century, cattle numbers in Kissidougou have generally increased during more recent times. In the south-east of the prefecture, this increase has now been reversed as savanna pastures have ceded to secondary forest thicket which is inhospitable to cattle. In the north, where savannas predominate, the vegetational impact of increased cattle numbers has been especially noticeable since the early 1980s. This period has seen an influx of Fula herders who had evacuated their cattle to Sierra Leone during Guinea's first post-independence regime, and who have now returned to settle in Kissidougou village territories.

Fire management has long been integral to the maintenance and management of these diverse vegetation types. In sparsely populated, drier northern regions, villagers cannot prevent the bush fires which pass through their savannas annually. Rather, they seek to turn these to their advantage by sequencing their own burning activities through the dry season. In January, early in the dry season when dew and green vegetation enable fire to be controlled, village authorities organize the protection of the village, forest island and certain sacred forest sites by burning limited areas to create fire-breaks. Farmers also take such steps to protect their own crops, gallery forests and, where deemed appropriate, fallow vegetation. Slightly later, in February, hunters also begin to set fires of limited extent in personal hunting grounds, both to attract game to the young grass shoots which soon appear, and to improve visibility. Later still, in March or April, farmers set fires for field preparation. Because limiting fire to within field boundaries cannot be assured, the village may co-ordinate its field burning. At this time, village groups also hunt cane rats (*Thyronomis swinderianus*, a crop pest which congregates in unburned swamps) and set fires on swamp margins to do this. Other fires set by wild honey collectors, smokers, and lightning strikes can also get out of control at this time. But by this hottest time of the dry season in April, when violent and more destructive fires would occur, much of the savanna upland has already been burnt. It is only when late fires threaten houses or property that villages mass-mobilize to extinguish them.

In the south and east of the prefecture, where dry seasons are slightly shorter and populations more concentrated, control of savanna fire has proved more feasible. Villagers can cut effective fire-breaks around field boundaries, assisted by the low boundary-to-area ratio of the blocks of contiguous village fields typical of Kissi farming organization in this area. Indeed, in certain areas such fire control has further assisted the conversion of savannas to secondary forest thicket.

Kissi and Kuranko use a wide range of gathered products as well as farm-sites from the diverse forest–savanna landscape shaped by these management processes. While the village forest island provides certain useful plant products, others are obtained from savanna (e.g. thatch, sauce leaves, toothbrush sticks, edible tree seeds), gallery forest fallows (e.g. building poles), and swamp vegetation (e.g. basketry and wrapping materials). Villagers also make use of the product availability afforded by agricultural management, collecting fuelwood, for example, from the dead branches left by upland field clearance. Certain trees which provide valuable wild products are carefully preserved during field clearance, and their distribution enhanced. The oil palm (*Elaeis guineensis*) is a prime example; once oil palms are present in an area, villagers multiply them both by deliberate sowing in forest islands and on soon-to-be-fallowed farmland, and by preserving animals (e.g. palm rats) known to distribute their seed.

Conclusions

Kissidougou's inhabitants use the diversity of vegetation forms in the forest–savanna mosaic in furnishing their everyday needs. By managing ecological processes involving fire, soils, animals and vegetation they have also been able to enrich the mosaic, improving the value of their environment in terms of agricultural productivity and other local priorities. This has involved converting savanna into forest successional vegetation, thus altering the balance between forest and savanna vegetation forms. It has also involved adapting the quality—species composition and structure—of each form to suit changing social and economic needs. Where ecological processes involving water (climate), soil and fire make conditions marginal for forest, leaving a precarious balance between forest vegetation regeneration and pyrogenic savanna, the Kissidougou case suggests that people's manipulation of these processes can tip the balance. Thus forest islands are the products of everyday life and management, not the last relics of a once great forest; and upland quality for agriculture and gathering has been improved, not

degraded, by local farming, fire and animal management practices. Given the extent to which inhabitants are actively shaping the forest–savanna mosaic to suit their needs, and have been doing so for centuries, studies of forest–savanna transitions should place local agro-ecological management centre-stage. Equally, environmental and sustainable agriculture policies designed without appreciation of local management skills, both overlook actual problems and possibilities, and risk undermining the very practices which have enhanced tree cover and agricultural productivity in the transition zone (Fairhead and Leach, 1993).

Acknowledgements

This chapter has been equally co-authored by Melissa Leach and James Fairhead, and draws on fieldwork carried out with Dominique Millimouno and Marie Kamano. The research was funded by ESCOR of the Overseas Development Administration, whom we gratefully thank. Opinions represented here are, however, the authors' own, not those of the ODA. Many thanks are also due to the villagers in Kissidougou prefecture with whom we worked and to our Guinean collaborators: Projet de Développement Rural Intégré de Kissidougou, Direction National des Forêts et de la Chasse, and the Direction National de la Recherche Scientifique.

Notes

1. Present rainfall is between 1500 and 2100 mm per annum, over a rainy season of 7–8 months, with both quantity and duration highly variable from year to year. It is this seasonality and variability, as much as total rainfall, which influences vegetation patterns.
2. Climate historians argue that climatic conditions drier than at present prevailed in this part of West Africa between 1100 and 1860, with the exception of a period between about 1500–1630 (Brooks, 1986; Nicholson, 1979).
3. With the notable exception in Ivory Coast of Spichiger and Blanc-Pamard (1973).
4. Fonio (*Digitaria exilis*) is a small grain cereal crop which was domesticated in West Africa. It is often known as 'hungry rice'.

James Fairhead and Melissa Leach

References

Aubréville, A. (1949) *Climats, forêts et désertification de l'Afrique tropicale*, Société d'Edition de Géographie Maritime et Coloniale, Paris.

Avenard, J.-M., Bonvallot, J. Latham, M. Renard-Dugerdil, M., and Richard, J. (1974) *Aspects du contact forêt–savane dans le centre et l'ouest de la Côte d'Ivoire: étude descriptive*, ORSTOM, Abidjan.

Boutrais, J. (1992) L'élevage en Afrique tropicale: une activité dégradante? *Afrique Contemporaine*, 161, 109–125.

Brooks, G. E. (1986) A provisional historical schema for Western Africa based on seven climatic periods, *Cahiers d'Etudes Africaines*, 101–102, 43–62.

Fairhead, J. and Leach, M. (1993) Degrading people: the misuse of history in Guinea's environmental policy, paper presented at the annual African Studies Association Conference in Boston, USA, December 1993.

Fairhead, J. and Leach, M. with Millimouno, D. and Kamano, M. (1992) *Managed Productivity: the technical knowledge used in local natural resource management in Kissidougou Prefecture*, COLA Working Paper 3, Kissidougou.

Furley, P., Proctor, J. and Ratter, J. (eds) (1992) *Nature and Dynamics of Forest–Savanna Boundaries*, Chapman & Hall, London.

Leach, M. and Fairhead, J. (1993) Whose social forestry and why? People, trees and managed continuity in Guinea's forest–savana mosaic, *Zeitschrift für Wirtschaftsgeographie*, 37(2), 86–101.

Morgan, W. B. and Moss R. P. (1965) Savanna and forest in Western Nigeria, *Africa*, 35(3), 286–293.

Nicholson, S. E. (1979) The methodology of historical climate reconstruction and its application to Africa, *Journal of African History*, 20(1), 31–49.

Spichiger, R. and Blanc-Pamard, C. (1973) Recherches sur le contact forêt–savane en Côte d'Ivoire: Etude du recru forestier sur des parcelles cultivées en lisière d'un ilôt forestier dans le sud du pays baoulé, *Candollea*, 28, 21–37.

15

Livelihood, sustainable development and indigenous forestry in dryland Nigeria

R. A. Cline-Cole

Introduction

Ideas about livelihood and sustainable development are useful for studying indigenous use and management of woodland and forest resources, and the combination of trees and shrubs with crops and livestock, in Nigeria's northern drylands. The direct and indirect contribution of this agri-silvi-pasture to the sustainability of both livelihoods and environment in these resource-poor drylands have long been recognized. However, sustained research and policy attention has only been devoted to questions of linkages between livelihood sustainability, environmental degradation and popular participation in the management of regional forestry resources since the 1970s.

Nigerian dryland farmers and pastoralists are also foresters, for whom 'it is difficult, if not impossible, to separate the management of production from the management of the environment'; together these form part of the livelihood strategy of households and groups (Redclift, 1993, p. 36). Sustainable development

offers a framework for combining livelihood considerations with conservation concerns in ways which do not devalue the contribution of such indigenous dryland forestry to environmental management (Redclift, 1993).

Livelihood and sustainable development

The concept of sustainable development (SD) has been continuously modified in the years since 1987, when it was initially publicized by the World Conservation Union in its *World Conservation Strategy* (WCU/IUCN, 1980). Current interpretations diverge widely, with the phrase taking different meanings in different contexts (Woodhouse, 1992; Vivian, 1994; Mitlin, 1992).

However, despite a multiplicity of *meanings* (more than 30); *goals* (social, political, economic, ecological); *components* (sustainability, development); *approaches* (populist, interventionist,

People and Environment in Africa. Edited by Tony Binns
©1995 John Wiley & Sons Ltd

neo-liberal); and *dimensions* (epistemological, political, economic), there is an emerging consensus that SD:

- is applicable at all geographic scales;
- is concerned with improving the living standards of the poor and disadvantaged;
- should promote equity within and between generations as well as between and within nations;
- facilitates popular participation in development or decision-making;
- combines socio-cultural, political, economic and ecological interests; and
- sometimes implies major political change.

Thus the sustainable use of forestry resources would involve

not only conserving biological diversity, fauna and flora, but also maintaining ecological functions such as soil quality, hydrological cycles, climate and weather, river flow and water quality. It also implies maintaining supplies of natural products—game, fish, fodder, fruits, nuts, resins, dyes, basts [fibre/matting], construction materials, fuelwood, etc.—which are indispensable to the livelihoods of local people (Colchester, 1994, p. 70).

Livelihoods are the means through which people obtain a secure living to meet basic needs for food, shelter, health, etc. They are secure when ownership of, or access to, the resources and income-earning activities on which they are based are safe or guaranteed (Redclift, 1993; Conway and Barbier, 1990). Income-earning activities, like cropping, livestock raising, trading, gathering, hunting, handicraft manufacture and off-farm work, all benefit from direct and indirect forestry inputs:

- trees and shrubs act as savings, which can be 'cashed' in an emergency (Mortimore *et al.*, 1990);
- the production, transport and trade of forest products provide employment and income for a large number of people;
- and while collected or hunted sylvan products add much needed variety to diets in 'normal' times, their value is considerably enhanced as 'famine foods' during periods of shortage.

Not surprisingly, even under conditions of increasing population size and density, stable livelihoods often encourage investment of labour and funds in conserving and improving trees, shrubs and other resources (Mortimore, 1993; Conway and Barbier, 1990). It is worth emphasizing, however, that livelihood activities involve dryland populations, resources, environment and development (PRED) in complex linkages and processes of change, some of which can and do threaten livelihood security. Thus, in fuelling forest and woodland clearance, the needs of an expanding or increasingly prosperous population for land and its associated resources sometimes exacerbate soil erosion, adversely affect soil and vegetation productivity, contribute to loss of biodiversity, and reduce forest product supplies.

Whether PRED linkages result in conservation or degradation of dryland forestry resources depends on the specific historical and geographic conditions which obtain in a given situation. They also depend on the consequences of processes like deforestation, and the selective elimination or adoption of flora for livelihood activities like crop, livestock, fodder or fuel production (Cline-Cole, 1994).

Indigenous dryland forestry

Dryland Nigeria

Nigeria's drylands occupy relatively homogeneous plateaux and plains north of latitude 11° N, which are interrupted by the channels of the Hadejia–Jama'are and Sokoto–Rima river systems (Figure 15.1, inset). Rainfall is concentrated in a single rainy season of up to seven months, although this can be as little as four weeks or less in the north-eastern part of these flat-to-undulating savannas. Average annual rainfall increases from north to south (from less than 500 mm to about 1500 mm), and is characterized by wide spatial and temporal variability. Periodic droughts are common and long-term rainfall averages are declining.

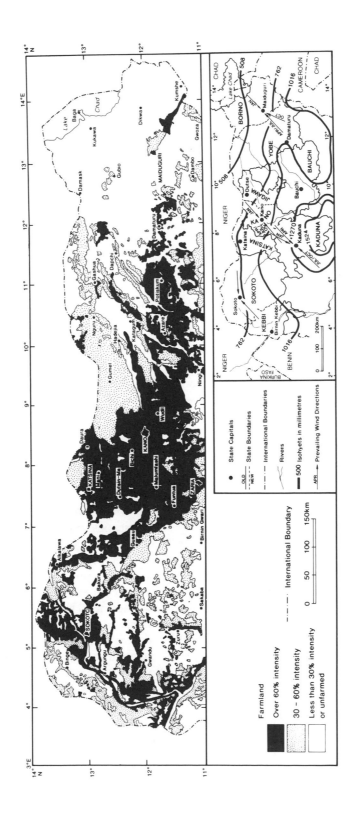

Figure 15.1 *Farming intensity in dryland Nigeria in the late 1970s. Based on vegetation and land-use maps by the Ministry of Rural Development, Federal Department of Forestry, Nigeria, 1977/78. Source: Mortimore (1989); Anderson (1987)*

173

Although levels of urbanization are increasing, and currently stand at around 25%, the region's *c.* 28 million people (1991 census) remain overwhelmingly rural and agrarian. Agriculture accounts for nearly half (48.3%) of regional land use (Silviconsult, 1990). Population totals and densities are increasing. Averages in excess of 200 per km^2 make Kano, Katsina and Jigawa the most densely populated dryland areas, the close-settled zones (CSZs), which can support densities in excess of 500 per km^2. There is a close correlation between human and livestock population density, land-use intensity and land insufficiency (Figure 15.1).

Livelihoods in dryland Nigeria

A diversity of income-earning opportunities helps to spread risk and stabilize livelihoods. Rural producers combine rainfed 'upland' (*tudu*) and irrigated 'lowland' (*fadama*) crop production, (semi-)sedentary livestock rearing, and a bewildering range of on-farm, off-farm and non-farm activity, in an integrated production system. Some of the latter involve short-term mobility.

Agricultural output is of three kinds: annual crops, minor root and vegetable crops, and residues from both sets of crops; livestock products; and miscellaneous sylvan products from cultivated and uncultivated land (Mortimore *et al.*, 1990). Dependence on non-agricultural income increases with harvest failure, livestock mortality, population density, farming intensity, land scarcity, and prox-imity to large urban centres (Mortimore, 1993). The collection, processing and sale of sylvan products from both agricultural and non-agricultural land make important contributions to non-agricultural income, with fuelwood being, arguably, the most important of these. Dryland forestry also contributes directly and indirectly to agricultural production and environmental protection.

The subsistence and commercial value of forestry products and services, and their contribution to livelihood security, income diversification and environmental protection can be summarized as: *direct use value* (timber and non-timber products; recreation, education and habitat resources); *indirect use value* (environmental functions), *non-use value* (cultural significance, aesthetic and biodiversity value); and *option value*, which refers to the conservation of forestry resources for their future use and non-use value (Pearce, 1990).

Forestry landscapes

Trees, shrubs, woodland, forests and grasses are core elements of the cultural landscape. Indigenous land use combines agriculture, sylviculture and livestock husbandry in time and space. Although dryland Nigerians make a clear distinction between humanized and wilderness landscapes, forestry is an integral part of both crop cultivation and pastoral production, and is a visible element of the landscape in and around settlements (Figure 15.2). Indeed, most dryland farmland consists of farm parkland, 'a landscape in which well-grown trees occur scattered through cultivated or recently fallowed fields' (Pullan, 1974, p. 119).

Table 15.1 matches the indigenous agri-silvi-pastoral landscapes of dryland Nigeria with general classifications of tropical dryland agroforestry systems and practices. The rest of this section examines these indigenous forestry landscapes and their component parts in some detail. First, summary information on landscape structure, composition, geographical distribution, socio-economic importance and environmental significance is presented; agri-silvi-pastoral management structures and dynamics are then discussed, with particular reference to the creation and maintenance of the landscapes identified. The discussion ranges freely between different scales of geographical analysis, and highlights the close and complex links between livelihood activities and environmental management.

Karkara

This is farm parkland, which dominates upland areas of intense land use (farmland of over 60%)

Figure 15.2 *Indigenous forestry in the Kano Close-Settled Zone. The agri-silvi-pastoral landscape shown contains scattered farm trees at variable densities, farm boundary plants, shade trees around farm compounds, live hedges adjoining cattle droves and localized grass fallows. Source: Pullan (1974), reproduced by permission*

intensity, Figure 15.1). It supports human settlement, and mature(ing) economic trees and shrubs at variable densities on annually cultivated farmland, which is grazed by domestic livestock and transhumant cattle after the annual harvest (Figure 15.3).

Farm trees and shrubs consist of a wide variety of species (more than 70 in the Kano CSZ alone) although some are locally dominant (e.g. locust bean (*Parkia biglobosa*), silk cotton (*Ceiba pentandra*), baobab (*Adansonia digitata*) and *Hyphaene thebaica* or *dum* palm). Table 15.2 lists some common farm trees and shrubs, and identifies their direct and indirect use, and non-use values.

Karkara plants are private property, which are sometimes owned separately from land. Farm trees and shrubs usually belong to smallholders, who are overwhelmingly male. However, *henna*

shrubs (*Lawsonia inermis*) and *Parkia* trees frequently belong to women, who have full control over the disposal of their products. *Karkara* trees and shrubs are inheritable, mortgageable and marketable; and transactions involving these trees/shrubs and their products are common, even between spouses and siblings. Ownership of farm trees/shrubs may be retained when plots are transferred (Mortimore *et al.*, 1990).

The environmental functions of farm parkland vegetation are influenced by species composition and plant density, the landscape configuration of plants (along field boundaries, around compounds and settlements, interspersed with crops, along cattle droves), and the mutual compatability of land uses (Figure 15.2). *Gamba* grass (*Andropogon gayanus*) farm boundaries stabilize the soil against dry-season harmattan winds and protect young grain crops against early rainy

Table 15.1 *Agroforestry systems, functions, landscapes and practices*

System practice[1]	Major output or function[1]	Common Nigerian dryland species involved	Equivalent indigenous dryland forestry landscapes
Agri-silvi-pastoral systems			
Tree–crop–livestock mix around homesteads (homegardens)	Production of food, fodder, livestock products, etc. for home consumption and sale	*Adansonia digitata, Acacia albida, Ficus* spp., *Mangifera indica*	*Karkara*; *saura*
Woody hedgerows for browse, mulch, green manure and soil conservation	Production of food, fodder, fuelwood; soil conservation	*Moringa oleifera, Balanites aegyptiaca, Lawsonia inermis*	*Karkara*; *saura*
Agri-silvi-cultural systems			
Multipurpose trees and shrubs on farmland	Wide range of sylvan products for subsistence and exchange; soil conservation and improvement; shade provision; farm boundary demarcation	*Parkia biglobosa, Anogeissus leiocarpus, Acacia albida, Diospyros mespiliformis*	*Karkara*; *saura*; *fadama*
Shelter-belts and windbreaks; shade trees in and around compounds and settlements; strips of trees/shrubs along the edges of contour terraces; woody hedgerows	Production of food, browse, fodder, fuelwood, medicinal products, mulch, (green) manure; soil conservation and improvement; (wind) erosion control	*Khaya senegalensis, Azadirachta indica, Mangifera indica, Moringa oleifera*	*Karkara*; *saura*
Silvi-pastoral systems			
Protein banks of multi-purpose trees/shrubs on or around farmlands, and grass and woodland fallows	Production of livestock fodder and food crops	*Acacia* spp., *K. Senegalensis, Demkon arguwa*	*Saura*; *karkara*; *daji*
Living fences of fodder, trees, shrubs and grass	Service function (fences); production of tree products	Vetiver grass, tussock grass	*Karkara*; *saura*; *fadama*
Trees and shrubs on pasture	Production of livestock fodder and pasture; wood, fruits, ethno-veterinary products	*Acacia* spp., *B. Aegyptiaca, Guiera senegalensis*	*Saura*; *daji*; *fadama*

[1]Source: Nair (1989)

season line squalls and localized windstorms (Swindell, 1986). But *gamba* also makes good grazing. Thus, where farm boundaries also line drove routes, they are more sensibly planted to shrubs and trees like *Demkon arguwa, Euphorbia balsamifera* and *E. lateriflora*, which livestock find unpalatable, and which also yield useful products (e.g. latex with medicinal value).

Figure 15.3 *A* karkara *landscape with a mix of millet (*Pennisetum typhoides*), guinea corn (*Sorghum bicolor*) and a cover crop of groundnuts (*Arachis hypogaea*) interspersed with irregularly-spaced trees near Ringim. The* Khaya senegalensis *in the foreground are part of a row of widely-spaced farm boundary trees. Photograph by author*

Leaf litter from most farm trees improve soil fertility. However, deep-branching (e.g. *Parkia* and mango or *Mangifera indica*) and halophytic (e.g. *Eucalyptus*, *Khaya senegalensis* or fig) trees and shrubs compete with annual crops. Clusters of such trees tend to be restricted to field boundaries, orchards, and land in and around settlements and farm compounds. Here, their 'umbrella effect' is a desirable indirect use value, which does not compete with their direct use value as producers of valuable timber and non-timber products. In contrast, agroforesters make strenuous efforts to increase the number, and improve the distribution of trees like *Acacia albida*, *Adansonia digitata* and *Tamarindus indica* on cropland. These trees maintain and enhance crop and/or livestock productivity through the redistribution of soil fertility.

The creation and maintenance of *karkara* favour economically useful species. At the same time, the conservation of mature farm parkland depends on a good representation of trees and shrubs which can be intensively exploited for their products with little if any adverse consequences for plant growth or vitality. Trees on *karkara* need to be sufficiently hardy to survive bark-stripping (for medicine, rope-making, dye-making), browsing (by free-ranging small stock) and leaf and fruit collection (for fodder, food and medicine).

Saura

Several of these characteristics are also essential to successful species survival in *saura* where,

177

Table 15.2 *Common farm trees and their use values*

Species	English/ Hausa name	Fuelwood, Charcoal	Utility wood	Food	Fodder	Medicine, repellents, poisons	Various raw materials	Protection, soil improvement	Cultural values
Acacia albida[4]	*Gawo*	*	*	—	*	*	*	*	—
A. nilotica[12]	*Gabaruwa*	*	*	*	*	*	*	*	*
Adansonia digitata[3]	Baobab	—	—	*	*	*	*	*	*
Anogeissus leiocarpus	*Marke*[6]	*	*	*	*	*	*	—	—
Azadirachta indica[2]	Neem	—	*	—	—	*	—	*	—
Balanites aegyptiaca	*Aduwa*[15]	*	*	*	*	*	*	*	*
Butyrospermum paradoxum[7]	Shea-butter	*	*	*	*	*	*	*	*
Ceiba pentandra[17]	Silk cotton	—	*	*	*	*	*	*	*
Celtis integrifolia	*Zuwo*	*	*	*	*	*	*	*	—
Combretum collinum	*Kantaka*	*	*	*	*	*	*	—	*
C. micranthum[20]	*Geza*	*	*	*	*	*	*	—	*
Diospyros mespiliformis[10]	Ebony	*	*	*	*	*	*	—	*
Ficus platyphylla	Fig	*	—	*	*	*	*	—	*
F. sycomorus[17]	Fig	*	*	*	*	*	*	—	*
F. thonningii	Fig	*	—	*	*	*	*	*	*
Guiera senegalensis[13]	*Sabara*	*	*	*	*	*	*	—	*
Khaya senegalensis[13]	Mahogany	*	*	—	*	*	*	*	*
Mangifera indica[5]	Mango	—	—	*	—	*	—	—	*
Moringo oleifera[15]	*Zogale*	*	*	*	*	*	*	*	*
Parkia biglobosa[1]	Locust-bean	*	*	*	*	*	—	*	*
Piliostigma thonningii	*Kargo*	*	*	*	*	*	*	—	*
P. reticulatum[8]	*Kargo*	*	*	*	*	*	*	*	*
Prosopis africana[12]	*Kirya*	*	*	*	*	*	*	—	*
Sclerocarya birrea	*Danya*	*	*	*	*	*	*	—	*
Tamarindus indica[9]	Tamarind	*	*	*	*	*	—	*	*
Vitex doniana[11]	*Dinya*	*	*	*	*	*	*	—	*
Ziziphus spina-christi	*Kurna*	*	*	*	*	—	*	*	*

* = use reported: — = use not reported: [12] = ranking in list of 20 most plentiful farm species (Silviconsult, 1990): *Source:* Updated from Cline-Cole *et al.* (1990, p. 90).

although species composition may be similar to that in *karkara*, farm trees are only just emerging from the sapling or shrub stage. Trees and shrubs here need to be more fire-resistant than *karkara* plants, if they are to survive regular controlled burning of undergrowth by hunters and livestock rearers. Grazing, burning and woodcutting are important land-use features in such areas, and land is sequentially or concomitantly grazed, fallowed and cultivated (Pullan, 1974). *Saura* are areas of immature parkland or fallow shrubland, which are farmed at 30–60% intensity (Figure 15.1).

Where *saura* is characterized by low land productivity and limited agricultural opportunities, the collection and sale of fuelwood to urban suppliers, the manufacture of mats, rope and baskets from the leaves of the *dum* palm, and bee-keeping may become important remunerative activities.

Daji

These 'wilderness' areas are either completely unfarmed or farmed at less than 30% intensity (Figure 15.1). They are important sources of both timber and non-timber forest products. *Daji* is most extensive in areas of low population density, higher rainfall or favourable edaphic conditions, and includes a diversity of habitats: uncultivable scrubland in *saura* and *karkara* (often devoid of trees), extensive areas of rangeland or tree savanna, riparian woodland, hill forest blocks, forest outliers, etc.

Direct use values of *daji* include building poles and construction timber for local and regional use; invaluable dry-season grazing and fodder resources for livestock; raw material for craft occupations like carving; and 'bush meat' (mammals and large birds), which constitutes an essential source of animal protein in locally wooded or forested areas. In addition, the role played by woodland and forests as gene pools; in protecting watersheds and regulating river flow; and in influencing local or regional climate represent good examples of their indirect use value.

Fadama

Fadama bears, like *daji*, the expanding (and intensifying) imprint of human and livestock activity. These seasonally flooded wetlands contain well-drained *saura* and *daji*, as well as irrigable and uncultivable marshland, in sometimes complex spatial and temporal mixes (Figure 15.4); Double-cropped *fadama* areas can be as intensively

exploited as *karkara*. The characteristic farm parkland landscape is sometimes identifiable in *fadama* areas, where bunded plots are interspersed with economic trees.

Economic trees and shrubs on floodplain parkland produce fodder, fuel, food, medicines, etc. Fruits like mango (*Mangifera indica*), guava (*Psidium guayava*), banana (*Musa sapientum*), custard apple (*Anona squamosa*) and pawpaw (*Carica papaya*) are cultivated for sale, where theft does not pose an insurmountable problem.

Uncultivated areas produce grasses for grazing and roofing material, which enter a thriving local and regional trade. Access to irrigable land for dry-season farming has to be negotiated separately from access to fruit trees, and from access to fuel and timber, and livestock grazing and watering resources.

The local and regional importance of *fadama* is often tied to the use value of forestry resources. Thus the Hadejia–Nguru wetlands on the Jigawa–Yobe border produce fish, contribute to groundwater recharge, and are important staging posts for migratory birds, as well as a natural habitat for native birds. But fuelwood, too, makes an important contribution to the value of economic production in these wetlands (Adams and Kimmage, 1992), which also produce and export *Eichinocloa stagnina* hay for use as feed for horses in Maiduguri and Kano (Adams and Hollis, 1987). In addition, the manufacture and sale of *dum* palm products generates substantial income for floodplain villagers and seasonal migrants from as far away as Niger (Barbier *et al.*, 1991). Similarly, floodplain and nomadic pastoralists (the latter from outside the floodplain and, sometimes, outside Nigeria) depend on natural alluvial grasslands and browse from trees for valuable dry-season grazing, on which the production of surplus meat for regional trade and consumption partly depends.

Management of forestry resources

The distribution, structure and dynamics of indigenous forestry landscapes emphasize not only

Figure 15.4 *A* fadama *fringed by* daji *in the distance.* Balanites aegyptiaca *shrubs can be seen in the foreground. Cultivation is prohibited in this communal grazing and watering area (*makiyaya*) south of Hadejia. Photograph by author*

that 'the management of woodland [is not] distinct from the management of trees on farmland', but also 'that in many cases farmland or rangeland, and woodland, cannot be separated' (Shepherd, 1992, pp. 10 and 11). The goals and techniques of indigenous forestry management are diverse; and their effects on species composition, structure and diversity complex and dynamic. Dryland forestry landscapes are products of a continuous process of selective elimination, protection and propagation of indigenous flora, and the equally careful adoption of exotic species. Their continued, if dynamic, existence serves a range of sometimes competing interests.

For farm parkland, tree and shrub selection and management extend beyond the early years of farm establishment (*saura*) into those of maturity (*karkara*), as permanent cultivation replaces fallows and previously undisturbed wilderness areas. The number of farm trees increases as the area under forest and woodland decreases: only 10% of farming households have no trees growing on their farms. Seedlings which regenerate spontaneously may be transplanted and/or protected from animal and other damage until they reach shoulder height: two-thirds of households tend such seedlings, which are sometimes propagated by domestic livestock. Landownership and security of tenure encourage the establishment of permanent field boundaries sown to border plants, and the propagation of perennial farm trees and shrubs, which maintain their value in relation to the cost of living: more than 90% of rural households, mostly owner-occupiers, plant trees (Mortimore *et al.*, 1990; Silviconsult, 1990).

As the species composition of the 20 commonest farm trees and shrubs in Table 15.1 shows, this combination of protection and propagation favours indigenous multi-purpose species. These species are selected primarily for food, fruit, fuel and fodder production, shade provision and erosion control (Silviconsult, 1990). With few exceptions (e.g. tussock grass, other border plants and orchards) farmland forestry management focuses on individual trees and shrubs, which are pollarded (Figure 15.5(a)), pruned (Figure 15.5(b)), lopped (Figure 15.5(c)) and coppiced (Figure 15.5(d)) to give products of different shapes and sizes. Pastoralists illegally lop fodder trees on farmland during the dry season, when they are also known to steal forage stored on farms.

The management of entire stands of woodland and forest is commonplace in *daji* and uncultivated *fadama*, where it also incorporates the management of associated resources of grass and water. Such wilderness areas are not dominated by the popular farm species, and are common property (CPRs) or communal resources, which are subject to collective rather than individual control. Community grazing and watering areas for sedentary or village livestock (*makiyaya*) are a notable example, which are subject to the ultimate supervision and protection of village heads (Figure 15.4).

Daji and uncultivated *fadama* are also managed by herders, who 'try to keep a wide range of species alive, and are interested in a range of fodders which are available at different times of the year, suit different kinds of stock, and vary in their nutritional content' (Shepherd, 1992, p. 11). Species which produce medicinal products for animals are also highly valued. Rangeland trees and shrubs like *Acacia seyal*, *A. tortilis* and *Balanites aegyptiaca* are lopped to produce browse at the end of the dry season, when pods and fruits are also collected for animal feed. These and other species also provide wood for constructing livestock enclosures, for fencing off cultivated plots, and for fuel. Significantly, neither customary tenure nor statutory land law provides title to grazing, water and fodder for transhumant

herds in wilderness areas; mobile stockowners depend on the tolerance of sedentary communities for access to these resources. Consequently, farmers collect and sell free rangeland fodder to pastoralists, who they also occasionally charge for access to enclosed alluvial dry-season grazing.

By and large, the morphology and species composition of wilderness areas are influenced by selective exploitation of tree species for timber and fuelwood; by selective clearance for cultivation; by selective browsing of livestock; and by fires started to create access routes for livestock, stimulate new browse, and flush out game (Wilkinson, 1991).

Trends in forestry resources and landscapes

The dominant form of land-use change is the conversion of woodland, shrubland and grassland to farmland: the area under cultivation doubled between 1965 and 1990 (Silviconsult, 1990). Consequently, the scale of vegetation transformation is most extensive, and the rate of change most rapid, in the least densely populated areas of the drylands. Here, extensive tracts of *daji* and *fadama* are being privatized by rich or powerful land speculators, and part-time or 'businessmen' farmers; *fadama* farming is expanding at the expense of pastoralism, which is increasingly squeezed into constricting rangelands; and both *daji* and farmland are currently under high and growing pressure to satisfy an insatiable regional fuelwood demand. In these areas, traditional systems of grazing, collecting, hunting and farming rights are being eroded, and forestry landscapes are undergoing rapid change.

However, in some of the most densely populated areas, where agriculture can account for up to 90% of local land use, *karkara* is proving remarkably stable in appearance and, in some cases, in species composition also. This is the case in the Kano CSZ, for example, where increasing population densities have combined with a host of place- and time-specific factors to act as a catalyst for investment in conservation measures

Figure 15.5 *Single tree management in the Kano Close-Settled Zone: (a)* Moringa oleifera *poles (b) Recently-pruned* Parkia *(c) Newly-lopped* Parkia *(d) Coppiced* Acacia albida *with signs of regrowth. Photographs by author*

like tree-planting and protection (Mortimore *et al.*, 1990). In some parts of the Kano CSZ tree numbers are actually increasing.

Overall, therefore, trends in forestry resources and landscapes are contradictory, with stable or expanding landscapes and increasing tree numbers in some areas coexisting with decreasing tree densities and contracting landscapes in others. Such spatial and temporal variations raise the crucial question of how indigenous forestry can integrate environmental stability with growth in productivity, while ensuring relative equity of access to productive assets and economic opportunities (cf. Egger and Majeres, 1993). In other words, how can sustainable forestry livelihoods be achieved and protected under these circumstances?

Towards sustainable forestry livelihoods

Livelihood security needs to be integrated with environmental conservation to achieve sustainable indigenous forestry. This requires various combinations of the following (cf. Hardoy *et al.*, 1992).

The conservation of specific types of forest, woodland, trees and shrubs

Indigenous foresters are very deliberate in their exploitation and management of trees, shrubs and wilderness areas for products and services. The latter frequently complement, but rarely, replace each other. In particular, 'dedicated' or uni-purpose species (e.g. *Eucalyptus*, *Azadirachta indica*) make inadequate substitutes for multi-purpose trees and shrubs, which make more efficient use of land and labour. Similarly, shade or boundary species cannot replace those, like *Acacia albida*, which can be profitably interspersed with crops. Hunters, herders, and collectors of timber, honey and medicinal products all express clear preferences for, and dislikes of, various forest/woodland communities and

tree/shrub species for a whole range of use and non-use values. Individual trees and shrubs, like (sub-)species and whole vegetation communities, are credited with identifiable characteristics, which influence their desirability for goods, services and material for propagation. The full range and diversity of species and forestry communities must be maintained, even expanded, if present and future needs are to be met.

The conservation of entire agri-silvi-pastoral landscapes

As important as the need to conserve individual forestry components, is the necessity for whole forestry landscapes to be conserved. Pastoral livelihoods depend heavily on access to, and movement between, the various components of indigenous forestry landscapes; agroforesters combine crop cultivation on upland with *fadama* farming and, in some areas, with fishing; and livelihoods of the landless and land-poor are heavily dependent on access to a variety of communal resources in different parts of the landscape. The conservation of entire landscapes not only facilitates livelihood diversity, it also influences macro- and micro-climatology and ecology, and enhances the conservation of individual landscape components.

A continuing ability to grow trees and shrubs

This involves considerably more than just detailed knowledge of the propagation and silviculture of dryland species (learned as part of farming), and the availability of planting material. Security of land and tree tenure is crucial to the ability to grow trees and shrubs. Tenant agroforesters and those experiencing land shortage do not invest in perennial farm trees. Similarly, where silvi-pastoralists neither own nor retain the right of exclusion over rangeland fodder resources, they are more likely to adopt 'passive' (simple, sometimes intensive, exploitation) rather than 'active' (conservation, regulation, skilful use of fire) measures in the 'management' of such resources. Thus agroforesters in some of the CSZs complain of the routine destructive lopping of fodder trees on farmland by pastoralists; this is relatively rare on rangeland, where it tends to be pronounced only during periods of drought and famine. Pressures on the state to resolve issues of pastoral land rights and the plight of the landless and land-poor are likely to intensify with population growth, agricultural expansion and the intensification of farming. This will benefit tree planting, which tends to increase at the expense of the simple tending of volunteer seedlings as land use becomes more intensive.

A capacity to sustain forestry production in all its diversity

While, for example, farm trees may produce enough fuelwood to meet rural needs, even in some of the most densely populated areas, urban fuel demand must be met from *daji* if it is to be satisfied in its entirety, and if periurban farm trees and agricultural land are to be conserved. However, the complete clearance of forests and woodlands leads to a loss of biodiversity and reduction in environmental complexity, and undermines the natural resource base, which supports livelihood diversity. The need to maintain a diverse forestry base cannot, therefore, be sufficiently emphasized, particularly in a drought-prone region where food shortages and famines are recurrent phenomena, and where drought and famine coping mechanisms depend heavily on knowledge of, and access to, sylvan products and environments. Sustaining forestry production in all its diversity contributes to sustainable livelihood security, which is enhanced by the ownership of the land, livestock or trees, and/or secure access or rights to grazing, cultivation, fishing, hunting or collecting.

Conclusion

Meaningful studies of dryland forestry must address the livelihood concerns of the inhabitants

of these resource-poor and ecologically vulnerable areas *as well as* the sustainability of these environments (Chambers, 1987). The two sets of concerns are inextricably linked in indigenous forestry managment. The latter distinguishes between farm and forest, but does not separate the management of farmland from that of forest: individual tree management can take place in *daji* (e.g. for bee-keeping) while whole stands of trees are managed on *karkara* and *saura* (e.g a live hedge). Management can be *passive* (simple collection of sylvan products) or *active* (protection or propagation of vegetation), with the latter increasing at the expense of the former as population density and land-use intensity increase, and as security of tenure is achieved.

The human-focused version of sustainable development used in this chapter offers a framework for studying these different elements of indigenous forestry, as the latter continues to evolve under a range of internal and external influences.

References

Adams, W. M. and Hollis, G. E. (1987) *The Hadejia–Nguru Wetlands Project. Hydrology and sustainable resource development of a Sahelian floodplain wetland*, University College, London.

Adams, W. M. and Kimmage, K. (1992) Wetland agricultural production and river basin development in the Hadejia–Jama'are valley, Nigeria, *Geographical Journal*, 158, 1–12.

Anderson, D. (1987) *The Economics of Afforestation: A Case Study in Africa*, Johns Hopkins University Press, Baltimore, MD.

Barbier, E. B., Adams, W. M. and Kimmage, K. (1991) *Economic Valuation of Wetland Benefits: the Hadejia–Jama'are floodplain, Nigeria*, International Institute for Environment and Development/London Environmental Economics Centre, London.

Chambers, R. (1987) *Sustainable Rural Livelihoods: a strategy for people, environment and development*, Commissioned Study No. 47, Institute of Development Studies, University of Sussex, Sussex.

Cline-Cole, R. A. (1994) Political economy, fuelwood relations and vegetation conservation in *Kasar* Kano, Northern Nigeria, 1850–1915, *Forest and Conservation History*, 38(2), 67–78.

Cline-Cole, R. A., Falola, J. A., Main, H. A. C., Mortimore, M. J., Nichol, J. E. and O'Reilly, F. D. (1990) *Woodfuel in Kano*, United Nations University Press, Tokyo.

Colchester, M. (1994) Sustaining the forests: the community-based approach in South and South-East Asia, *Development and Change*, 25(1), 69–100.

Conway, G. R. and Barbier, E. B. (1990) *After the Green Revolution. Sustainable agriculture for development*, Earthscan, London.

Egger, P. and Marjeres J. (1993) Local resource management and development: strategic dimensions of people's participation, pp. 304–324 in D. Ghai and J. M. Vivian (eds), *Grassroots Environmental Action. People's participation in sustainable development*, Routledge, London.

Hardoy, J. E., Mitlin, D. and Satterthwaite, D. (1992) *Environmental Problems in Third World Cities*, Earthscan, London.

Mitlin, D. (1992) Sustainable development—guide to the literature, *Environment and Urbanization*, 4(1), 111–124.

Mortimore, M. J. (1989) *The causes, nature and rate of soil degradation in the northernmost states of Nigeria, and an assessment of the role of fertilizer in counteracting the processes of degradation*, Working Paper 17, Environmental Department, World Bank, Washington.

Mortimore, M. J. (1993) Population growth and land degradation, *Geojournal*, 31(1), 15–21.

Mortimore, M. J., Essict, E. U. and Patrick, S. (1990) *The Nature, Rate and Effective Limits of Intensification in the Smallholder Farming System of the Kano Close-settled Zone*, Federal Agricultural Coordinating Unit, Ibadan, Nigeria.

Murdoch, J. (1993) Sustainable rural development: towards a research agenda, *Geoforum*, 24(3), 225–241.

Nair, P. K. R. (1989) Agroforestry systems, practices and technologies, pp. 53–62 in P. K. R. Nair (ed.) *Agroforestry Systems in the Tropics*, Kluwer Academic Publishers, Dordrecht, The Netherlands.

Pearce, D. W. (1990) *An Economic Approach to Saving the Tropical Forests*, LEEC Paper 90/6, London Environmental Economics Centre, London.

Pullan, R. A. (1974) Farmed parkland in West Africa, *Savanna*, 3(2), 119–151.

Redclift, M. (1993) Sustainable development and popular participation: a framework for analysis, pp. 23–49 in D. Ghai and J. M. Vivian (eds) *Grassroots Environmental Action. People's participation in sustainable development*, Routledge, London.

Shepherd, G. (1992) *Managing Africa's Tropical Dry Forests: a review of indigenous methods*, Overseas Development Institute, London.

Silviconsult Ltd (1990) *Northern Nigeria Household Energy Study*, Silviconsult, Bjarred, Sweden.

Swindell, K. (1986) Population and agriculture in the Sokoto–Rima basin of northwest Nigeria: a study of political intervention, adaptation and change, 1800–1980, *Cahiers d'Etudes Africaines*, 26(1–2), 75–112

Vivian, J. (1994) NGOs and sustainable development in Zimbabwe: no magic bullets, *Development and Change*, 25(1), 167–194.

Wilkinson, R. (1991) A case for the conservation of forest outliers in the Jema'a area, Kaduna State, pp. 131–138 in E. A. Olofin, S. P. Patrick and J. A. Falola (eds) *Land Administration and Development in Northern Nigeria: case studies*, Bayero University, Kano, Nigeria.

Woodhouse, P. (1992) Environmental degradation and sustainability, pp. 97–115 in T. Allen and A. Thomas (eds), *Poverty and Development in the 1990s*, Oxford University Press with the Open University, Oxford.

World Conservation Union (IUCN), World Wide Fund for Nature (WWF), United Nations Environment Programme (UNEP) (1980) *World Conservation Strategy*, IUCN, Gland, Switzerland.

16

Soil and fertilizer use among small-scale farmers on the Jos Plateau, Nigeria

Kevin D. Phillips-Howard

Introduction

The management of soil fertility in Africa has long been of interest to agronomists (e.g. Nye and Greenland, 1960; Allan, 1965), geographers (e.g. Beyer, 1980; Osunade, 1988) and anthropologists concerned with agricultural ecology and indigenous knowledge (e.g. Richards, 1985). In an applied context these interests also correspond with the people-oriented theme of rural development studies (e.g. Chambers *et al.*, 1989).

Soil fertility management is a basic ecological task of all arable farmers. It is essential for sustained crop production and the improvement of the farmers' livelihoods. To achieve these ends, farmers manipulate nutrient levels and soil physical conditions to meet the needs of their crops. This requires substantial knowledge of the local environment, including crops, fertilizers and soils. The utility of such indigenous knowledge, as shown in this case study, has become an important focus of people–environment relations in Africa.

Among small-scale farmers on the Jos Plateau, Nigeria, soil fertility is managed so as to gain as much edible and sellable crop as possible within

limited but changing circumstances. Many of these farmers are 'resource-poor', with little cash, simple technology and limited access to inputs. However, they are often 'rich' in ecological knowledge, which enables them to exploit opportunities through strategies and tactics well fitted to their circumstances.

The study area

The Jos Plateau (Figure 16.1) comprises 8600 km^2 of central Nigeria about 1200 m above sea level. The monthly mean temperatures of 20–24 °C are low for the latitude (10° N), while the rainfall of 1000–1500 mm per annum is comparatively high. The area comprises an undulating plain of Basement Complex rocks into which younger granites and basalts intrude to form rocky hills (Morgan, 1979). The plain is continually cultivable where water is available, but its deep, sandy soils are generally poor and susceptible to erosion. The more fertile flood terrace (*fadama*) soils are also cultivable in the dry season, which lasts from October to April.

People and Environment in Africa. Edited by Tony Binns
©1995 John Wiley & Sons Ltd

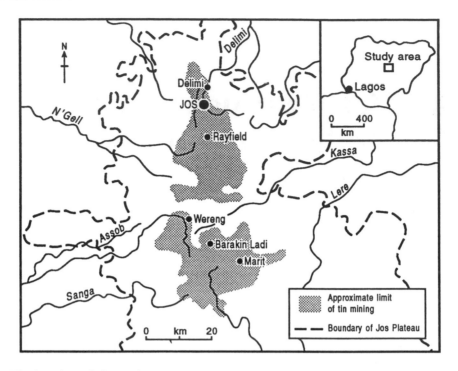

Figure 16.1 *The location of the study area*

The natural savanna vegetation has been removed from both the plain and many of the hills. The present non-cultivated vegetation on most of the plain comprises complexes of grass, shrub and woodland. There are 'economic trees' on the farmland and plantations, mainly of *Eucalyptus*. Whereas about 53% of the Jos Plateau is actively cultivated, the non-cultivated areas comprise: woodland, 37%; shrub/grassland, 6%; shrubland, 4%.

Ecological changes on the Jos Plateau

One of the main changes on the Jos Plateau has been the growth and decline of large-scale tin mining. Commercial tin mining began there in 1904 and peaked in 1943 when more than 15 000 tonnes of tin ore were produced. Subsequently mining declined, though it still continues on a small scale. Some 316 km² of minespoil was created, including various heaps, tailings and paddocks. Through the levelling of spoil heaps and filling of paddocks, about 10% of the mineland was restored or reclaimed, often with *Eucalyptus* plantations (Figure 16.2). The remaining spoil and the mine-ponds are now recognized as resources for agricultural and other uses (Figure 16.3).

Agriculture on the Jos Plateau also changed greatly during the twentieth century. This involved increases in the areas cultivated, numbers of farmers and variety of crops grown, with production becoming more intensive and market-oriented. Over most of the plain, the proportion of cultivated land increased to 75–90% by 1990 and both wet- and dry-season farming expanded on to former mineland. From the late 1980s, this 'informal reclamation' was encouraged by Nigeria's Structural Adjustment Programme (SAP) and an agricultural policy that focused on

Figure 16.2   *Abandoned mineland with eucalyptus plantations on the Jos Plateau*

small-scale farmers. General increases in the production of maize and irrigated dry-season crops also occurred and the Jos International Breweries outgrower scheme encouraged irrigated barley cultivation (Porter and Phillips-Howard, 1994) (Figure 16.4).

Despite this dynamism, small-scale agriculture was subject to severe constraints including poor soils, lack of capital and shortages of fertilizer and labour. The strategies and tactics discussed below represent the farmers' attempts to overcome these in order to improve their livelihoods.

Strategies and tactics

The information presented below is drawn from studies conducted in 1990 and 1991. The first of these (Phillips-Howard and Kidd, 1991) was a case study involving a short questionnaire survey and semi-structured interviews among 31 farmers along a section of the Delimi River. This was a 30% sample of the farmer population there. The second (Phillips-Howard, 1994) involved semi-structured interviews with 90 'contact farmers' in one of the Jos Plateau's extension areas; this sample represented 5% of all contact farmers in that area.

Soil conditioning

In tropical Africa, soil physical properties are especially important to crop yields. Often, more labour is allocated to provide physical conditions suitable for crop growth than to the improvement of soil fertility by organic means (Richards, 1983).

Figure 16.3 *Abandoned mineland with Fulani cattle drinking from a mine-pond*

On the Jos Plateau, large amounts of labour are invested in preparing the land using hoes. At the beginning of the wet season ridges are constructed, especially for maize, millet and sorghum. These ridges (1 m wide and 0.5 m high) maintain soil aeration, prevent waterlogging and facilitate stormwater runoff. They are constructed along the lines of earlier ditches and incorporated sediment that had accumulated in them. Grass and other growing vegetation is either turned in or covered during ridge construction, so providing organic manure. Smaller ridges are constructed for *acca* (the small-grained cereal *Digitaria exilis*), and larger ones for yams. Cocoyams are often grown in rectangular-shaped raised beds. Ridge construction is strategic in that it is sequential and includes ties, which help to minimize soil erosion.

The dry-season soil-conditioning strategy of farmers along the Delimi River near Jos transforms barren minespoil into productive farmland within a few years (Figure 16.5). In fact, though the farmers readily distinguish several types of soil (Table 16.1), they said that 'they are all the same if there is fertilizer' (Hausa: *dukansu dayome in da taki*) and 'there is none that surpasses the other in importance' (*ba wadda yafi wani amfani*). This was because, to them, 'farming is on the hand' (*gona na hannu*), meaning that soil management was more important than soil type. It was jokingly said that all soils, even 'rocks' (*dutse*), can be made suitable for dry-season farming.

Land clearance was said to have several purposes: provision of space to plant crops; assistance for crops to grow well; supply of plant

190

Figure 16.4 *Dry season barley on the Jos Plateau*

Table 16.1 *Delimi farmers' characterization of some soils*

Type (in Hausa)	Characteristics
Tabo	Sticky, holds water, black, red or white, good for crops. Can irrigate at 3–4 day intervals
Yashi	Loose, 'like guinea corn', well drained, needs more frequent irrigation, sometimes daily
Laka	Similar to *tabo*, but softer, can be formed into a ball
Yumbu	Clay for making pots
Para kasa or *taya rago*	Best soil for crops. Whatever is planted will grow well
Palele	Whitish, fine and shiny, cannot retain water, needs frequent irrigation, not fertile
Rai rai	Very soft soil
Sakuwa	Stony soil
Gabako or *kisitdano*	Reddish soil

Note: The soils are distinguished by colour, water-holding characteristics and irrigation requirement, 'softness' and suitability for crop growth.

Figure 16.5   *Dry season vegetables on the Jos Plateau*

nutrients; removal of pests, sticks and stones. This is highly labour-demanding and involves cutting bush, digging up grass and roots, extraction of stones, breaking of subsoil and burning. The latter provides fertilizer in the form of ash. Other fertilizers, cropping practices and the inclusion of trees may also have soil-conditioning effects. Certain of the tasks, like digging up roots, breaking of subsoil and stone removal, have cumulative effects on soil condition over several years.

Tillage and basin construction begins with thorough digging, further stone removal and hoeing of the soil into a fine tilth. The area is then levelled and, where there is a significant slope, small terraces are built. Basin construction involves creating a series of intersecting ridges to form square or rectangular basins, often 8–12 m^2 in area. Again, this has cumulative effects where basins are reconstructed yearly, the cultivated area is expanded and terraces are further developed.

Fertilizer combination

Fertilizer use on the Jos Plateau is complex and usually involves the combination of two or more types. Dry-season farmers around Jos apply various kinds of inorganic fertilizer plus ash derived from urban refuse. Many also apply organic manure of various kinds. The mixing of fertilizers is an old and well-established practice among dry-season farmers. Before the arrival of modern fertilizer it was common to mix sawdust, ash and cow manure together. Fertilizer combination seems to be an adaptation to uncertain nutrient availability. It allows avoidance of risks due to overdependence on one nutrient source.

According to the farmers, some of the benefits of fertilizer combination are softened soil, better crop growth and savings in fertilizer costs. Before considering these benefits in more detail the farmers' classification of fertilizer types is presented.

Fertilizer classification

The Delimi dry-season farmers recognize many different fertilizers (Hausa: *taki*) which are distinguished according to their characteristics and usefulness. Figure 16.6 gives the farmers' classification of fertilizers, with the major types: *takin zamani* (modern fertilizer) and *takin gargajiya* (traditional fertilizer). The latter is subdivided into two main classes *toka* (ash) and *kashi* (manure), in addition to *shara* (sweepings) and *bola* (domestic refuse).

Most traditional fertilizers are identified according to their source. This is also true of some modern fertilizers, in terms of their city of origin, e.g. *Dan* (son of) *Lagos*, *Kaduna* or *Port Harcourt*. Several modern fertilizers are identified

by their chemical name (e.g. CAN, *supa*, DAP). NPK 27 : 13 : 13 is called *waka da shinkafa* (beans and rice), because of its likeness to that food. This corresponds with the concept of fertilizer as *abincin kasa* (food of the soil). A preferred fertilizer is named *shinkafin gona* (rice of the farm).

The farmers' have their own criteria for distinguishing the different types of fertilizers. These are:

1. *karfi*—strength or power;
2. *zafi*—'hot', can 'burn' crops ('cold' is *sanyi*);
3. *baki*—blackness or dark-greenness of the crop;
4. *dadewa gona*—persistence on the farm;
5. availability;
6. *kama amfani*—usefulness;
7. *kuzari*—energy (growth of crops);
8. cost;
9. *ja*—red (redness of crops);
10. *laushe*—softness (of the soil).

Of these ten criteria, six relate to characteristics of the fertilizer (1, 2, 4, 5, 6, 8), three refer to effects on crops (3, 7, 9) and one is an effect on soil

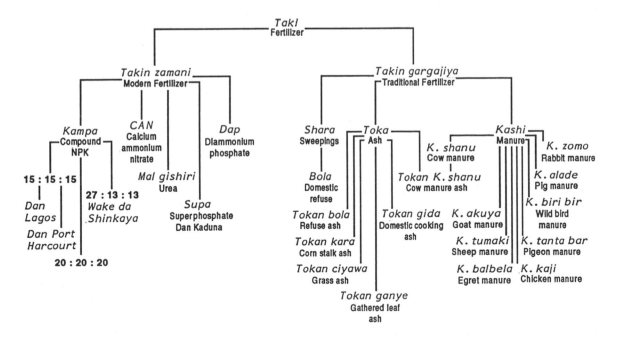

Figure 16.6 *The Delimi farmers' fertilizer classification. (After Phillips-Howard and Kidd, 1991)*

193

condition (10). Farmers can readily rank the fertilizers according to these criteria. The number of types used range from five to nine and always include a combination of modern fertilizer, refuse ash and manure.

Fertilizer ranking

The mean rankings of fertilizers in order of preference provided by 10 farmers were as follows: pig manure, NPK, DAP, Egret manure, goat manure, refuse ash, urea, *supa*, CAN, chicken, sheep and cow manure. Refuse ash is regarded as a cheap, highly available fertilizer which softens the soil. This material has a high pH (10.2), which tends to neutralize soild acidity and may contribute to the soil-softening effect.

NPK is thought to be strongest, among the most useful and available, but also most expensive, of the inorganic fertilizers. DAP is regarded as a very strong, crop-darkening and most useful fertilizer, which persists on the farm but is relatively unavailable in the market. By contrast, CAN is considered of little use though more available; it is regarded as comparatively weak yet 'hot', with the effects of reddening crops and hardening the soil.

Cow manure is rated low against most criteria, but its lack of use by the Delimi farmers is attributed to its seed content which necessitates extra labour costs in weeding. Egret manure is ranked among the strongest, hottest, most energy-giving and crop-darkening of all the fertilizers, characteristics associated with the rich, insect diet of the cattle egret; although it is relatively unavailable (only collectable under the birds' roosts) and known to harden the soil. Ironically, pig manure is ranked first and highly rated against most criteria, but it is said to be 'taboo' among the Muslim farmers.

Fertilizer mixing

Neither modern fertilizer nor refuse ash alone is considered as effective as a mixture of the two. Refuse ash is also mixed with sheep or goat manure. These mixtures are equated with *supa* plus CAN, and DAP alone, in terms of their strength. The farmers agree that CAN and *supa* should be combined with each other as well as with refuse ash. Though readily available, CAN is not much used by dry-season farmers, because of its 'hotness' and water-absorbing character. However, it is mixed with *supa* and together these two 'weak' fertilizers are considered as strong as DAP. Among the traditional fertilizers: cow manure plus chicken manure is equated with egret manure; chicken and goat manure are commonly mixed; cow, goat and sheep manure (all 'cold') are considered equivalent and interchangeable.

The study of 'contact farmers' (CFs) visited by village extension agents (VEAs) also found that fertilizer mixing is considered important for gaining satisfactory yields from little fertilizer. The CFs commonly report reductions in the total costs and amounts of fertilizer applied as a result of mixture.

Among the inorganic fertilizers known by the CFs, NPK 15 : 15 : 15 is most widely used, again mainly in mixtures. The commonest combination of NPK is with *supa*. This allows the NPK to persist in the soil and enables the CFs to eke out their fertilizer to attain satisfactory crop yields with minimal waste of capital.

The CFs also have a range of tactics used to maintain or improve soil fertility within their operational constraints. These include ways to: buy more inorganic fertilizer; use inorganic fertilizer more effectively; or use organic fertilizers or other traditional techniques (Table 16.2).

Implications for agricultural extension

The farmers' strategies and tactics are little understood by the VEAs, who are intent on encouraging the adoption of a few standard messages on 'optimal' fertilizer application. These messages include only inorganic types, which are either scarcely available or supplied too late. They also ignore the farmers' shortage of capital and labour. The farmers generally reject messages on fertilizer use and sometimes chase VEAs away because they cannot provide the necessary inputs.

Table 16.2 *Fertilizer use tactics of the contact farmers*

1. To buy more fertilizer:
   - struggle to buy fertilizer with cash available
   - sell dry-season harvest, or goats, to pay for fertilizer
   - mine and sell tin to pay for fertilizer
   - secure a paid job, e.g. labouring, to pay for fertilizer
2. To use available inorganic fertilizer more effectively:
   - weed thoroughly to minimize losses of fertilizer to weeds
   - plant beans below the placement of fertilizer
   - mix soil with fertilizer, especially for growing maize
   - apply inorganic fertilizer to small areas and cover with soil
   - reduce the size of fertilizer applications if there is little
3. To use organic fertilizers and other traditional techniques:
   - use organic manures, e.g. manure, ash, refuse and sweepings
   - grow *acca*, which requires comparatively little fertilizer
   - rotate maize, guinea corn, *acca* and millet
   - dig deeply (with a tractor) to bring nutrients to the surface
   - store manure for a year prior to use to destroy weed seeds
   - burn manure prior to use to destroy weed seeds
   - construct effective drainage to minimize fertilizer leaching
   - cultivate and mound up soil carefully to increase crop yields
   - grow soy beans to improve soil fertility
   - space plants more widely to exploit soil fertility fully

The limited role of the extension service in the improvement of fertilizer use on the Jos Plateau could be increased by greater involvement of farmers. As Tamang (1993) also notes, with regard to soil fertility management in Nepal, outsiders should learn from farmers' approaches to problems and help to strengthen their existing practices. This would enable the farmers' knowledge and priorities to generate more relevant messages and technologies. Greater farmer participation could transform the interaction between VEAs and CFs, without extra demands on the time of either. A more facilitatory extension service may need the support of an efficient fertilizer distribution system and reactivated farm service centres.

Conclusion

Soil fertility management among small-scale farmers on the Jos Plateau involves two general strategies, soil conditioning and fertilizer combination, and various lesser tactics. These all contribute to the development of productive agriculture on former mineland.

The importance of considering local circumstances, particularly the constraints to production, was indicated by the marginal relevance of the extension service's messages. These overlooked the farmers' need to be frugal with limited resources as in the mixing of fertilizers to eke them out and reduce costs. This strategy resembles that of Filipino farmers, who applied fertilizer so as to maintain rice crop 'health' at minimum cost (Perrot-Maitre and Weaver, 1992). In both cases, the farmers' strategies involved ingenious use of limited amounts of fertilizer rather than the recommended 'optimal' applications.

Clearly, small-scale farmers can successfully adapt their fertilizer use towards survival and livelihood goals within their production constraints. For such adaptive ingenuity to be encouraged, the work of extension services needs to be reoriented and made more relevant to farmers' circumstances. Such reorientation should be based on full participation of the farmers in the adaptation and development of fertilizer and soil-conditioning technologies. This process should be complemented by policies and institutions which can effectively deliver the fertilizer and other inputs sought by the farmers.

Acknowledgements

This work was supported by the Jos Plateau Environmental Resources Development Programme (JPERDP), a linkage project between the University of Jos, Nigeria and Durham University, UK; it was funded by the European Development Fund, Project No. 5106.53.41.001 and the University of Jos.

Kevin D. Phillips-Howard

References

Allan, W. (1965) *The African Husbandman*, Oliver and Boyd, London.

Beyer, J. L. (1980) Africa, pp. 5–37, Chapter 2 in G. Klee (ed.), *World Systems of Traditional Resource Management*, Winston, New York.

Chambers, R., Pacey, A. and Thrupp, L. A. (1989) *Farmer First: farmer innovation and agricultural research*, Intermediate Technology Publications, London.

Morgan, W. T. W. (ed.) (1979) *The Jos Plateau: a survey of environmental and land use*, Occasional Publications (New Series), No. 14, Department of Geography, University of Durham, Durham, 45 pp.

Nye, P. H. and Greenland, D. J. (1960) *The Soil under Shifting Cultivation*, Commonwealth Agricultural Bureau Technical Communication No. 51, Harpenden.

Osunade, M. A. A. (1988) Soil suitability classification by small farmers, *The Professional Geographer*, 40(2), 194–201.

Perrot-Maitre, D. and Weaver, T. F. (1992) Indigenous knowledge and fertiliser strategies in Leyte, Philippines. Implications for research and demonstration trials, *Journal for Farming Systems Research—Extension*, 3(1), 21–34.

Phillips-Howard, K. D. (1994) Training and visit extension and fertilizer use: the case of the Jos Plateau, Nigeria, *Applied Geography*, 14(3), 245–263.

Phillips-Howard, K. D. and Kidd A. D. (1991) *Knowledge and Management of Soil Fertility among Dry Season Farmers on the Jos Plateau, Nigeria*, Jos Plateau Environmental Resources Development Programme, Interim Report, No. 25, University of Durham, Durham, 21 pp.

Porter, G. and Phillips-Howard, K. D. (1994) Outgrower barley cultivation on the Jos Plateau, Nigeria: a case study of agricultural innovation under 'SAP', *Geographical Journal*, 160(3), 319–327.

Richards, P. (1983) Farming systems and agrarian change in West Africa, *Progress in Human Geography*, 7(1), 1–39.

Richards, P. (1985) *Indigenous Agricultural Revolution*, Hutchinson, London.

Tamang, D. (1993) *Living in a Fragile Ecosystem: indigenous soil management in the hills of Nepal*, International Institute for Environment and Development Gatekeeper Series No. 41, London.

17

Adapting to environment and market: trade and marketing in northern Nigeria

Gina Porter

Introduction

This chapter uses field research and colonial archives to chart the spatial pattern of local and long-distance trade in Borno,[1] north-eastern Nigeria, over the last century or so. Local cultural conditions, state policy, transport technology and external international influences are all significant forces shaping Borno trade. However, the evidence presented here illustrates that environmental factors have played, and continue to play, a particularly fundamental role in the development of trade in this region, as elsewhere in Africa (see Chapter 18).

Ecologically based long-distance trade has long been a feature of the continent. The diverse environments of tropical forest, savanna and desert stimulated indigenous trade centuries before external penetration of the continent occurred (Curtin, 1984, Chapter 2; Little, 1992, Chapter 3). In West Africa historical research indicates a particularly intensive zone of pre-colonial trading activity across the Sahel, linking communities of nomadic pastoralists to the north with sedentary farmers of the savanna and tropical forests to the south (Lovejoy and Baier, 1975; Baier, 1980; Lovejoy, 1980). Grain and manufactures were

exported from the savanna to the desert edge in return for salt and dates. Resources of the forest zone, notably kola, were brought north and exchanged for a diversity of produce from areas like Borno and Hausaland: textiles, livestock, leather goods, slaves, natron, dried onion leaves and shea butter. A complex pattern of re-exporting took desert-side produce to the forest, and forest products up to the desert edge. Such trade was well established and highly organized by the eighteenth century. Additionally, there were important trade routes across the Sahara linking the savanna regions to Morocco, Tunisia, Libya and the Mediterranean coast (Figure 17.1).

For the cultivators resident in the northern savannas, where the dry season is lengthy, participation in long-distance trade became an especially important element in household incomes. Some entrepreneurs established themselves along the trade routes and in distant trade centres and, in their role as landlords to the members of visiting caravans, became important links in extended trade diasporas. Islam played a vital role in the development of this trade through its unifying ideology and its influence on commercial procedures (Lovejoy, 1980, 144–145).

People and Environment in Africa. Edited by Tony Binns
©1995 John Wiley & Sons Ltd

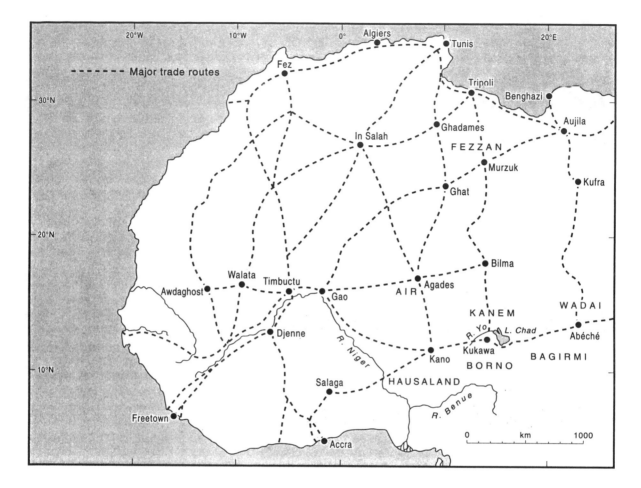

Figure 17.1 *West Africa in the pre-colonial period*

The imposition of colonial rule subsequently reshaped both long-distance and local trading patterns to some degree, through the establishment of boundaries, the introduction of new transport technologies, the exploitation of different resources and markets, and indirectly through its influence on population growth and redistribution. Nonetheless, broader constraints imposed by physical environment and resource endowment have remained a backcloth against which the interplay of political, economic and socio-cultural elements influencing both long-distance and local trade takes place.

Borno, located in the far north-east corner of Nigeria, provides a fascinating case study of changing patterns of trade. Most of the region is sparsely populated Sudan savanna (possibly still averaging under 50 persons per km²), with a rainy season largely restricted to five months, from May to September. Average annual rainfall at the state capital, Maiduguri (latitude 11 ° 51′ N), is about 660 mm (26 inches) but variability from year to year is considerable. The discussion here focuses mainly on the area occupied by the emirate of Borno, roughly coincident with the Borno state established in 1976 (i.e. before its partition into two states—Borno and Yobe—in 1991).

Trade and environment in pre-colonial Borno

Water availability has played a critical role in the economic development of Borno. In the nineteenth century, although Borno was notorious for its part in the trans-Saharan slave trade, this was an enclave activity of the urban-based ruling class. The majority of the indigenous Kanuri population were probably more deeply involved in the local economy and, to a lesser extent, in long-distance trade within West Africa. The extraction of salt and potash from the borders of Lake Chad and the region north of the River Yobe, and its transport westwards to Hausaland and southwards to the Benue was a particularly important activity. Extraction and trade in these commodities were encouraged by the length of the dry season and the consequent need for dry-season occupations to supplement wet-season cultivation. The majority of the salt workers were free migrant labourers who moved northwards in the dry season and established temporary camps at the salt workings (Lovejoy, 1986). Kanuri and Hausa traders transported potash westwards to Hausaland as a return load for kola—used as a mild stimulant—from the Volta Basin, and tobacco, cotton cloth and clothing from Hausaland. Other important regional economic enterprises included pastoralism, notably around the shores of Lake Chad, and horses, bred by Shuwa Arabs. Borno was the principal exporter of horses to other regions of present-day Nigeria and also supplied places as distant as Salaga and the Fezzan (Figure 17.1).

However, in this period the whole of Borno appears to have been suffering from the aftermath of the mid-eighteenth century 'Great Drought' and continued climatic deterioration. Lovejoy (1978) ascribes Borno's position as an 'economic satellite' of the central Hausa country, by the end of the nineteenth century, principally to the deteriorating environmental conditions. A number of Kanuri traders had left the region and relocated their enterprises in Hausaland early in the nineteenth century, possibly encouraged by better climatic conditions further west. The density of population in many rural areas appears to have been inadequate to support a thriving rural economy and a substantial export trade. The region's vulnerability to drought was already an important constraint on production and trade.

Colonial change

In the dry season of 1902 a British expeditionary force entered Borno, and nearly 60 years of colonial rule followed. The prospects for the region were perceived to be limited; it is 'flat, stale and unprofitable: no hills or rivers' (Borno Emirate Assessment Report, 1913). Colonial records in the Nigerian national archives—district notebooks, officers' touring diaries, assessment reports, etc.—from the early 1900s through to independence record the vital significance of water for economic development; indeed, for survival. Drought was an important theme: in 1913, the region (along with much of the Sudan zone from Senegal to Ethiopia) experienced severe drought, the worst since the eighteenth century, though deaths from starvation in Borno Province were reported only in Bedde, to the west of Borno Emirate. The severity of its impact on production and trade was recorded in government and trading company reports; it continues to be recalled even today among indigenes of the region. The total population of the emirate declined from 499 000 in 1913 to 354 061 in 1914, mainly through temporary migration, according to provincial reports of 1915. Statistics indicate a decline in *village* (not nomad-owned) cattle to nearly one-third, and of village sheep and goats to under one-twentieth of former numbers, between 1912 and 1915, on the far north-western edge of Borno (Machena assessment report, 1919). The London and Kano trading company representative in Kano wrote home to headquarters on 21 September 1914: '[the famine] is especially bad in Bornu . . . this will have a bad effect on our Canteen [retail merchandise] trade'.

Even in less harsh years, colonial officers observed the close relationship between population distribution and water supply in Borno. The assessment report of 1912, for example, records that population distribution was 'thickest near streams'. In favoured areas indigenous irrigation of vegetable crops was practised (notably by the Shuwa Arabs, an important minority group in Borno) and the produce was sold in local markets (Mongonu district notes, 1922). In areas with shallow wells, migration of population was inevitable when the water supply was exhausted (Gumsu district report, 1923). The colonial administration rapidly commenced well-sinking at selected locations to encourage permanent settlement and indigenous trade, both seen to be necessary for political stability and exploitation of the region's resources. By 1919 the sinking of six or seven wells had 'materially aided in the development of the market' at Potiskum (annual report, 1919). In the early 1930s a major well-sinking programme was under way (annual report, 1931).

The problems of water shortage were particularly evident in the pastoralist industry, which the colonial administration sought to foster. The distance of the majority of Borno from major lines of communication suggested the wisdom of focusing on the development of pastoralism. Animal ownership among the semi-nomadic Shuwa, Fulani and Kwoyam and the settled Kanuri and Shuwa was substantial and it was envisaged that hide and skin production could be developed for export. Unfortunately, Borno hides were subsequently judged the poorest quality in Nigeria, because of the poor grazing of the semi-arid rangelands and the scratching of animals' hides by acacia thorns as they fed. Shortage of water at slaughter caused additional damage through staining of skins (Hides and Skins Mission, 1948; Colonial Office: Report of a tanner's mission to Nigeria, 1956). The improvement in water supply achieved through the well-sinking programme did not solve the problem. Overgrazing was a serious concern in the late 1950s, despite an intensive borehole programme in which holes were drilled at approximately 16 km intervals to tap artesian and subartesian water. At that time there were 74 artesian boreholes and 13 subartesian boreholes. However, the average density of artesian wells in

Borno, overall, was still only one for every 313 km^2. Shortly after independence, a Borno Native Authority report on rural water supply (1962) remarked upon on the imminent arrival of the geographer, A. T. Grove, to examine the problems of overgrazing in the artesian area. The problems were exacerbated, however, by a major campaign of rinderpest inoculation in 1960–63, and the good rains of the 1960s, both of which contributed to further enlargement of herds (Grove, 1985, pp. 164–165).

Although water supply was probably the most critical environmental constraint for resource development in colonial Borno, the importance of another factor, accessibiity, became increasingly apparent. This had two interconnected aspects: the development of motorized transport within Borno, and the broader problem of links between Borno and the southern coast of Nigeria. The British pursued a policy of reorientating trade with world markets from north (over the Sahara) to south (the sea route to Europe). Thus whereas Borno, in pre-colonial times, had an equal advantage with Hausaland in terms of distance to the Mediterranean coast via the Sahara, it occupied a peripheral position in the colonial state of Nigeria.

Many parts of Borno experienced considerable accessibility problems because of local soil conditions. The water-retentive clays of the *firki* (black cotton soil) areas, while ideal for dry-season sorghum production, became impassable in the wet season. The light *kesa* sands were difficult for motorized transport even in the dry season. The construction of paved roads thus became increasingly critical to Borno trade, especially since the region was not deemed sufficiently resource rich to merit the early construction of a rail link to the coast. In 1905 Flora Shaw (wife of the first High Commissioner of Nigeria, Sir Frederick Lugard) recommended the construction of a light railway from the Niger to Kano, 'when the markets of this district [are] worked it would perhaps be time enough to extend a similar cheap service from Kano to the capital of Bornu' (Shaw, 1905, p. 499). This comment was representative of prevailing attitudes towards Borno.

Although a railway extension from Kano to Nguru, on the western edge of Borno, was opened in 1930 (initiating a local boom in groundnut production), central Borno did not obtain a rail link with the rest of the country until after independence. One of the first all season roads (to Jos) was opened in 1925/26. At that time it took three days to travel the 553 km route between Kano and Maiduguri (Migeod, 1924). The Jos route, and subsequent road construction (principally after independence), had a major impact on the Borno economy. Grain and other foodstuffs from Borno were sent in increasing quantities to the food-deficit tin-mining areas of the plateau. The live cattle trade expanded enormously in response to growing markets for meat in the forest zone of southern Nigeria, though this trade was largely dominated by the Hausa, especially from western Borno. The dried fish trade from Lake Chad continued to be hampered by poor access until the opening of the all-weather Maiduguri to Baga road in 1969; dried fish production rose from 6.4 million kg in 1969 to 26.5 million kg in 1971 (Osuji, 1976).

Despite changes wrought by colonial rule, some traditional indigenous long-distance trade along the old routes to the north continued, at least in the early years following colonization. Along the northern border of Borno, interaction was tenuously maintained with the desert-side economy, despite occasional closures of the Niger–Nigeria boundary. At Nguru's camel market, the remnants of this trade were observed with the Tibbu continuing to bring down camels from Niger to exhange for sugar and tea (Provincial Office report, 1936). Even surreptitious, illegal, movements of slaves northwards into Niger were sporadically detected, as was noted in a Kanembu district touring report of 1935.

The long dry season continued to favour trading expeditions and *cin rani* (dry-season migration). *Masu cin rani* are savanna people who migrate to find employment and income in the dry season when agricultural activities at home are at a minimum, thus helping to conserve food supplies (Prothero, 1957; Mortimore, 1989, pp. 196–199). The district and touring reports refer to the prevalence of *cin rani*, particularly to the salt deposits, and also cite many examples of dry-season trade, which in the early years was normally conducted using donkey transport. In the Dapchi area traders generally made three journeys to Kano per dry season in the 1920s, while in the 1930s Magumeri traders made three journeys *per month* to more local centres: either to Potiskum with potash (returning with corn) or with skins and hides to Maiduguri (returning with scents, used in quantity by men). In Gujba district, potash and salt were traded in the dry season, traders making a five-day journey with potash purchased (for three shillings per block) at the district's main market, Goniri, four blocks per donkey, south to Ashaka (on a tributary of the River Benue), where it could be sold at double the price, and a return-load of salt purchased.

Problems since independence

Since independence in 1960, low rainfall and the peripheral location of the region in the Federal Republic of Nigeria have continued to hinder development in Borno. The belated arrival of the railway at Maiduguri in 1964 had only a short-term impact on export trade, because it was followed by severe drought in the early 1970s, which brought an immediate halt to hitherto expanding groundnut and cattle production. During the ensuing oil boom (c. 1974–81) considerable sums, generated by the export of petroleum from the oilfields of south-eastern Nigeria, were invested in road construction throughout northern Nigeria. The introduction of a uniform subsidized petrol price in 1973, and the wage rises initiated by the government's Udoji pay awards to public sector employees in 1975, encouraged substantial growth in the transport sector; vehicle ownership rose rapidly and many new transport companies commenced operation. These changes influenced local patterns of trade, perhaps most obviously through their impact on the rural periodic market system. Field surveys of markets in four rural districts surrounding the state capital, Maiduguri, in the late 1970s and early 1980s, showed a substantial reorganization of trade through the movement of settlements and markets to the roadside (Porter, 1988). Throughout the region, such flexibility has been assisted by the limited infrastructural investment in villages and markets in Borno.

In the many areas with water supply problems, however, water remains a critical second factor for market growth. Lack of a good supply can threaten market trade even in a settlement endowed with the advantages of location on a paved road. Water is required by cultivators in the settlement, but also by visiting pastoralist groups, who contribute to the market trade in many settlements. The experience of the village of Auno,

on the main Maiduguri–Potiskum–Kano road (Figure 17.2), provides clear illustration of this point. This settlement has an administrative function, as headquarters for the surrounding district, and there are two boreholes, drilled about 1979. Trade grew in Auno's weekly Sunday market (established prior to independence) following its removal to a new site on the edge of the village, and assisted by the expansion of traffic along the road, the establishment of a secondary school in 1982 and the construction of a dispensary. In 1984 the region was again in the grips of severe drought, 1983 being the driest year in the locality this century (Kolawole, 1987). Attendance at the market declined rapidly

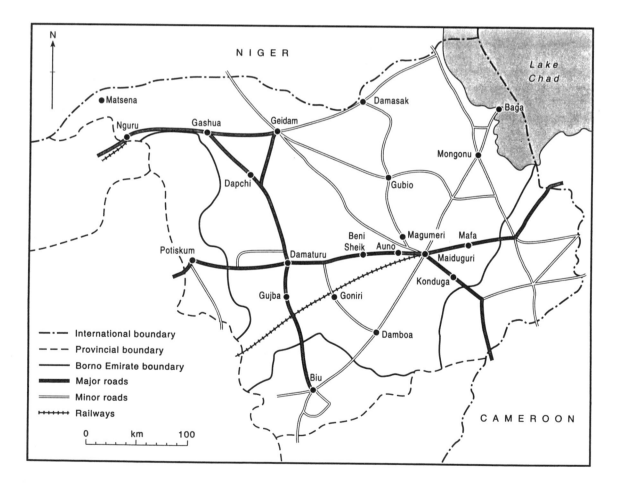

Figure 17.2 *The Borno region*

following the breakdown of pump engines which put both boreholes out of action for over six months. A visit to the settlement in June 1984 found richer members of the community purchasing their water from Maiduguri (nearly 34 km distant) at the exorbitant cost of 2N per drum (at prevailing exchange rates, about £1.60). Poorer villagers were forced to take all their water from a hole normally used principally for watering animals. Many people were suffering from water-borne infections which reduced their capacity to farm. The slaughter house at Auno was closed due to lack of water, animals could no longer be slaughtered in the market, and meat had to be brought from Maiduguri. The market was empty. In nearby Mafa district about 15 boreholes had been drilled by the state government between 1977 and 1984, but three-quarters were not functioning in the 1984 drought due to pump failure, some having been out of action for two years!

Not surprisingly, in a state-wide survey of rural development, Ijere (1983) found water to be the main constraint on settlement. Settlement location is still closely related to perennial streams and lakes and areas where the water table is sufficiently close to the surface to permit well sinking. The 1980s was the driest decade this century in Borno. The South Chad Irrigation Project, a large and costly scheme which commenced in 1974, has been severely affected by declining rainfall in the Chari–Logone catchment areas which feed Lake Chad. The scheme contributes little to agricultural production in the region because it depends on water pumped from the lake. In 1984–85 the edge of Lake Chad retreated many kilometres from the canal intended to take water to the extraction pipes, thus leaving the irrigation system stranded. However, cultivation (of maize and cowpeas) and grazing on the lake floor expanded substantially following the lake's recession, ameliorating the effects of the drought for local people. Recessional cultivation and grazing on the lake shore have long been traditional strategies for coping with drought in the region. Now many settlements, some fairly permanent, have been established on the lake floor, which appears to have enormous agricultural potential (Kolawole, 1987, 1988).

Since the collapse of oil prices and the imposition of a national Structural Adjustment Programme in mid-1986, Borno has experienced further difficulties, particularly with reference to accessibility. The remoteness of off-road areas has intensified, because transporters and traders are increasingly reluctant to risk their vehicles beyond the paved road. New vehicles are exorbitantly costly and spare parts difficult to come by. Only 68 new commercial vehicles were purchased in Borno state in 1986, according to federal government statistics, compared with 2287 in 1982. This is, of course, a common problem of remote areas in the many African countries currently undergoing structural adjustment programmes (Harral, 1988).

In the harsh environmental conditions of Borno, and the broader context of national development strategies which for many years focused resources on urban areas, it is hardly surprising that mobility remains an important coping strategy. (Michael Mortimore (1989) has demonstrated this particularly effectively in a detailed study of the Manga village of Dagaceri, on the far north-western border of Borno.) Mobility takes the form of both local settlement migration—for example from old shoreline locations on Lake Chad to the lake floor—and longer distance dry-season migrations to urban and rural areas, though the urban areas are not the magnet they were in the oil boom. Flexibility is similarly exhibited in the continuing widespread importance of pluri-activity. In my Borno market surveys in the late 1970s and 1984, 20 different combinations of occupation were identified among traders, many of which were pursued concurrently.

Conclusion

Historical research suggests that environment played an important part in the development of trade in pre-colonial Borno. Problems of water supply and, increasingly, accessibility are pervasive themes of the colonial records. More recent field study in rural Borno indicates that the significance of these factors has persisted in the post-colonial era, despite considerable state expenditure on boreholes and roads. The Borno economy remains plagued by drought and the region's peripheral location.

Notes

1. Borno is now the official spelling for Borno state and the Borno region. In the colonial and early independence period the region was known as 'Bornu'.

A note on archival sources

The majority of archives referred to in this study are deposited in the Nigerian National Archives, Kaduna, Nigeria (NAK). Exceptions include the London and Kano trading company correspondence, held in the Picton Archives, Liverpool (PA), and Colonial Office reports on the Nigerian hides and skins industry, held by the Public Record Office, London (PRO). Specific references are as follows:

● NAK: SNP 10, 286p/1913 Bornu Emirate assessment report; SNP 10 169p/1915 Bornu annual report 1914; SNP 10 63p/1915 Quarterly report, December quarter 1914; SNP 17, 12168 Machena district assessment report 1919; SNP 15 Acc 317 Mongonu district notes *c.* 1922; SNP 9 2350/1923 Gumsu district special report; SNP 74p/1919 Bornu annual report 1918; SNP 16817 vol. 1 Bornu annual report 1931; SNP 4883 Hides and skins missions, 1948 and 1954; SNP 4335 Hides and skins trade; BORNUNA 296/S.1 1961; MAIPROF Maiduguri Provincial Office report 1817 1936; MAIPROF 3300 Kanembu district touring report 1935; MAIPROF 187 Borsari district assessment report 1928; MAIPROF 521 Gujba district report 1927; MAIPROF 18A Magumeri district assessment report 1934.

● PA: 380 LON Box 1 Correspondence Kano–Liverpool 380 1/1/1–1/1/155.

● PRO: CO 852/1197/5 Report of a tanner's mission to Nigeria, 1956; CO 852/996/4 Cattle mission to Nigeria.

References

Baier, S. (1980) Ecologically based trade and the state in precolonial Africa, *Cahiers d'études africaines*, 20, 149–154.

Curtin, P. D. (1984) *Cross-cultural Trade in World History*, Cambridge University Press, Cambridge.

Grove, A. T. (ed.) (1985) *The Niger and its Neighbours*, Balkema, Rotterdam.

Harral, C. (1988) *Road Deterioration in Developing Countries: causes and remedies*, World Bank Policy Study, World Bank, Washington, DC.

Ijere, J. A. (1983) Local organisations as mechanisms for rural development in Borno State, Nigeria: analysis of spatial processes and patterns, unpublished Ph.D. thesis, Michigan State University.

Kolawole, A. (1987) Environmental change in the South Chad Irrigation Project (Nigeria), *J. of Arid Environments*, 13, 169–176.

Kolawole, A. (1988) Cultivation of the floor of Lake Chad: a response to environmental hazard in eastern Borno, Nigeria, *Geographical J.*, 154, 243–250.

Little, P. (1992) *The Elusive Granary: herder, farmer and state in northern Kenya*, Cambridge University Press, Cambridge.

Lovejoy, P. E. (1978) The Borno salt industry, *Int. J. of African Historical Studies*, 11(4), 629–668.

Lovejoy, P. E. (1980) *Caravans of Kola*, Ahmadu Bello University Press, Zaria.

Lovejoy, P. E. (1986) *Salt of the Desert Sun: a history of salt production and trade in the central Sudan*, Cambridge University Press, Cambridge.

Lovejoy, P. E. and Baier, S. (1975) The desert-side economy of the central Sudan, *Int. J. of African Historical Studies*, 8(4), 551–581.

Migeod, F. W. H. (1924) *Through Nigeria to Lake Chad*, London.

Mortimore, M. (1989) *Adapting to Drought: farmers, famines and desertification in West Africa*, Cambridge University Press, Cambridge.

Osuji, F. N. C. (1976) The dried fish commerce in Nigeria, *Nigerian Field*, 41, 3–18.

Porter, R. E. (1988) Perspectives on trade, mobility and gender in a rural market system: Borno, north-east Nigeria, *Tijdschrift voor Econ. en Soc. Geografie*, 79(2), 82–92.

Prothero, R. M. (1957) Migratory labour from north-western Nigeria, *Africa*, 27, 251–261.

Shaw, F. L. (1905) *A Tropical Dependency*, James Nisbet, London.

18

Ecological diversity and its impact on rural marketing channels in the Bamenda Highlands, Cameroon

Graham Hollier

Introduction

Prior to the modern era of rapid urbanization, the greater part of any trade in foodstuffs in Africa was between rural communities living in different ecological zones. Mutually exclusive farm products could be exchanged, or craft goods could be procured in return for produce. Trade has been, and continues to be, conducted over considerable distances, as between the forest and savanna and Sahel zones of West Africa (Hopkins, 1973; Onyemelukwe *et al.*, 1977; Lovejoy, 1980), as well as over much shorter distances where sharp differences in relief, climate and vegetation create opportunities for intra-regional commodity movements. Such a case is provided by the marketing channels found in and close to the Bamenda Highlands of Cameroon.

In the last quarter of the nineteenth century the first European explorers in the Bamenda Highlands found trade flourishing in a complex network of periodic rural markets. Today, the greater part of the staple food stuffs that pass through these same market-places is destined for towns at higher levels in the country's urban hierarchy. The periodic rural markets are structured to allow rural consumers wider access to manufactured goods brought in by itinerant urban-based traders, but more importantly, they are linked in such a way as to facilitate the sale and distribution of local farm produce. They act as collection points for local produce and as magnets for bulk-buying traders from the urban centres. Some part of the produce on display, however, continues to fulfil a longer-standing role in an essentially rural to rural distribution, between different ecological zones within a spatially more restricted area than is often the case in rural to urban marketing channels. The intention in this chapter is to examine how ecological variations within a relatively restricted geographical area can continue to exert influence on the pattern of marketing between rural communities, even when the bulk of commodity flows are destined for a major urban market.

The environmental context

The Bamenda Highlands is part of the mountainous backbone of Cameroon that stretches from

People and Environment in Africa. Edited by Tony Binns
©1995 John Wiley & Sons Ltd

Mount Cameroon in the south by way of the Adamawa Massif to the Mandara Mountains in the north (Figure 18.1). The highest point of the Bamenda Highlands exceeds 3000 m, but the dominant feature is a lava plateau above 1400 m. This is an open grassland area that in colonial times led to the whole region now administered as the North-west Province being known as the Grassfields. Elevations below 300 m occur only in the far north of the province, in the valleys of the Donga, Metchum and Katsena Ala rivers. The Mbaw Plain is between 720 and 800 m in elevation, and is ringed on all but the south-east side by a steep escarpment rising by almost 1000 m to the high plateau country around Ndu and Kumbo.

To the south lies the Ndop Plain, a relatively flat area at a mean altitude of 1200 m, much now submerged beneath the Bamendjing reservoir. At the foot of the west-facing escarpments below Mount Neshele is an undulating plain drained to the north by the Mezam and Metchum rivers, and to the west by streams flowing towards the rainforests that lie to the south-west of the province.

The range of elevations and a general decrease in both precipitation and humidity from the south-west to the north-east of the region produces a climatic and ecological diversity that is unique in West Africa (Gleave and Thomas, 1968). There are a series of wet south-west-facing zones, and

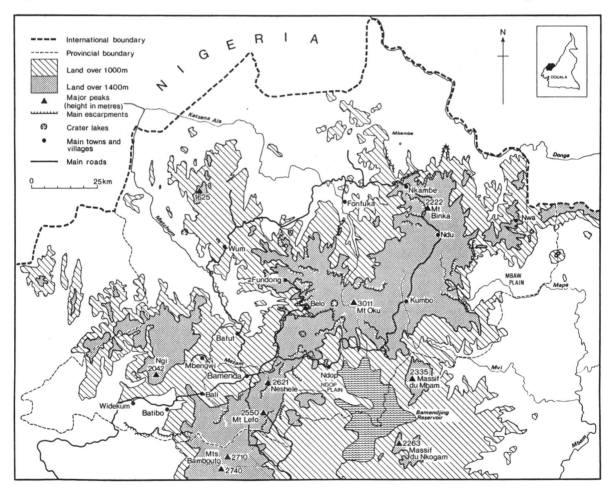

Figure 18.1 *The Bamenda Highlands, Cameroon*

north-east facing rain shadows. Batibo, for example, receives 3264 mm of rainfall a year on average while Ndop averages only 1545 mm. Several distinct climatic zones have been identified from extremely hot and relatively dry in the north to hot, very humid and extremely wet in the forest areas of the south-west, with much of the high plateau being cool and cloudy and not without highly localized climatic patterns, especially on the escarpments. There is a marked seasonality in rainfall with a rainy season extending from May until October.

The ecological and agricultural significance of the climatic zonation is considerable, since within a few kilometres it is possible to pass from luxuriant tropical rainforest to montane grassland, and alpine bamboo forest. The ecological diversity is reflected in the variety of crops, both tropical and temperate, that can be cultivated successfully in the Bamenda area. The oil palm grows in the warm, very wet zones of the south-west, below an altitude of about 1200 m, and in the even hotter areas of the Mbaw Plain, the Metchum Valley and the Mbembe forests north of Nkambe. The same areas produce good crops of banana, plantain, cocoyam and cassava, while the very hot and sunny conditions of the Ndop Plain favour groundnuts and maize. The main subsistence crop of the high plateau is maize, which has now almost completely replaced guinea corn. The cool and misty conditions of the high plateau allow extensive cultivation of the 'Irish' potato, and a wide range of 'European' or temperate vegetables. Potatoes have become an important cash crop, rivalling coffee as a major source of domestic income. These crops are indicative of the range cultivated in the province, and of the potential for trade between areas with different ecological characteristics.

The foodstuffs marketing system

Within an area of some 18 000 km^2 there are more than 300 market-places, though less than one-fifth are large enough to attract traders from outside the immediate locality and thus become foci for significant movements of produce. The foodstuffs marketing system can be structured as a model in which different types of traders form the links between markets, enabling produce to move either up the urban hierarchy or between rural markets located in ecologically different areas, thus creating a vertically and horizontally integrated network of markets (Figure 18.2). Each market-place has to be seen in the context of its position within several different commodity distribution channels, for the markets function according to how different groups of traders meet the variety of urban and rural demands.

Of relatively minor significance, in terms of total quantity and value of foodstuffs marketed in the province, are the sales of produce by farmers either at the farm-gate, or in the small village markets normally beyond the reach of bulk-buying wholesalers. Under certain circumstances, these markets can act as feeder markets to the major periodic rural markets, with intermediaries fulfilling a useful function in bulking small consignments of staple foodstuffs into loads worthy of the attention of professional traders at the larger markets. The majority of commodity transactions between producers and buyers take place within the confines of 50 or so major periodic rural markets. Bamenda, the provincial capital and the principal urban settlement, with a population of perhaps 100 000, is the focal point of the province's market network and the destination for the largest share of foodstuffs marketed in the province. Typically, Bamenda-based traders travel out to one or more periodic rural markets each week to buy produce which will later be sold either wholesale to urban retailers, or direct to urban consumers. The other important categories of traders to be found in the major rural markets are those from outside the province, who are mostly bulk-buying wholesalers supplying the urban markets of Douala and elsewhere to the south, and traders from essentially rural areas elsewhere in the province, seeking produce unavailable in their own areas. It is this last group whose activities will be examined in more detail.

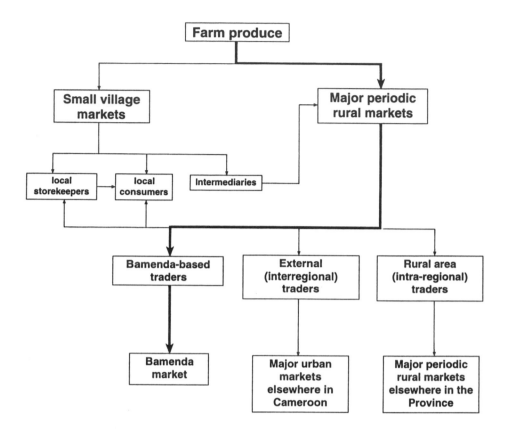

Figure 18.2 *Principal foodstuffs marketing channels in the Bamenda Highlands*

Palm oil marketing

The main agricultural commodity traded between rural areas is palm oil. Few areas above 1250 m can grow the oil palm, and as groundnut oil is expensive, there are large tracts of the high plateau where demand for cooking oil has generated a substantial trade in palm oil from the low-lying regions (Hollier, 1984). Most of the oil marketed in the province is produced in just three zones: the south-western forests, the Metchum Valley and Mbembe. The first is climatically best suited to the oil palm, and output is least affected by the generally slower dry season production of fruit. The marketing of palm oil has been an important aspect of economic life since before colonial times, and although the greater part of marketed oil output is destined for Bamenda, this area continues to attract traders from all parts of the

high plateau as far north as Kumbo and Fundong, and south-east towards the provincial boundary. Production in the Metchum Valley is much less oriented towards urban Bamenda as it is usually more expensive, and in the dry season, less regular in supply, than oil from the south-west. However, it continues to stimulate two important rural distributions: to the higher ground around Wum, and to the east of Bafut among linguistically and culturally affiliated villages. Bafut is the main periodic market of this area, and small-scale rural traders compete for supplies of oil with larger-scale operators from Bamenda. For the most part, the amount these traders can purchase is limited by their ability to convey oil without recourse to vehicular transport. This improves their trading margins, but clearly limits their turnover. By contrast, traders moving oil to the high plateau from the markets at Widikum,

Batibo and Mbengwi depend upon public transport or private haulage contractors. Their scale of operation is similar to successful Bamenda-based traders who supply the urban market. Some operate from Bamenda, but do not maintain fixed trading establishments, while others are based in the rural areas of demand. Typically, the latter are proprietors of general provisions stores.

There is one producer market of note in the forests of Mbembe, but because of the extreme problems of vehicular access most of the palm oil from the area is carried by the producers to the major periodic markets on the high plateau, notably Nkambe (Hollier, 1990), from where it is sold on to other localities in the north-east of the province. Some oil produced in Mbembe may still cross the Nigerian border as it did routinely from pre-colonial times until independence, reflecting the greater physical barrier posed by the northern escarpment of the high plateau than the River Donga to the north. Although these three zones account for an overwhelming proportion of marketed palm oil in the province, the area of oil palm forest is much more extensive and there are many smaller flows which point to continuing interaction between the high plateau and surrounding lower-lying areas such as the Mbaw Plain and the valleys of the upper Katsena Ala.

The marked seasonal fluctuation in palm oil prices of around 100% places extreme pressures on large-scale, longer-distance traders supplying rural areas. Put simply, fewer of their rural customers have the purchasing power of the urban population to withstand the significant increases in retail prices as the dry season progresses. Demand is cautioned by a problem of cash flow, for most of the consumers are farmers whose disposable income is regulated by their own fluctuating sales of staple foodstuffs in the market-place, and of coffee to the co-operative.

Gari marketing

Cassava (or manioc), the root crop from which *gari* is prepared, has a number of features in common with palm oil. Its cultivation is restricted by altitude (though not within such severe limits), and much labour must be invested in turning the raw material into a marketable commodity. As with palm oil, and in contrast to cocoyams or maize, *gari* is purchased by the consumer in a form that can be cooked without further preparation. Like maize, cassava is a crop of New World origin, and it did not begin to make serious inroads into traditional cultivation and dietary patterns in the region until the middle years of the present century, and then, largely as a hungry season standby. Its more recent success here, as elsewhere in Africa, is partly due to its resilience on very poor soils, but its diffusion may owe as much to urbanization as the ease of cultivation. *Gari* has become an important urban staple, not least because it is quick and easy to prepare, and is a cheap and filling staple of eating houses. The main production zones, certainly those which produce a surplus for marketing, lie off the high plateau. Production is most concentrated in a belt stretching from the forest fringe to the west and south of Batibo, through Bali, and north to Mbengwi and Bafut. Second in terms of total output is the Ndop Plain, though the more diffuse nature of marketing underplays the area's importance.

The most striking feature of *gari* distribution within the Bamenda Highlands is the rural to urban direction of the majority of flows, over 80% destined for Bamenda (Hollier, 1986). The main examples of rural to rural distribution are the links between the producer markets of Bafut and the Ndop Plain, and the consumer villages of the high plateau in an arc from just east of Bamenda to Fundong, and the trade between the Mbaw Plain and Ndu. Much of this trade is small-scale and carried out on foot, but it is an important entry to a trading way of life for many young men in these areas. Low-income, low-demand rural markets cannot be supplied by the same scale of trader as supplies urban markets, since demand is below the threshold required to offset additional transport costs. A small-scale rural trader secures a niche in rural to rural marketing by substituting labour for capital (transport costs), but his geographical range is restricted by the distance he can cover in a day, and his stock by headload or bicycle capacity.

The large periodic rural markets in Wum, Nkambe and Kumbo attract thousands from their surrounding hinterlands each week. As administrative centres they had begun to assume certain urban characteristics by the mid-1970s. With a growing population not directly dependent on farming, the demand for *gari* has stimulated some trading activity, especially when stocks of maize, the preferred staple of these localities, are low. This has led to at least a seasonal movement of *gari* from the far north into Nkambe and Wum, and from Bali and the Ndop Plain into Wum and Kumbo.

The production and seasonal distribution of maize

The seasonality found in some of this *gari* trading is a further context in which the marketing pattern is influenced by the marked environmental contrasts in the region. This is particularly apparent in the production and distribution of maize. The spatial distribution of maize production is perhaps the widest of all the staple foodstuffs, though total production is rather less than for cassava or cocoyams. Production is greatest on the rich alluvial soils of the Ndop plain, in the Bali area, and on the high plateau between Kumbo and Nkambe, where it is not uncommon to find extensive tracts of land above 1700 m given over exclusively to maize. Supplies to Bamenda are maintained for much of the time by the staggered harvests, made possible by the later onset of the rains as one proceeds from south-west to north-east across the highlands, and by the possibility of a second harvest in the Ndop Plain. There is little rural to rural movement of maize, as few rural areas have a consuming population prepared to pay the price of importing maize during times of local scarcity. However, some stocks from Bali are marketed in the Wum area, where demand is sustained by the resident Hausa population and the temporary dry-season influx of nomadic Fulani (Ako) pastoralists. Maize bought in the Ndop Plain is carried across the mountains

to Fundong, to meet a similar demand from a people whose dietary preference for maize is so strong that they shun the opportunity to purchase cheaper root crop alternatives. Unlike the sedentary population in the area, they can meet the premium on price by occasional sales of cattle.

Conclusion

It is often overlooked that the fundamental characteristics of existing market systems predate the emergence of significant rural to urban commodity flows. While new circumstances have spawned new markets and marketing mechanisms, the network of traditional periodic rural markets has been remarkably resilient, adapting to new demands, but retaining their historical role in intra-regional rural to rural distribution. Although traders engaged in this activity are responsible for only a fraction of the total produce movement in the Bamenda Highlands, they demonstrate how market-places can fulfil different roles in commodity distribution. Market-places are part of several different chains of distribution as befit the demands placed upon them by different types of traders. Despite the competition from rural to urban commodity flows these market-places continue to facilitate the movement of foodstuffs between ecological zones. The diversity of crops, farming techniques and agricultural strategies in the Bamenda Highlands strongly reflects the environmental character of the region. The marketing system is, in effect, a link between different environments. What this study shows is the way in which African farmers and traders exploit the economic opportunities that arise when markedly different environments and production regimes are found within a relatively restricted geographical area.

References

Gleave, M. B. and Thomas, M. F. (1968) The Bagango valley: an example of land utilization and agricultural practices in the Bamenda Highlands, *Bulletin de l'Institut Fond d'Afrique Noire*, Series B, 30, 655–681.

Hollier, G. P. (1984) The marketing and distribution of palm oil in North-West Province, Cameroon, *Scottish Geographical Magazine*, 100, 171–183.

Hollier, G. P. (1986) The marketing of gari in North-West Province, Cameroon, *Geografiska Annaler*, 68B, 59–68.

Hollier, G. P. (1990) Rural distribution channels in West Africa, pp. 52–65 in A. M. Findlay, R. Paddison and J. A. Dawson (eds), *Retailing Environments in Developing Countries*, Routledge, London.

Hopkins, A. G. (1973) *An Economic History of West Africa*, Longman, London.

Lovejoy, P. E. (1980) *Caravans of Kola: the Hausa kola trade, 1700–1900*, Ahmadu Bello University Press, Zaria.

Onyemelukwe, J. O. C., Filani, M. O. and Abumere, S. I. (1977) Interstate trade in major foodstuffs of Nigeria, *Nigerian Journal of Economic and Social Studies*, 19, 325–350.

Section IV
Southern Africa

The Amphitheatre in the Drakensberg mountains of Kwa Zulu-Natal, South Africa. (Photograph: Tony Binns)

19

Sustainability of smallholder food production systems in Southern Africa: the case of Zimbabwe

Lovemore M. Zinyama

Introduction

Since the 1980s, an increasing number of African governments have come to recognize the futility of earlier post-independence development strategies that emphasized urban-based industrialization at the expense of agriculture and the rural sector. There is now a general consensus among policy-makers that the key to the continent's current economic malaise lies in the transformation of agriculture, strengthening the smallholder farming sector, a return to domestic food self-sufficiency, and more generally the development of the rural areas in order to make them attractive places in which to live and work. However, one also recognizes the wide margin between intent as enunciated in policy statements on one hand and actual implementation, such that success in pursuit of these objectives is very patchy across the continent. Even where attempts have been made to improve smallholder agriculture and ensure food security at both national as well as household levels,

questions remain about the sustainability of African food production systems for a variety of reasons. This chapter examines the issue of sustainability with reference to the smallholder or peasant agricultural sector in Zimbabwe.

In most African countries, the question of sustainablity assumes significance from the fact that their peasant farmers, who comprise the majority of the population, are directly dependent on their natural resource base for not just mere welfare, but for their very survival. Discussion of the sustainability of African agriculture must centre on how to improve the social well-being of the population, given the fact that the poor lack economic alternatives to the current excessive exploitation of their natural resource base. Sustainability here is considered within the framework provided by the Brundtland Commission which defined sustainable development as 'development that meets the needs of the present without compromising the ability of future generations to meet their own needs' (WCED, 1987, p. 43).

People and Environment in Africa. Edited by Tony Binns
©1995 John Wiley & Sons Ltd

Lovemore M. Zinyama

Post-1980 agricultural changes in Zimbabwe

At independence in 1980, the new black government in Zimbabwe came to power committed to transforming the national economy and society, to redress the inherited social and spatial inequalities between the rich (overwhelmingly white) minority and the poor black majority, and in particular to raise the quality of life in the subsistence communal farming areas where a little over half the population live. It immediately embarked upon a dual rural development strategy involving, on the one hand, the redistribution of land and resettlement of land-hungry peasants on former white-owned large-scale commercial farms (see Chapter 20) and, on the other, increased support for peasant farmers within the existing communal farming areas. Throughout the 1980s, considerable progress was made towards improving agriculture and general living conditions in both communal and resettlement areas inhabited by black peasant farmers. The measures adopted included the provision of educational and health services, improved water and sanitation facilities, decentralization of, and increased access to, government services, the provision of transport and agricultural marketing facilities, agricultural extension and credit services (Zinyama, 1986a, 1992).

Four agricultural subsectors exist within Zimbabwe, namely (a) the large-scale commercial farming sector, (b) the small-scale commercial farming sector, (c) the communal farming sector and (d) the resettlement areas (Figure 19.1). The large-scale commercial sector currently occupies some 11 million ha of land and comprises some 4000 farming units which range in size to over 8000 ha, mostly under freehold tenure. Previously, it comprised exclusively white farmers, but in recent years a small number of newly affluent blacks have become landowners within the sector. The small-scale commercial sector comprises some 8500 units on land that was set aside during the colonial period for the few blacks who wished, and could afford, to acquire land under freehold or leasehold tenure. The farms are generally small, with an average size of between 150 and 200 ha. The sector occupies some 1.4 million ha of land.

The communal farming sector occupies some 16.4 million ha of land and supports about 51% of the national population of 10.4 million (1992 census), mostly through susbsistence crop production. The average size of arable holdings in the communal areas is about 2 ha, held under usufructuary rights. In addition, the inhabitants have access to communal grazing for their livestock, mostly cattle, goats, sheep and donkeys. Among the approximately 1 million households scratching a living from communal lands, are many families of urban migrant workers who continue to retain their rights to rural land which is cultivated by their wives and children. They work the land in a desperate effort to supplement meagre household incomes from urban employment as well as a means of securing their land rights. Access to land is also a means of social security in times of unemployment or old age. Land cultivation, combined with urban wage employment (if available), enables low-income households 'to take advantage of the opportunities offered in both the urban and rural milieu, and to minimize risks' (Potts and Mutambirwa, 1990, p. 678). Migrant husbands maintain contact with their rural homes and agricultural activities of their households through regular return visits at weekends and month-ends (Zinyama, 1986b).

The fourth sub-sector, covering the resettlement areas, is a post-independence development. By the end of the 1980s, the resettlement areas covered 3.5 million ha allocated to some 53 000 farming families. The current second phase of the land reform programme envisages the transfer of a further 5 million ha from the large-scale commercial sector for redistribution to an additional 110 000 black peasant households. At the end of the programme, the resettlement areas will occupy a total of 8.5 million ha of land; conversely, the large-scale commercial sector will be reduced from 15.5 million ha at independence in 1980 to 5 million ha for the production of strategic (primarily in terms of export earnings) and capital-intensive crops such as tobacco, wheat and horticultural products.

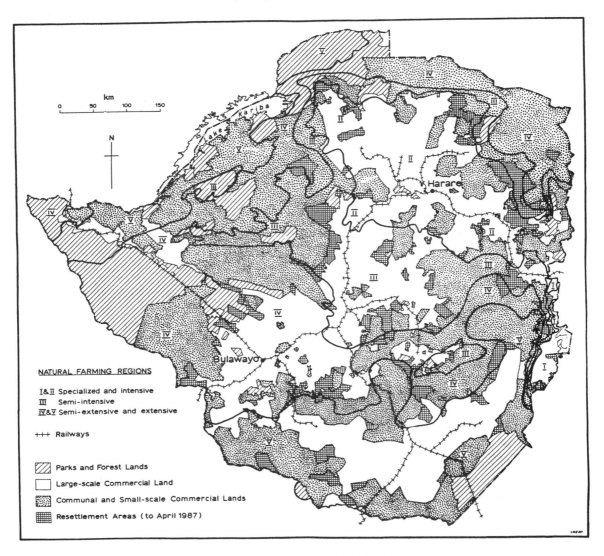

Figure 19.1 *Zimbabwe—major land divisions and agro-ecological regions*

The transformation of the communal farming sector in Zimbabwe since 1980 has received wide acclaim from most observers, the international community and development aid agencies. It has been described as one of the few agricultural success stories in Africa, made more spectacular against the backdrop of a deteriorating food production and supply situation, widespread famine and malnutrition over much of the continent (Eicher, 1982; Macgregor, 1990). Whereas before 1980 peasant farmers' share of national agricultural output was very insignificant, by the mid-1980s they were contributing substantially to overall agricultural production, national food security as well as industrial crops. The principal crops grown in the peasant sector are maize (the country's staple food crop), cotton, sunflower seeds and other small grains. Before independence, black small-scale farmers contributed less than 10% of the maize that was sold to the government-controlled marketing organization, the Grain Marketing Board (GMB);

217

since then, their share has increased to between 40 and 60% of the maize sold each year (Table 19.1)

However, these trends and developments at the national level, while impressive, hide substantial spatial and social disparities in the transformation of the country's peasant farming sector. The continuing uneven distribution of land by race across the principal agro-ecological regions exerts a considerable differentiating influence on the emerging spatial patterns of agricultural development within the peasant sector. The bulk of the agricultural land in the ecologically more favourable eastern and central parts of the country remains within the large-scale commercial sector (Figure 19.1)[1]. It is those few peasant households who are fortunate to live in communal areas situated in these regions who have had the largest

and most consistent increases in crop sales since the early 1980s, and hence have benefited most from the state-assisted agricultural transformation that has taken place (Gobbins and Prankerd, 1983; Stanning, 1987; Zinyama, 1987, 1988a).

Intra-community differences by age, gender and economic status have also been reported in studies of the peasant agricultural sector in Zimbabwe. Generally, three categories of peasant farming households have been found to be particularly disadvantaged, namely, (a) young families with little or no arable land, few or no cattle to provide both draught power for land preparation as well as manure, and those without farming implements, (b) female-headed households, and (c) families of some low-income urban labour migrants who may be vulnerable to labour constraints at peak labour demand periods. These

Table 19.1 *Maize sales to the Grain Marketing Board by agricultural sector, 1974–75 to 1991–92 intake years*

Intake year*	Large-scale commercial sector		Small-scale commercial, communal and resettlement sector		Total sales (tonnes)
	tonnes	%	tonnes	%	
1974–75	1 290 253	96.5	46 683	3.5	1 336 936
1975–76	957 588	95.1	49 358	4.9	1 006 946
1976–77	886 018	91.3	83 982	8.7	970 000
1977–78	856 799	91.0	84 265	9.0	941 064
1978–79	813 420	92.7	63 605	7.3	877 025
1979–80	473 736	92.5	38 184	7.5	511 920
1980–81	728 582	89.4	86 296	10.6	814 878
1981–82	1 650 574	82.0	363 269	18.0	2 013 843
1982–83	1 021 892	73.4	369 374	26.6	1 391 266
1983–84	464 486	75.3	152 414	24.7	616 900
1984–85	551 612	58.6	390 001	41.4	941 613
1985–86	1 008 971	55.2	819 140	44.8	1 828 111
1986–87	911 945	57.2	682 429	42.8	1 594 374
1987–88	246 735	61.3	155 802	38.7	402 537
1988–89	440 733	36.8	755 948	63.2	1 196 681
1989–90	510 686	43.8	654 841	56.2	1 165 527
1990–91	357 414	45.8	423 594	54.2	781 008
1991–92	233 731	38.6	371 764	61.4	605 495

* = The GMB intake year, which runs from 1 April to the following 31 March, is the year following that of production, i.e. the crop planted in November 1980 for the 1980–81 growing season was delivered to the GMB during the 1981–82 intake year.
Sources: Agricultural Marketing Authority *Grain Situation and Outlook* (annual reports), Harare; Grain Marketing Board, *Annual Reports*, Harare.

households continue to experience low production levels, especially if they live in the drier southern and western regions of the country where droughts are recurrent, coupled with increasing population pressure and widespread land degradation. Food shortages are common, forcing many to seek recourse in government food relief programmes each year. The large mismatch across agro-ecological regions between production and consumption—the most densely populated areas are in the drier parts of the country—necessitates high transport costs in moving grain from surplus to deficit areas. Given the social and spatial disparities in food production and distribution, it is not surprising that malnutrition remains a major public health problem in many parts of rural Zimbabwe (Republic of Zimbabwe, 1986), despite the food surpluses at the national level. In brief, the progress in raising agricultural production within the peasant sector of Zimbabwe since the early 1980s has been highly skewed both socially and spatially, and does not seem to provide for sustainable rural development in the long run.

Major environmental problems in Zimbabwe

The past century has shown that the physical environment in Zimbabwe is highly fragile and sensitive to human mismanagement. The degradation of the country's natural resources has been brought about by a combination of human factors, and in particular it bears the imprint of racial discrimination and the politics of land alienation by the white settlers during the colonial period (1890–1980). Today, the commercial farming areas which were alienated for white settlement generally have high standards of resource conservation and management, hand in hand with substantial underutilization of land (Weiner *et al.*, 1985; Whitlow, 1988). The areas that were set aside for black peasant farming, now known as the communal farming areas, present the most intractable problems of environmental degradation. The communal areas are characterized by widespread soil erosion and river siltation, loss

of genetic diversity due to vegetation clearance for human settlement, cultivation and fuelwood for a rapidly expanding population with an average annual growth rate of 3.1%. These processes are not independent of each other, and a retrogressive change in any one may result in degradation in some or all other areas. As observed by Young and Burton (1992), it is this multiplicity of impacts that makes the management of the natural resource base so complex.

Large areas of the communal lands are occupied by domed inselbergs and other granitic landforms; in some cases as much as 50% of the land area is occupied by these landforms, thereby reducing the amount of suitable land available for cultivation (Whitlow, 1980). The steep slopes promote rapid surface runoff and soil erosion and the development of shallow sandy skeletal soils which are highly susceptible to degradation when cultivated or stocked without proper management. Without adequate cash to purchase inorganic fertilizers to apply to these inherently infertile soils, crop yields quickly decline, thereby compounding the threat of food shortages especially in the drier southern and western regions of the country. In order to mitigate these recurrent food shortages, rural households adopt a variety of coping strategies (Campbell *et al.*, 1989; Zinyama *et al.*, 1990). Unfortunately, due to a lack of viable alternatives, some of these coping mechanisms—e.g. fluvial gold panning or fuelwood vending—entail further over-exploitation of the rural resource base and environmental degradation. A survey of the extent of soil erosion in Zimbabwe by Whitlow (1987) showed that 23.2% of the communal areas were experiencing extensive to very extensive erosion while a further 19.6% were subject to moderate erosion. The respective figures for the (former white) commercial farming areas were 1.3 and 3.4%. Only 36.9% of the communal areas were subject to very little or no erosion, compared with 79.4% of the commercial farming areas. Increasing population pressure and land shortage over the past century have driven many peasant families to clear marginal land for cultivation on steep slopes and along watercourses, thereby adding to the incidence of soil erosion and siltation of rivers and dams (Whitlow and Zinyama, 1988; Zinyama, 1988b). Meanwhile, woodland clearance for cultivation and fuelwood also deprives people of supplementary food resources such as wild fruits, berries, roots and leaves, thereby reducing their overall food supplies and nutritional status, especially in times of acute food shortages (Gomez, 1988; Zinyama et al., 1990).

It is apparent that the communal areas present the most severe environmental problems in Zimbabwe. The dilemma facing the country is therefore one of attempting to increase agricultural output and land productivity from an impoverished and rapidly degrading natural resource base. Any consideration or national debate about the long-term sustainability of agriculture within the communal areas must therefore address several related issues including the systems of land tenure, patterns of landownership and land use, control of and access to common resources at the local community level as well as population control. Surveys in different parts of Zimbabwe have shown that while some of the gains in peasant agriculture in the 1980s arose from the adoption of new farming technologies (principally hybrid seed varieties and chemical fertilizers) (Zinyama, 1992), they were also partly due to an extension in the area under cultivation arising from the growth in the farming population (Rohrbach, 1987). More and more marginal land has been turned over for cultivation to meet the demand for arable land by a rapidly increasing population (Whitlow and Zinyama, 1988). Today, suitable agricultural land is very scarce in most communal areas of Zimbabwe. This must imply that production can only be sustained in the future more through increased productivity per unit of land than from the extension of the area under cultivation.

An additional problem facing small-scale agriculture in Zimbabwe is that crop production is entirely rain-fed and output in any one year is dependent upon the total amount as well as the seasonal distribution of rainfall. Thus, even where farmers may have purchased the necessary

chemical fertilizers and hybrid seeds, their harvests remain tied to the vagaries of the weather. Since the early 1980s, Zimbabwe (and Southern Africa generally) has experienced more years of low and variable rainfall with some severe droughts which resulted in widespread food shortages. The years 1981–84, 1985–87 and more recently 1991–2 were particularly dry. These drought years are indicated in Table 19.1 by the dramatic falls in the quantities of maize sold to the GMB in the subsequent marketing years. More significantly, a large part of the decline in maize sales from the commercial farming sector since the mid-1980s has been due to poor real prices offered by government and reduced profitability of maize production vis-à-vis other enterprises such as horticulture and game farming (whose prices were not controlled by the government) (Herbst, 1988). In contrast, small-scale farmers lack alternative opportunities to diversify, and continue to depend on grain production regardless of agro-ecological conditions, seasonal rainfall patterns or producer prices. The high annual variability of both crop yields and sales from the small-scale farming sector compared with the large-scale commercial sector as shown in Table 19.1 has serious implications for national food security. Following the 1991–92 drought, Zimbabwe was turned from a net regional food exporter to an importer. It became necessary during 1992–93 to import over 2 million tonnes of maize, plus sorghum, sugar, wheat and other foodstuffs at a total cost in excess of Z$3 billion. This compared with the much smaller quantities of 268 900 and 83 200 tonnes of maize imported in 1984–85 and 1991–92 respectively to meet shortfalls in domestic production arising from previous droughts. Following the premature cessation of the 1993–94 rainy season in mid-February, large parts of the communal areas again experienced widespread crop failure in 1994. By May, over 1 million rural dwellers had registered for government relief food and the number was expected to increase, as even those families who had managed to harvest a little exhausted their supplies later in the year (The Herald, 28/5/94).

Economic reform, poverty and agricultural sustainability

The year 1990 saw a major change in government economic policies, from the socialist rhetoric of the 1980s to a more market-oriented economy. The 1980s had been characterized by slow and sluggish economic growth, lack of investment and rising unemployment. It is estimated that during the decade to 1990, the population in the 15–64 age category grew by an annual average of 3.9%, while formal sector employment grew at a much lower rate of 1.6% per year (Republic of Zimbabwe, 1991). Hence in 1990 the government, with the backing of the World Bank, the International Monetary Fund (IMF) and other aid organizations, began implementation of the economic structural adjustment programme aimed at revitalizing the economy, attracting both domestic and foreign capital investment in order to create more employment opportunities for the growing numbers of young unemployed. An integral part of the structural adjustment programme is the reduction of government expenditure, with drastic cuts already effected in subsidies for basic foodstuffs and essential social services such as health and education. The emphasis is now on full cost recovery from users of such public social services, price deregulation and commercialization of the operations of agricultural and other parastatals, some of which are being privatized.

While structural adjustment is intended to benefit the economy in the long run, in the short term it has brought considerable hardship to the poor in both rural and urban areas as a result of inflationary price increases following the removal of government price controls and subsidies, and the retrenchment of workers in both public and private sectors. For many low-income families faced with the threat or reality of retrenchment, the lack of alternative employment opportunities, and the escalating cost of living in urban areas, the possession of a piece of arable land in the communal areas assumes even greater significance in the 1990s. For the time being at least, the economic reform programme has exacerbated the problems of poverty, thereby making an even larger number of families more dependent on the land for their survival. This in turn puts more pressure on the land and adds to its degradation. On the other hand, land degradation exacerbates their poverty in so far as it depletes the very source of their livelihood. Thus increased poverty becomes both a cause and a consequence of land degradation within the communal areas. In the short term, the economic reform programme may therefore contribute towards the unsustainability of small-scale agriculture by driving on to the land many more people than can be supported under the current land-use and management practices. As noted by Young and Burton (1992), a further consequence of poverty is not just resource degradation, but also a lack of resource regeneration. Capital is needed to restore degraded lands, and thereby increase its sustainable productivity, but the poor do not have the necessary capital.

Conclusion

Poor farmers are dependent to a large extent on their natural resources and environment because they lack alternative means for obtaining a livelihood. Poverty and environmental degradation in Africa are closely intertwined and should be viewed as one complex crisis whose interrelated facets should be tackled simultaneously. The interlocking problems include poverty and the lack of development, rapidly rising population, food insecurity, acute ecological stress and drought, inappropriate national policies, as well as 'a global economic system that takes more out of a poor continent than it puts in' (WCED, 1987, p. 6). In Zimbabwe, commendable achievements have been made since 1980 to alleviate rural poverty and raise incomes through increased agricultural production. However, as discussed above, there are grave doubts about the sustainability of these gains under the current smallholder food production system. Environmental degradation within the communal areas continues largely unabated, thereby depleting the very resource base upon which the inhabitants depend for their livelihood. This downward spiral means that, contrary to the concept of sustainable development as defined by the Brundtland Commission (WCED, 1987), the ability of the present generation, let alone those in the future, to meet their needs is seriously compromised. Issues such as land tenure, landownership and land-use patterns, population growth and population control, which so far have not featured intimately in the debate on strategies for communal lands development, need to be more closely integrated in the effort to raise agricultural production and productivity and in combating land degradation. Even the programme of land distribution, which has been going on since 1981 and has occupied the national centre-stage since 1989, has been debated primarily within the political context of giving the land back to the indigenous inhabitants of the country.

Note

1. Zimbabwe is divided for commercial farming purposes into five agro-ecological zones, commonly known as 'natural farming regions'. The division is based primarily on rainfall amount and reliability. Conditions become increasingly marginal for farming from natural region I to natural region V as rainfall decreases in both amount and reliability. Regions IV and V, with less than 650 mm of rain per year, are subject to severe seasonal droughts and are considered suitable only for extensive livestock and game ranching, supplemented in region IV by the cultivation of drought-resistant small grains such as millet and sorghum. Of the 25.2 million ha in natural regions IV and V, communal farmers occupy 48%, the remainder being large-scale commercial farmland, urban land, state land, national parks and state forests. Natural regions I–III, the principal agricultural regions, cover 13.8 million ha, of which 30% is communal land. At independence, large-scale white commercial farmers occupied 58% of the land within these three agro-ecological regions. Overall, 74% of all the communal land is located within natural regions IV and V.

References

Campbell, D. J., Zinyama, L. M. and Matiza, T. (1989) Strategies for coping with food deficits in rural Zimbabwe, *Geographical Journal of Zimbabwe*, No. 20, 15–41.

Eicher, C. K. (1982) Facing up to Africa's food crisis, *Foreign Affairs*, 61(1), 151–174.

Gobbins, K. E. and Prankerd H. A. (1983) Communal agriculture: a study from Mashonaland West, *Zimbabwe Agricultural Journal*, 80(4), 151–158.

Gomez, M. I. (1988) A resource inventory of indigenous and traditional foods in Zimbabwe, *Zambezia*, 15(1), 53–73.

Herbst, J. (1988) Societal demands and government choices: agricultural producer price policy in Zimbabwe, *Comparative Politics*, 20(3), 265–288.

Macgregor, J. (1990) The crisis in African agriculture, *Africa Insight*, 20(1), 4–16.

Potts, D. and Mutambirwa, C. (1990) Rural–urban linkages in contemporary Harare: why migrants need their land, *Journal of Southern African Studies*, 16(4), 677–698.

Republic of Zimbabwe (1986) *First Five-Year National Development Plan 1986–1990*, Harare.

Republic of Zimbabwe (1991) *Second Five-Year National Development Plan 1991–1995*, Harare.

Rohrbach, D. D. (1987) A preliminary assessment of factors underlying the growth of communal maize production in Zimbabwe, pp. 145–184 in M. Rukuni and C. K. Eicher (eds), *Food Security for Southern Africa*, UZ/MSU Food Security Project, University of Zimbabwe, Harare.

Stanning, J. (1987) Household grain storage and marketing in surplus and deficit communal farming areas in Zimbabwe: preliminary findings, pp. 245–291 in M. Rukuni and C. K. Eicher (eds) *Food security for Southern Africa*, UZ/MSU Food Security Project, University of Zimbabwe, Harare.

WCED (World Commission on Environment and Development) (1987) *Our Common Future* (Brundtland Commission Report), Oxford University Press, Oxford.

Weiner, D., Moyo, S., Munslow, B. and O'Keefe, P. (1985) Land use and agricultural productivity in Zimbabwe, *Journal of Modern African Studies*, 23(2), 251–285.

Whitlow, J. R. (1980) Land use, population pressure and rock outcrops in the tribal areas of Zimbabwe Rhodesia, *Zimbabwe Rhodesia Agricultural Journal*, 77(1), 3–11.

Whitlow, R. (1987) A national soil erosion survey for Zimbabwe, *Journal of Soil and Water Conservation*, 42(4), 239–242.

Whitlow, R. (1988) Soil conservation history in Zimbabwe, *Journal of Soil and Water Conservation*, 43(4), 299–303.

Whitlow, R. and Zinyama, L. (1988) Up hill and down vale: farming and settlement patterns in Zimunya Communal Land, *Geographical Journal of Zimbabwe*, No. 19, 29–45.

Young, T. and Burton, M. P. (1992) *Agricultural Sustainability: definition and implications for agricultural and trade policy*, Economic and Social Development Paper 110, FAO. Rome.

Zinyama, L. M. (1986a) Agricultural development policies in the African farming areas of Zimbabwe, *Geography*, 71(2), 105–115.

Zinyama, L. M. (1986b) Rural household structure, absenteeism and agricultural labour: a case study of two subsistence farming areas in Zimbabwe, *Singapore Journal of Tropical Geography*, 7(2), 163–173.

Zinyama, L. M. (1987) Gender, age and the ownership of agricultural resources in the Mhondoro and Save North communal areas of Zimbabwe, *Geographical Journal of Zimbabwe*, No. 18, 1–14.

Zinyama, L. M. (1988a) Commercialization of small-scale agriculture in Zimbabwe: some emerging patterns of spatial differentiation, *Singapore Journal of Tropical Geography*, 9(2), 151–162.

Zinyama, L. M. (1988b) Changes in settlement and land use patterns in a subsistence agricultural economy: a Zimbabwe case study, 1956–1984, *Erdkunde*, 42(1), 49–59.

Zinyama, L. M. (1992) Technology adoption and post-independence transformation of the small-scale farming sector in Zimbabwe, pp. 180–202 in D. Drakakis-Smith (ed.), *Urban and Regional Change in Southern Africa*, Routledge, London.

Zinyama, L. M., Matiza, T. and Campbell, D. J. (1990) The use of wild foods during periods of food shortage in rural Zimbabwe, *Ecology of Food and Nutrition*, 24(4), 251–265.

20

Government policies and the population–environment interface: land reform and distribution in Zimbabwe

Jennifer A. Elliott

Introduction

The conditions under which people live, the manner in which resources are utilized and the prospects for conservation in the future are all in part influenced by the fundamental features of national government and the policies for economic and sectoral development pursued. For the estimated 80% of the African population who depend on agricultural livelihoods, government policies regarding extension, conservation, pricing, infrastructural provision and even urban shelter, are among the factors in the explanation of the specifics of population–environment relations at any one place or time.

Government policies of land reform intervene very directly between population and the environment. They seek to restructure the system of land tenure, together with the size, distribution and spatial arrangement of landholdings in an area (King, 1977). In addition to changes in the ways in which people hold land, land tenure reform may involve change to the rules governing people's rights to land and the institutions which administer those rights (Downs and Reyna, 1988). Land tenure reforms have been undertaken in Africa for a variety of political, economic and social reasons,

often in combination and sometimes in conflict. Reform of traditional land tenure systems was seen as the prerequisite for the economic development of African farming areas in Kenya in the 1950s for example, when a programme of land consolidation was implemented. The inherently political nature of land reform is confirmed by the number of governments who express commitment to such policies and the tendency historically, for significant land reform programmes to follow major political upheavals (for example, post-revolution Ethiopia in 1974 and on independence in Zimbabwe in 1980).

The impacts of such policies on population–environment relations are as diverse and dynamic as the motivations for undertaking them. In peasant agriculture, land is often the key factor of production and access to land a major correlate of political and social prestige within such societies. Land reform intervenes in these established relationships between people and the land. Furthermore, policies of land reform often involve the movement of people to new lands and/or settlement areas with potentially differing local ecologies and social circumstances. Unfortunately, the 'social' and 'environmental' impacts of land reform policies are regularly

People and Environment in Africa. Edited by Tony Binns
©1995 John Wiley & Sons Ltd

overlooked in the planning stages and are not subject to systematic monitoring.

In 1980, Zimbabwe initiated a programme of land reform. Changing the existing population–environment relationships within agriculture was central to the objectives of the resettlement policy. Fifteen years into the programme, this chapter identifies key features of the policy in terms of planning and practice as related to achieving these population–environment goals. Recent survey work is used to highlight aspects of the impact of the policy on population–environment relations at the household level as expressed through changes in the use of woodland resources.

Land reform in Zimbabwe

At independence, access to land resources among the population in Zimbabwe was highly inequitable as a result of colonial policies of land apportionment dating back to 1890. In 1980, 47% of the total farmland of the country was reserved for the large-scale (European) farming sector (totalling less than 7000 individual farmers). In contrast, over 700 000 African farmers within the communal areas had access to only 49% of the total farmland, much of it in less agriculturally suited regions. Addressing the 'lost lands issue' (Moyo and Skalnes, 1990) which had been a primary mobilizing force for the guerrilla movements in the years up to independence, was therefore an urgent political task for the newly elected government. Land redistribution through the purchase of commercial farmlands for the resettlement of Africans was seen as the way to overcome this legacy and return lands to their rightful owners. The original target for the programme was to voluntarily resettle 18 000 families on 1.1 million ha of land. More recently, a ceiling has been set for the transfer of lands to the resettlement sector of 8.3 million ha involving a total of 162 000 households (Government of Zimbabwe, 1989). The location of the early resettlement scheme areas is shown in Figure 20.1.

Radical land reform through the resettlement programme was also a key element of the independent government's commitment to a socialist future for the country based on 'growth with equity' (Ministry of Economic Planning and Development, 1981). Priority for movement within the programme was in the first instance to be given to the poorest groups in society, including those displaced by the war and those without access to land. New relations of production were planned within the programme, for example, through the target for 70% of resettlement to take place under 'Model B', encompassing co-operative farms operated on a collective basis (Republic of Zimbabwe, 1982). The resettlement policy was therefore a central key in the proposed socialist transition of agriculture which would enable the integration of rural producers as active participants into the national development process (Munslow, 1985).

From the outset, there was also the intention that population movement through the resettlement policy would assist in the alleviation of pressure on communal area environments from which the majority of settlers would be drawn. Average population densities in these areas at independence were in excess of 25 persons per km^2, in comparison with densities of less than 8 persons per km^2 in the commercial farming sector (Central Statistics Office, 1984). In addition, 74% of the communal farming areas of the country were located in regions defined as suited only to extensive cattle ranching and the cultivation of drought-resistant crops. Since independence, national surveys of deforestation and soil erosion (Whitlow, 1980, 1988) have highlighted the strong spatial continuities between environmental degradation and land tenure, the most severe problems being concentrated in the communal sector. The resettlement policy was seen as an essential element in rectifying this situation. Where possible, land was to be acquired for resettlement adjacent to communal areas with particularly severe problems of population pressure and environmental degradation (Ministry of Lands, Resettlement and Rural Development, 1981). Within subsequent amendments to the policies and procedures of resettlement, this link has been strengthened through the integration of a

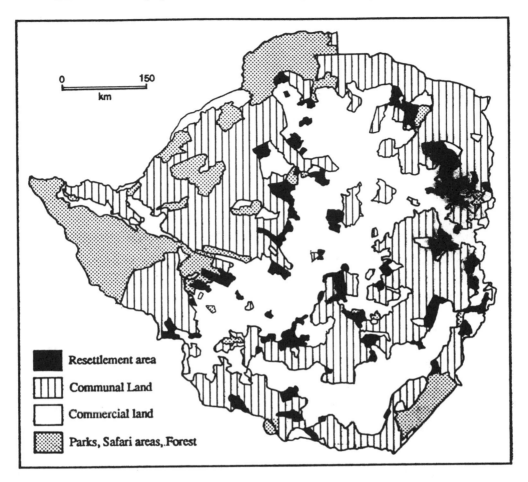

Figure 20.1 *Resettlement areas in Zimbabwe, 1983*

programme of communal area reorganization and development with the policy of population movement through resettlement (Department of Rural Development, 1992).

Progress to date

In 1988, an Overseas Development Administration evaluation report concluded that the resettlement programme had 'so far proved a considerable success' (Cusworth and Walker, 1988, p. 37). In terms of the UK's financial commitment to the programme, it was suggested that 'there can be few of ODA's rural development projects that have been as effective in achieving such a sustained rate of expenditure' (p. 17).

In practice, the pace of land transfer and settlement in Zimbabwe has been slower than targeted. By the beginning of the 1990s, 52 000 families had been moved within the programme to an area of 3.3 million ha of land (largely former commercial farmland). In part, the relatively slow pace of resettlement has been due to the restriction until 1990 of the government to a market-bound process of land acquisition; the private property provisions of the Lancaster House constitution effectively constrained land purchases in the first 10 years to a 'willing-seller/willing-buyer' basis. As a result, the government had little control over the type or location of land acquisition, which in practice was largely of abandoned and marginal lands often in fragmented rather than contiguous blocks.

The legislative constraint on the pace and location of resettlement has now been removed with the cessation of the Lancaster House constitution and the passing of the Land Acquisition Bill (1992) which enables the compulsory purchase of land for state purposes. Financial and political factors are likely to be of primary concern in the future. For example, in the context of declining donor funding, the programme will depend increasingly on the resources of the national government (undergoing structural adjustment). There is no doubt that the comtemporary policy context of resettlement in Zimbabwe is also now substantially different from that at independence. As Moyo (1986) states, there is a 'much more complex configuration of issues, realities and determinations of the land question' (p. 165). For example, it is suggested that the political force of the 'lost lands issue', which fuelled land transfers in the early years, has lost some impetus as large-scale landownership by African businessmen and politicians has risen.

The impact of the resettlement programme on the socialist transformation of agriculture in the country has been limited. In practice, Model A resettlement (based on individual family farms with common grazing resources) accounted for over 80% of total expenditure within the programme to 1987 (Cusworth and Walker, 1988, p. 6) and 85% of settler placement to 1991 (Ministry of Lands, Agriculture and Rural Resettlement, 1992, p. 19); In 1991, settler take-up on Model B schemes was only 42% of planned capacity (p. 19). Since 1983, and the refusal of the British government (the major international donor for the resettlement programme up until 1987), to fund co-operative villages, the Model B schemes have been resourced entirely by the Zimbabwean government. The problems of management, finance and infrastructural development experienced within these schemes 'have resulted in this model being considered unfavourable to most potential settlers' (Ministry of Lands, Agriculture and Rural Resettlement, 1992, p. 19). In 1992, the government recommended that resettlement on the basis of Model B be restricted to a very few schemes meeting a number of criteria and that action be taken to deregister those co-operatives under existing schemes which are judged to have failed (Department of Rural Development, 1992, p. 40–41).

Assessments of the performance of settlers within Model A schemes have also suggested that those families who bring least to the resettlement schemes in terms of resources and agricultural skills have fared worst within the programme; 'the allocation of land to people without resources is not the best solution to solving their destitution' (Ministry of Lands, Agriculture and Rural Resettlement, 1992, p. 99). Recent changes in the policies and procedures of resettlement (Department of Rural and Urban Development, 1992) have included new criteria for the selection of settlers encompassing both 'need' and 'suitability'. Priority within the programme will in future be given to households who can demonstrate the 'skills required for the enterprise they are to be engaged in' (Government of Zimbabwe, 1989, p. 89). Resource efficiency and financial concerns (including the prospect of the government implementing a cost-recovery programme) are now taking precedence over earlier concerns for equity.

Early progress towards the alleviation of population pressure in the communal areas through resettlement was limited primarily due to the wider problems of obtaining land for the programme. In addition, since the majority of resettled families were those without land in the communal areas, their movement did not lead to any substantial release of lands in these areas. It is also recognized that there are no formal procedures for the identification of settlers in relation to population pressure in their home areas or for the disposal of land utilized by them prior to resettlement. Research shows that the majority of settlers do not give up their rights to land in the communal areas, as required by their resettlement permits, for a variety of social and cultural reasons (Jinya, 1991). At the national level, the pace of resettlement cannot be expected to contribute substantially to the relief of population pressure with the rate of natural increase in the country exceeding 3.1% per annum (Central Statistics Office, 1992).

The impact of resettlement on household use of woodland resources

In 1992–93, a survey of 439 households in two resettlement scheme areas of Zimbabwe was conducted to assess changes in the use, collection and management of woodland resources on resettlement. Questions focused on contemporary experience, a recall of such activities when resident in the communal areas and the respondents' explanation of any change over the period. Selected findings of the research are presented to illustrate the impact of the resettlement policy on one aspect of the population–environment interface at a particular scale, i.e in terms of household use of woodland resources.

Some of the most widespread changes on resettlement for the sample as a whole included an increase in total wood use, decreased distances travelled in collection, an increased reliance on individual rather than communal sources, a rise in shared responsibility for wood collection and greater active selection of species for particular wood-using activities. There was, however, diversity in the explanations of such changes given by respondents. These included reference not only to aspects of environmental change on resettlement, but also political-economic and social factors associated with the policy and the experience of movement. For example, some respondents prioritized the improved availability of woodland sources as explanation for their more frequent participation in certain wood-using activities or their use of more wood now in cooking for longer or in brewing 'better tasting beer'. However, other respondents reported factors on resettlement

such as the time demands of agricultural activities, a lack of knowledge concerning the regulations on resource use in the area and a commitment to new religious faiths, as serving now to exclude or reduce their participation in certain activities.

In addition to the varied explanations of change in wood use as identified by respondents, any single factor of political-economic, social or environmental change had a very diverse impact at the household level. This is shown in Table 20.1 with respect to the impact of environmental change on the responsibility for and technology adopted in resource collection. It is evident that a number of 'human' factors such as the perception of 'accepted' gender roles, access to technology, socio-economic well-being, the time available for resource collection and the social composition of the resettled community, serve to regulate the impact of environmental change on the woodland collection activities at this level.

Table 20.1 *The explanation of change in responsibility for fuelwood collection*

'Trees were scarce in the communal areas, so we had to combine our efforts unlike here'

'In communal areas, men went because the trees had to be cut down. Now women are taking over'

'Now I cannot burden my wife with carrying fuelwood while I can use a scotchcart (a two-wheeled cart pulled by oxen)'

'In the communal areas, there was not much work to do as we had no fields, so women collected wood. Here we have fields and are busy so everyone collects wood'

'We are now using a scotchcart to transport wood, but we were unable to do this in the past because the area was too mountainous'

'Women are best at carrying bundles, but now wood is nearby, anyone can go'

'Men are taking responsibility from women as trees are bigger here and therefore require the use of a scotchcart'

'Women now collect fuelwood, but in the communal areas, men went because the distances travelled were so great'

'At home, people did not work as a community, but here it is different and one can just ask to borrow a scotchcart'

Jennifer A. Elliott

Conclusion

Land reform policy in Zimbabwe has affected population–environment relations at the national level in a number of respects. For example, the resettlement sector now constitutes almost 10% of the total agricultural land area of the country. This represents a significant change in terms of access to resources for particular groups over the situation at independence. At this scale, however, the pace of resettlement has not contributed to the relief of population pressure in the communal areas. This does not discount the possibility of such effects at the village scale, for example. Agricultural production in the scheme areas remains dominated by family-based production rather than the co-operative, but in the main, settler households achieve higher levels of productivity and enjoy improved standards of living over residents of the communal areas.

This chapter has also indicated that land reform policy impacts on population–environment relations at the level of the household. Changes in the use of woodland were attributed by respondents themselves to a range of political-economic, social and environmental factors. Some of these factors of change were related to the resettlement policy itself, such as the conditions of permits and the improved access to resources facilitated by participation in the programme. In addition, factors of local ecologies and the specific characteristics of the household concerned were important in determining the nature of change experienced and in turn, the impact on decision-making regarding woodland use.

The case study has shown that the impacts of a government policy of land reform on population–environment interactions are diverse and diffuse. It is evident also that the achievement of 'population' or 'environmental' objectives through resettlement in Zimbabwe is closely interrelated.

Acknowledgement

The author would like to acknowledge the assistance of the ODA in funding the fieldwork on which this chapter draws.

References

Central Statistics Office (1984) *1982 Population Census: A preliminary assessment*, CSO, Harare.

Cusworth, J. and Walker, J. (1988) *Land Resettlement in Zimbabwe: a preliminary evaluation*, ODA Evaluation Report EV434, ODA, London.

Department of Rural Development (1992) *Policies and Procedures: Resettlement and the Reorganisation and Development of the Communal Lands*. Ministry of Local Government, Rural and Urban Development, Harare.

Downs, R. E. and Reyna, S. P. (1988) *Land and Society in Contemporary Africa*, University of New England Press, London.

Government of Zimbabwe (1989) *National Land Policy*, Ministry of Lands, Agriculture and Rural Resettlement, Harare.

Jinya, M. S. (1991) *Resettlement Schemes Permits Administration and Management: a diagnostic study of permit violations*, Monitoring and Evaluation Unit, Department of Rural and Urban Development, Harare.

King, R. (1977) *Land Reform: a world survey*, Bell & Son, London.

Ministry of Economic Planning and Development (1981) *Growth with Equity*, Government Printer, Harare.

Ministry of Lands, Agriculture and Rural Resettlement (1992) *Second Report of Settler Households in Normal Intensive Model A Resettlement Scheme*, Monitoring and Evaluation Unit, Harare.

Ministry of Lands, Resettlement and Rural Development (1981) *Resettlement Programme: policies and procedures*, Harare.

Moyo, S. (1986) The land question, pp. 165–203 in I. Mandaza, (ed.), *Zimbabwe: the political economy of transition 1980–86*, Codesria, Senegal.

Moyo, S. and Skalnes, T. (1990) *Zimbabwe's Land Reform and Development Strategy: state, class bias and economic rationality*, Zimbabwe Institute of Development Studies Research Papers No. 3, Harare.

Munslow, B. (1985) Prospects for the socialist transition of agriculture in Zimbabwe, *World Development*, 13(1), 41–58.

Republic of Zimbabwe (1982) *Transitional National Development Plan 1982–1985*, Ministry of Finance, Harare.

Whitlow, J. R. (1980) *Deforestation in Zimbabwe: problems and prospects*, Supplement to *Zambezia*, University of Zimbabwe, Harare.

Whitlow, J. R. (1988) *Land Degradation in Zimbabwe: a geographical study*, report prepared for Department of Natural Resources, Harare.

21

Environment as weapon: land, labour and African 'squatters' in rural South Africa

Charles Mather

Introduction

Conservation and environmental preservation have always been linked to broader political imperatives in the South African countryside (Beinart, 1989; Brooks, 1992). Efforts to conserve fragile ecologies were, for example, used to maintain the division between 'black' and 'white' land legislated under the Land Acts of 1913 and 1936. In the areas reserved for Africans, only 13% of the total land in South Africa, the priority was to prevent widespread soil erosion and overcome environmental problems associated with too many people on too little land. By preserving soils and preventing erosion, the state hoped to secure the material base for the policies of segregation and, after 1948, apartheid in rural South Africa. However, attempts by state officials to impose conservation methods, that were often ill-suited to local conditions, often led to open confrontations between African communities and local administrators (de Wet, 1989; Hendriks, 1989). In the decades after the election of the apartheid government in 1948, the massive population removals of Africans from 'white' to 'black' rural areas led to new and increasingly unpopular conservation measures to deal with the influx of

people on to land which was already overcrowded and under stress (Yawitch, 1981; Platzky and Walker, 1985). Environmental conservation for African farmers during the 1920s, 1930s and 1940s in what would become South Africa's bantustans several decades later was thus always controversial and highly politicized.

In the 'white' rural areas, attempts to conserve fragile soils and ecosystems must be seen in the context of the state's ideal of a countryside populated by white family farmers (Keegan, 1991; Clynick, 1994). But the state had a particular kind of white farmer in mind: a progressive individual who paid workers wages rather than in kind and farmed economically viable pieces of land (Murray, 1987). To this end, the state passed legislation during the 1940s to prevent the division of farms into plots so small that environmental damage was inevitable. Laws to discourage African workers from using, and by implication degrading, privately owned land were also passed. These legal measures were complemented by huge subsidies for conservation and a programme to educate white farmers on the preservation of soils and pastures (Beinart, 1989).

But the division of the countryside and conservation policies into 'white' and 'black' was never

People and Environment in Africa. Edited by Tony Binns
©1995 John Wiley & Sons Ltd

entirely successful or uncontested: there were numerous categories of land in 'white' South Africa that defied this division enshrined in the statute books. On unoccupied company-owned farms, proclaimed mining ground, state-owned Crown land and game reserves, ownership and control on the ground were not always congruent, especially in remote rural regions. While white landowners or the state may have owned these farms, the land was farmed, settled and controlled by Africans. In the Barberton district, where the colonization of land by whites was slow and geographically uneven, there remained a great deal of Crown land available for African settlement in what was ostensibly a 'white' rural area (Figure 21.1). Through the 1920s, 1930s and 1940s, the struggle between white commercial farmers and African rent tenants over land and labour on these farms is a crucial chapter in the agrarian transformation of the region (Mather, 1992). Significantly, white farmers' demands for the

resources controlled by African 'squatters' (the pejorative term of the period) were mediated by the discourse of environment and conservation. This chapter is about how the struggle for land and labour in a district of South Africa interacted with broader environmental and conservation issues.

Contested spaces

Crown land was one of numerous contested spaces in the South African countryside during the first half of the twentieth century. This was land held by the state and sold or leased mainly to white farmers. The extent of Crown land in any particular district depended on the agricultural potential of the soil and the prevalence of diseases that affected humans and livestock. On the eastern Transvaal highveld, for example, where diseases were less common and the potential for maize

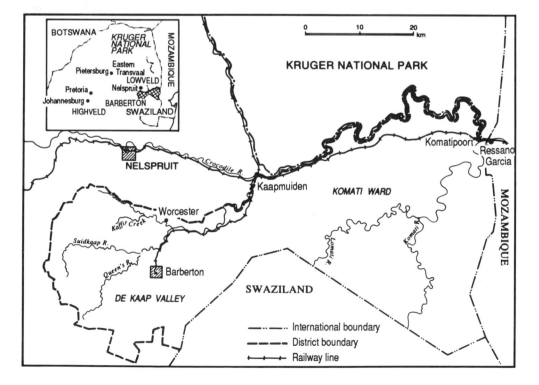

Figure 21.1 *Location of study area*

farming was high, virtually all of the land in the region was owned privately by the 1920s. Crown farms were a rarity in a region where 90% of the land was owned by white farmers or landowners. In the Barberton district, by contrast, where malaria epidemics were more common and outbreaks of cattle diseases plagued white and black farmers alike, there was a great deal of Crown land still unoccupied by white landowners. It is difficult to assess with any degree of accuracy how much Crown land was available at any one time in the Barberton district. Nevertheless, in the early 1920s over two-thirds of the land in Barberton was still in the hands of the state. By the late 1940s, there was still almost 150 000 ha of Crown land in the district. While this category of land was ostensibly held for white settlers, Africans were permitted to use these farms for an annual rental paid to the state.

For Africans forced off white commercial farms, unoccupied Crown farms provided a refuge where cattle could graze, seeds could be sown and crops could be harvested. Crown farms also provided a space where rural Africans could avoid the demands by white farmers for unpaid labour. Local state officials used Crown land as a resource to slow the inevitable overcrowding of land reserved for Africans under the Land Acts. By directing dispossessed Africans on to Crown farms not yet occupied by white settlers, the local Native Commissioner in Barberton could ease the impact of agrarian transformation, if only in the short term. For white commercial farmers growing labour-intensive crops like cotton, vegetables, tobacco and citrus, Crown farms provided an important source of seasonal wage workers. With short, but very intensive demands for labour, white farmers were dependent on the young black men and women from these areas who worked for two or three months harvesting cotton, tobacco and fruit. These areas were 'one of the sources whence derived seasonal labourers, who washed like spring tides through farms for harvesting and shearing' (Bradford, 1988, p. 36).

Wage labour from Crown farms was, however, more difficult to control and mobilize than was the case for permanently resident farm workers on white-owned land. While some white commercial farmers entered into strategic alliances with African chiefs on Crown land for labour—an arrangement that usually involved some form of compensation—these accords were usually very tenuous. A second problem for white farmers was that harvesting tobacco and subtropical fruit during the summer coincided with African subsistence agriculture on Crown farms. Labour was more difficult to mobilize in this season. During years of poor rainfall and when crops failed, more labour was available as African households were forced to purchase food with cash. But even during years of severe drought and crop failure, farmers still complained of labour shortages. When the state provided Africans in reserves and on Crown land with maize, it apparently left white farmers 'with a bitter feeling of wrong done to them, of betrayal of their interests in favour of pusillanimous petting of the natives and of encouraging the natives in indolence and evasion of man's duty to labour'.[1]

The key to the relationship between white commercial farmers and 'squatters' on Crown land in the Barberton district was that these were spaces where Africans could sell their labour under conditions more of their own choosing. The improved bargaining position of Africans off white farms was always recognized by the white farming community. Contracts, when they existed, were often based on a weekly or monthly ticket system allowing workers to shift from farm to farm, or to even refuse to work for particular farmers. Migrant workers also used information networks and nicknames to avoid particularly harsh working environments, low wages and poor conditions. It was unwise, for example, to work for *Mdisipansi* (Don't sit on your ass!) or for *Mashaibongolo* (Donkey killer) because conditions were hard and dangerous. Working for *Mazibambela* (Keep working) might have been hard, but at least it was fair.

From the perspective of white farmers, Crown farms were areas where 'squatters' avoided work on farms and where undesirable activities could not be controlled. Crown farms were spaces where 'squatters' could take 'refuge' from work. They also provided a 'sanctuary' to those evicted from white-owned farms and a place where 'natives were not subject to any form of control'.[2] One white farmer even suggested that African rent tenants were part of the 'leisured classes', a situation that was unacceptable to whites given the context of the Great Depression where millions of whites were 'half-starved slaves' in comparison.[3] White farmers complained that African rent tenants on Crown land influenced workers who lived permanently on white-owned farms. In a petition to the Native Commissioner in Barberton, they complained that Africans on Crown land set 'a very bad example to the natives we have residing on our land.'[4] Indeed, white farmers often blamed Monday morning hangovers on the activities of their employees on Crown farms at the weekends. The control of African tenants by white farmers, already problematic and incomplete, was complicated by rent tenants on nearby Crown farms.

Farmers linked their inability to encourage Africans to work on their farms to the cash-generating activities in these uncontrolled spaces. Entire households were allegedly involved in illegal activities including beer brewing, cultivating cannabis, crop thieving from nearby white-owned farms, and prostitution. These areas were also 'widely believed to harbour stock-thieves' (Wilson, 1971, p. 129). In a strongly worded memo, the Secretary for Lands described in detail the economy that existed on Crown land in the Barberton region: 'Between 700 and 800 of these squatters roam about on proclaimed land, chop down trees, and transport wood to the nearest mine and sell it there, plant dagga (cannabis) and carry on illegal trade in that plant, brew kaffir beer and hold beer parties.'[5]

The link drawn between the refusal of African 'squatters' to work on white farms and the economic activities that supported them was almost certainly true. Many Crown farms were close to mine workers' housing in the Barberton district, where a ready market existed for beer, food, cannabis and the purchase of sex. Some Crown farms were close to the small, but burgeoning, town of Barberton where there were economic opportunities for Africans not living under a white farmer (MacMillan, 1989). There is also evidence that Africans on Crown land maintained cattle herds for households on white farms who were not permitted to own livestock. But not all Africans in these settlements were involved in what officials considered vice activities. The Native Affairs Department usually distinguished the 700–800 Africans who 'roamed about the district' from those 'decent and law abiding types who live on the land and their stock.'[6] A proportion of these rent tenants worked on the local mines and farms on a regular basis and used Crown land to sustain cattle herds and plant substantial fields. Indeed, in the late 1940s almost 70 ha of maize was being planted by the residents of one Crown farm. Crown land was also generally free from the restrictions imposed on livestock and agriculture by the Native Affairs Department in the areas reserved for exclusive African occupation. African 'squatters' on Crown land were more free, not only with regard to the sale of their labour, but also in terms of their life on the land.

The struggle between white commercial farmers and African tenants during the 1920s and early 1930s was sporadic and uneven. Dogged by droughts, local and global depressions, plant diseases and uncertain markets, white farmers lacked the economic power to challenge the independence of African rent tenants on Crown land. Without predictable markets and steady incomes, white farmers also failed to convince the state to act against African 'squatters' and tip the balance of power in their favour. By the late 1930s and early 1940s, however, the economic climate for farming improved markedly with a new system of marketing for white farmers and a huge demand for food during the Second World War. Both economically and politically, white commercial farmers were in a better position to mobilize the state against African rent tenants on Crown land. The reason why the state intervened is significant: white farmers claimed that African 'squatters' in the Barberton district were eroding fragile soils, destroying endangered trees and wiping out wild animals. The implication of their charge was that if African rent tenants overcrowded, overworked and overstocked these farms, they would be irreparably damaged for future white settlers.

Environment as weapon: the assault on African 'squatters'

It is hardly surprising that the discourse of environment was used against African rent tenants in the late 1930s and early 1940s. This was a period of extreme concern over the impact of erosion and degradation in the 'white' countryside. Much of this environmental damage was caused by white settlers overstocking fragile ecologies and dividing farms into plots so small that degradation was inevitable. The state responded by passing the Soil Conservation Act in the 1940s and by amending the Land Settlement Act which prevented the subdivision of farms. By the mid-1940s the state had also subsidized conservation works to the tune of £2.5 million. In this context, farmers' claims that African 'squatters' were degrading land destined for white settlement, had an immediate impact on state officials.

Significantly, the source of many complaints concerning Africans damaging the environment originated from white farmers who could not control rent tenants on Crown land. In one publicized report a white farmer was having difficulty forcing African 'squatters' to provide him with free labour for six months every year. He also failed to convince the tenants of the Crown farm to decrease the size of their herds so that there would be sufficient grazing for his sheep in the winter. When the tenants refused both demands, the white farmer responded by lodging a formal complaint with the police accusing the tenants of destroying endangered trees, killing wild animals and overgrazing. He went so far as to suggest that the 'squatters' had a cache of weapons on the farm which they used to kill wild

animals. Another farmer, who was having 'trouble' convincing African tenants on a Crown farm to work for free, reported that they were ploughing on the slopes of mountains and cutting down endangered *kiaat* trees.

Were the accusations by the white farming community justified? Were the farms being degraded by African 'squatters'? Between the 1920s and the early 1940s most of the reports of environmental degradation were either exaggerated or entirely false. They reflect instead the inability of white farmers to use African-controlled land and to encourage 'squatters' on to their farms as labour. By the late 1940s and early 1950s, however, conditions on Crown farms had changed substantially. With the progressive colonization of the region by white settlers, many African tenants were forced off Crown farms and onto other farms or into the reserves. Those still on Crown land found conditions deteriorating rapidly as new tenants arrived with a need for pastures and arable land. By the late 1940s, some of these farms were undoubtedly overstocked and overgrazed. On one 2500 ha farm there were 39 households with 500 cattle, 50 sheep and 900 goats. Conservative estimates were that the farm could at most hold 200 cattle and 100 small stock. Agricultural plots were also overworked and there was widespread evidence of erosion. In spite of reports like these, it would be incorrect to blame the degradation of flora and fauna on African agricultural and hunting practices. Instead, the evidence suggests that the origins of environmental damage on Crown farms must be located in the demands by white farmers for access to land already in use. White stock farmers, rather than African 'squatters', were responsible for placing grazing land and pastures under severe stress. Where there was overcrowding by Africans on Crown farms, which eventually led to soil erosion and degradation, the root cause of ecological damage was the state's policy of settling white farmers in the countryside at the expense of African rent tenants on Crown farms.

In spite of the deteriorating conditions on Crown land, there were sound reasons why African tenants refused to move off Crown land in the Barberton Valley in spite of the dwindling resource base. First, with overstocking and overcrowding in the areas reserved for Africans in the Barberton district, those evicted from Crown land or white farms faced the devastating prospect of decreasing the size of their herds. African households with cattle were reluctant to move to these reserves and lose a resource that was so crucial to their economic and social well-being. Second, there were stringent restrictions with regard to agricultural production in the areas reserved for Africans that were not generally enforced on Crown land. Finally, the economic opportunities for selling beer, wood and other commodities to wage earners on the mines would be lost in the remote region reserved for exclusive African occupation.

Ignoring the root cause of damage to soils, pastures and animals, state officials responded promptly to the letters and police reports from farmers in the Barberton district. The regional Inspector of Lands, whose thinking was similar to the white farming community, was ordered to investigate the situation in the Barberton district. His response foreshadowed what was to come:

In my outings I find that there are a lot of Kaffirs on proclaimed Crown Land. They don't work on the mines but are those who left white farms. They take refuge on this land where they live unhindered without any duties. They take out plants to plant their own crops; the wild animals are also being hunted out; they are there illegally and should be evicted.[6]

The inspector stepped up his efforts to evict Africans from Crown farms by appointing three additional rangers and declaring that all Crown farms should be 'freed' of African 'squatters'. Evicting African rent tenants from Crown land was, however, easier said than done. It was impossible, for example, to prevent Crown farms in remote rural areas from being immediately resettled by those ordered off the farm. And even after the appointment of three additional rangers in the 1940s, the inspector was still understaffed to patrol the entire Barberton district.

The inspector's attempts to evict tenants in the region of Worcester reflect the problems faced by state officials and highlight the crucial role of African resistance in rural transformation. The region around Worcester had apparently become 'a sort of sanctuary for natives who leave employment [on white farms]'.[8] In 1939 the inspector responded by ordering 24 African households and their 558 cows and sheep off two farms and directing them to the 'black' areas in the Komati ward. In a remarkable display of resistance and defiance, the tenants refused to leave the farm arguing that they had lived on the land for years, had large livestock herds, and had invested a great deal of time and resources on the land. Faced with this strong resistance, the inspector was forced to extend their permission to remain on the farms until the end of 1940. After 1940 the tenants would have to leave the Crown farm unconditionally. As a precautionary measure, he warned the clerk at the magistrate's office not to accept any further payments for rent from the residents of the farm. But when the clerk was temporarily replaced, eight of the families took the opportunity to pay Crown rents for the following year, thereby ensuring their continued residence on the land. The infuriated inspector declared that the 'natives have not behaved properly'. He patronized the residents further by demanding that they 'render themselves' to white farmers as farm workers. The residents of the farm rose to the challenge and refused. By the end of 1941 the resistance of the residents around Worcester had become 'so strong that definite action had to be taken'.[9]

The archival record is silent on the experiences of Africans who were removed by white farmers from Crown land to the overcrowded reserves or to other privately owned farms in the late 1940s and early 1950s. Oral testimony sheds some light on the process of dispossession and the interaction between white farmers and African peasants on the land. It also suggests that as white settlement in the region progressed, many more households were forced to leave Crown farms. Take for example the case of the Vilikati family. During the 1920s and 1930s, the household head worked on a local mine on a full-time basis and owned a respectably large herd of livestock that included cattle, donkeys and horses. The household also produced a wide range of crops for personal consumption including maize, jugo beans, ground peanuts, cowpeas and sweet potatoes. Some time after the Second World War the Crown farm was leased to a white farmer who planned to use the land to graze sheep. When the farmer arrived on the farm he demanded unpaid work from the Vilikati children during the winter months. He also informed all the residents of the farm that their cattle herds would have to be thinned out since there was insufficient grazing for his sheep and the tenant's cattle. But Mr Vilikati refused to allow his children to work for the farmer because it would interfere with the school year. He was also unwilling to decrease the size of his herd and remain on a farm where the grazing land would be under severe stress. Faced with this intransigence, the farmer gave the Vilikatis the option of tending the sheep in winter or leaving the farm. In the late 1940s, the household moved, with a number of others, to a farm closer to Sheba mine, presumably another smaller, but more crowded, Crown farm. With less grazing and more pressure on the land on the new farm, Vilikati was forced to significantly decrease the size of his herd. As more Crown farms were sold to white settlers who had served in the Second World War, many more households felt the brunt of new white farmers and an increasingly determined state.

By the early 1950s hundreds of African households had been forced off Crown farms and into the reserves. While some were forced off in the same way as the Vilikatis, after 1950 many were evicted by the state, which was spurred on by the huge demand for government land from white settlers and by persistent allegations that Africans were cutting down forests and burning pastures. Their new methods of evicting 'squatters' were more concerted and even vicious: those tenants who refused to move after an initial warning were fined the sum of £10, a huge amount by any standard in those days. To prevent Africans from moving from one farm to the next, the Inspector of Lands started a programme of house burning. Houses constructed of stone and corrugated iron were removed with tractors and bulldozers. By the mid-1950s the Secretary for Lands claimed that most rent tenants had been removed from Crown land in the Barberton district. Preserving land for white settlers and the claims that Africans were degrading soils and pastures were the basis of this process of dispossession.

Conclusion

The theme of land and labour is integral to the agrarian transformation of South Africa. Simply put, when African communities could retain access to land for subsistence, it made them more independent of the demands by white farmers for unpaid labour. Retaining some control over land also allowed Africans in the rural areas to maintain cattle, a resource which was crucial to their economic and social reproduction. Crown land was one category of land in rural South Africa that provided the basis for this independence and allowed rent tenants to survive on an uneven and shifting mix of remittances from migrant labour, wages earned on local mines and farms, agricultural production, and other informal activities. Crown farms also provided a refuge from white farmers who demanded a labour force that could be better controlled. What makes the struggle between African rent tenants and white commercial farmers in the Barberton district unique is the way in which the discourse of environment was used against African 'squatters'. Unable to control the labour of Africans on Crown lands, white commercial farmers blamed 'squatters' for the degradation of soils and pastures and the wanton destruction of wild animals. Given the heightened awareness of conservation during the 1940s, the state moved quickly to evict Africans from Crown land in the fear that these farms would be damaged for future white settlement. The cause of environmental destruction on some farms in the Barberton district cannot, however, be laid at the feet of African 'squatters', as the white farming community argued. The degradation of pastures must be seen in the context of white farmers' demands for grazing land for sheep and cattle. Similarly, soil erosion and forest denudation on Crown farms was not a result of poor African agricultural practices; rather it was due to the progressive colonization of land by white settlers and the dispossession of Africans on to less and less Crown land.

The historical geography of dispossession and conservation in the Barberton district from the 1920s to the 1950s confirms the political content of ecological preservation. In this district, the discourse of conservation was closely tied to attempts to control African labour and evict African 'squatters' from Crown land. Conservation in post-apartheid South Africa will almost certainly become as politicized in both rural and urban contexts.

Acknowledgements

This research would not have been possible without the financial assistance of the Social Sciences and Human Research Council of Canada, the International Development Research Council of Canada and the University of Bophuthatswana. I am also grateful to Jerry Segage in the field, and Cecile Badenhorst, Jonathan Crush and Gordon Pirie for comments on an earlier draft of this chapter. Finally, thanks go to Phil Stickler for drawing the map.

Notes

1. Central Archives Depot Pretoria (CAD), Native Affairs Department (NTS) 32/336. Famine in the Barberton District. Komati Agricultural and Industrial Society to Prime Minister J. B. Hertzog, 4/7/1927.
2. CAD, NTS 878/323. Crown and Mining Ground: Removal of squatters From. Inspector of Lands to Secretary for Lands, 16/10/1941.
3. *Barberton Herald*, Editorial, 9/2/1931.
4. CAD, NTS 878/323. Petition by Local Farmers to Native Commissioner in Barberton, 10/7/1941.
5. CAD, NTS 878/323. Secretary for Lands to Secretary for Native Affairs, 24/10/1944.
6. Ibid. Native Commissioner, Barberton to Chief Native Commissioner, Pietersburg, 3/5/1948.
7. CAD, Department of Lands (LDE) 33360. Inspector of Lands, Nelspruit to Secretary for Lands, 16/10/1941.
8. CAD, NTS 878/323. Secretary for Lands to Secretary for Native Affairs, 30/12/1941.
9. Ibid. Native Commissioner, Barberton to Secretary for Native Affairs, 18/7/1941.

References

Beinart, W. (1989) The politics of colonial conservation, *Journal of Southern African Studies*, 15, 143–162.

Bradford, H. (1988) *A Taste of Freedom: the ICU in rural South Africa, 1924–1930*, Ravan Press, Johannesburg.

Brooks, S. (1992) The environment in history: new themes for South African geography, pp. 158–172 in C. Rogerson, and J. McCarthy (eds), *Geography in a Changing South Africa*, Oxford University, Cape Town.

Clynick, T. (1994) Creating rural space for a Boerestand: modernisation and the racial order on the white Platteland, *c.*1959, unpublished paper, University of Bophuthatswana.

De Wet, C. (1989) Betterment planning in a rural village in Keiskammahoek, Ciskei, *Journal of Southern African Studies*, 15, 326–345.

Hendriks, F. T. (1989) Loose planning and rapid resettlement: the politics of conservation and control in Transkei, South Africa, 1950–1970, *Journal of Southern African Studies*, 15, 306–325.

Keegan, T. (1991) The making of the rural economy: from 1850 to the present, pp. 36–63 in Z. A. Konczacki, J. L. Parpart, and T. M. Shaw, (eds), *Studies in the Economic History of Southern Africa*, Vol. 2: *South Africa, Lesotho and Swaziland*, Frank Cass, London.

MacMillan, H. (1989) A nation divided? The Swazi in Swaziland and the Transvaal, 1865–1986, pp. 289–323 in L. Vail, (ed) *The Creation of Tribalism in Southern Africa*, James Currey, London.

Mather, C. (1992) Agrarian transformation in South Africa: land and labour in the Barberton district, 1920–1960, unpublished PhD. thesis, Queen's University, Kingston.

Murray, C. (1987) Review article: landlords, tenants and share-croppers-agrarian change in regional perspective, *Journal of Southern African Studies*, 14, 153–159.

Platzky, L. and Walker, C. (1985) *The Surplus People*, Ravan Press, Johannesburg.

Wilson, F. (1971) Farming 1866–1966, pp. 104–171 in M. Wilson, and L. M. Thompson (eds), *Oxford History of South Africa*, Vol. II, Oxford University Press, Oxford.

Yawitch, J. (1981) *Betterment—the myth of homeland agriculture*, South African Institute of Race Relations, Johannesburg.

22

Development and change: irrigation and agricultural production in Dinokana village, North West Province, South Africa

J. H. Drummond

Introduction

A major concern of geographers, as well as other social scientists, in recent years has been the analysis of the problems of Africa's rural areas and its so-called agricultural crisis. A favoured solution to this crisis is the development of irrigation schemes. Geographers have contributed to studies of irrigation development in Africa, including the analysis of large-scale irrigation schemes, which in general have not been as successful as anticipated (Briggs, 1978; Adams, 1982, 1988; Adams and Grove, 1984) and the consequent reorientation towards small-scale irrigation (Adams and Carter, 1987), particularly where this builds on indigenous irrigation systems (Adams and Anderson, 1988; Adams *et al.*, 1994). Irrigation projects are often seen as one way of contributing to agricultural commercialization, agricultural production, food security and rural development.

The present study of declining agricultural production and changing irrigation systems in Dinokana village, North West Province, South Africa (formerly Bophuthatswana bantustan) is located within the broad field of studies on African agricultural policy and production which has been reviewed in depth by Hinderink and Sterkenburg (1987). Just as Hinderink and Sterkenburg (1987) have covered the historical literature relating to their main theme of agricultural commercialization, it is argued here, that, especially in the former bantustans of South Africa, a historical perspective is essential to understand the nature of contemporary agricultural collapse. It is suggested that a geography which employs both historical and political economy approaches, and moreover focuses on micro-level case studies which take account of local resource management strategies, would be a valuable contribution to debates on the nature of past, present and future agricultural development in the former bantustans.

People and Environment in Africa. Edited by Tony Binns
©1995 John Wiley & Sons Ltd

Bophuthatswana agriculture

Although the regime of Lucas Mangope was overthrown in March 1994 and Bophuthatswana was reincorporated into South Africa in April 1994 (Lawrence and Manson, 1994), there has to date been little material change in Dinokana under the new ANC-dominated North West provincial government. It is therefore still pertinent to dwell on the policies and programmes of the previous regime in attempting to analyse patterns of land and water use.

A major thrust of Lucas Mangope's administration was to try and gain diplomatic recognition for Bophuthatswana. Since the bantustans were an integral component of the apartheid system, they were unrecognized by any country other than South Africa. This, however, did not deter Bophuthatswana from allocating considerable resources in pursuit of its recognition goal (Drummond, 1991). One of the ways in which Bophuthatswana tried to proclaim its 'independence' was to promote agricultural policies which would lead to self-sufficiency in food production. The Department of Agriculture in the Bophuthatswana Legislative Assembly (the forerunner to Bophuthatswana), had been set up in 1972 and was responsible specifically for agricultural planning, betterment schemes and extension. At 'independence' in 1977 this became the Bophuthatswana Department of Agriculture. To pursue the aim of 'national' self-sufficiency, a second agricultural body was established in 1978, the parastatal Agricultural Development Corporation of Bophuthatswana (Agricor), 'originally with the primary goal of feeding the Nation in the shortest possible time from its own resources' (Agricor, 1984, p. 2).

In those rural areas selected to host 'development' in the form of agricultural projects, traditional patterns of land use and resource allocation were often radically transformed. One such area was Dinokana in the Lehurutshe district,[1] the home of the Hurutshe people which, before 'independence', was known as Moiloa's Reserve (Figure 22.1). This area was chosen for agricultural development in the early 1980s by both the Department of Agriculture and Agricor, primarily because of its rich groundwater resources, which it was decided could be harnessed for irrigation schemes. This was in spite of the fact that there was a network of irrigation furrows, first developed in the 1840s, which ran through the villagers' gardens and fields. It is interesting to note the direct influence of the former President of Bophuthatswana, L. M. Mangope, whose home area is close to Dinokana, in the establishment of the projects. By 1981 agricultural production in Dinokana was in severe disarray and Mangope recommended that the Bophuthatswana Department of Agriculture devise an agricultural project using the water for irrigation.

At that time, Bophuthatswana was coveting ties with Taiwan, and invited a number of agricultural advisers to Bophuthatswana. Subsequently rice production got under way at three locations, one of which was Dinokana; chosen because of the availability of water from the Dinokana 'eye' (a fountain or spring with an average yield of 352 l/s). The initial aim of the projects was to make Bophuthatswana self-sufficient in rice production. To this end the Dinokana project became operational on an experimental basis in December 1981, and by 1983 120 farmers were organized on a co-operative basis to farm rice and vegetables under Taiwanese guidance on an area of 48 ha. The site chosen was immediately adjacent to the village, close to the groundwater spring, and was on an area of tribal land, which had been intensively cultivated by the villagers up to the 1970s. The initial experience was the failure of the crop, but by 1983 the project farmers 'were encouraged and had much confidence in the rice plantation' (Chang, 1983, p. 1). The rice was successfully marketed locally in Bophuthatswana and in other parts of South Africa, while neighbouring Botswana also proved to be a very important market. The project was strongly supported by the local extension officers and by the Department of Agriculture officials at head office. To date, the project has been regarded as fairly successful by those involved with it, and has the enthusiastic support of the members of the farmers' co-op.[2] However, the rice project has

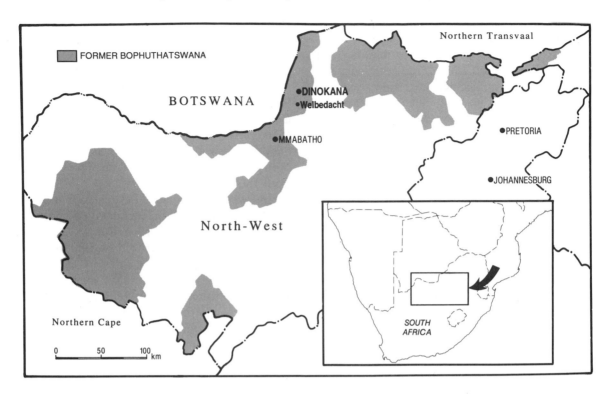

Figure 22.1 *Location of study area*

not always been seen in such a positive light by the villagers and the tribal council. There has been some resentment against the project because it is felt it uses 'too much water' in the sense that it takes water away from the villagers' irrigated gardens.[3] However, the rice project, the fields of which are often flooded for irrigation, only draws water from the Dinokana lower 'eye' which is linked to and has a much lower yield than the main upper 'eye'. The waters of the upper 'eye' are much in demand by the Agricor irrigation project, the growing nearby settlement of Welbedacht and by the villagers themselves. Considerable conflict over the allocation of this water has been manifest in the village for over a decade and continues to the present day.

In 1984 Agricor's agricultural development strategy was in full operation and again the intervention of President Mangope was crucial in the decision to establish another agricultural development project in Dinokana. Under political pressure from Mangope, Agricor rushed through established planning procedures and within nine months set up a vegetable-growing project close to Dinokana in August 1984, called the Lehurutshe Irrigation Scheme. The aim of the president, it seems, was to have a project which would supply cheap vegetables for the people of Bophuthatswana; a laudable enough aim. However, Agricor could not plan the project in detail quickly enough. They therefore hired managing agents, the Israeli agribusiness company Agri-Carmel, who recommended the installation of an expensive computer-controlled drip irrigation and fertilizer system, which was Israeli built.

The capital costs of the project were R2.3 million and Agricor officials have acknowledged that this figure was too high for the project to be financially successful in the short term. In the first season Agricor stuck to the president's brief and planted popular cheap vegetables such as cabbages, onions, carrots and beetroot. Although production was excellent, Agricor could not make enough profit from the sale of cheap vegetables to cover the capital costs of the project. Agricor, not given to altruism, decided after one season to switch production to high-value crops such as green and red peppers and water melons to try to improve profits and the financial viability of the project.

Very quickly the aim of the project was abandoned, as villagers could not afford prices of peppers and melons, and instead Agricor openly competed on the South African produce markets. Understandably, these markets fluctuate greatly and Agricor has had severe problems with timing harvesting and delivery of the crops to markets while prices are high. Consequently, the project has been plagued by financial troubles and still has not recovered its initial outlay.[4] In terms of meeting Agricor's national strategy of agricultural development to make Bophuthatswana self-sufficient in food, the project may be seen as being successful in that the actual production of food is considerable. However, the water needs of this project are substantial, as a computerized drip irrigation system is used on 48 ha, and the more wasteful system of sprinkler irrigation is used on 50 ha of land. This has a negative effect on Dinokana village, since the supply of water running through the village irrigation furrows has been reduced. Indeed, water is only allowed to run down the furrows one day a week. In the era before this project was commissioned, a greater supply of water was available to the villagers. Agricultural production in the village itself has therefore declined.[5]

Historical review of agriculture in Dinokana

In order to get a clear picture of the reasons why it was felt necessary to establish projects in Dinokana in the early 1980s, it is useful to reconstruct a picture of the changing agricultural landscape up to this period. The dominant view of contemporary South African social historians who are concerned with the nature of the development of African agriculture, is that the reserves were deliberately underdeveloped in order to encourage Africans to sell their labour on the mines, factories and farms of an industrializing South Africa (Wolpe, 1972; Legassick, 1977). It is often argued that the South African peasantry at first responded to the opportunities created by this economic development by increasing their production for the market (roughly the period from the 1880s to the 1920s).

However by the 1930s, it is generally held that a fully fledged and independent peasantry no longer existed in South Africa (Bundy, 1988). This argument has been challenged by Simkins (1981) who has analysed the statistics of agricultural production and concluded that the rapid decline and disintegration of the South African peasantry only set in during the late 1950s. Available evidence from Dinokana would tend to support this view (Drummond and Manson, 1993).

The pre-colonial system of agricultural production began to be modified by the arrival of missionaries among the Tswana. In 1843, David Livingstone of the London Missionary Society (LMS) established a mission station at Mabotsa, on the Manwane stream near Gopane, about 15 km north of Dinokana. Under the direction and guidance of Livingstone the local people developed a network irrigation system for agriculture. One of Livingstone's biographers, Blaikie (1903, p. 56), records that Livingstone, writing to his father on 27 April 1844 about a lion attack at Mabotsa, told how the attacks of the lions 'drew the people of Mabotsa away from the irrigating operations they were engaged in'. That the Tswana quickly realized the advantage of this technique is not in question. This can be seen from the writings of Livingstone himself who, writing of an irrigation scheme under the Tswana chief Bubi, recalled:

The doctor and the rainmaker among these people are one and the same person. As I did not like to be behind my professional brethren, I declared I could make rain too, not however by enchantments like them, but by leading out their river for irrigation. The idea pleased mightily, and to work we went instanter. Even the chief's own doctor is at it, and works like a good fellow, laughing heartily at the cunning of the 'foreigner' who can make rain. . . . This is, I believe, the first instance in which Bechuanas have been got to work without wages. It was with the utmost difficulty the other missionaries got them to do anything (Blaikie, 1903, p. 37).

The probable reason for the Tswana working without wages is that they realized the advantages of building irrigation canals for their agricultural prospects. From Mabotsa, knowledge of irrigation quickly spread to Dinokana.

The missionaries of the LMS were expelled from the Transvaal in 1852, and replaced by those of the German Hermannsburg Missionary Society (HMS), who set to work in Moiloa's Reserve in 1859. That the Hurutshe continued with their irrigation works in the absence of the LMS missionaries is apparent from the observations of the HMS missionary Zimmerman who, on his arrival in Dinokana in 1859 observed,

this wonderful wide valley (with) Dinokana just about in the centre. The land brings enormous amounts of corn as the people concentrate more on agriculture. Dinokana is surrounded by many large vegetable gardens. The Bahurutshi already know how to irrigate. The Bahurutshi are generally well off, some even really wealthy, because they have their cattle farming as well as many good lands. They have bought many wagons and ploughs.[6]

In 1859 the Hurutshe were competent in the use of irrigation and were keen to expand their agricultural production through the adoption of new technology such as the plough. That the people of Moiloa's Reserve had many wagons also indicates that they were in fact involved in trading networks and were producing for markets (Manson, 1990). The Hurutshe continued to expand their agricultural production throughout the latter half of the nineteenth century. In particular, they boosted production to take advantage of the new markets created by the diamond discoveries at Kimberley in 1867 and the opening of the Witwatersrand gold fields in 1886. Evidence to support this is provided by the observations of contemporary travellers and writers of the period. Emil Holub, a Czech

traveller, visited Dinokana in March 1874 and April 1875. On his first visit Holub reported that the Hurutshe 'have become the most thriving agriculturalists of all the Transvaal Bechuanas' (Holub, 1881, vol. I, p. 416). This prosperity was based on irrigation, as can be seen from Holub's account that

the people have turned the Matebe springs to good account; not only have they conducted the water into the town so as to ensure a good supply for domestic purposes, but they have cut trenches through their fields and orchards, thereby securing a thorough irrigation (Holub, 1881, vol. I, p. 418).

Moreover, passing through Dinokana after harvest time in 1875, Holub noted that

the Bahurutshe in Dinokana gathered in as much as 800 sacks of wheat, each containing 200 lbs., and every year a wider area of land is being brought under cultivation. Besides wheat, they grow maize, sorghum, melons and tobacco, selling what they do not require for their own consumption in the markets of the Transvaal and the diamond fields (Holub, 1881, vol. II, p. 22).

By 1875, the Hurutshe had quite clearly responded to new opportunities in agriculture. In this the Hurutshe were not unique. It has been demonstrated by Bundy (1988) that the South African peasantry as a whole responded to the opening of markets by increasing agricultural production. However, whereas Bundy (1988) suggests that the independent peasantry no longer existed by the 1930s, Dinokana seems to have been an exception to this rule. Although there would have been booms and slumps in agricultural production associated with climatic factors, agriculture in Dinokana seems to have remained fairly stable and productive throughout much of the twentieth century. The general health and relatively prosperous position of Dinokana in the first decade of the century, when infant industrialization was taking place, can be judged by the contemporary observation that

placed in the centre of a great amphitheatre of hills is Dinokana (the place of many waters). It is very fertile and there are seven streams. Where the land can be irrigated the people grow tobacco, figs, fruit of all sorts, melons and so on and it seemed to be a most fertile and well cared for place.[7]

The continued fertility and productivity of Dinokana in the era up to the Second World War can also be gauged from an examination of the relevant archival material. For example, in 1930 the Moiloa Reserve Local Council applied for and received a grant of £1550 from the Minister of Native Affairs for agricultural improvements. These measures included the construction of dams and irrigation furrows, the erection of a dairy hut to facilitate the marketing of cream, the purchase of stud bulls, the provision of a fumigation outfit to protect citrus trees against disease, and the sinking of a number of boreholes, as well as the maintenance of roads in the reserve. Commenting on these developments, the local Native Commissioner stated that the 'Reserve bids in a fair way to become a model native area'.[8] State support for African agriculture continued and a further boost was occasioned by a subsidy scheme to increase crop production during the Second World War. However, not all farmers benefited equally and it was a class of male progressive farmers who further developed commercial agriculture in alliance with the government Native Affairs Department (Drummond and Manson, 1993).

In the period up to 1957, Dinokana had not crumbled into the unproductive labour reserve economy so typical of many South African bantustan areas. According to a survey made by the South African ethnographer P. L. Breutz (1953, p. 161) in the early 1950s, 'the tribe has an elaborate irrigation system. As there is more water they also grow European vegetables, such as cabbages, peas, tomatoes, carrots, radish, onions, and they have various kinds of fruit trees. There is also sufficient grazing around Dinokana.' However, this relatively sound position needs to be tempered with archival evidence, which suggests that the broader productive base was selectively narrowed at Dinokana, and the women especially, felt threatened by continuing state support through betterment planning, for male progressive farmers (Drummond and Manson, 1993).

Agricultural decline

From a probable high point of production during the wartime subsidy period (Drummond, 1992) decay set in. Possible reasons for the decline in agricultural production stem initially from a major change in policy associated with the coming to power of the National Party government in 1948. Previous high levels of support were gradually withdrawn in the late 1940s and 1950s. Also, in 1957 the South African government attempted to force African women to carry passes. This action was strongly resisted by the women of Dinokana, who symbolically burned their passes in protest, and by the majority of the community. The state reacted to this with force and large numbers of people were detained. This caused severe dislocation in Dinokana and consequently dealt a strong blow to agriculture as many people went into hiding or fled to neighbouring Botswana (Hooper, 1960). One Dinokana farmer pointed out that 'in 1957 my harvest was very bad, only eight bags. I usually got 50 or 60' (Manson, 1983, p. 37).

Before the people of Dinokana could recover from this shock to the agricultural system, they were faced by an unfortunate chain of events. There was a severe drought in the years 1962–66, while simultaneously there was an outbreak of disease among the villagers' fruit trees, which were an important source of food as well as providing some cash income from the sale of fruit.[9] The fact that neighbouring Botswana received independence in 1966 was also a blow to the economy, since this was accompanied by the strict enforcement of the previously open and fluid border between Moiloa's Reserve and the Bechuanaland Protectorate (Drummond and Manson, 1991). In turn, this reduced the resources available to the people of Dinokana, since previously they had maintained cattle posts (grazing lands) near Kanye in Botswana.[10]

Apartheid policies, such as influx control and forced removals, added substantially to land hunger during the 1960s and 1970s. The present-day settlement of Welbedacht only came into existence in 1969, when labour tenants and 'squatters' were moved there from white farms in the western Transvaal (Surplus People Project, 1983). In addition, under influx control, people were moved from the Witwatersrand to Welbedacht. These removals added over 13 000 people to the reserve's population, contributing to overcrowding, the erosion of pastures, and a fall in crop yields. One Dinokana farmer, Piet Mohalelo, remembers noticing a large increase in population 'from '65 ja, people are so moving on to the reserve that I don't know in five years' time how the place will be. It will be overpopulated.'[11]

Although not taking land resources away from the original Hurutshe inhabitants, water, perhaps a more precious resource, was redirected from Dinokana to the resettlement area of Welbedacht. Every house in Welbedacht had a tap, and for a number of years, water was supplied free from the Dinokana 'eye'. The diversion of water away from the villagers affected irrigated cultivation, further hampering the potential to grow crops all year round. The villagers resented 'their' water going to Welbedacht, to people who are not Hurutshe. One villager, referring to Welbedacht, complained:

The land is ours, but some of the people who occupied that township are from white farms . . . and some are from other tribes. . . . Things will only improve if they (Dinokana villagers) can complain, if they organise themselves and negotiate they will get their water back . . . the villagers here just waited until Welbedacht was built and the water was pumped into the Welbedacht dam. It is then that they started to complain, they should have complained earlier . . . there should be time that they pump water to the people. Not always to the projects and Welbedacht.[12]

The impact of apartheid migration and population policies was severe. The effects of dumping 13 000 people at Welbedacht, a location choice surely influenced by the availability of water, has undoubtedly had a negative impact on agriculture. Population increase in Dinokana, not relieved by the option of permanent urbanization, was compounded by influx control and forced removals, factors over which those who still wished to irrigate had no control. Furthermore, the transfer of administrative functions from the South African Department of Bantu Administration and Development to the Bophuthatswana Department of Agriculture, resulted in the decline of extension support to progressive farmers. Allied with increasing population and concomitant reductions in water supply, the remaining progressive farmers battled to farm on a commercial basis in the 1970s and 1980s.

Although the precise chronology and causes of the collapse of agriculture at Dinokana are difficult to unravel, evidence of its extent is available from air photographs. Simplified land-use maps derived from these for 1957 and 1984 offer some illustration of the collapse of the agriculture. These indicate that the area of cultivated land, as measured using a planimeter, declined from 470 ha in 1957 to 206 ha in 1984—a 56% contraction. Through ground truthing, it is the author's perception that this estimate errs on the conservative side.

Conclusion

The experience of agricultural development in Dinokana suggests a contradiction in terms of agricultural goals and planning. Both projects may be seen as a partial success in fulfilling their 'national' political goals, that is in terms of increasing food production, but they have had negative impacts on Dinokana village (which was supposed to benefit from these projects). Consequently, the issue of whether any 'development' has taken place is a moot point. This contradiction is not unique to Dinokana, but resonates to wider experiences of agricultural development elsewhere in Africa.

Planners of Bophuthatswana's rural development projects of the 1980s had little idea of the rich and complex agrarian history of Dinokana. A knowledge of local agricultural history certainly ought to inform development planning under the new North West provincial government. For example, information on previous cropping and irrigation strategies could inform contemporary decisions taken by (ahistorical) land-use planners. Rather than seeking a rural development mould from Israel or Taiwan, as was the case at Dinokana in the 1980s, or the present tendency to listen to whatever country comparisons the World Bank deems appropriate, technical, social and political constraints on production could better be identified via a thorough analysis of the local situation.

Acknowledgements

I wish to thank Phil Stickler, University of the Witwatersrand, for drawing the figure. Financial assistance for this research from the University of the North West is gratefully acknowledged.

Notes

1. Lehurutshe refers to a district (formerly Moiloa's Reserve) but, in addition, Lehurutshe is the official name for a proclaimed urban settlement, formerly known as Welbedacht. The latter name is still in widespread use in the district, therefore to avoid confusion, Welbedacht is used in the text to refer to the urban settlement.
2. Interview with R. Jordan, Director of Extension, Bophuthatswana Department of Agriculture, by J. H. Drummond, Mafikeng, 31/5/1988.
3. Interview with P. Montshosi, lifelong resident of Dinokana, by J. H. Drummond and A. H. Manson, 18/6/1987 (interpreters L. Mosadi and T. Gwai).
4. Interview with N. de Smidt, Agricor district manager for Lehurutshe, by J. H. Drummond, Welbedacht, 5/8/1988.
5. Interview with P. Montshosi, 18/6/1987.
6. From Hermannsburg Mission Records, unnumbered, 1864, p. 138 and cited in Manson (1990, p. 30). It should be noted that the term Bahurutshi is an old convention which has been replaced by the contemporary term Hurutshe.
7. See letter from Native Commisioner, Zeerust, to the Secretary for Lands, Pretoria, 8/7/1936. Transvaal Archives, Pretoria, NTS Vol. 8537, Moiloa Reserve Local Council Erection of Citrus Packing Shed 37/360F.
8. Ibid.
9. Interview with P. Montshosi, 18/6/1987.
10. Ibid.
11. Interview with Piet Mohalelo, by A. H. Manson, Dinokana, 3/12/1982 (South African Institute of Race Relations Oral History Archive, William Cullen Library, University of the Witwatersrand, Johannesburg).
12. Interview with P. Montshoshi, 18/6/1987.

References

Adams, W. M. (1982) Managing to irrigate Nigeria? pp. 37–44 in H. G. Mensching (ed.), *Problems of the Management of Irrigated Land in Areas of Traditional and Modern Cultivation*, International Geographical Union, Hamburg.

Adams, W. M. (1988) Rural protest, land policy and the planning process in the Bakolori project, Nigeria, *Africa*, 58, 315–336.

Adams, W. M. and Anderson, D. M. (1988) Irrigation before development: indigenous and induced change in agricultural water management in East Africa, *African Affairs*, 87, 519–535.

Adams, W. M. and Carter, R. C. (1987) Small-scale irrigation in sub-Saharan Africa, *Progress in Physical Geography*, 11, 1–27.

Adams, W. M. and Grove, A. T. (eds) (1984) *Irrigation in Tropical Africa: problems and problem solving*, Cambridge University Press, Cambridge.

Adams, W. M., Potkanski, T. and Sutton, J. E. G. (1994) Indigenous farmer-managed irrigation in Sonjo, Tanzania, *The Geographical Journal*, 160, 17–32.

Agricor (1984) *Temisano: developing the community through co-operative agriculture*, Agricor, Mmabatho.

Blaikie, W. G. (1903) *The Life of David Livingstone*, John Murray, London.

Breutz, P. L. (1953) *The Tribes of Marico District*, Government Printer, Pretoria.

Briggs, J. A. (1978) Farmers' response to planned agricultural development in the Sudan, *Transactions, Institute of British Geographers* 3, 464–475.

Bundy, C. (1988) *The Rise and Fall of South African Peasantry* (2nd edn), David Philip, Cape Town.

Chang, M. H. (1983) *Dinokana Rice and Vegetable Project Report*, Department of Agriculture, Mmabatho.

Drummond, J. H. (1991) The demise of territorial apartheid: re-incorporating the bantustans in a 'New' South Africa, *Tijdschrift voor Economische en Sociale Geografie*, 82, 338–344.

Drummond, J. H. (1992) Changing patterns of land use and agricultural production in Dinokana village, Bophuthatswana, unpublished MA dissertation, University of the Witwatersrand, Johannesburg.

Drummond, J. H. and Manson, A. H. (1991) The evolution and contemporary significance of the Bophuthatswana–Botswana border landscape, pp. 217–242 in D. Rumley and J. Minghi (eds), *The Geography of Border Landscapes*, Routledge, London.

Drummond, J. H. and Manson, A. H. (1993) The rise and demise of African agricultural production in Dinokana village, Bophuthatswana, *Canadian Journal of African Studies*, 27, 462–479.

Hinderink, J. and Sterkenburg, J. J. (1987) *Agricultural Commercialization and Government Policy in Africa*, KPI, London.

Holub, E. (1881) *Seven Years in South Africa: travels, researches and hunting adventures, between the diamond-fields and the Zambezi (1872–79)*, Vols I and II, Sampson Low, Marston, Searle and Rivington, London.

Hooper, C. (1960) *Brief Authority*, Collins, London; reprint, David Philip, Cape Town (1989).

Lawrence, M. E. and Manson, A. H. (1994) 'The dog of the Boers': the rise and fall and legacy of Mangope in Bophuthatswana, paper presented to the History Workshop, University of the Witwatersrand, Johannesburg, July 1994.

Legassick, M. (1977) Gold, agriculture and secondary industry in South Africa, 1885–1970: from periphery to sub-metropole as a forced labour system, pp. 175–200 in R. Palmer and N. Parsons (eds), *The Roots of Rural Poverty in Central and Southern Africa*, University of California Press, Berkeley and Los Angeles.

Manson, A. H. (1983) *The Troubles of Chief Abram Moilwa: the Hurutshe resistance of 1954–1958*, South African Institute of Race Relations, Johannesburg.

Manson, A. H. (1990) The Hurutshe in the Marico District of the Transvaal, 1848–1913, unpublished Ph.D. thesis, University of Cape Town.

Simkins, C. (1981) Agricultural production in the African reserves of South Africa, 1918–1969, *Journal of Southern African Studies,* 7, 256–283.

Surplus People Project (1983) *Forced Removals in South Africa, the Surplus People Project*, Vol. 5: *The Transvaal*, Surplus People Project, Cape Town.

Wolpe, H. (1972) Capitalism and cheap labour power in South Africa: from segregation to apartheid, *Economy and Society*, 1, 425–456.

23

People and drought in South Africa: reaction and mitigation

Coleen H. Vogel

Introduction

Droughts are endemic features in Southern Africa. Periodic dry spells have occurred in the 1920s, 1940s, 1960s, 1980s and more recently in the early 1990s (Tyson, 1986). The early 1980s drought has been identified as one of the most severe on record (Dent *et al.*, 1987). Between 1982 and 1993 two rainy seasons recorded less than 75% of normal rainfall, in 1982/83 (average rainfall, 408 mm) and 1992/93 (average rainfall, 484 mm) (Laing, 1992).

The causes of these climatic phenomena have been well documented in the literature (e.g. Tyson, 1981, 1986; Harrison, 1984, 1986; Lindesay, 1988a, b; Schulze, 1988; Mason, 1990). In contrast, however, very little has been documented about the impact of such events on the rural poor (Abrams *et al.*, 1992; AFRA, 1993; Vogel, 1994a, b). In this chapter the reaction to and mitigation of drought, through time, is examined for South Africa. The argument advanced here is that a lack of detailed knowledge of indigenous drought-coping strategies short-circuits any well-intentioned drought relief interventions.

Official response to drought

Pro-active changes in drought planning and the need for a multi-faceted approach to droughts have been slow in coming to South Africa (Vogel, 1994a; Walters, 1993). The focus of much drought relief and planning in the past has been on livestock farmers, while others engaged in commercial agriculture and subsistence agriculture in black rural areas, have been largely ignored.

Prior to the 1980s, drought assistance was given to stock farmers in those districts proclaimed as drought-stricken areas, according to fixed criteria. The purpose of these schemes was to assist farmers in the maintenance of a herd during exceptionally dry times. Drought assistance was given by the state in successive phases: firstly rebates on transport costs, then loans, and finally subsidies at increasing rates as drought persisted (the Phase Drought Relief Scheme). Seasonal drought impact however, was to be carried by farmers as their own responsibility (Bruwer, 1990), with drought relief given only in times of prolonged, severe drought.

Since 1980, attention has focused on devising a more long-term drought assistance scheme and a much-needed re-evaluation of the drought policy in the country has been undertaken (Bruwer, 1990; Walters, 1993). This new approach has been praised by some for its conservation focus (Smith *et al.*, 1992; Tube, 1993). The primary objective of the revamped drought scheme is to ensure the optimal utilization of resources without detrimental effects on pasture lands, and also

People and Environment in Africa. Edited by Tony Binns
©1995 John Wiley & Sons Ltd

to encourage research and the monitoring of rural drought impacts. References to farm management and the need to recognize that climatic variability, and particularly drought, are natural and frequent occurrences, have also been made.

Despite a renewed effort to improve farm management and thereby possibly reduce drought impact, much state drought relief has remained biased towards white commercial farmers (Table 23.1). There has been a reluctance to acknowledge that drought impacts are not only physically induced, but are also linked to levels of development in certain areas. A long-awaited change in drought relief, has however, begun to emerge as a result of the efforts of the Management Committee for Co-ordinated Drought Action established in 1992, in response to the severe drought of the time and the involvement of the National Consultative Drought Forum (Abrams *et al.*, 1992; Vogel, 1994b).

The need to locate drought relief within a broader rural context, which also includes black farmers and the rural poor, has thus finally emerged after decades of inadequate drought response in the country: 'The pronounced agricultural bias of previous aid policies has led to insufficient consideration being given to the protection of the rural poor against threats posed to their security in terms of water supply, food and employment' (Walters, 1993, p. 14). In a detailed investigation of recent state expenditure on drought relief, Rimmer (1993, 25) notes that:

Current drought policy, distorted towards the commercial sector needs to be reviewed . . . much of the programme (debt relief and drought relief of the 1990s) seeks to address problems related to inefficiency and low profitability rather than rainfall variations. For the future, drought policy will need to address the social and economic costs of drought induced vulnerability in a far more focused way than hitherto.

Earlier references to official thinking on drought, clearly illustrate misperceptions of drought impacts and an absence of a holistic understanding of drought that has prevailed in South Africa since the 1920s (Vogel, 1994a). Much of this misperception has been rooted in broader socio-political thinking. With the recent political developments in the country, and a growing awareness and motivation to include the rural dimension in drought planning, a dramatic change in drought thinking has occurred. It is, however, precisely in this area that data and research about people's responses to periods of environmental stress are most lacking. In this chapter an attempt is made to redress these shortcomings.

Table 23.1 *State allocations: drought relief 1992/93*

Programme	1992/93 Allocation R (million)	% Allocation
Assistance to white farmers	1093.6	64.25
Assistance to industries	20.0	1.18
Assistance to water supply task force	2.0	0.12
Assistance to Nutritional Development Programme	440.0	25.85
Assistance to self-governing territories	130.0	7.64
Not allocated	16.4	0.96
Total	1702.0	100

Source: Abrams, Short and Evans (1992)

Indigenous drought-coping strategies

Much investigation into the relationship between drought and indigenous coping strategies has been undertaken in other African countries (including Watts, 1983; Corbett, 1988; Downing, 1987, 1988, 1990; de Waal, 1989; Mortimore, 1989; Campbell, 1990; Campbell *et al.*, 1989; Cekan, 1990; Devereux, 1992). However, relatively little detailed, *local*, assessment to date, has been undertaken of household food security and coping strategies during droughts.

Coping strategies employed by households vary spatially and temporally. Thus several coping strategies and adaptive strategies may evolve as a crisis develops (Corbett, 1988; Davies, 1993).

Colson (1979), working among the Gwembe Tonga of Zambia, observed a sequence of people's food preparation during dry periods (Campbell *et al.*, 1989; Zinyama *et al.*, 1990). In northern Nigeria, Watts (1983) illustrated a progression of coping strategies, with earlier ones including the borrowing of grain, progressing to permanent outmigration, as the crisis intensified. These different coping strategies have also been shown to depend on the degree of household vulnerability, including such aspects as access and entitlement to food (Watts, 1983; Dreze and Sen, 1989; Watts and Bohle, 1993; Naerra *et al.*, 1993).

Changes and adaptations in drought-coping mechanisms have occurred and factors such as colonialism, socio-political and economic influences, have been shown to play a part (Downing, 1988; Freeman, 1988, Campbell *et al.*, 1989; Zinyama *et al.*, 1990; Chen, 1991). In settler colonies, for example, changes in cash crop production and land tenure have altered the relationships between rural society and environment. Labour migration, particularly strong in South Africa and neighbouring countries, 'had a profound effect upon traditional patterns of production and upon the availability of labour to apply to coping strategies' (Zinyama *et al.*, 1988, p. 198). Government intervention to circumvent food crises, and the existence of farmer support groups in certain areas (Brattan, 1987; Freeman, 1988), have also served to alter local and traditional coping strategies. Food parcels and intervention, moreover, have become expected sources of aid. Such changed strategies and increased dependence during periods of ecological stress were recognized as early as the mid-1930s in Southern Rhodesia: 'the saying had become common "why worry? The government will feed us"' (Southern Rhodesia, 1933, p. 3; quoted in Zinyama *et al.*, 1988).

Drought-coping mechanisms among the Tswana

When examining indigenous drought-coping strategies in South Africa, it is evident that certain modifications and adaptations to traditional strategies have occurred. As Davies (1993) clearly illustrates, there is a difference between what is meant by coping strategies during periods of drought and in wetter years. 'Coping' is thus defined as a short-term response to an immediate decline in access to food, whereas 'adapting' means a longer-term change in the mix of ways in which food is acquired, irrespective of the year in question.

Several adaptations to the prevalence of drought have, for example, occurred among the Tswana. Traditional ways of coping with food shortages included *letsema* and *mafisa* (Breutz, 1956; Hitchcock, 1979; Freeman, 1988; Stacey, 1992).[1] The *mafisa* system, a system of communal building and ploughing (Breutz, 1956), ensured a wider distribution of livestock among the population, particularly during times of food shortage and droughts. The system entailed lending cattle to people who used them for milk and draught power. The system therefore enabled cattle owners to spread their risks, thus reducing the impact of drought, epidemics or heavy predation (Hitchcock, 1979). *Letsema*, a system of sharing cattle and looking after stock, included assisting members of the group with seasonal agricultural tasks such as harvesting and weeding. Other strategies involved the collection and storage of grain (Molete, 1987); the sale of cattle; allowing the land to lie fallow, and only ploughing that which may yield produce (Bothloko, 1987).

More recent investigations of local drought-coping strategies over a 10-year period, conducted in the villages of Disaneng (Molopo district) and Khunwana (Ditsobotla district) of Bophuthatswana,[2] indicated that several of these strategies have changed in importance. Household interviews in Disaneng and Khunwana revealed some adaptations in response to drought and also a failure to improve 'drought-proofing' over time.

Survey results indicated that several households were unable to cope with the drought of the 1990s (Vogel and Drummond, 1993), notwithstanding previous drought interventions by the state (drought relief) in the 1980s. As noted in the study of the early 1980s (Freeman, 1988), prayer remained high on the list of relief measures. Of particular significance, however, was the decline of community support structures, with both village communities indicating that they had no collective strategy to combat drought (Table 23.2).

The absence of a collective drought strategy has also been recorded in other parts of Africa, such as in Sudan, where it was shown that:

The respondent households were vulnerable not only because their crops failed, livestock died or were sold to meet the rising cost of grain, but also because *community cohesion* and the resources upon which the cohesive mechanisms depended diminished, which led to a failure of support locally (Pyle and Gabbar, 1993, p 141, italics added).

Similarly in the Edongo study area of Namibia, Naerra *et al.*, (1993, p. 97) noted that:

A significant observation made during field work was the large degree to which respondents claimed to have worked together for common benefit in years gone by, but the decline in the formal economy and the drought had made it increasingly difficult to help anyone but themselves. Almal sukkel alleen (Everyone struggles alone).

Village drought relief mechanisms have clearly not improved over time. Freeman (1988, p. 202), observing drought-coping in Bophuthatswana in the 1980s, noted that:

if villagers were warned of a forthcoming drought their activities would not be radically different from those adopted during the present drought. The main reason for this apparent lack of forward planning is that in a future drought, villagers expect their circumstances to be fairly similar to present circumstances, with access to a similarly constrained number of alternative courses of action.

One possible reason put forward for the lack of a collective response at the time of the 1990s drought in Bophuthatswana, was that of political fear of repressive measures if collective action was taken:

it is difficult for the communities to establish self-help projects especially in Bop areas because due to the political background of Bop, people are not allowed to initiate their own projects . . . People . . . are idelling [*sic*] and sitting under trees because of lack of funds to initiate any project (Drought and Development Forum, Northern Cape, 1993, p. 2).

A state of total apathy is therefore apparent in some rural households. Communities no longer appear to have a *collective* strategy of coping with drought and resort instead to individual methods of lessening drought impacts, such as selling their labour and resources derived from their immediate environment. Some respondents during the 1990s drought, for example, stated that they had resorted to selling sand, obtained from the river, for income. This lack of a collective drought strategy and individual desperation in the face of drought, is even more worrying considering that most of these districts were targeted for drought relief in the 1980s drought, with food and work programmes (Vogel and Drummond, 1993).

The lack of effective mechanisms for coping with drought need, however, to be viewed in their historical context. There are indications that various adaptations to drought impacts have occurred with time in these areas. Former assistance from the chief in times of food shortages and droughts, for example, has been replaced over time by a greater reliance on state

Table 23.2 *Coping strategies during extreme drought periods in Disaneng and Khunwana (1982–92)*

Year	Village	Coping strategy (%)			
		No strategy	Pray	Sell stock	Government aid
1980s (Freeman	Disaneng	71	72	22	29
	Khunwana	82	85	32	26
1990s (Vogel)	Disaneng	78	72	22	26
	Khunwana	30	78	68	54

Ranking of coping strategies expressed as a percentage of total number of respondents. *Source*: Vogel (1994b).

assistance. Chiefs have not always been viewed as being of assistance, and such observations were noted as early as the 1900s:

Neither the chiefs nor headman, excepting one or two . . . pay any regard to this state of things (drought) (Letter from Rev. P. Wookey, Kuruman, 15 September 1903, Cape Archives, Native Affairs 633, B2162).

There is a kind of terror amongst the lower classes of people lest if they report, chiefs should come down on them (Letter from Rev. P. Wookey, 23 September, 1903, Cape Archives, Native Affairs 633, B2162).

Chiefs were, moreover, referred to as being 'indolent', 'lazy' . . .

The headmen are perfectly useless and unless the Native Affairs Department take the matter in hand the Reserve will go from bad to worse (Letter to the Superintendent Mafeking from Sgt Mitchelson, Kraaipan, 28 January 1923, Central Archives Depot, Native Affairs 783 7/336).

Government assistance has grown significantly in popularity among the indigenous people over time:

In order to relieve the scarcity in the Mafeking district occasioned by repeated droughts and locust invasions, the magistrate recommends that assistance be given the Natives in the form of advances of seed mielies and Kaffir corn (Letter to the Secretary Finances, Pretoria, from the Secretary Native Affairs, 27 November, 1924, Central Archives Depot, Native Affairs 783, Vol. 2).

Food assistance needs, however, to be carefully evaluated. Direct assistance, in the form of food aid, is not an ideal panacea for hunger in the long term and is often misappropriated. Food parcels have not always reached all the people for whom they were targeted. Several reports of food aid failing to reach those in need were noted during the drought efforts of the 1980s in Bophuthatswana (Freeman, 1988).

Migration, although commonly regarded as an important coping strategy in arid or semi-arid areas during droughts, also requires closer investigation. Permanent, immediate outmigration is not a popular choice among residents of Khunwana and Disaneng. The idea of mass outmigration to city areas, during times of drought, is a more complicated process often involving a variety of reasons for moving. More than half the responses (67%) from both villages,

for example, indicated that they would not move during the 1990s drought. Reasons given for remaining in Khunwana for example, included violence in urban areas and retrenchments from mines (Table 23.3). Some, who had been prompted by drought to seek alternative work, had returned to their villages because of the difficulties cited above. The majority stated that there were no jobs available, either on farms or in urban areas.

These findings are supported by similar reports from Northern Transvaal of a tendency for rural people to 'sit out' a drought (R. van den Heever, 1993, pers. comm.) and Kimberley (S. Legodi, 1993, pers. comm.). Although it is extremely difficult to authenticate these reports with other statistics, such as official migration figures, survey data indicate that the number of people propelled into city areas from rural poor areas, as a consequence of drought, is not as high as first estimated.

The lack of immediate migration as a response to drought is not uncommon. Research undertaken in villages in Zimbabwe (Matiza *et al.*, 1989) during the 1980s, and in Kenya (Downing, 1987) also indicates that migration as an option is complicated by a number of socio-economic factors and has altered over time. Kin networks now appear to be less extensive and less able to support families in times of drought, compared to several decades ago (Downing, 1987). As a result few households were observed leaving their villages.

Similar indications, of a preference to remain close to families during periods of stress, were also noted in other areas of the country during past droughts:

Table 23.3 *Migration as a coping strategy in Disaneng and Khunwana (1982–92)*

Year	Village	Migration options
1980s		Seek work 65%
	Disaneng	
1990s		Seek work, no success 50%
		34% remain at home
1980s		Seek work 36%
	Khunwana	
1990s		Seek work, no success 100%
		therefore remain at home

Source: Vogel (1994b).

In times of stress Natives are more reluctant than usual to leave families and proceed to distant centres of employment (Letter to the Native Chief Commissioner, King Williamstown, 12 February 1925, Central Archives Depot, Native Affairs, 6/336).

Although the debate about rural–urban migration as a result of drought, is more complex than previously thought, this must not be interpreted as suggesting that no migration may be triggered by drought. The mushrooming of squatter settlements in South Africa's metropolitan areas reflects a complex set of urban growth processes, which include both the natural growth of the existing urban population and a rural migration influx. If a severe and prolonged drought were to occur, and agricultural and other sources of livelihood were greatly stressed, then outmigration from rural areas might occur. Such movements, however, would probably be the last drought-coping mechanism adopted. Strong evidence of migration from poor rural areas during drought periods, as often portrayed in the media, has, however, not been found. Rather, a range of alternative coping mechanisms are adopted as communities turn to other forms of employment in their rural villages, to government aid and in several cases resort to 'sit out' the drought.

Conclusion

Severe droughts occur regularly in South Africa. Much is known about the causes of droughts, but very little is documented about the impacts of, and response to, such events. In particular little is known about drought impact in rural poor areas, including information on local water demand patterns, health and nutritional changes prior to and during droughts. Recent involvement by government, trade unions, church groups and other interested parties, in the shape of the National Consultative Drought Forum,[3] has meant that the focus of drought has at last shifted to include such aspects. People–environment relationships have therefore now been placed high on the agendas of several development forums.

However, an essential element that is still missing from much hazard research, is a detailed assessment of how people respond and cope with periods of environmental stress. Traditional views of drought-coping mechanisms among indigenous people are poorly understood. Interviews among two rural communities in the North Western region of South Africa have indicated that many myths about drought impact and coping mechanisms persist. Migration is often not a popular option for groups and families. An impoverished economy, lack of employment, inadequate education and heightened political violence in city areas, all add to the disincentives to move. This reluctance to move, moreover, is not something new and has been noted in the past, both in South Africa and elsewhere in Africa. Effective communal response to drought also appears to be declining. Whereas collective coping strategies were evident in the past, such as *mafisa* and *letsema*, these appear to have gradually diminished over time. Rural poor households in South Africa today exhibit few collective mechanisms with which to withstand droughts and instead prefer to 'sit out' droughts, often relying on government aid.

Failure to investigate and understand local drought-coping strategies has often proved to be expensive both for funding agencies and policy-makers. Changes in coping strategies and adaptations, both spatially and temporally, have occurred and much more attention needs to be given to them in the future. Actual responses to environmental stresses must be carefully monitored, rather than relying on outdated information. Detailed examination of inter- and intra-household vulnerability before and during periods of food stress is also essential. A more sensitive appreciation of how people interact with their environment could drastically reduce the impacts of similar events in the future. What is urgently required is a concerted effort by geographers and others, to investigate and document the dimensions of indigenous people–environment interactions, so that negative impacts associated with periods of stress, such as droughts, are reduced.

Notes

1. The Tswana occupy several areas including the presently demarcated North West Province, parts of the Northern Cape and Botswana.
2. Today the black homeland of Bophuthatswana is known as the North West Province and forms part of South Africa.
3. From 1994, the National Consultative Drought Forum has become the National Rural Development Forum, reflecting its new emphasis on rural development issues.

References

Abrams, L., Short, R. and Evans, J. (1992) *Root Cause and Relief Constraint Report*, National Consultative Forum on Drought, Johannesburg.

AFRA (Association for Rural Advancement) (1993) *Drought Relief and Rural Communities*, Special Report, No. 9, Pietermaritzburg.

Bothloko, J. (1987) Interview of John Bothloko by George Stacey, Interview No. 19, Mareetsane Moditsaatsile, Institute for Advanced Social Research, Oral History Collection, University of the Witwatersrand, Johannesburg, 15 July 1987.

Brattan, M. (1987) Drought, food and the social organisation of small farmers in Zimbabwe, pp. 214–244 in M. H. Glantz, *Drought and Hunger, Denying Famine a Future*, Cambridge University Press, Cambridge.

Breutz, P. L. (1956) *The Tribes of the Mafeking District*, Government Printer, Pretoria.

Bruwer, J. J. (1990) Drought policy in the Republic of South Africa, pp. 23–38. in *Workshop on Drought*, Du Pisani, A. L. (ed), *Proceedings of the SARCCUS Workshop on Drought*, June, 1989.

Campbell, D. J. (1990) Community-based strategies for coping with food security: a role in African famine early warning systems, *GeoJournal*, 20, 231–241.

Campbell, D. J., Zinyama, L. M. and Matiza, T. (1989) Strategies for coping with food deficits in rural Zimbabwe, *Geographical Journal of Zimbabwe*, 20, 15–41.

Cekan, J. (1990) The use of traditional coping strategies during famine in sub-Saharan Africa, *Drought Network News*, 3, 5–6, Nebraska.

Chen, M. (1991) *Coping with Seasonality and Drought*, Sage, New Dehli.

Colson, E. (1979) In good years and in bad: food strategies of self-reliant societies, *Journal of Anthropological Research*, 35, 18–29.

Corbett, J. (1988) Famine and household coping strategies, *World Development*, 16(9), 1099–1112.

Davies, S. (1993) Are coping strategies a cop out? *IDS Bulletin*, 24, 60–72.

Dent, M. C., Schulze, R. E., Wills, H. N. M. and Lynch, S. D. (1987) Spatial and temporal analysis of drought in the summer rainfall region of southern Africa, *Water South Africa*, 13, 37–42.

Devereux, S. (1992) Household responses to food insecurity in northeastern Ghana, unpublished D. Phil. thesis, University of Oxford.

De Waal, A. (1989) *Famine that Kills*, Clarendon Press, Oxford.

Downing, T. E. (1987) The drought and famine, 1984–1985, pp. 243–268 in J Downing, L. Berry, L. Downing, T. Downing and R. Ford (eds), *Drought and Famine in Africa: 1981–1986*, Clarke University, Worcester.

Downing, T. E. (1988) Climatic variability, food security and smallholder agriculturalists in six districts of central and eastern Kenya, unpublished Ph.D. thesis, Clarke University, Worcester.

Downing, T. E. (1990) African household food security: What are the limits of available coping-mechanisms in response to climatic and economic variations, pp. 39–67 in H. G. Bohle, T. Cannon, G. Hugo and F. N. Ibrahim (eds), *Famine and Food Security in Africa and Asia*, Bayreuther Geowissenchalfliche Arbeiten, vol. 15, Bayreth.

Dreze, J. and Sen, A. K. (1989) *Hunger and Public Action*, Oxford University Press, Oxford.

Drought and Development Forum, Northern Cape (1993) Report on the status of the Northern Cape region, including Bophuthatswana areas, *Fourth Meeting of the National Consultative Forum on Drought*, Development Bank of Southern Africa, 26 January.

Freeman, C. (1988) The impact of drought on rural Tswana society, unpublished MA dissertation, University of the Witwatersrand, Johannesburg.

Harrison, M. S. J. (1984) A generalised classification of South African summer rain-bearing synoptic systems, *Journal of Climatology*, 4, 547–560.

Harrison, M. S. J. (1986) A synoptic climatology of South African rainfall variations, unpublished Ph.D. thesis, University of the Witwatersrand, Johannesburg.

Hitchcock, R. K. (1979) The traditional response to drought in Botswana, pp. 91–976 in H. T. Hinchey, (ed.), *Proceedings of the Symposium on Drought in Botswana*, 5–8 June, 1978, Botswana Society, Botswana.

Laing, M. (1992) Drought update 1991–1992, South Africa, *Drought Network News*, Nebraska, 4, 15–17.

Lindesay, J. A. (1988a) The Southern Oscillation and atmospheric circulation changes over southern Africa, unpublished Ph.D. thesis, University of the Witwatersrand, Johannesburg.

Lindesay, J. A. (1988b) Southern African rainfall, the Southern Hemisphere semi-annual cycle, *Journal of Climatology*, 8, 17–30.

Mason, S. J. (1990) Temporal variability of sea surface temperatures around southern Africa: a possible forcing mechanism for the eighteen-year rainfall oscillation, *South African Journal of Science*, 86, 243–252.

Matiza, T., Zinyama, L. M. and Campbell, D. J. (1989) Household strategies for coping with food insecurity in low-rainfall areas of Zimbabwe, pp. 209–221 in G. D. Madimu, and R. H. Bernsten (eds), *Household and National Food Security in Southern Africa*, University of Zimbabwe, UZ/MSU Food Research in Southern Africa Harare.

Molete, K. (1987) Interview by George Stacey, Gannalaagte, Institute for Advanced Social Research, Oral History Collection, University of the Witwatersrand, Johannesburg, 14 July 1987.

Mortimore, M. (1989) *Adapting to Drought: farmers, famines and desertification in West Africa*, Cambridge University Press, Cambridge.

Naerra, T., Devereux, S., Frayne, B. and Harnett, P. (1993) *Coping with Drought in Namibia:* Informal social security systems in Caprivi and Erongo, 1992, Namibian Institute for Social and Economic Research, Namibia.

Pyle, A. S. and Gabbar, O. A. (1993) Household vulnerability to famine: survival and recovery strategies among Berti and Zaghawa migrants in northern Dafur, Sudan, 1982–1989, *GeoJournal*, 30, 141–146.

Rimmer, M. (1993) *Debt Relief and the South African Drought Relief Programme: an overview*, Land and Agricultural Policy Centre, Policy Paper 1, Johannesburg.

Schulze, G. C. (1988) El Nino en La Nina—die seun en die dogter (the son and the daughter), *South African Weather Bureau Newsletters*, 475, 7–8.

Smith, D. I., Hutchinson, M. F. and McArthur, R. J. (1992) *Climatic and Agricultural Drought: Payments and Policy*, Centre for Resource and Environmental Studies, Australian National University, Canberra.

Stacey, G. (1992) The origins and development of commercial farmers in the Ditsobotla and the Molopo regions of Bophuthatswana, M.Sc. dissertation, University of Pretoria.

Tube, J. (1993) An attempt at understanding the circumstances governing communal cattle ownership and how we could improve them, unpublished mimeo, Development Research, Agricor, Mmabatho, Bophuthatswana.

Tyson, P. D. (1981) Atmospheric circulation variations and the occurrence of extended wet and dry spells over southern Africa, *Journal of Climatology*, 1, 115–130.

Tyson, P. D. (1986) *Climate Change and Variability in Southern Africa*, Oxford University Press, Cape Town.

Vogel, C. H. (1994a) (Mis)management of droughts in South Africa: past, present and future, *South African Journal of Science*, 90, 4–5.

Vogel, C. H. (1994b) *Consequences of Drought in Southern Africa, 1960–1992*, unpublished PhD thesis, University of the Witwatersrand, Johannesburg.

Vogel, C. and Drummond, J. (1993) Dimensions of drought: South African case studies, *GeoJournal*, 30, 93–98.

Walters, M. C. (1993) Present state policy in the RSA and possible areas of adaptation, paper presented at a seminar on Planning for Drought as a Natural Phenomenon, Mmabatho, Bophuthatswana, 28 January 1993.

Watts, M. (1983) *Silent Violence: food, famine and peasantry in northern Nigeria*, University of California Press, Berkeley.

Watts, M. J. and Bohle, H. G. (1993) The space of vulnerability: the causal structure of hunger and famine, *Progress in Human Geography*, 17, 43–67.

Zinyama, L. M., Campbell, D. J. and Matiza, T. (1988) Traditional household strategies to cope with food insecurity in the SADCC region, pp. 183–205 in M. R. Rukuni, and H. Bernsten, (eds), *Southern Africa: food security policy options*, Food Security Research Report, Department of Agricultural Extension, University of Zimbabwe, UZ/MSU, Harare.

Zinyama, L. M., Matiza, T. and Campbell, D. (1990) The use of wild foods during periods of food shortage in rural Zimbabwe, *Ecology of Food and Nutrition*, 24, 251–265.

24

Health and health care in the 'new' South Africa

Garrett Nagle

Introduction: approaches to the study of health and health care

A geographical approach to the study of environment, health and health care offers a unique appraisal of the conditions operating in a given location at a particular time. It operates at a variety of temporal and spatial scales from the individual or community health survey to national health policy and global food programmes. It takes into account the multi-disciplinary nature, causes and effects of ill health and analyses the delivery of health care as a spatial, social, economic and political entity. Moreover, it synthesizes and, in an accessible way, presents data from a variety of primary and secondary sources.

The two main geographical approaches to health and health care are disease ecology (epidemiology) and the provision of health care services. These have often been isolated from each other, although some recent studies have adopted a more interdisciplinary approach and have linked the two during regional investigations into patterns of health and health care (Nagle, 1992, 1995a).

Such an approach has particular relevance in studies in South Africa where a number of factors

have combined to generate much ill health, especially in the former 'homelands', periurban and rural areas. These range from the legacy of separatist policies under the apartheid regime to the limited carrying capacity of the natural environment.

Health and health care in the 'new' South Africa

The election of Nelson Mandela as South Africa's first black president in 1994 marked the beginning of a new era in South Africa. However, although apartheid, a policy of separate development for different races, officially ended with President de Klerk's reforms in 1993, it is likely that much segregation will remain *de facto* if not *de jure*. The white minority of *c.* 5 million continue to retain considerable privileges against the black, coloured and Indian populations (27, 3, and 1 million respectively) (Table 24.1). The effects of past discrimination are still evident at a macro-scale, the former 'homelands', areas reserved for the sole occupancy of blacks and through which they were expected to fulfil their political aspirations, and at a meso-scale, an urban level, in which there has

People and Environment in Africa. Edited by Tony Binns
©1995 John Wiley & Sons Ltd

Table 24.1 *Basic indicators of well-being in South Africa*

	Black	White	Coloured	Indian
Life expectancy	63	73	63	67
Infant mortality rate	52.8	7.3	28	13.5
Total fertility rate	4.7	1.7	2.8	2.3
Health care expenditure per head (R)	138	597	356	340
Mean monthly income (R) 1994 (5R = £1)	662	3931	1279	2005

Source: SAIRR (1993).

been segregation of residential and commercial areas, as well as services such as health care facilities.

Since the early twentieth century the disease pattern of South Africa has followed very clearly defined racial lines and, in general, this has persisted to the present with minor modifications in recent years. It ranges from degenerative diseases, mostly among whites, to contagious ones, mostly among blacks and coloureds. For whites, diseases such as cerebrovascular diseases (strokes), cardiovascular disease (heart) and carcinoma (cancers) are the main causes of morbidity and mortality, accounting for over two-thirds of deaths. By contrast, a very high proportion of the coloured and black population suffer high rates of infectious, contagious diseases such as TB, gastroenteritis and respiratory infections. Increasingly, however, urban blacks are at risk from strokes, heart diseases and cancers, a pattern resembling that of whites. Moreover, the 'self-destructive' diseases related to drugs, prostitution and alcoholism are taking an increasing toll among the black population (SAIRR, 1992).

Geographically, some areas fare worse than others. Homelands, resettlement camps, and periurban areas harbour infectious diseases, especially during rapid population influx. Such epidemics relate to a highly unstable social and economic environment characterized by low incomes, inadequate diets, overcrowded housing and poor water and sanitation facilities.

Similarly, health care in South Africa clearly reflects the nature of society, both in terms of political development and market forces. It illustrates the imprint of separatist policies, with four provincial health departments, ten health and welfare departments for each of the homelands and three 'own affairs' departments for whites, coloureds and Indians. In general, health care for whites is based on the Western model: high technology, curative orientation and frequently privately run. By contrast, much health care available for blacks and coloureds is publicly run, especially for those in the homeland areas.

Moreover, there are many inequalities in the health services, as the figures in Table 24.2 show. More hospital beds and doctors are available per capita for whites than for blacks and facilities in homeland hospitals and clinics are often inferior to those in 'white' hospitals. Indeed, there are inequalities in the private market: although 75% of whites are covered by medical aid only about 5% of blacks have such cover (SAIRR, 1993).

Welcomewood and Ndevana: two examples from Ciskei

The 1913 Native Land Act and the 1936 Native Trust Land Act set aside 13% of the land area of South Africa for the black population. These areas, the former 'homelands', currently accommodate about 40% of the South African population, but account for 8% of employement and 6% of production by value. One such

Table 24.2 *Inequalities in health care provision, South Africa*

	RSA*	Ciskei	Lebowa	QwaQwa
Hospital beds per 1000 population	4.0	4.2	2.1	2.8
Doctors per 1000 population	0.6	0.4	0.0	0.1
Nurses per 1000 population	4.5	3.3	1.9	1.9

*Including all 10 homelands.
Source: SAIRR (1993, pp. 79–280).

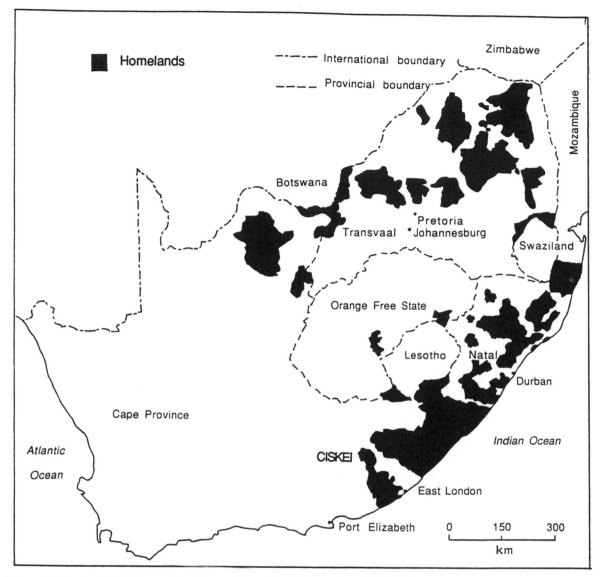

Figure 24.1 *South Africa and the former 'homelands' (based on South Africa, 1989, p. 172)*

'homeland' is Ciskei (Figure 24.1), an artificial construct developed by apartheid legislation.

It is a small area (7760 km^2) of limited environmental quality. It is divided into four major geographic regions: the coast belt, the dissected coastal plateau, the Amatola Basin and the semi-arid mountainous north. Only the basin has much potential for production. Soils are generally unsuitable for cultivation and most of the vegetation provides poor quality grazing although suitable for browsing. Rainfall figures are generally quite low ($\leqslant 800$ mm) and occurs mostly in December and January, i.e. summer convection storms ($> 70\%$). However, the area was badly affected by drought in the late 1980s and early 1990s, reducing the agricultural potential even further. Thus the land's carrying capacity is limited by a combination of suboptimal climatic conditions and steep slopes.

Nevertheless, population densities are high, on average 100 per km^2 but up to 320 km^2 in the south-east. This greatly exceeds the carrying capacity of the land, estimated at *c.* 80 per km^2. Moreover, population growth is rapid: in the 1970s it increased at an annual rate of 6% and in the 1980s between 2 and 3%. A considerable amount was due to forced removals, the rest due to a high birth rate. Some 45% of Ciskeians are under the age of 15 years and in rural areas it is as high as 51%. There is also a high femininity ratio: women outnumber men by 53:47, a result of the large number of absentee migrants (Nagle, 1995b).

Welcomewood is a rural settlement camp of 1000 people (Figure 24.2). Housing density is generally quite high (mean 6.2, maximum 14) and plot sizes (1.7 ha) allow some subsistence agriculture. The houses are mostly made from wood or wattle and daub. Water is provided to the settlement by means of a single tap and fuelwood is collected from 4 km away (by women and children). Neither electricity nor sanitation are provided in the village. Local sources of employment are limited to the school, clinic and shop, in all less than 15 jobs. Welcomewood is particularly vulnerable to unemployment given the lack of oppportunities in the village and its remoteness from centres of employment, such as King William's Town, and the expense of getting there.

Cultivation is primarily of a subsistence nature. However, only about 35% of households cultivate their plots. The large number of absent males (45%) creates a labour shortage, hence agriculture is frequently abandoned. A substantial amount of land is unused for a number of reasons: theft, low yields, inability to afford the inputs and lack of land rights.

By contrast, Ndevana is a periurban area, a settlement having a large population size and density but lacking in urban facilities, services or infrastructure. The houses are a mixture of wattle and daub, flotsam and jetsam (Figures 24.4–24.7). It was also a resettlement scheme, and grew rapidly during the 1970s and the 1980s, creating a number of problems regarding health, employment and service provision. Its population is officially estimated at 20 000, although workers in the area claim it is much higher.

The ability of the land to cater for its inhabitants is very limited. Housing density is high (mean 6.6, maximum 15) but resources are scarce. The provision of water in Ndevana is better than in Welcomewood. Over 95% have access to taps along the roadside. Plots in Ndevana are used for a mixture of vegetables, mealies and squatter shacks. The latter, known as shack farming, represents a secure regular income from a small plot of land (< 0.25 ha), since more money is received, and regularly, from letting land than from agriculture. However, it has led to severe overcrowding and breakdown in the provision of basic amenities such as water and sanitation.

Ndevana typifies a periurban area by its lack of facilities. Regular employment is limited to the police, schools, clinic and shop. Indeed, most of those working in the service sector of Ndevana live in the emerging 'middle class' area of Phakamisa. However, there are informal activities such as taxiing, brewing, domestic service and gardening. The majority of those employed work in King William's Town or East London: an added burden is the high cost of transport (18 and 70% of the average monthly income to King William's Town and East London respectively).

Morbidity

Research by the author between 1989 and 1991 showed that in Welcomewood 39% of children under the age of five years were wasted (underweight), 12% severely so; 44% of children were considered to be stunted (low height or long-term nutritional deficiency) and 28% were severely stunted. The proportion of children who were both severely stunted and severely wasted was much lower, 3% although 27% were moderately wasted and stunted. Ndevana provided a similar picture: 29% were wasted, although only 4% severely so; 34% were stunted, 11% severely and 16% moderately wasted and stunted, 2% severely. Households with malnourished children were characterized by absent fathers. They were more likely to be having fewer meals, a less varied diet, and in many cases the mother was herself malnourished.

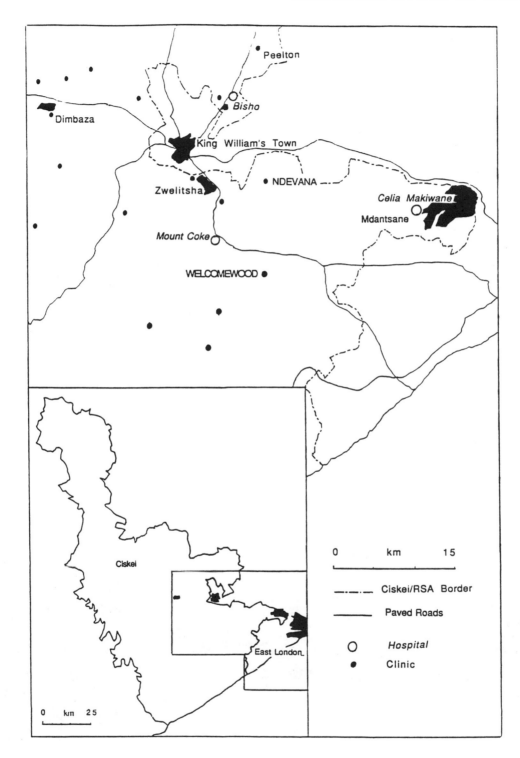

Figure 24.2 *Welcomewood and Ndevana*

Figure 24.3 *Structure of Ciskei Health Service*

The major forms of illness were nutritional, respiratory and skin infections. These accounted for nearly 75% of all treatments. Others included measles, burns and accidents. Malnourished and severely malnourished children were at increased risk of contracting a variety of diseases. They were also more likely to have longer episodes of the illness and recurrent bouts.

Patterns of disease also followed a seasonal and age-based pattern. Enteritic complaints were more likely in the summer, associated with reduced and/or contaminated water supplies and more parasitic viral pathogens (Figure 24.8). Children below the age of six months were less at risk of enteritis, possibly due to breast-feeding practices. Over the age of six months there were increasing bouts, caused in part by unhygienic methods of food preparation and, in part, by increased hand to mouth activity.

By contrast, respiratory complaints were concentrated in the winter months of June to

Figure 24.4 *Wattle and daub housing under construction in Ndevana, Ciskei*

Figure 24.5 *A squatter shack, Ndevana, Ciskei*

August, affecting three-quarters of all children. Similarly, skin infections were common in winter and the region appeared to be in the midst of an epidemic, caused by poor sanitation, inadequate water supply, malnutrition, overcrowding and a lack of heating. Likewise in winter there was a small but significant rise in the number of children, notably toddlers and babies, treated for burns.

Women constitute an extremely vulnerable population. They are especially vulnerable to illness, given their low socio-economic standing. many mothers are young, unmarried, malnourished and under tremendous stress. Of those surveyed, 77% were nervous, tense and worried, 73% suffered frequent headaches and 69% claimed to be tired all the time. Many were unable to sleep, had a poor appetite and lacked emotional stability.

Mortality

Mortality patterns were analysed using data from the Ciskei Department of Health (1989) and from the Cecilia Makiwane and Mount Coke hospitals, and Grey Hospital, King William's Town. Cause and time of death among infants varied. In Mdantsane, the principal causes of childhood death were gastroenteritis (20%), kwashiorkor and marasmus (12%) and pneumonia (12%): similar findings were found at Mount Coke and Keiskammahoek hospitals, both serving rural populations. In each hospital undernutrition was considered to be a key condition in other deaths, notably TB and measles. At Grey Hospital approximately 50% of patients were Ciskeian and during the period 1978–88 the main causes of infant death were gastroenteritis, malnutrition, respiratory diseases and measles, accounting for

Figure 24.6 *Informal housing, Ndevana, Ciskei*

c. 70% of black infant deaths, whereas congenital malformations and asphyxia accounted for all white infant deaths. Moreover, the majority of black deaths were in the neonatal period (up to four weeks) and post-neonatal period (four weeks to one year), while white deaths occurred in the first week after birth, reflecting congenital malformations and immaturity. Similarly, the child mortality rates indicated high death rates for the enteritic, nutritional, respiratory and infectious diseases. Between 1976 and 1988, 85% of black deaths were in these categories.

Health care

The provision of health care in Ciskei produced many constraints upon those providing the service and those requiring it. The Ciskei Health Department is funded by South Africa, which

therefore maintains some degree of control over the practices. Moreover, South Africa also achieves a degree of control through secondment of staff and loans of equipment. The health sevices have a very hierarchical structure (Figure 24.3). The regional hospital, Cecilia Makiwane, located in Mdantsane, acts as a specialist referral hospital and as a nurse-training institution. The second tier of hospitals, such as Mount Coke, developed out of small mission hospitals, and serve a number of clinics and sub-clinics in the region. These clinics represent the bottom rung of the health ladder. For example, Mount Coke provides doctors, ambulance services and various health personnel to 18 rural and 4 urban clinics. These clinics are designed to offer a comprehensive health service providing general medical care, family planning, nutrition education, TB treatment, antenatal care and obstetrics. Generally, they comprise a waiting room, a maternity room, consulting room and toilet facilities.

Figure 24.7 *Periurban location, Ndevana, Ciskei*

Both Ndevana and Welcomewood possess a clinic, the former serving over 20 000 people and the latter 2000–3000. The Welcomewood clinic contained only a consulting room, waiting room, store and staff quarters. It had neither electricity, running water nor indeed any sanitary facilities. Although the clinic at Ndevana was better, in practice both operated under a number of constraints. Staff shortages were a serious problem, leading to reduced efficiency and a poor image of the health services. When staff levels decreased attendance at the clinics decreased, owing to increased waiting time, lack of care and attention, and reduced hours of opening. The quality of staff also raised some concerns. Poor staff training resulted in a failure to spot potentially ill people and offer preventative medicine. Staff morale was low, owing to lack of resources, poor motivation and inadequate wages. Other provisions missing included transport

facilities, telephone, weighing scales, stethoscopes, road-to-health cards, vaccine and proper sewage systems.

The presence of a clinic did not guarantee its use. In both places those furthest from the clinic used it least. In Welcomewood two months passed between the doctor's visit to the clinic (in theory on a weekly basis). Nursing assisants and village health workers were poorly paid and motivation was low. There was considerable friction in one clinic, with allegations that powdered milk supplies were given to those unentitled to them. Traditional practitioners were common especially in Ndevana and the perceived high cost of treatment (the fare of getting to the clinic and the opportunity cost of missing or seeking work) reduced the numbers using the health services. Despite these comments it must be pointed out that the health services in Ciskei, and in these settlements, reach a large number of people and

265

Figure 24.8 *Water for drinking, washing, cleaning and bathing, Welcomewood, Ciskei*

have a beneficial effect on their health. There is a full health strategy and in general this is quite successful. However, problems will arise and these are likely to be felt disproportionately in small communities, where there is a limited provision, and in communities with rapid population growth.

Future prospects

The year 1994 heralded the start of a new political era in South Africa. The apartheid policies have been dismantled, the African National Congress are the majority power and Mr Mandela is the first black president of South Africa. Sanctions have been lifted, disinvestment has declined somewhat and all groups have equal rights within South Africa. Among many South African blacks there is great optimism about the future and aspirations are high. In reality, there is little room for optimism. Population growth remains high, 2.5% per annum, especially among blacks and coloureds. Levels of violence remain high and this is having a detrimental effect on new investment. Political change brings instability and new investors continue to wait some time before taking the plunge.

Meanwhile there are many social and economic factors which prohibit many South Africans from achieving full health: unemployment, under-employment, population growth and population pressure continue. It is likely that for a great majority of those in the homelands, the vulnerable communities, political change will have very little effect on their social and economic position. Ciskei, for example, remains peripheral in South Africa, in terms of its location, economy and political strength. Although the homelands have already lost much autonomy and have been subsumed in wider economic regions, it is very doubtful whether their material position will improve. Ciskeian people will remain poor and thus discrimination *de facto* will continue. Levels of health will remain low and possibly deteriorate with increasing stress. If blacks leave homelands and move to the periurban areas they may experience similar pressures as they left behind, only further intensified.

Despite the political reforms of the early 1990s, the health care system in South Africa still retains many of the characteristics developed during the apartheid era: excessive fragmentation, excessive state intervention, market-curative orientation, urban bias and white dominance. Although the ANC manifesto states that it wants to have a health service which provides basic health care for all people, it will find that there is a vast number of programmes that have to be implemented, such as housing and education, and these may take priority over health. Thus the 2.5 billion rand (£500 million) announced by Mr Mandela on 24 May 1994 to kick-start the redevelopment of South Africa might not go very far when spread over a plethora of projects. As regards health, the physical infrastructure and health personnel that already exist will have to be used in the best way possible. It is unlikely that there will be sudden shifts in policy and if there are it could signal a move of personnel from the public to the more lucrative private sector. The prospects for health and health care in the 'new' South Africa are, on the one hand, exciting, but on the other, frightening.

Acknowledgements

I would like to thank Angela and Rosie for their support and patience while I have been writing this chapter, and for being there. For Mary and Sean, for all they have done.

References

Ciskei (1988) *Annual Report: Department of Health*, Government Printer, Bisho.

Nagle, G. E. (1992) Malnutrition in the Zwelitsha area of Ciskei, Unpublished D. Phil. thesis, University of Oxford.

Nagle, G. E. (1994a) Challenges for the 'new' South Africa, *Geographical (Analysis)*, 66(5), 45–47.

Nagle, G. E. (1994b) Regional Inequalities in the 'new' South Africa, *Geographical (Analysis)*, 66(9), 49–50.

Nagle, G. E. (1994c) South Africa's demographic timebomb, *Geographical (Analysis)*, 66(10), 52–54.

Nagle, G. E. (1995a) Trends in health and health care in South Africa, in A. Lemon (ed.), *The Geography of Change in South Africa*, Wiley.

Nagle, G. E. (1995b) Population dynamics in Ciskei, *Geography Review*, 8(4).

SAIRR (1992) Race Relations Survey, 1991–1992, South African Institute of Race Relations, Johannesburg.

SAIRR (1993) *Race Relations Survey 1992–1993*, South African Institute of Race Relations, Johannesburg.

South Africa (1989) *Official Yearbook of the Republic of South Africa*, Bureau for Information, Pretoria.

Epilogue

Tony Binns

I very much hope that the 24 contributions presented in this volume have interested and informed the reader. The diversity of locations and topics covered, together provide a wealth of empirical material, which I trust will make a significant contribution to existing literature on people–environment relationships in Africa. Between them the chapters have raised many issues in different environmental contexts, and I believe we can learn some useful lessons from the evidence presented.

Many of the contributions have revealed the complexity of people–environment interactions and the livelihood systems within which they function. These systems are far from being simple and static, as so often was assumed in the past. Flexibility, in the shape of different crop varieties and mixtures, rotations, non-farm occupations and mobility of people and livestock, are, for example, just some of the many risk aversion strategies adopted. We have seen how trees and tree crops are frequently highly valued and nurtured, how soil fertility can be enhanced and maintained, and how ecological diversity can be exploited by both production and trading systems. The importance of social, economic and political factors in shaping, and at times, constraining people–environment interaction has also been demonstrated. The roles of the state and various traditional and modern institutions have been particularly apparent in the studies from South Africa and Zimbabwe, but institutional influences are manifested in different ways elsewhere, for example, in community allocation of responsibilities according to age or gender.

While there is understandably a widespread concern among poor people with low-level technology to avoid risk and ensure survival, there is no shortage of evidence of long-term planning and spontaneous innovation. 'Sustainability' may be the 'buzz-word' among the development fraternity in the 1990s, but many Africans have long been aware of whether or not their livelihood systems are sustainable and have taken steps, in many different ways, to enhance sustainability so as to ensure future survival.

So, having presented the evidence, we might ask, 'where do we go from here, if living standards in Africa are to be improved?' Governments and development agencies need to take note of the messages contained in these studies. In particular, the starting point for formulating any development strategy must be a detailed appreciation of what the specific situation is like now. More effective and democratic data collection methods need to be encouraged, such as participatory rural appraisal (PRA), championed by Robert Chambers, and now being widely used by non-governmental organizations (NGOs), such as ACTIONAID, as we have seen. Such methodologies ensure that information, viewpoints and aspirations come directly from those who will hopefully benefit from subsequent development intervention. 'Ask the people', must be the catchphrase of the future, but so many development programmes in the past have neglected to do just this.

Data collection methodologies must also take in the whole picture, so that relationships between different elements within a livelihood system might be appreciated. For example, efforts to improve rice production in The Gambia would not get very far without involving women, who are traditionally responsible for the crop and have a rich fund of knowledge. The indigenous institutional context would also need to be fully understood. By taking a holistic approach to data collection, the systemic effects of how innovating in one element of the system might impact elsewhere, can be detected. The value of data collection at the micro-level has also gained more support in recent years within development circles. Whether the focus is the village, or the household, it is often only at this level that the real complexity of decision-making processes can be fully appreciated.

Finally, I would like to make a strong plea for further work to be undertaken on people–environment relationships in Africa. In a continent where technology is generally limited and unequally distributed, many poor people are in a sense so 'close to environment' in their daily lives that coping and adapting are constant concerns. I believe that geographers, both by themselves and also working in multidisciplinary research teams, have an important part to play in further elucidating people–environment linkages in Africa, since for me it is this interface which should be the essential focus of all good geographical investigation. There is scope for much greater collaboration in this field between African, British and other geographers, and an opportunity to bring together similar research from different parts of the continent. For example, the work on drought and land degradation in the Sahel might usefully be examined in the light of similar work undertaken in Southern Africa. This same topic is one where physical and human geographers, such as have been brought together in this collection, might also collaborate more closely and effectively in the future.

Future possibilities for research, publishing and teaching on people–environment relationships in Africa are considerable. Let us hope that more of this work will be undertaken, that African governments and development agencies will take it seriously, and that the schemes, projects and other interventions which follow will play a meaningful role in advancing living standards among Africa's people.

Index

Numbers in *italics* refer to illustrations

Index compiled by Margaret Binns